DEFENDER OF THE FAITHFUL

THE TAUBER INSTITUTE SERIES FOR THE STUDY OF EUROPEAN JEWRY

The Tauber Institute Series is dedicated to publishing compelling and innovative approaches to the study of modern European Jewish history, thought, culture, and society. The series features scholarly works related to the Enlightenment, modern Judaism and the struggle for emancipation, the rise of nationalism and the spread of antisemitism, the Holocaust and its aftermath, as well as the contemporary Jewish experience. The series is published under the auspices of the Tauber Institute for the Study of European Jewry—established by a gift to Brandeis University from Dr. Laszlo N. Tauber—and is supported, in part, by the Tauber Foundation and the Valya and Robert Shapiro Endowment.

For the complete list of books that are available in this series, please see brandeisuniversitypress.com/series-list/

Arthur Green
Defender of the Faithful: The Life and Thought of Rabbi Levi Yitsḥak of Berdychiv

Yosef Hayim Yerushalmi in Conversation with Sylvie Anne Goldberg
Transmitting Jewish History

Charles Dellheim
Belonging and Betrayal: How Jews Made the Art World Modern

Cedric Cohen-Skalli
Don Isaac Abravanel: An Intellectual Biography

ChaeRan Y. Freeze
A Jewish Woman of Distinction: The Life and Diaries of Zinaida Poliakova Glikl: Memoirs 1691–1719

Dan Rabinowitz
The Lost Library: The Legacy of Vilna's Strashun Library in the Aftermath of the Holocaust

Jehuda Reinharz and Yaacov Shavit
The Road to September 1939: Polish Jews, Zionists, and the Yishuv on the Eve of World War II

Adi Gordon
Toward Nationalism's End: An Intellectual Biography of Hans Kohn

Arthur Green

DEFENDER *of the* FAITHFUL

The Life and Thought of Rabbi Levi Yitsḥak of Berdychiv

Brandeis University Press / Waltham, Massachusetts

Brandeis University Press

Manufactured in the United States of America
Designed by Mindy Basinger Hill
Typeset in Minion Pro

Library of Congress Cataloging-in-Publication Data

Names: Green, Arthur, 1941– author.
Title: Defender of the faithful : the life and thought of Rabbi Levi Yitshak of Berdychiv / Arthur Green.
Description: First edition. | Waltham, Massachusetts : Brandeis University Press, 2022. | Series: Tauber Institute series for the study of European Jewry | Includes bibliographical references and index. | Summary: "Defender of the Faithful is an intellectual and religious biography of Levi Yitshak of Berdychiv (1740–1809), one of the most fascinating and colorful Hasidic leaders of his time. Featuring examples of Levi Yitshak's extraordinary texts alongside insightful analysis, Arthur Green examines both Levi Yitshak's theology and broader philosophy"—Provided by publisher.
Identifiers: LCCN 2022020858 | ISBN 9781684581016 (cloth) | ISBN 9781684581023 (ebook)
Subjects: LCSH: Levi Isaac ben Meir, of Berdichev, 1740–1809. | Rabbis—Ukraine—Berdychiv—Biography. | Hasidim—Ukraine—Berdychiv—Biography.
Classification: LCC BM755.L44 G74 2022 | DDC 296.8/332092
[B] —dc23/eng/20220608
LC record available at https://lccn.loc.gov/2022020858

5 4 3 2 1

למורי וחברי —

Dedicated to the many teachers and friends, both living and dead, from whom I have learned so much.

And especially to the memories of Ada Rapoport-Albert and Tsippi Kauffman, who should have been among the first readers—and critics—of this work.

CONTENTS

PREFACE AND ACKNOWLEDGMENTS

I had intended to write a book on Levi Yitsḥak of Berdychiv shortly after completing *Tormented Master: A Life of Rabbi Naḥman of Bratslav*, published in 1979. I was deterred from doing so by the conundrum of sorting out issues of history and folklore. I questioned how much could be known of the historical person of Levi Yitsḥak and whether it was possible—or even desirable, for that matter—to pick apart the powerful figure of legend from the author of one of the early collections of Hasidic sermons, a work still widely read and reprinted in contemporary Hasidic circles. I feared that the historical sources might be too dry, diminishing the figure so well known to the Jewish imagination, and that a legendary account would be burdened with so much romance and glory that the historical personage would be lost within it. Various other projects and concerns then delayed this writing even further, and I am grateful that I have been given the length of days that has allowed me to come back to it.

The long delay has given me the privilege of reading and teaching Levi Yitsḥak over the course of many years. Conversations with students have contributed much toward my understanding of him. Foremost among these is Or N. Rose, who has also written on Levi Yitsḥak. Others include Ebn Leader, Ariel Evan Mayse, and David Maayan. So too the group of Hebrew College rabbinical students to whom I taught a seminar on *Kedushat Levi* in 2021. One of those, Micah Friedman, has served as my research and editorial assistant in the final stages of this project. I am particularly grateful to him. Three colleagues in the field of Eastern European Jewish history have read through the first part of this manuscript and offered various helpful suggestions. I acknowledge my thanks to Immanuel Etkes, ChaeRan Freeze, and Yoḥanan Petrovsky-Shtern for those comments. Responsibility for the final text of the volume is, of course, entirely my own.

I am also grateful to Sylvia Fuks Fried and Eugene Sheppard for the interest that Brandeis University Press has shown in this volume since I suggested it to them. As a twice-over alumnus of Brandeis and a member of its faculty, I take particular delight in its appearance in a Brandeis series.

DEFENDER OF THE FAITHFUL

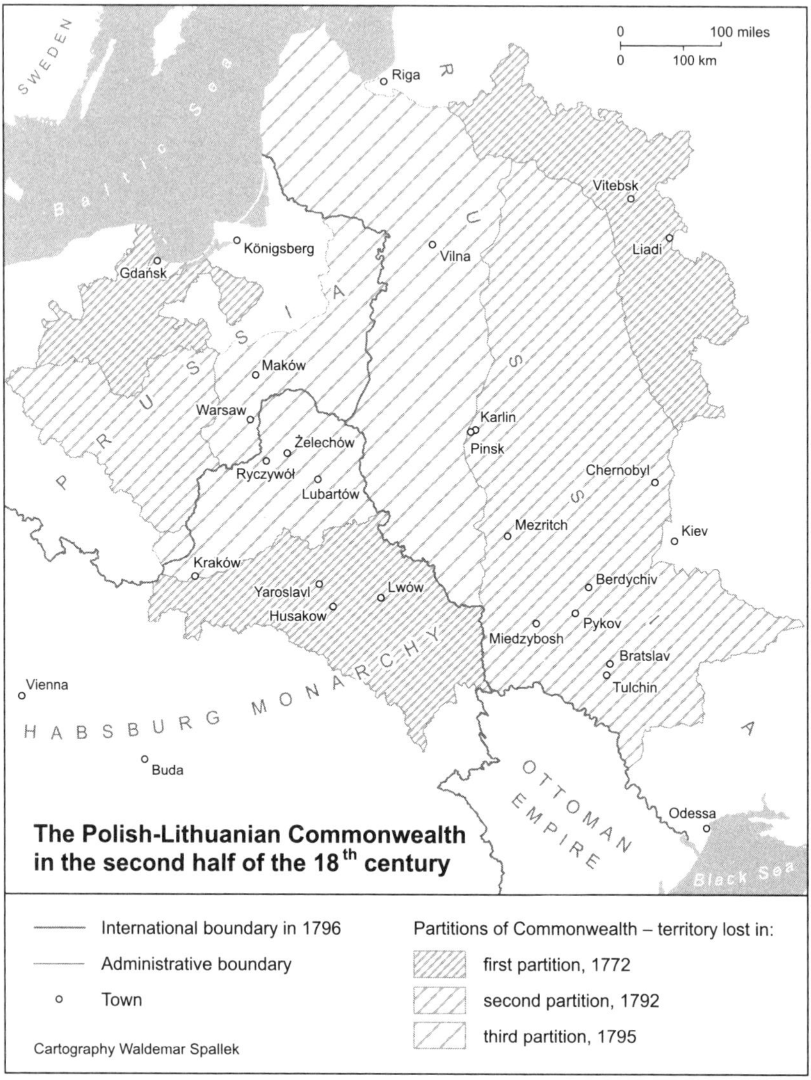

The Polish-Lithuanian Commonwealth in the second half of the 18th century

INTRODUCTION

I

Levi Yitsḥak of Berdychiv is one of the great figures of the Hasidic imagination. It would be no exaggeration to say that for Jews living in Eastern Europe in the decades just preceding the great changes of the early twentieth century, and down through the Holocaust era, he was the second best known and revered personality of the Hasidic legacy, following the Ba'al Shem Tov himself. This was true despite the remarkable fact that his memory was not borne aloft by a powerful dynasty of descendants that came in his wake, as was the case with so many others.

Hasidism in our era has moved in different directions. Perhaps better known these days are Levi Yitsḥak's younger contemporary and friend Rabbi Nahman of Bratslav and the recently deceased R. Menahem Mendel Schneersohn, the last rabbi of Lubavitch or ḤaBaD. These have both become the central figures of significant outreach movements, attracting large numbers of seekers and newly pious Jews to the ranks of their devotees. The various Hasidic dynasties originating in both Poland and Hungary also continue to thrive, largely peopled by their astounding rates of natural increase. These groups and their heroes are somewhat exclusive of one another. You will almost never hear R. Nahman quoted in a text or lesson of ḤaBaD; the Lubavitcher *rebbe* will not be referenced, at least not in a positive way, in circles of Gur or Satmar. But the name of Levi Yitsḥak continues to be revered by all of these groups. Tales of him continue to be told throughout the Hasidic world and beyond.

There is reason to believe that the events following 1881–82, more than seventy years after Levi Yitsḥak's death in 1809, were crucial in affirming his place in the pantheon of Jewry's spiritual heroes. In the wake of the frightening pogroms that broke out across the Ukrainian provinces of the tsarist empire in those years, the majority of Jews who remained traditionally pious were in need of a figure to rally around parallel to those who were beginning to come to the fore among the secularized intellectuals of emerging Jewish socialism and Zionism and in the new literature being created in both Hebrew and Yiddish. Levi Yitsḥak of Berdychiv was the perfect religious folk hero for this era.[1] Tales about him began to appear in abundance, both in collections along with others and in volumes devoted to him alone. This stream of ever-expanding and creative storytelling has never ceased.

This was the case because of two interrelated traits long associated with Levi Yitsḥak: his love for Jews, including the most ordinary and unlettered among them, and his willingness to argue on their behalf, both in this world and before the heavenly Throne of Glory. The later legends expanded on these themes far beyond anything present in the historical record about the rabbi of Berdychiv, but they were built around a kernel of historical truth. Levi Yitsḥak the defender of Israel became Levi Yitsḥak the protestor against divine injustice, serving as the clarion call that gave voice to new generations of Jews crying out their pain as the era of *shtetl* life was being destroyed by forces far beyond their control. The voice of Levi Yitsḥak as a figure of protest only grew louder over the bloody first half of the twentieth century as survivors of the first World War, the awful pogroms that followed it, and finally the Holocaust, continued to call him forth to express their horror at what felt like divine indifference to their endless suffering. In the wake of the Holocaust, several modern writers cast him as God's unforgiving judge, the embodiment of their own struggles to believe, as children of Abraham, that the burning castle in which we live indeed has a Master.[2]

But our interest here is in Levi Yitsḥak the historical figure, a man born in 1740, thus raised in an era before the shadow of modernity had yet cast itself over a Jewry living within the feudal society of the old Polish kingdom. He lived through the great changes wrought in Jewish life in the wake of the partitions of Poland and was a key Jewish leader in that turbulent era. Levi Yitsḥak died in 1809, just as the armies of Napoleon, as well as the forces of Western Enlightenment, were sweeping across the plains of Eastern Europe, about to change their landscape forever.

II

The history of Hasidism in the late eighteenth century has been widely studied since the turn of the twentieth century, when inner Hasidic hagiography began to give way to modern historical research. A clear line between these two only began to emerge in the succeeding decades and continues to this day to remain somewhat elusive. Simon Dubnov, long recognized as the pioneer historian of Hasidism, was in active communication with rabbis who worked as gatherers of sources for him while at the same time serving as editors of collections of Hasidic traditions and tales, published for the believing Hasidic community. Shmu'el Abba Horodezky, the leading figure in Hasidic research in the next generation, was himself a descendant of the Chernobyl dynasty and a bearer of living oral traditions from within his family. My own revered teacher, Abraham Joshua Heschel, was a careful and responsible scholar of early Hasidism, along with his various other areas of intellectual endeavor. He too, however, brought personal memory and family-held traditions to bear on his research.

The systematic study of Hasidic thought, as distinct from research into Hasidism as a social movement, began with the students of Gershom Scholem, who described Hasidism as "The Latest Phase" in the long history of Jewish mysticism. While Scholem devoted rather little of his extensive oeuvre to Hasidism, two of his disciples, Joseph Weiss and Rivka Schatz-Uffenheimer, did important pioneering work. Their school of research has been carried on by such scholars as Rachel Elior, Ron Margolin, and the late Ada Rapoport-Albert and Tsippi Kauffman, to whose memory I have dedicated this volume.

Historical monographs devoted to the lives and thought of individual figures within eighteenth-century Hasidism have begun to emerge in recent years. My own *Tormented Master: A Life of Rabbi Nahman of Bratslav* was the first undertaken in a critical mode. The Ba'al Shem Tov has been the the subject of significant studies by Moshe Rosman, Immanuel Etkes, and Rachel Elior. Etkes is also the author of a major study of R. Shne'ur Zalman of Liadi, whose thought has been studied by Elior as well. The works of Gadi Sagiv on R. Menaḥem Naḥum of Chernobyl and Uriel Gelman on R. Ya'akov Yitsḥak of Lublin have also made significant contributions. Zvi Mark has contributed greatly to our further understanding of R. Nahman and the movement around him.

Much has changed in research on Hasidism in the more than forty years since I first thought of writing a book about Levi Yitsḥak. It is now clear, thanks in part to the work of Rapoport-Albert, that Hasidism, both as an ideology and as a popular religious movement, began to develop largely after the death of Hasidism's second great leader, R. Dov Baer of Mezritch, in 1772, and was dominated by the school of his disciples. They, along with other circles, such as those of Korets and Zloczow, sowed the seeds of what was to become a dominant force in Eastern European Jewish life after the turn of the nineteenth century. As I shall demonstrate in these pages, Levi Yitsḥak played a clear and self-conscious role in the leadership and building of that movement.

What we know of the historical Levi Yitsḥak is based on a variety of early sources, which I now need to present to the reader. In contrast with the special case of Nahman of Bratslav, here we do not have a careful contemporary chronicler who recorded every available detail of his master's life. While we do have substantial historical records referring to Levi Yitsḥak, who was rabbi of major communities and a well-known figure in his day, much of the information we have about him has to be sifted carefully from among later and much-embellished legends. This can be done by a combination of careful selection from among those sources and reading with a discerning eye.

First and foremost, however, we will learn about Levi Yitsḥak through a careful reading of his own words, some published within his own lifetime and others preserved in manuscripts and appearing after his death. Chief among these is his volume of collected teachings, entitled *Kedushat Levi,* a name by which he himself came to be called within Hasidic circles. Levi Yitsḥak published one section of that work himself in Slavuta in 1798. That slim volume, now a treasured rarity among Hebrew book collectors, contains his homilies on the miracles of Hanukkah and Purim. The larger part of that work, consisting mostly of teachings arranged around the weekly Torah reading cycle, appeared two years after its author's death, edited by his son, in Berdychiv, 1811.[3]

These two parts of *Kedushat Levi,* always published together since 1816, should really be considered separate works. The 1798 volume may be called a treatise. He offers multiple homiletically based readings on each of the two festivals, and the work is filled with inner cross-references and consistent themes (to be discussed below) that make it a single work. The 1811 volume, more similar to most Hasidic publications of the time, is a collection of homiletical comments on the Torah. Some are full sermons, running several pages in length. Many more are brief remarks built around single insights into a biblical word or phrase. Were these comments he made in the Berdychiv *yeshivah*, preparing students for the weekly Torah portion to be read on Shabbat? Were they said casually, by the wayside, to his disciples and then written down? How wide or narrow was the intended audience for a particular sermon or remark? All this is beyond our ken, but we must endeavor to consider it nonetheless. We will return frequently to this question of intended audience.

Such collections of homiletic comments on the annual Torah reading cycle are considered the classics of Hasidic literature, and the *Kedushat Levi* is highly regarded among them. In most cases, these homilies were originally delivered orally and in Yiddish, the single spoken language of Eastern European Jews within their own communities.[4] Later, abbreviated Hebrew versions of them were prepared for publication based on oral memory and notes, sometimes by the preacher himself and in other cases by sons or disciples. Often, including in the case of Levi Yitsḥak, they were published shortly after the author's death.[5]

Later Hasidic tradition has it that *Kedushat Levi*,[6] including the posthumously published sections, was written by Levi Yitsḥak himself, unlike many other compilations of Hasidic homilies. This is certainly true of the 1798 volume. Regarding the sermons on the Torah, it is difficult to determine. There is no obvious indication of an editor's hand, something that is often found in other works. The writing is in a fairly clear and straightforward rabbinic Hebrew, and it is considered one of the more readily comprehensible of Hasidic works.

Even before the first section of *Kedushat Levi*, Levi Yitsḥak authored his brief commentary on the *Six Remembrances* (six things a Jew is obliged to recall each day) for publication. That was his first work to appear in print.[7]

Much later, on the eve of Eastern European Jewry's terrible destruction, there appeared a slim volume called *Shemu'ah Tovah*, printed in Warsaw, 1938, chiefly from a manuscript (subsequently lost) in the library of the Kozhenits Hasidic dynasty. It is attributed by its editor to Dov Baer, the Maggid of Mezritch, and Levi Yitsḥak, without further specification. Included within it is a series of sermons, most dated to the summer months of 1773 and 1774, the two years following the Maggid's death. I have demonstrated elsewhere (to be summarized below), by comparison to passages in *Kedushat Levi*, that these are indeed by the young Levi Yitsḥak. So too are a few questions on matters of Kabbalistic doctrine addressed to his teacher Dov Baer of Mezritch. These sermons turn out to be an extremely significant historic source, one that until now has received almost no scholarly attention.[8]

This means that we have writings of Levi Yitsḥak completed when he was thirty-three or thirty-four years old, treatises he published at ages fifty-four and fifty-eight, and collected writings, including some later material, published after his death at age sixty-nine. These will give us an opportunity to look at the development of certain themes within his thought.

Short homilies and statements attributed to Levi Yitsḥak are also found in several compendia of Hasidic teaching composed in the years shortly following his death. He is also quoted in a book by his son R. Yisra'el of Pikov and in works by several of his disciples, especially in R. Aharon of Zhitomir's *Toledot Aharon.*[9] In addition to his own Hasidic teachings, Levi Yitsḥak was author of a large number of *haskamot* or encomia, what today we might call "blurbs," recommending and authorizing the publication of works by others. These were considered crucial to the publication success of rabbinic writings, and Levi Yitsḥak's recommendations were highly sought. The historical significance of these lies particularly in the fact that they usually indicated the date of writing and were likely to include both the location where written and the title of the recommender.

As rabbi of several important communities, Levi Yitsḥak was necessarily active in the field of *halakhah*, or Jewish praxis, as well. Given the positions he held, he left behind a surprisingly small corpus of halakhic writings. These have been the subject of recent study and add to our understanding of their author and his circumstances.[10] There are also references to Levi Yitsḥak in letters, anti-Hasidic denunciations by rabbinic authorities, and various other Jewish writings of the era. As a communal rabbi and a well-known personality in his own day, Levi Yitsḥak is also occasionally featured in documents preserved in Polish and Russian archives of the era. These too can be significant fonts of information, sometimes offering a very different coloration to events than those found within the Jewish sources.

When it comes to learning from the legendary sources, one first needs to distinguish among various collectors and reporters of them. Simon Dubnov relied on rabbis like Yisra'el Levinstein to serve as careful gatherers of both documents and oral traditions that were still available at the turn of the twentieth century. That does not mean, of course, that these can be treated as evidence of exactly what took place a century earlier, but they do preserve memory as it was handed down over several generations in a fairly stable and undisturbed local environment. This is also the case with a work like the memoirs of R. Yoshe Shub, a Slonim *ḥasid* writing in the 1880s but whose work was only printed in stencil form a century later. Sources like these need to be distinguished from works by figures such as Aharon Tseygengold and Yudl Rosenberg, among the many who published Hasidic stories in the pre-World War I period. These are essentially works of fiction inserting the names of Hasidic *tsaddikim* into plots woven of bits of folk memory and much of the authors' own imagination. Their main purposes were to entertain and inspire, especially to turn the attention of pious readers away from the newly emerging secular literature in both Hebrew and Yiddish. Most of the later collections of Hasidic tales, including the well-known collections by Yisra'el Berger, published under such titles as *'Eser Orot*, *'Eser Tsaḥtsaḥot*, etc.,[11] lie somewhere in the middle.

With regard to Levi Yitsḥak in particular, the first attempt at semi-modern biography was by his descendant Matityahu Guttman (1891–1972), published under the title *Tif'eret Beyt Levi* in 1910. There the young author is still identified as the son of the rabbi of Jassy in Romania. Guttman, who later bore the title of ADMoR (Hasidic *rebbe*) of Buhusi, lived in Tel Aviv and went on to write works about several other Hasidic figures. While the purpose of his book is clearly hagiographical, it is based on a close reading of earlier sources, along with family traditions, and there is much to be gleaned from it. Numerous recent pious biographies of Levi Yitsḥak, published in Israel, are of considerably less value, using the late legendary sources uncritically as the basis for their understanding.[12] An earlier English work by Samuel Dresner combines some careful research, evident in his notes, with an attempt to present its hero as a model for contemporary Jewish living.

III

In addition to being a rabbi and an influential leader of the Hasidic movement, Levi Yitsḥak was one of the most profound and original thinkers that movement produced in its early years. A major purpose of this book is to present his thought, both as a representative of the Mezritch school in early Hasidism and as a distinct figure within it.

The central texts of Hasidism, among which *Kedushat Levi* is certainly to be counted, have been well-known to the Hasidic faithful ever since their first publication. The fact of their frequent reprinting indicates that they continue to have a large reading public both within the Hasidic community and beyond it. But that public, especially in more recent generations, is not known for careful reading of these sources, either for historical context or for ideational content. Hasidic homilies are treated as a somewhat lighter form of reading, offering inspiration for the ongoing life of piety rather than being examined as sources of intellectual challenge and spiritual innovation.[13] While Talmud is still studied carefully within that community, and legal texts are given much critical examination, the same is usually not true of those texts that define Hasidism itself.

Modern historical scholarship that seeks to read these works more carefully and critically is, as mentioned above, a rather recent enterprise. The classic study of the Maggid's school is *Hasidism as Mysticism* by Rivka Schatz-Uffenheimer, first published in 1968. In that work, texts from a wide range of early Hasidic sources, both within the Mezritch circle and beyond it, are placed side by side with little attempt to distinguish between them. More recent scholarship has begun to distinguish diverse intellectual currents within that group, running across multiple fault lines.[14] This book continues in that tradition.

Reading collections of Hasidic sermons for ideational content is not a simple task. While the particular Torah passage that forms the nub of the sermon often affects the teaching's message, we need to remember that preachers are not biblical commentators. Their chief concern is with the lives of their hearers, for which the text before them is largely a foil. In the Hasidic case, this often refers to their followers' inner lives and moral conduct. The word *torah* means "teaching," the authors frequently remind us and then go on to ask, "What is this verse coming to teach us today?" Other aspects of the homily's setting or occasion, sometimes obvious but most often opaque to the latter-day reader, also play a role in the way things are said. Consistency is not an item high on the value list of these authors; often something found in one homily will seem directly in conflict with things found elsewhere within the same volume. Add to this the fact that our sources are highly abbreviated versions of oral originals translated into somewhat rudimentary Hebrew, a language that existed solely as a literary vessel. New and daring ideas, to the extent that they are found in these sources, come dressed up in quotations from older rabbinic sources in order to give them a sense of normative respectability.

All this means that the scholar has to read these sources with great care and insight, not jumping to conclusions due to the appearance of a particular term or turn of phrase. Comparison of passages, both by the same author and among contemporaries, especially within the same circle, can also be a useful tool. Within a particular author's writings, the question of preponderance is important to consider. Yes, there may be a few pious statements that speak of messiah's arrival—but that does not make him an ardent messianist. How frequent is that theme—or the call for ascetic renunciation, for example, or denunciation of it—when compared with other views and when compared with other figures within the circle? Descriptions of themes to be found in such works should also not devolve into presenting them as though forming a systematic theology, something very far from what these sources have to offer.

Hasidism emerged in the eighteenth century as a popular movement of mystical revival. Its preachers and authors used snippets of teaching from the prior traditions of Kabbalah, which many of them knew quite well, but they did not advocate for it in a totalistic fashion. The secret universe of Kabbalistic doctrine had become extraordinarily complicated and abstruse by this point in its development, far beyond the reach of the audience that Hasidism was seeking to engage. In some ways it may even be depicted as tottering near collapse, partly due to its role in the Sabbatian debacle but even more because of its own inner overelaboration. The Hasidic masters picked and chose from within this vast body of teachings and images, always interested above all in those elements that would excite the hearts of their listeners.

Those of us who are used to hearing today's sermons may be surprised at how little reference there seems to be in the Hasidic authors to the great historic transformations amid which they lived. Levi Yitsḥak's career saw the decline of the Polish kingdom and its eventual partition, beginning in 1772; the new situation of his Jews as subjects of the tsarist empire; the French Revolution and the early years of Napoleon; and the early rise of both *haskalah*, or Western Enlightenment, and calls for civil emancipation among European Jews. None of these, however, is openly mentioned in his sermons. Rabbinic Judaism from the early centuries of the common era expressed an alienation from, including a certain disdain for, events occurring within history, especially that of the surrounding non-Jewish world. The tradition depicted itself as existing in a degree of long-term suspended animation, living in the days of exile after the destruction of the Temple and prior to the arrival of messiah. It thus was not considered proper to openly mention worldly events on the political stage in the context of sermons. Needless to say, it might also have been risky to do so, particularly in those prominent communities in which Levi Yitsḥak served. More highly valued than the calendar of history were Judaism's twin sacred calendars: that of the weekly cycle of public readings from the Torah and that of festivals and fast days scattered through the year. It was to these that preachers and thinkers were to devote their attention, and it is around these, particularly the former, that most works of Hasidic teaching are organized.

The fact is, however, that none of us, however isolated, exists totally outside the realm of history. Both knowledge of ongoing events and the changing spirits of the times find their way into the preachers' words, even though one often has to read between the lines and engage in a degree of educated guesswork to draw them forth. Such relatively rare passages in Levi Yitsḥak's writings will be given special attention in the course of our readings throughout this volume.

The book is divided into two sections, the first considering its subject's life and the second devoted to an analysis of his thought. The opening chapter, longer than any other, constitutes a brief biography, constructed as best we can from existing historical documents. Use of the legendary sources, where I thought them to be of potential historical value, is limited and carefully documented in the notes. The following three chapters, primarily based on Levi Yitsḥak's own writings, place him in the context of the early Hasidic movement, seeking to describe his crucial role in its self-understanding and growth over the course of his career. The concluding chapter of section I, turning back to sources outside *Kedushat Levi*, places our author in the context of a well-documented dispute that emerged among Hasidic leaders in the years 1797–1805, giving us a larger picture of some of the issues that engulfed the movement as it was beginning to achieve success.

The second section deals with Levi Yitsḥak as a religious thinker, examining key questions in his teachings set in their historical context. But biography remains the focus. The aim is to view his treatment of themes and ideas as a way of understanding him as a person, with special attention given to his concept of his own role as leader and teacher. It begins with Levi Yitsḥak's intellectual/spiritual roots in the mystical teachings of his master, Dov Baer of Mezritch. We then seek to ask how these profound teachings related to the broad popular movement that Levi Yitsḥak had a key role in creating. This takes us especially to the question of miracles and how a sophisticated mystical thinker like Levi Yitsḥak sought to negotiate a relationship with the emerging notion of *tsaddik* as wonderworker, surely a key factor in the movement's spread. As we see the distinctive religious personality of Levi Yitsḥak emerge from his writings, we go on to take note of his positions with regard to several key questions that engaged the circle of the Maggid's disciples in the course of the decades following his death. In a movement that emphasized serving God with joy, it is no surprise that these include issues of pleasure and power (both for God and for the devotee) in the religious life, the role of the commandments, and freedom of reinterpretation of the Torah. The volume concludes with Levi Yitsḥak's particularly radical notion of the *tsaddik*'s powers and what that might have meant in the particular context of the times in which he lived.

PART I *Levi Yitsḥak as Hasidic Leader*

1

THE LIFE AND TIMES OF AN EIGHTEENTH-CENTURY RABBI

This opening chapter will summarize the life and rabbinic career of Levi Yitsḥak. But before turning to biography itself, we need to turn our attention to the word "rabbi" (translating *rav*) and what it meant in eighteenth-century Eastern Europe. In that context, we shall have to distinguish between *rav* and Hasidic *rebbe*. Levi Yitsḥak, although known to history as a great leader of Hasidism, served throughout his life in the career of *rav*, not *rebbe*.

The town rabbi in most places was designated as *rav av bet din*, "chief justice" of the local Jewish community. He functioned in a combination of legal, educational, and official roles, with the legal being the most significant. He was required to have formal ordination to serve in this role, which came from one of his teachers. All legal issues and disputes within the Jewish community were brought before and adjudicated by the rabbinic court, with the rabbi at its head. These included a great variety of business and financial matters, including disputes and competition among merchants, violations of contract, local business privileges, and many more. Marriage, divorce, and other areas of personal status within the Jewish community were also under rabbinic jurisdiction.[1] This meant that a very high degree of legal scholarship, covering a great variety of areas, was required for a successful rabbinic career. It was understood, in fact, that the rabbi was to spend most of his time studying, perhaps even composing books of commentary on Talmudic tractates or compendia of responses to legal questions that arose.

In the first years of Levi Yitsḥak's rabbinic career, there was still a weak but functioning regional body, called the Council of Four Lands, reaching beyond that of the local rabbinic court, which held a place of some authority, especially in commercial matters. But that body was disbanded in 1764 in a process parallel to the weakening of central authority in the declining Polish state itself.[2] Generally, even prior to that date, each rabbi was the final authority for the interpretation and fulfillment of Jewish law within his local community. In practice, however, younger or less prominent rabbis would write letters containing legal questions addressed to greater authorities or to specialists in a particular domain of law, and the latter would respond, perhaps then even publishing their responsa in scholarly volumes to be consulted by others.

In addition to matters of business and personal status, rabbis were expected to see to it that high standards of ritual behavior were observed within their communities. This meant supervision of kosher slaughterers and butchers, the maintenance of proper bathhouses for men and women, seeing to it that the Sabbath was not publicly violated, dealing with questions regarding women's menstrual purification, and much more. In larger communities, there would be a number of lesser officials who worked under the supervision of the rabbinate. These might include scribes, meat inspectors, and others. They would be employees of the *kahal*, or organized Jewish community, as was the rabbi himself. But he was seen as standing at the top of this pyramid, having to maintain a general sense of communal order and respectability.

Education was also a part of the communal rabbi's responsibility. While elementary schools (*ḥadarim*) and houses of study (*battey midrash*) were independent and largely without supervision, the rabbi was expected to offer classes on Talmudic law for the leading scholars of the city and to provide learning opportunities for unusually talented young men, the sort who might one day be future colleagues. Twice a year, on the Sabbaths preceding Pesaḥ and Yom Kippur, the *rav* was expected to offer a public discourse on legal matters related to these occasions. Other than that, preaching was not seen as a necessary part of the rabbinic role, although some chose to do so more frequently.

While much of the actual power within the Jewish communities remained in the hands of wealthy merchant-class lay leaders who appointed the rabbi, he too had a role as the proper Jewish legal authority within his town and the surrounding district. There were situations in which that authority came into contact, sometimes including conflict, with that of the state. The latter was much more intrusive after the partition of Poland and the inclusion of so many Jewish communities within the tsarist empire.

The reader familiar with today's rabbis and their tasks will notice that what we would call the "pastoral" function of the rabbinate is missing from this list. Responding to the personal needs of community members, whether in illness, mourning, or other forms of personal struggle (poverty, hunger, etc. among them), was not seen as the rabbi's particular responsibility. These were concerns of the community as a whole, not particularly those of the rabbi. As a practicing Jew, he had the obligation to fulfill such *mitsvot* as visiting the sick, comforting mourners, and burying the dead, but no more so than others. In larger communities, there were lay societies that dealt with these matters, only consulting the rabbi if some halakhic question came up in the course of their activities. A wide discrepancy thus existed between the potential needs of many within the community and the willingness or ability of its rabbinic leaders to fulfill those needs. The highly intellectualized world of rabbinic learning in Eastern Europe did little to support the people's desire for the rabbi as a "holy man." The typical *rav* was not expected to give out blessings or even to reassure those wavering in their faith because of personal troubles. Training in "spiritual leadership," one might say, was not part of the curriculum that led to the rabbinate.

Regarding the *rebbe*, it should first be noted that *rebbe* is an entirely informal title. Originally it simply means "teacher." One could be a *rebbe* in a *kheyder*, an elementary school, for example. To call someone your *rebbe* in Yiddish is simply to acknowledge him as your teacher, not necessarily implying anything Hasidic. It is in origin another form of the word *rav*; only once Hasidism became institutionalized were they truly distinguished from one another.

A Hasidic *rebbe* in the eighteenth century fulfilled none of the above-listed rabbi's functions. On the contrary, he came about precisely to fill those large gaps left by the rabbinate. Hasidism was founded around the image and memory of R. Israel Ba'al Shem Tov (c. 1698–1760), who had been a healer, an inspiring teacher, and one who offered blessing. *Ba'al shem*, in the generations immediately preceding Hasidism, had been seen as a profession, that of folk healer. A *ba'al shem* (literally "master of the name") knew how to use a combination of amulets, rituals, and natural herbs to effect healings in a place and time where modern medicine had not yet made its mark. Many of the *ba'aley shem* were also shamans or magicians, and their power to both bless and curse, including dealing with evil spirits, was widely accepted. The Hasidic *rebbe* is a descendent of the *ba'al shem*, renamed and transformed in early Hasidism into a spiritual guide, but one who also retains the power to bless and heal.[3]

In the late eighteenth century, when the young revivalist movement was just beginning to establish itself, there were essentially two ways of earning a living as a *rebbe*. Many of the future Hasidic leaders started out in the role of *maggid*, or communal preacher. These were paid a rather meager salary by the *kahal* in exchange for offering weekly sermons in the synagogue, usually delivered on Shabbat afternoons. These sermons were forms of erudition, especially in the realm of moral behavior, but had some function as venues of communal entertainment as well. Even semi-educated craftsmen and merchants enjoyed hearing a skillful preacher weave together disparate passages from the Bible, Talmud, and an array of prior homiletic sources in order to make his point, hopefully one of some originality. Listening to the preacher was considered a good and respectable way to spend time on a Shabbat afternoon, especially during the long Sabbaths of the summer months.

To be a *maggid* required a lesser but also a somewhat different education than that of a rabbi. Most were learned in the aggadic or narrative sections of Talmudic lore but less so in the heady and intricate arguments of the legal passages. Midrash, Zohar, and varying degrees of further Kabbalistic knowledge were also parts of the *maggid*'s education. Such preachers might also function as teachers of children in order to supplement their income. A distinct feature of the *maggid* in early Hasidism, as we shall see, was wandering about amid towns that were too small to have full-time preachers of their own and offering words of teaching, either on the Sabbath or during brief weekday visits, when they could also appeal for funds. Such gifts were also given in exchange for personal blessings. Many of these *maggidim* were also healers, and the combining of the roles of *maggid* and *ba'al shem* (although interestingly no longer called that) was characteristic of early Hasidism. These preachers began to develop a popular following, especially among these small-town and rural Jews, and that led to their evolution into Hasidic *rebbes*.[4]

Other *rebbes* served as neither rabbis nor preachers but chose to be supported by their disciples alone and were thus able to devote themselves fully to the teaching and propagation of Hasidic ideas and the cultivation of expanding circles of followers, what we today might call "movement building." These included two people very close to Levi Yitsḥak: R. Shne'ur Zalman of Liadi, the founder of ḤaBaD (or Chabad) Hasidism; and R. Elimelekh of Lezajsk. It was also true of R. Naḥman of Bratslav, a young *rebbe* to whom Levi Yitsḥak took a liking. Shne'ur Zalman, who certainly had the learned credentials to have been a successful communal rabbi, eschewed that career in order to create a wide-ranging network of personal devotees, who supported him and his court in a highly organized and disciplined fashion.[5] As Hasidism became more widespread and successful after the turn of the nineteenth century, this became the dominant model.

Levi Yitsḥak was a *rav*. As such, he was hired by communal boards, leaders of the *kahal*. As his hirers, they also had the power to fire him, which, as we shall see, they did more than once.

Levi Yitsḥak was born in 1740 in the town of Husakow in eastern Galicia (today western Ukraine),[6] where his father Meir served as the local rabbi. Both R. Meir and his wife, Sarah Sosia, were descended from rabbinical families and were thus members of the educated elite corps that, together with wealthy merchant families, stood at the helm of Jewish communal leadership in the eighteenth century. Their son's education certainly began at home, but Levi Yitsḥak's father died when he was quite young, and he was sent off to learn in the houses of study in somewhat larger towns, first in nearby Yaroslawl and later in Lubartow in the Lublin district, which had a particular reputation for maintaining a high level of Talmudic learning.

In Lubartow, probably in mid-adolescence, he met several people who were to have significance in his later life. Yissakhar Ber, later rabbi of Zloczow, was a friend and study partner. Both Levi Yitsḥak and Yissakhar Ber were young scholars in the *bet midrash* who impressed members of the wealthy Peretz family, leading merchants in the town and well-known in the district beyond. While still in their teens, the two young men were married to the daughters of two of the Peretz brothers. Levi Yitsḥak's bride was named Perl, daughter of Yisra'el Peretz.[7]

Typically, early marriage for budding scholars in Eastern European Jewish society was followed by a period of *kest*, full-time learning supported by the young scholar's father-in-law.[8] The length of this support was negotiated as part of the marriage contract. This was an easy task for someone like Yisra'el Peretz, who must have seen the "acquisition" of such a learned young man for his daughter as elevating the social standing of the Peretz family. Levi Yitsḥak probably continued to study in the local *bet midrash*. At the same time, marriage into this very prominent family probably meant that the young scholar was exposed to the family's business affairs as well.[9] Merchants of this class were much involved in travel and participated in periodic regional fairs, places where scholars as well as merchants often met, exchanging ideas along with merchandise.

It was while in Lubartow, or perhaps in the course of such travels, that young Levi Yitsḥak heard the reputation of, and then became acquainted with, R. Shmelke Horowitz, rabbi of Ryczywol.[10] R. Shmelke, fourteen years older than Levi Yitsḥak, was a significant halakhic scholar but had also become imbued with the spreading but still inchoate spirit of religious revival that would coalesce a decade later into the emerging Hasidic movement.[11] Levi Yitsḥak was also attracted to the thinking and new forms of religious praxis that were developing in these circles. At some point, probably shortly after the death of the Ba'al Shem Tov in 1760, R. Shmelke was drawn to the group of disciples forming around Dov Baer, the Maggid (or "preacher") of Mezritch (Mezhyrichi). Levi Yitsḥak eventually saw himself as a disciple of R. Shmelke, who in turn brought him, along with some other future leaders, into the Mezritch circle.[12]

Around 1761, when R. Shmelke was appointed to another, presumably more prestigious or lucrative, position as rabbi of Sienawa, the twenty-one-year-old Levi Yitsḥak took his place in Ryczywol. His rather youthful appointment to that post was most likely the result of the combined efforts of his mentor and the extended Peretz family. The Ryczywol community was losing a rabbi who was both an increasingly respected scholar and a member of the elite Halevi Horowitz clan, one of the most important rabbinic and merchant families of Poland. The fact that he recommended his disciple for the role was surely significant, but it probably helped that the Peretz family could offer the sort of contribution that was expected on such occasions. A town rabbinate was a source of prestige and secure income for a young scholar and usually had to be bought as well as intellectually earned.[13]

The appointment in Ryczywol determined the course of Levi Yitsḥak's professional career for the rest of his life. Although we think of him in retrospect as a Hasidic master, his only professional career was that of town rabbi, one he played out in a succession of four communities, the latter two of which were in fact very prominent rabbinical posts.

An interesting bit of drama in the Peretz family is recorded in a letter written to the first major historian of Hasidism, Simon Dubnov, by Rabbi Joseph Levinstein, one of his great informants and a master of local oral traditions. While Levi Yitsḥak was serving in Ryczywol, his father-in-law got into some serious financial difficulty with his patron, the nobleman who owned the town of Lubartow. Although the amount he owed was not huge, he was threatened with imprisonment unless he could pay it off. His daughter, Levi Yitsḥak's wife, turned to the nobleman, promising to pay off the debt with her husband's rabbinic salary. As a form of collateral, she even agreed, according to Levinstein's account, that if the sum was not properly paid, she would convert to Christianity! Her husband cosigned the note without properly understanding what was in it. When she told him, he was deeply shaken. Immediately he began wandering from place to place, seeking funds to pay off the debt. In the course of that wandering, however, he also shared the teachings of Hasidism, which began to make a great impression.[14]

In about 1765, the young rabbi made the first upward move within his rabbinic career, going from Ryczywol to the somewhat larger and commercially more significant town of Zelechow.[15] We do not know the precise circumstances of this move, but there is nothing to indicate that he had run into any trouble in his first post. The move to a rabbinate in a more prosperous place is in no way surprising. A prior rabbi of Zelechow had been a brother of R. Shmelke.[16] It would have been quite natural for him to have recommended his brother's protégé. This move might again have been greased by the financial connections of the Peretz family.

In 1765, Hasidism did not yet exist as anything one might describe as an organized religious movement. Stories of the Ba'al Shem Tov were beginning to circulate five years after his death, many of them about his miraculous healings and extraordinary powers of perception, but some also telling of his unique approach to spiritual questions. He had achieved fame partly for being a mystical teacher who rejected the harsh ascetic practices that had previously been associated with those who studied and practiced Kabbalah. He was known also as a lover of ordinary Jews who encouraged directness and simplicity in coming before an ever-present God. Intense and ecstatic prayer, often accompanied by gestures, shouts, and song, were also associated with him and with those around him. A few figures who had been his disciples or colleagues were beginning to spread his teachings, mainly in the southeast region of the Polish kingdom, quite far from Zelechow. Oral teachings, perhaps accompanied by small informal treatises on pious behavior or lists of devotional practices, were beginning to circulate from hand to hand.

Sometime during the course of his rabbinate in Zelechow, Levi Yitsḥak began to take on the practices associated with those emerging circles. We do not know whether this happened when he was still under the influence of R. Shmelke and a small circle around him or only after he had met R. Dov Baer of Mezritch, who was to become his most significant teacher.[17] The most important traditional account of Levi Yitsḥak's life describes his Zelechow period in these words:

> His practices and holy ways were a source of great wonder to the people of Zelechow. It is known that he was enflamed with sparks of godly fire, especially when at prayer. He was utterly enthusiastic, in a great and awesome way. He would shout aloud from the depths of his pure heart; anyone who heard him would feel his own heart melt away. He caused many to return from sin as they beheld his holiness and his constant attachment to the One who lives forever. Beholding his teachings and his devotion, which were his life and pleasure, the love of God took root in their hearts as well. The righteous of his generation said that he possessed the soul of Rabbi Akiva, of whom the Talmud reported that "if one left him praying in one corner of a room, one would find him in the other corner because of his many bowings and prostrations."[18]

While there is no reason to attribute specific accuracy to this late and very enthusiastic description, it does capture something of the moment it is meant to describe. The young rabbi was acting publicly in ways that were alien to Jewish life as the townspeople of Zelechow had known it. Perhaps practices like these, shouting and jumping about during prayer, were beginning to spread in places like Korets (Korzec) and Zloczow, far to the southeast of Zelechow (and they were being denounced there as well), but nothing like them had been seen in central Poland, and they seemed disturbing, perhaps even abnormal, to the leaders of the community. This behavior in prayer was to characterize Levi Yitsḥak throughout his life and is reflected throughout the legends. The phrase "he caused many to return from sin" in fact echoes language to be found in Levi Yitsḥak's own early sermons, as we shall see below, and may be translated as "he was spreading Hasidic practice among the people."[19]

A later local historian of the Zelechow community claims that Levi Yitsḥak was particularly remembered in the town for working with local charitable societies and emerging workingmen's guilds, features of Jewish life that were growing in importance in the late eighteenth century.[20] While these accounts may reflect the local societies' later attempts to link themselves to their town's famous onetime rabbi, they do fit in with the way Hasidism was typically spread: its messengers going around the strictly traditionalist leadership and spreading the new teachings and practices "from below" by dedicating time and attention to groups within the community that were usually neglected by their learned and wealthy leaders.

By insisting on spreading his Hasidic views and practices, alien to the ways of tradition as the local Jewish establishment understood them, Levi Yitsḥak succeeded in undermining his position as the community's rabbi. While organized opposition to Hasidism was just beginning to emerge in somewhat remote Lithuania and Belorussia, here it seems that the locals themselves reacted against the import of these strange and extreme-seeming Hasidic ways. There was a nearby rabbi named Uziel Meisels, later himself a devotee of Hasidism, who may have had a hand in legitimizing this opposition.[21] In any case, Levi Yitsḥak's contract as rabbi was terminated, and he was rather aggressively forced to leave the city.[22]

It was in the course of the Ryczywol and Zelechow years that Levi Yitsḥak and Perl became parents of seven children (perhaps also of others who did not survive childhood, as was typical).[23] Of their three sons, two became rabbis. Yisra'el, the eldest, became rabbi in the Ukrainian town of Pikov. After Levi Yitsḥak's death, he served for a short while as rabbi of Berdychiv, though he always retained his former title. He died in 1818. His book,[24] in which his father is frequently cited, appeared a year after his death. The second child was Meir, named for his grandfather. He, somewhat surprisingly, published his own little book of Torah insights in the Hasidic style when he was quite young.[25] We shall have occasion to refer to it, as well as to a teaching of his, below. Several of his short Talmudic interpretations are also included in *Kedushat Levi*. He died in 1806, during his father's lifetime, leaving behind a wife and four children. He does not seem to have held a rabbinic position.[26]

The fact that a deposed and somewhat controversial rabbi landed on his feet rather quickly, attaining a rabbinate far more prominent than that of Zelechow, is quite surprising. In 1775,[27] Levi Yitsḥak was appointed rabbi of Pinsk, one of the two leading cities of Polesia, the southern part of Belorussia. Pinsk was a long-established Jewish community, and this was a rabbinate that had been occupied by prominent figures in the past.[28] Of special significance is the fact that Pinsk was historically seen as one of five key cities that were under the domination of the Lithuanian rabbinate. The centers of that rabbinic authority lay in Vilna and Brest-Litovsk (Brisk), bastions of opposition to Hasidism. Just three years prior to Levi Yitsḥak's appointment, the Vilna authorities, partly at the urging of Rabbi Eliyahu, known as the Vilna Gaon, had published fierce denunciations and bans against the emerging movement.[29]

As was the case with Zelechow, it is hard to determine just how and why this much more significant appointment came about. Again, both religious and socioeconomic elements may be part of the picture. The area around Pinsk may be considered one of the original hotspots in the early Hasidic-Mitnaggedic conflict. One of the first disciples of R. Dov Baer of Mezritch brought his teachings to the area, establishing a Hasidic center in the nearby town of Karlin. He was active there by the late 1760s, perhaps earlier. R. Aharon of Karlin created a strong local following, so much so that in some of the anti-Hasidic documents that began to appear in 1772, the *ḥasidim* altogether are referred to by the term *Karliner*. R. Aharon died quite young in that same year, predeceasing his master by several months; he was the only one of the disciples to die before R. Dov Baer himself. His place was taken by his own follower, also a member of the Mezritch circle, R. Shlomo of Karlin. R. Shlomo offered a strong sort of folk Hasidism that attracted a growing base of support both within Pinsk itself and especially in the surrounding towns and countryside. This Hasidism, similar to that modelled by various Ukrainian *tsaddikim*, was later to offer a popular alternative to the much more intellectual ḤaBaD Hasidism that was centered to the north of Pinsk.[30]

Under the influence of the Karlin center, there were some members of the rabbinic elite in Pinsk who were also sympathetic to Hasidism. This was the case with Levi Yitsḥak's predecessor R. Raphael, who was leaving Pinsk for the very prestigious rabbinate of AHU, the three affiliated communities of Hamburg, Altona, and Wandsbeck in northwest Germany.[31] The head of the local *yeshivah*, R. Eliezer Ha-Levi, was close to some of the Hasidic *tsaddikim* as well. It may be that the influence of these local circles prepared the groundwork for the acceptance of a rabbi who publicly identified with Hasidism, in contrast to the situation in Zelechow. There Levi Yitsḥak had been a strange and somewhat alienating figure because of his Hasidic leanings. Here he was particularly welcomed by one element within the controversy-riven community, who got the upper hand with his appointment. From the beginning, however, there were those who opposed him, following the word coming so strongly from Vilna.

But there were other reasons that may initially have made this appointment attractive, even to those communal supporters who were not personally inclined toward Hasidism. Under the authority of the Council of Four Lands, Pinsk had been considered a major community, and Jews in a wide swath of nearby towns were held under its sway. This meant that the rabbi of Pinsk was their chief legal authority, but also that they paid taxes to the Pinsk *kahal*, significantly increasing its income and prestige.[32] Once the council was disbanded in 1764, the smaller communities began to rebel against this outside authority, whose power over them was no longer enforceable. Tax revenues decreased, and the Pinsk community found itself increasingly in debt. Typically, Hasidism first spread in smaller Jewish communities, unlike the cities, where elite rabbinic leadership held greater sway. It may well have been that Levi Yitsḥak, surely very much the candidate of the growing Hasidic populace of those towns, looked attractive to the leadership partly out of the hope that he might be the right personality to reaffirm their loyalty to his rabbinate and hence to the Pinsk community itself that employed him.

Levi Yitsḥak served as rabbi of Pinsk for about nine years. We do not have a lot of information about his life in that community. He seems to have conducted a *yeshivah* there, as would have been expected, and to have developed a number of local followers. He is also said to have continued to visit Zelechow, where he retained claim to the rabbinic title for reasons not entirely clear. There, too, he seems to have retained a personal following.[33]

A major event that occurred during Levi Yitsḥak's years in Pinsk was a public debate about the merits of Hasidism that took place in Praga, the Warsaw suburb where Jews were permitted to live, in 1781. This debate was conducted in the context of the second round of anti-Hasidic denunciations that took place in that year, beginning with the *ḥerem* of Grodno, issued on the third of Elul. The anti-Hasidic voice, representing the Vilna Gaon and the Lithuanian rabbinate as a whole, was R. Avraham Katzenellenbogen of Brisk, the other major community of southern Belorussia. The choice to hold the debate in greater Warsaw seems to indicate that it was to be presented as a major public event, perhaps one that would attract the attention of educated Poles as well as Jews. We do not know how Levi Yitsḥak was chosen (or "chose" himself) to be the Hasidic spokesman for that event, but his placement there is an indication of his position among early figures within the emerging movement. In that period, Levi Yitsḥak was the only one of the Maggid's disciples, the leading group that was promulgating Hasidic teachings, to be rabbi of a major community within the district of Hasidism's growth. R. Shmelke, Levi Yitsḥak's original mentor, was by this time in Mikulov (Nikolsburg), in Moravia, far away from the center of Hasidic spread and disputation. The others were mostly *maggidim*, a position of much less prestige. Levi Yitsḥak must have been looked upon as the "success story" of the growing Hasidic movement, a rabbi of a community of parallel importance and prestige to that of his opponent.

We do not have a surviving protocol of that debate. There is, however, a letter that Katzenellenbogen wrote to Levi Yitsḥak in 1784 proclaiming his victory and restating his objections to Hasidism.[34] He does so because it has become clear that the *ḥasidim*, including their spokesman, did not see themselves as having been defeated in that debate. He therefore repeats his objections to Hasidism and its innovations, essentially the same list as had been put forth in the bans of both 1772 and 1781. He looks upon Hasidism as a sect (*kat*), one that is turning Jews aside from the way of their righteous ancestors and also dividing the Jewish people. He treats Levi Yitsḥak with a degree of respect as a learned but seriously misguided colleague and urges him to repent and change his ways.

There is no remaining textual evidence of Levi Yitsḥak's side of that debate. If he replied to the Brisk rabbi's questions in writing, that document has not been preserved, and we have no way of knowing whether such a text once existed. Katzenellenbogen's statement regarding the debate itself, to the effect that Levi Yitsḥak could not open his mouth and had nothing to say in response to his accusations, may simply be his own triumphalist version of the encounter. But it is also possible that the lack of response, in writing as well as orally, points to a deeper spiritual strategy on Levi Yitsḥak's part, one of responding in silence. If we look through the earliest Hasidic teachings that were then circulating in manuscript, later to be edited into what is now called the "Conduct Literature" of Hasidism,[35] we will see that the value of *hishtavvut*, "indifference," is among the most often cited as key to a self-definition of the *ḥasid*. "It should make no difference whether people praise you or speak ill of you," these formulations often read, and some specifically urge silence in the face of one's opponents. It may be that this was the way Levi Yitsḥak chose to respond. In doing so, he would have been exemplifying one of the new movement's primary values, an act of witness more significant to his growing audience than anything he could have said in words might have been. Among the practices associated with some circles in early Hasidism (particularly around R. Avraham Kalisker, a fellow-member of the Mezritch circle) there were also acts of public self-humiliation as tactics to defeat pride, a sin that the *ḥasidim* often associated with the elite circles of the learned, including people like the rabbi of Brisk.[36] "Let them defame you," these texts urge. "Your silence in response is indicative of a deeper strength than any words you might offer." Of course, there is no way to prove that this is the case; the document might simply be lost.

While we have no response by Levi Yitsḥak himself to the charges made in the debate, we do have a most interesting letter in defense of Levi Yitsḥak written by R. Eleazar, the son of Levi Yitsḥak's friend Elimelekh of Lezajsk, at his father's behest and quoting his father at length. The text was published as an appendix to the first edition of the father's *No'am Elimelekh* in Lviv, 1788, shortly after R. Elimelekh's death.[37] Although it takes the form of response to a query, there is no indication of an addressee in the letter, and it is undated. One has a sense that it was intended as a public statement, serving as the Hasidic answer to the accusations against the growing movement. It is not clear whether it was written as early as the late 1770s in response to Levi Yitsḥak's difficulties in Zelechow or whether it was composed after 1781 to defend both Levi Yitsḥak and the emerging movement from the accusations of the rabbi of Brisk.[38] This document is the best articulation we have of the Hasidic view of the controversy. It is several pages in length, and we therefore will need to quote from it selectively.

> The pages written in your holy hand have reached me. There it is requested that I inquire of my lord, father, master, and teacher (May his light shine forth forever!) concerning the controversy that has been awakened, due to our many sins,[39] around that brilliant rabbi and famous *ḥasid*, head of the rabbinic court of Zelechow (May his light shine!).[40] I asked my father . . . and he responded in these words: "Why do you consider this new? Things like this have gone on forever! We find that our father Abraham, of blessed memory, was cast by Nimrod into a fiery furnace [a discussion of the sufferings and trials of Abraham goes on for about a page]. . . . How would you respond to all these difficult and astonishing matters?
>
> "But I will say this to you, and it is the truth. When a *tsaddik* serves God in awe and in love, a love that brings him nearly to madness, as in 'Infatuated with love of her always' (Prov. 5:19), [he may behave] as we find King David did, 'whirling with all his might [before YHWH]' (II Sam. 6:14).[41] That *tsaddik* ever rises from one level to the next, day by day, and the blessed Holy One acts toward him with renewed love each

day, whether above or below, according to his rung. But the blessed Holy One gives that love only by means of trials. This is because of [heavenly] accusations, since 'There is no *tsaddik* on earth who has not sinned' (Eccles. 7:20).[42] The Accuser finds some cause [to condemn] the abovementioned *tsaddik*, rising to accuse him. [The Accuser does so] even though God [surely] forgives him, since it is the way of the *tsaddik* to think immediately of repentance, regretting [any sin] and being strict toward himself down to every hairsbreadth.

"Surely, he will have repented! How then can the Accuser inform against him? He stands up there and says that he [the *tsaddik*] has done so only for the sake of being praised and glorified in the eyes of people. But if people would stand up against him and confound him, he would not be able to withstand the test. This would be proof that he had sinned. This is why the blessed Holy One tries him, so that he withstand such a test. In this way, God brings the *tsaddik* to a higher rung each day. . . . [Here follows a disquisition on the merits of the *tsaddik* versus the penitent.]

"The trials that God offers are in most cases brought about through wicked people since '[an accusation of] liability is caused by one who is himself liable.'[43] This follows the scripture 'The righteous will walk in them [God's ways], but sinners will stumble in them' (Hos. 14:10). . . . [Further learned disquisition.]

"'Lies have no legs'[44] and the wicked one is killing [only] himself. So long as the blessed Holy One can save him by means of some merit, He will do so. The final trial of Abraham was that of having to bind his son [upon the altar], so that his merit and the ashes gathered on that altar stand for all generations.

"Thus may merit all those who serve God and have opponents [*mitnaggedim*] who stand over them with lies and altercations. Our eyes see their righteousness as their prayers are answered, just as were those of earlier generations. May we merit to eat the fruits [of those prayers] and may their merit protect us."[45]

> There may be a leader of his generation great in both learning and ancestry, who is nevertheless a quarreler. It may be because he committed a sin and forgot to repent. It may also be due to a sin of his youth, requiring great repentance and self-humbling. Who is greater to us than King David, of blessed memory, who was constantly praying over the sins of his youth, as in "the sins of my youth" (Ps. 25:7)?[46]
>
> What could I do? I was forced to say these things in order to justify the *tsaddik*. This was originally based on the responses of my lord, father, teacher, and master, may his light shine.

Levi Yitsḥak, in short, is the innocent victim of a wicked accuser. Yes, he surely has sinned at some point in his lifetime, as has every person. As a *tsaddik*, however, he has certainly repented of any such sins, and God has forgiven him. Still, there is a need to explain why the *tsaddik* suffers. God continues to test him as a way of spurring on his constant spiritual growth. God does this by seeking out a truly wicked person, Levi Yitsḥak's accuser, and having him speak lies about him. Ultimately only the liar will be harmed by them. He has been given this role, undoubtedly, due to some truly terrible sin of his own.

R. Eleazar's letter then goes on to justify Hasidic changes in the liturgy and other matters not directly related to Levi Yitsḥak but responding to specific charges made by the *mitnaggedim* in the debate and the bans, including those repeated in the letter from the rabbi of Brisk. He does, however, make two other remarks that are especially worthy of mention. He claims that each generation of Jews looks back toward those that came before it, claiming that then there were true *tsaddikim*, even that *ruaḥ ha-kodesh*, the holy spirit, was present among them. They are unable, however, to see that the same is true of their own generation.[47] The disciples of the Maggid reported experiencing the presence of such a holy spirit around their master's table. He also claims that the evil inclination toward idolatry, which the Talmud asserts had been abolished in ancient times,[48] was now manifest again in a new sort of idolatry, the growing lust after money. This form of "evil inclination"—perhaps we would call it "human nature"—was a tendency that Hasidic leaders like R. Elimelekh sought vigorously to combat, both by teachings and (unlike some other *rebbes*) by personal example.

In 1784, the elders of Pinsk refused to extend their rabbi's contract. Once again,

Levi Yitsḥak was forced the leave the community he had led, apparently amid more disgrace. There is no question that this dismissal came about in part as the result of continued pressure from without, particularly from the circle of the Gaon in Vilna. There is a surviving letter from the leadership in Vilna dated 6 Tammuz 1784 demanding that the leaders of the Pinsk *kahal* remove their rabbi. While no name is mentioned, this unquestionably refers to Levi Yitsḥak. This letter gives the impression that it is a final warning in an ongoing exchange on this matter.[49] The language of the letter is uncompromisingly fierce and urges the community to chase him out of town. There is evidence that the community resisted such pressure when the second round of bans was first issued in 1781, but the anti-Hasidic authorities would not be assuaged. Finally, three years later, they gave in.[50]

In addition to the internal Jewish sources discussing this conflict in Pinsk, the local governmental archives preserve a pair of Polish-language documents that outline it in great detail.[51] As can be expected, these records reflect no awareness of the Hasidic-Mitnaggedic debate and the different readings of Jewish tradition that the two sides represented. They present it as an interpersonal conflict between the rabbi, his sons, and the town elders. The two sides are presented in these court documents as plaintiffs and respondents. This means that the conflict between the community and its rabbi was brought before the local Polish court. It had to be adjudicated by an outside authority since the accused himself was the head of the rabbinic court of the city. In any case, this was a matter that had come to concern the city itself, not just the Jews within it.

The harsh accusations reflected in these documents, both internal and external, clearly point to a deeper ongoing conflict between the rabbi and the communal authorities. It is not clear whether this conflict was entirely about the Hasidic-Mitnaggedic debate, about which the Polish court would have cared little and hardly understood, or whether there were other unrelated issues that divided them as well. The documents seem to indicate the latter case. The matter raised in these documents, as will be made clear by their publication, is ultimately one of judicial integrity. The rabbinic courts had no secure way in which to defend the integrity of how their judicial rulings were accepted or enforced.[52] The rabbi was indeed an employee of the *kahal*. He had no enforcement mechanism independent of the communal authorities who had hired him. If the town elders, as it appears in this case, supported the losing side in one of his adjudications, he was quite powerless to stand up against them. The issue here looks very much like one of judicial independence and integrity.

We have no way of determining the balance between these two elements in bringing Levi Yitsḥak's career in Pinsk to a bitter and abrupt end. It is also not clear how the separate issues of Hasidic practices and judicial integrity might have become bound up with one another. Previous scholarship has noted, however, that we have Levi Yitsḥak's signature on two printed encomia for authors, one signed in Pinsk on the 18th of Tammuz, 1785, and the other in Berdychiv on the 25th of that month.[53] It has been suggested that the Pinsk *kahal* most likely allowed its rabbi to complete his second five-year tenure in order to avoid paying fines for breaking his contract.[54] The signature in Berdychiv just a week later gives clear indication that his appointment there had been arranged some time in advance. Once it was clear to Levi Yitsḥak that he could no longer hold on in Pinsk, he sought another position, this time in a place where his by now well-known adherence to Hasidism would not be an issue.

The reception that Levi Yitsḥak received in Berdychiv, in a district where Hasidism was much less controversial, is found in an anonymous introduction to his first little publication, a commentary on the Six Remembrances, six items a pious Jew is supposed to recall each day. We shall have occasion later to examine that text in detail, but here it is the opening of that introduction that interests us. Although published in Levi Yitsḥak's ninth year as rabbi of Berdychiv, it gives the impression of having been written earlier, closer to his appointment there:

> We praise God all the day! This is the day we have hoped for; we have found and seen what our soul loves. Our glorious master and teacher, that brilliant rabbi, glory of Israel, father of mercies, pride of the holy, crown of the *ḥasidim*, the famous saintly *ḥasid* our teacher Levi Yitsḥak, may his light shine, formerly head of the rabbinic courts in Zelechow and Pinsk, has been publicly raised up as head of the rabbinic court and righteous teacher in our holy community of Berdychiv, may God protect it. He walks the royal [i.e., "godly"] path of endless devotion to study and worship, in God's holy service taking upon his shoulders the burden of the entire people, to be their shield and protector.

Levi Yitsḥak was to serve as rabbi of Berdychiv for twenty-four years, until his death. It is with this town that his name is permanently linked. It may even be said that the town's name itself has become famous in Jewish history because it is joined to the name of its most famous rabbi.[55]

The move from Pinsk to Berdychiv might best be described as a lateral one from the point of view of a rabbi in those times. Pinsk was certainly a more famous place in prior Jewish history. Its rabbinate was highly respected and it had long been known as a center of Jewish learning. The Wolhyn district to which Levi Yitsḥak was moving did not have the same reputation in rabbinic circles.[56] Only the rabbinate of Ostrog, the district capital located somewhat to the west, was known as a seat of distinguished scholars. But what Berdychiv did not have in prestige and history, it did have as a commercial center. The scholars who have studied it most closely have described Berdychiv between the 1780s and the 1840s as "the most developed trade and economic center in eastern Poland, on a par with the key market centers in central Europe."[57] The Radziwill family, a branch of which continued to own the town even after the area passed from Polish to Russian sovereignty in 1793, sponsored monthly fairs in the town in addition to the large annual fair, the most important in the entire region. Business at these events, as well as in the local market, was almost entirely dominated by Jews, who also worked as craftsmen and artisans, as was typical throughout Eastern Europe. There were multiple synagogues and houses of study in the town, and there certainly was a small number of full-time Torah scholars within them, but this was not Berdychiv's strength. There were about two thousand Jews living in Berdychiv when Levi Yitsḥak arrived in 1785; that number probably increased severalfold during the twenty-four years of his tenure, largely due to the economic opportunities it offered.

For the town's rabbi, this would have meant a busy courtroom docket. The presence of so many travelling merchants in town would have made for lots of cases of competition and trespass of established rights (*hassagat gevul*). One can imagine victims of alleged price gouging or receivers of inferior merchandise at these fairs frequently turning to the rabbinic court.[58]

Levi Yitsḥak also conducted a *yeshivah* for Talmudic and halakhic studies in Berdychiv. Unfortunately, we lack information about its organization, duration, or any special curriculum of study. We would love to know, for example, how much he allowed his own devotion to Hasidic teachings to impinge upon the course of study for those under his supervision. Would they have studied such works as those of the MaHaRaL of Prague, the Zohar, or the Lurianic writings, still circulating in manuscript, that clearly influenced Levi Yitsḥak himself? Or did he insist on sticking to the bare bones (or "meat and potatoes," depending on your point of view) of *GeFeT*, Talmud and commentaries, within the *yeshivah*?

On this point, we do have a very interesting testimony from none other than Levi Yitsḥak's son Meir. In the introduction to his little *Keter Torah* volume, published in 1803, he begins by presenting himself as the son of Levi Yitsḥak, adorned with a full array of honorary titles, and then adds, "The whole world knows that he has raised up several thousand students, having taught them *GeFeT* and the legal decisors. Their hearts were enflamed with devotion as they heard his holy teachings, guiding them in a straight path toward His service."[59]

Here we have what may be seen as an answer to our question. While the formal curriculum of the *yeshivah* seems to have remained quite traditional, the students there were exposed to Levi Yitsḥak himself as a religious personality. Ever committed to spreading the message of Hasidic revivalism, he must have found this an especially valuable setting in which to do so. In Berdychiv, where he was well established in his rabbinate and had no ideological opposition from the communal leaders, he was able to use his position as rabbi and *rosh yeshivah* to influence a whole generation of future leaders who had come to study there.

Levi Yitsḥak did not have anything like a Hasidic court in Berdychiv; he did not function as a *rebbe*. He also did not have a dynasty following him to aggrandize his memory, a matter we shall presently discuss. Nevertheless, he became known throughout Eastern Europe as one of the central figures of Hasidism. How did that happen? It may be that these few words by his son contain a key to resolving that question. Levi Yitsḥak used his prominence *as a rabbi* and an educational model to promulgate the style and content of Hasidism. It is likely that young men from smaller communities where Hasidism was beginning to gain influence chose to study in Berdychiv for that reason, and that others, not previously aware of the passionate and demonstrative prayer life and bold, creative, readings of Torah that characterized Levi Yitsḥak's teachings, were exposed to them and won over.

In a certain sense, Levi Yitsḥak may be seen as having redeemed and transformed the image of the *rav* for a generation of Ukrainian Jews. Instead of being tied up in ivory tower learning and holding himself aloof from the community, which was so frequently the case, he used his rabbinate as a way of passing on his intense devotional life to the students who surrounded him. Below, we shall offer some careful readings of the teachings to which these students listened with such rapt attention. As we shall see, these are filled with concern for ordinary people and responses to their needs. In Berdychiv, the key messages of Hasidism—passionate worship of God and love for ordinary "weekday" Jews—were carried forth by the rabbi himself. In doing this, Levi Yitsḥak became a model for many who came after him.

It is clear from Levi Yitsḥak's literary output that his own intellectual life was preoccupied mainly with mystical theology and creative interpretation of the Torah, as we shall see below. He authored a very fragmentary Mishnah commentary, really just a series of notes to the text published in a Berdychiv edition, but nothing more in the realm of Talmudic or halakhic studies.[60] In one place in the *Kedushat Levi*,[61] the author mentions that he intends to publish a volume of Talmudic and halakhic novellae, something that might have been expected from a rabbi of his stature, but it never came to be. This may be an indication that he indeed did have ideas in this area, as did his sons, but that other matters took precedence for him.

That precedence forces us to call into question the assertion with which we opened this chapter: the claim that Levi Yitsḥak was a *rav*, not a *rebbe*. While that is true regarding his professional status, his written legacy leads completely in the other direction. He writes as would a *rebbe*, not a *rav*. We do not know how much of the *Kedushat Levi* reflects an oral *Vorlage*. Many of the teachings are brief insights he might have shared with students in his *yeshivah* or perhaps around the table or along the road, as did many a Hasidic *rebbe*. Others look like fuller sermons, but we do not know before what congregations they might have been preached. Recalling that regular preaching was not part of the rabbi's task, there was also nothing to have prevented him from doing so, if he was so inclined.[62]

Among Levi Yitsḥak's leading disciples, some are known exclusively for Hasidic leadership and teachings, while others excelled in rabbinic knowledge as well. The name usually first mentioned among his followers is that of Aharon of Zhitomir, *maggid* in said nearby town until his passing in 1815. Aharon was originally from Lithuania, and he had first been a follower of the Gaon of Vilna. He became close to Levi Yitsḥak while he was rabbi in Zelechow, and then followed him to Pinsk and Berdychiv. He is also said to have travelled with him on visits back to Zelechow.[63] His book, collected sermons called *Toledot Aharon*, was published in Berdychiv two years after his death, like that of his master. He frequently cites Levi Yitsḥak, and it is clear that the values he expresses are very much those of his master. It is likely that the very important collection of teachings attributed to both Levi Yitsḥak and Aharon published in 1821 under the title *Ge'ulat Yisrael* was composed in the circle of his disciples.

A very different follower of Levi Yitsḥak was Rabbi Avraham David Wahrman of Buczacz (d. 1840). He was one of the earliest rabbis within the Hasidic sphere known to have had something of a secular education along with his extensive Torah knowledge. He is said to have known both Polish and German and to have taken an interest in mathematics and modern science. He composed several important halakhic works, including *Da'at Kedoshim*, the name by which he is known in rabbinic circles, as well as a Hasidic-style collection of homilies called *Birkat David*.[64]

The figure from within Levi Yitsḥak's circle who was most successful as a Hasidic leader in the next generation was Moshe Zvi Guterman of Savran (1775–1838). The rabbi of Savran was one of the most powerful and popular leaders of Hasidism in Ukraine in the 1820s and '30s. Alongside Levi Yitsḥak, he was also a follower of such figures as R. Barukh of Miedzybozh and the Elder of Shpola, who represented a very different sort of Hasidism. While claiming the prestige of discipleship to Levi Yitsḥak, it is probably fair to say that in practice he more represented the folk Hasidism of his other masters. He was a rabbi, however, and supposedly a person of significant learning. For some period, he even served as rabbi of Berdychiv. His only work is a brief collection of Hasidic teachings called *Likkutey Shoshanim*. He is remembered in history especially for his fierce enmity to Rabbi Nathan of Nemirov and the *ḥasidim* of Bratslav.[65]

Another follower of Levi Yitsḥak in his final years was the future R. Yitsḥak of Neskhiz (Nesukhoyshe), the son of R. Mordechai, an early Hasidic leader from outside the Mezritch circle. R. Yitsḥak married a granddaughter of Levi Yitsḥak four years before the latter's death. He became part of the household and passed on various traditions in the name of his grandfather-in-law. These were published in 1892 in a little book called *Zikhron Tov*, containing some interesting and significant material. This includes a firsthand memoir of Levi Yitsḥak's personal demeanor:

> On Shabbat *'ekev* in 5627 [= summer of 1867, a year before his death], he recounted that the rabbi of Berdychiv was always in a happy state [*sharui be-simḥah*]. It was by this power that he [had the strength to] work at praying. Our master said that once he saw him sitting at his table on the eve of Yom Kippur, singing very lovely tunes. Just two tears, no more, flowed out of his eyes. Afterwards, they brought before him the stuffed fish, and he said, "May God fulfill all our wishes!" Then they brought some gravy, called *yeikhel*, and he began to call out loudly, "Let Israel

> hope [*yaḥel*] in God!" He went on, being very, very happy. All of his devotion was with incredible joy.[66]

The rabbi of Neskhiz also reports that the Berdychiver opposed the excessive use of fasting as an ascetic practice. The desire to fast, he said, "was an act of the evil urge, seeking to weaken the body so that one not be able to serve God."[67]

Among the other important disciples of Levi Yitsḥak were R. Shmuel Kaminka and R. Hayyim Krasner. A late legendary source preserves a memory of R. Elimelekh of Lezajsk reprimanding Levi Yitsḥak for "stealing" his disciples. It appears that a number of members of the Lezajsk circle began visiting Berdychiv as well. Levi Yitsḥak responded to his elder colleague in a deferential way: "Whose disciple am I, after all? If they come to Berdychiv, they are coming to a disciple of their master."[68]

In Berdychiv, the opposition that Levi Yitsḥak faced was not from the Jewish communal leadership, as in his previous two posts, but from the Polish owner of the town, Prince Radziwill. The multibranch Radziwill family was among the most prominent within the Polish nobility, but the particular branch that held ownership of the estates that included Berdychiv was somewhat impoverished and deeply in debt, partly due to the bad management of Micolai Radziwill's mother, Eleonora. As her son took over control of the increasingly wealthy town in the early 1790s, he tried to squeeze its population as much as possible in order to repay his debts and maintain the lifestyle and honors he considered appropriate to his station. He did this partly through Jewish leaseholders, who paid him an annual sum and therefore themselves felt they had a right to retrieve their costs from the townsfolk, and partly through direct taxation. Jews complained to the tsarist authorities about this double burden, but the general policy of the new Russian overlords at that point was to respect the privileges of the Polish nobility.

This conflict has been described in great detail by Yoḥanan Petrovsky-Shtern. Following is a brief excerpt:

> Mateusz Mikolai Udalryk Radziwiłł (ca. 1762–after 1835), who Russified his name and presented himself in his letters to the Russian government as Nikolai Radziwiłł, was a typical representative of the great Polish magnate family in decline. . . .
>
> . . . He introduced new taxes, raised the payment for lease-holding contracts, including the position of the town rabbi. Because he loved

to live and spend lavishly, accrued debts without measure and had no consideration for the economic benefit of the town, he taxed the merchants on items never taxed before under the current state regulation. In addition to a regular residential tax, he also introduced special taxes for repairing old and building new houses. He demanded more and more from his leaseholders, for example, from the candlemaker, who had to increase the price of candles by 25 percent. He allowed only his own weights and measures on the market square for which people had to pay the leaseholder—or, if they preferred to use weights and measures of their own, they could pay 150 rubles to the town owner instead. . . .

In almost every plea and complaint of the Jews of Berdychiv, whether detailed or brief, one of the most painful issues was that of the taxation that the town owner imposed on the practice of Judaism . . . "Our religion is leased by the [town] owner. In order to conduct our own religious service we are obligated to pay money to those who have leased our creed from the Prince [Radziwiłł]. Even the consciousness of each of us is not free to express its religious needs." And in a different plea: "Radziwiłł has appropriated the boxes for alms and for orphans." And again: "Even our religion and rabbinic positions are leased." And in greater detail: "The rabbinate itself is leased so that when a rabbi is elected we are obligated to pay the lessee. Jews have repeatedly complained of this to the authorities but they have obtained no protection."

. . . Despite an old privilege allowing Jews to elect rabbis and requiring rabbis to pay the town owner some 1,000 zloty annually, Radziwiłł repeatedly tried to appoint his protégés to the post. . . . Radziwiłł then commanded the town rabbi—that is, Levi Yitsḥak—to pay at least 500 zloty, or risk imprisonment. In 1793, he appointed four Jews . . . as "judges," purportedly to settle the issue of the tax on the rabbi's position; the real purpose was to lease to them the 4,000-zloty tax for the post, thereby enabling them to choose the town rabbi who best suited their interests. In fact, Radziwiłł did his best to establish a new type of rabbinic court absolutely independent of the chief town rabbi, routinely fulfilling the role of the head of the rabbinic court. In 1794, he directly accused Rabbi Levi Yitsḥak of inciting local Jews against the town owner. He demanded that the rabbi immediately sell his property and leave town. After another strong protest on the part of the local community and intercession of the town's financial elite, Radziwiłł acquiesced and allowed the town rabbi to stay, though he claimed that the 4,000-zloty tax was the price for his benevolence.[69]

As rabbi of the town and as a defender of judicial integrity against bribes and rampant corruption, Levi Yitsḥak was caught in the middle of this controversy. The dispute between Radziwill and Levi Yitsḥak was protracted and ugly. In the course of "milking" Berdychiv for every ruble he could, including the selling and reselling of privileges, Radziwill found that the town had a rabbi who ran honest courts and stood up for his community. He tried to convince the new tsarist overlords to allow him to dismiss this rabbi and choose one of his own, to whom he would sell this worthwhile position. All this came to a head in 1793–94. But his efforts did not succeed. It would seem that the Jews of Berdychiv, including most of the leadership, in this case rallied around their rabbi and saved him from the fate of losing yet another position. But the conflict surely took its toll.

Berdychiv, and the Wolhynian district of which it was a part, came under tsarist control in the second partition of Poland in 1793. This change was to be a decisive one in the history of Jews throughout Eastern Europe. Instead of the weak and disorganized Polish government, where real authority over a town or district was in the hands of the noble family that legally "owned" it, a centralized imperial bureaucracy took an increasingly strong hand in all areas of governance, including matters that concerned the status of the Jews. While the imposition of this new authority was slow and incremental, it clearly worried Jews, who generally anticipated in it a worsening of their condition and an erosion of their relative independence under the old system.[70]

We are told by a later Hasidic source that in this same year, 1793, the usually well-disposed rabbi of Berdychiv went through a period of *ḥalishut ha-da'at*, literally "weakened consciousness," that he "prayed quickly from a small prayer-book," and that "his mind was somewhat shut down."[71] In the idiom of the time, this probably means an episode of mental exhaustion or depression but possibly even what we might term a nervous breakdown, one in which he set aside the attempt at attaining mystical heights and just managed to hold on, praying simply to fulfill his obligation. It is likely that this reflection of inner torment in that year was partly related to the political and legal threats he was under and a fear that he and his family might again become wanderers.[72] The source that reports it, however, attributes this situation to Jews who belonged to the *'erev rav*, the "mixed multitude," who were unworthy to be in the *tsaddik*'s presence. While this term had been used in the recent past to describe both Frankists and *ḥasidim*,[73] here one wonders if it might not refer to activities of early *maskilim* in Berdychiv. Is it possible that their growing presence in this city that had become such a commercial center and was clearly liable to influences by travelers and the new ways they brought with them might have become too much for the city's rabbi to handle, especially while he was at the same time doing battle with the gentile overlord and having to adjust to the new Russian regime?[74] Quite a series of events, and they seem all to have come to a head at once in that year.

In the long run, the Russian authorities seem to have sided with the townspeople, and the prince withdrew his attempt to replace Levi Yitsḥak with a candidate of his own for the Berdychiv rabbinate. This seems to have initiated a long period of relative peace and success for Levi Yitsḥak, parallel to the growing prosperity of the town itself. Berdychiv continued to prosper through the latter years of Levi Yitsḥak's rabbinate, as it did well into the first half of the nineteenth century. It was a major hub of commerce and eventually of finance as well.

One industry for which Berdychiv became well-known and that Levi Yitsḥak had a major hand in shaping was the printing of Hebrew books.[75] Hebrew printing had become a widespread phenomenon in the Ukraine beginning in the 1770s. Many towns housed small printing houses, some of them lasting only a few years before their owners got a better offer from a nearby nobleman or community and moved their presses to a new location. Place names such as Korzec, Ostrog, and Slavuta, all of them not far from Berdychiv, became known in the Jewish world through the distribution of books printed in them. Given its general commercial prominence, Berdychiv was somewhat late in establishing a printing industry. The first Hebrew book published there appeared in 1807.[76] Its publisher was Shmuel ben Yissachar Ber Segal, a wandering printer who had previously been associated with books appearing in several other places. The book was the opening tractate *Berakhot* of the Babylonian Talmud, apparently printed with the intent of inaugurating the new printing house with the grand gesture of an edition of the entire Talmud. The volume was published with an enthusiastic approbation by Levi Yitsḥak in support of the endeavor, but no more of the set appeared. The Berdychiv printing house was a long-range success, however, remaining open until 1821. In 1815, a second printing house was opened by Berdychiv native Yisra'el Bak, later famous as the pioneer of renewed Hebrew printing in the Holy Land.

As rabbi of such an important community, on at least two occasions Levi Yitsḥak also seems to have played a public role in interactions with the Russian government. Both of these were around attempts at legislation to change the status of the Tsar's newly acquired Jewish subjects. In 1791, Levi Yitsḥak was in Warsaw to lead an assembly of both prayer and *shtadlanut* (influencing government officials) in response to a new "constitution" affecting the Jews' status. Until the Holocaust, memory was preserved of the synagogue where Levi Yitsḥak had prayed and the *shtender* (standing-box) he had used on that visit.[77] In 1803, when major changes were introduced restricting the residence and livelihoods of Jews in the Pale of Settlement, the rabbi of Berdychiv hosted a conference in Berdychiv that included both Hasidic *rebbes* and some early *maskilim*, making common cause in this case to protect the rights of village Jews. The conference did not succeed, but memory of that joint effort was long remembered, and a description of it is found in the memoirs of Ukrainian *maskil* Avraham Baer Gottlober, composed some seventy years later.[78]

From the internal Jewish sources, most of them sermons and religious teachings, it is hard to judge any particular eighteenth-century person's level of interest in and contact with the surrounding non-Jewish world. But we should also remember that Hebrew books printed in the tsarist empire were subject to government censorship, as were all publications. Many books appearing in the late eighteenth and early nineteenth centuries had some version of the following notice printed right on their title pages:

> The wise will understand on their own that the nations [*goyim*, also "gentiles"] who existed in the time of the Talmudic sages, of blessed memory, are not like those nations in whose lands we live [today]. They worshipped stars and constellations and were involved with all sorts of abominations. They did not know God or recognize His holy scriptures. But the nations in our times are God-fearing. They give honor to His Torah and administer judgment and justice in their lands. They are compassionate with the Jews who dwell under their wings. God forbid that we should say or write anything derisive about them. Anywhere in these books that the word *goy* or *nokhri*, "foreigner," or anything like it appears, they refer to the idolators who existed in the time of the Mishnah.

Preachers and authors had to be very careful what they said or wrote with regard to the outside authorities or the political surroundings amid which they lived. They therefore developed very subtle ways of making such references, so much so that even careful readers cannot say with certainty that they in fact refer to such events or situations. With this in mind, we should look at the following interpretation Levi Yitsḥak offers of the biblical Moabites' refusal to allow Israel to traverse their territory on the way to the Land of Israel:

> "Moab feared the people greatly because they were many; Moab detested the Children of Israel" (Num. 22:3). Why is Scripture precise in first referring to "the People" and only afterwards saying "the Children of Israel"? It is known that in the Midrash and the Zohar, "the people" often refers to the mixed multitude [who came out of Egypt with Israel]. "Moab feared the people," fearing that wherever Israel dwelt, people joined them as converts, like the mixed multitude, who were converted. That is why they were afraid to let Israel into their borders. Some of their nation might convert as well! Lest you say, "What difference would that make to them?" Scripture adds, "Moab detested the Children of Israel"; they hated Jews extremely.[79]

As mentioned, Berdychiv and the Wolhynian district surrounding it was joined to the Russian empire in 1793. Shortly afterwards, in December of 1794, the Jews who had come to live within Russia's borders from the former Polish territories were restricted to remaining within those newly acquired provinces, deemed the Pale of Settlement.[80] Jews were not allowed to settle anywhere in the Russian interior and needed special permission even to travel there. "Why is this?" Levi Yitsḥak must have heard his people asking. "Why do they hate or fear us so much?" The answer, he is telling them, is that they have a fear of such conversions. Indeed, the tsarist state, since the late fifteenth century, had persecuted what were termed "Judaizing heresies," elements within the Russian community that were adopting Old Testament practices, creating sects that were somewhere between an unrecognized Judaism and a primitive Christianity.[81] The Russian Orthodox hierarchy was deeply threatened by this phenomenon and caused the state to forbid Jews from dwelling on Russian soil, even though there is no evidence that this internal Russian development was a result of ongoing proselytizing by Jews.

It is likely that Levi Yitsḥak, an educated person who had contact with the outside world, was aware of this history. Can we *prove* that this is the object of his comments on the behavior of the Moabites? We cannot. But had it been stated in a way that was more obvious, the rabbi of Berdychiv could have faced big trouble. We need to remember when reading Hasidic teachings that these are the work of *preachers*, not biblical interpreters. What concerns the preacher are things happening in his hearers' lives. Often, in the Hasidic sources, this refers to their inner lives, their struggle for deeper faith or religious awareness, but not always. Sometimes, interpreting the text is a way of commenting on current happenings, either within the Jewish community or beyond it, from within the tradition. Keeping this in mind, I think we find Moab's fear of Jewish proselytization to be a fairly transparent stand-in for tsarist Russia.[82]

Rabbinic tradition has it that there are seventy nations in the world, an essentialist or conventional number. Each of these nations has a heavenly ruler, a *sar* or angel who is responsible for the fate of that particular nation and its people; only Israel is ruled by God directly. Each nation, Levi Yitsḥak notes (he does not distinguish ethnic from religious groupings), also has a distinctive script that belongs to it: the sacred Hebrew letters to the Jews, the Latin alphabet to the Poles or Catholics, Cyrillic to the Russians, and so forth. When one nation is defeated by another, he claims, both its angel and its script have been defeated: "The script and language are the means by which the angel receives divine bounty, and the nation receives it from him. Once the angel falls, that nation has no more script or language. It is known [i.e. obvious] that any nation that no longer governs but is ruled over by another no longer has an angel."[83]

He then illustrates his point by reference to a Talmudic comment on the fate of Babylon. But there seems to be little doubt that he also has in mind the defeat of Poland. As official rabbi of an important town, he was certainly aware, after 1793, that official documentation now had to appear in Cyrillic rather than Latin script.

In the same passage, he goes on to say that there have been some *tsaddikim* among the Jews who were able to master all seventy of the world's scripts and tongues, thus giving them the potential of power over all those opposing angels. The biblical Joseph and Mordecai serve as his examples. It would not seem at all farfetched to see this as the rabbi's justification for his own attempt to master the language of Berdychiv's new masters, an effort that would have been considered taboo by later and less enlightened generations of *ḥasidim* who were to follow.[84]

Levi Yitsḥak did a good bit of travelling across Eastern Europe over the course of his lifetime.[85] Later accounts (in these it is hard to separate fact from legend) place him as having visited Hungary quite early, perhaps during the Ryczywol or Zelechow years. Of course, he spent significant time with the Maggid in Mezritch and Rovno in the years prior to the latter's death in 1772. He is said to have visited Zelechow several times after he left; he seems to have had supporters there who remained faithful to him long after he was gone.[86] He refers at least once in *Kedushat Levi* to a visit to Lithuania,[87] a region to which he likely travelled more than once. Legend has him in various other places, often supporting his fellow Hasidic leaders or just seeking out the welfare of simple Jews. It is told that he once visited the Transylvanian district called Siebenburgen (today northwestern Romania). This was an area that by the mid-nineteenth century had a quite varied Jewish community, parts of it Hasidic and quite religiously extreme, but other parts where linguistic and cultural assimilation had already progressed significantly. Hasidic tradition has it that wherever Levi Yitsḥak had visited, tradition was upheld. It was only those places he had skipped where modernity managed to make inroads.[88] Whatever the historical value of that claim, it is indeed an indication that the rabbi of Berdychiv, wherever he travelled, had a great impact on the ongoing spread and popularity of Hasidic faith and practice.

Levi Yitsḥak died in Berdychiv on the 25th of Tishrey in 1809 at the age of 69. At some point shortly after his passing (perhaps a year or two later), his son Yisra'el, established as rabbi of much smaller Pikov,[89] was given the title of rabbi of Berdychiv. He seems to have served there for several years until his death in 1818,[90] but without leaving a strong mark on history. Despite this, there is no evidence of any attempt by him or his own children to establish anything like a Berdychiv dynasty. This fact in itself is somewhat curious in an age where that was increasingly becoming an accepted practice within Hasidism.

For a possible explanation, we turn to a most interesting document by Levi Yitsḥak's son Meir, who had predeceased him. This belongs to a group of a few short teachings by Meir that were included in his father's book. Meir is commenting on a Talmudic discussion of the verse in Psalm 86:2, in which King David (the presumed author of the Psalms) says, "Guard my soul, O Lord, for I am a *ḥasid*." Could it be, the Talmud asks, that David would have been so immodest as to refer to himself in that way? It responds by claiming that David in fact functioned as a rabbi (*moreh hora'ah*), in contrast to other kings, whose task was to wage war. It was because of this that he was right in considering himself a *ḥasid*, here meaning a pious person. But if he was in effect a rabbi, Meir asks, how could God have promised him that his descendants would succeed him? A well-known authority, the *Magen Avraham*,[91] had decided that the post of a rabbi, one who issues legal opinions, should not pass by inheritance, because decisions will have to be issued and they demand the person of greatest wisdom rule on them rather than someone who has the post by inheritance. David's case, Meir winds up saying (after long further discussion), was an exception to this rule since his son Solomon turned out to be the wisest of all men.

One might take this text simply as another little exercise in Talmudic mental gymnastics, along with several others that are brought in Meir's name. But I think it has to be looked at in historical context. Levi Yitsḥak chose to publish this little *pilpul* by his son in 1798, just at the time when the dynastic principle of succession was starting to establish itself in the Hasidic world. That was the very year when Mordechai of Chernobyl succeeded his father, Menaḥam Naḥum, the first step in creating the extensive Chernobyl dynasty that so dominated Hasidic life in Ukraine. The sons of Yeḥiel Mikhl of Zloczow were also acting already as *rebbes*. True, those were successions of a *rebbe*, not a *rav*. But it may be that this document reflects a distaste that Levi Yitsḥak, at that point probably the most prominent figure in the Hasidic world, cultivated in his sons for the notion of passing on either sort of post by succession. He was also at odds with R. Barukh of Miedzybozh, who was trying to assert his rule over all the *tsaddikim* because he was grandson of the Ba'al Shem Tov. Inheritance, after all, was also the source of the authority of Prince Radziwill, whom he had had to resist so strongly. A man who cared as much as Levi Yitsḥak did about the integrity of the halakhic system would have agreed with this ruling by the *Magen Avraham*, one that was ignored then, as it often is now. Perhaps Levi Yitsḥak discouraged the formation of a dynasty, wanting leadership to pass on, in good rabbinic fashion, to disciples rather than to sons and hopefully to the wisest among the next generation.[92]

2

LEVI YITSḤAK IN THE MAGGID'S CIRCLE

The Challenge of Leadership and the Hasidic Response

Levi Yitsḥak of Berdychiv was a key member of the circle of disciples surrounding R. Dov Baer of Mezritch (1704–1772), generally known simply as the Maggid, or "preacher." It was chiefly out of this circle that Hasidism achieved its fame and grew to be a major phenomenon on the Jewish historical stage. While Dov Baer presented himself as a disciple of Israel Ba'al Shem Tov and inner Hasidic historiography attributes the founding of Hasidism to the BeSHT, as he is called, it is clear to historians today that it was chiefly members of the Mezritch circle who conveyed the teaching and religious experience of their master's small spiritual/intellectual hothouse to ever-widening circles of listeners and readers, creating a large-scale religious and social movement. It was they who turned outward during their master's lifetime, and even more fully after his death, to extend the Hasidic message over broad areas of territory and to articulate its message. In the years following 1772, that message was made accessible to ordinary Jews as well as to the sort of learned and enthusiastic devotees to whom the Maggid had originally addressed himself. In the various controversies and debates about Hasidism, lasting until the end of the eighteenth century, it is always the Maggid's disciples who are in the foreground. Almost all of the major schools and dynasties that came to dominate Hasidic life have their ultimate origins in Mezritch.[1]

The Mezritch years (c. 1764–1772) represent the formation of a close spiritual brotherhood, a group of young men intensely devoted to their master, to a set of ideals, to the task of spreading religious revival, and (for the most part) to one another. The Maggid was seated at the center of the first Hasidic "court," a place to which confirmed and would-be disciples could come to hear his teachings and behold something of his glory.[2] While the Maggid's court was quite informally organized, and we are unclear as to who among his disciples were there together at any particular time, the later writings by members of the circle attest to the formative importance of those early years in the lives of its participants. Members of the circle continued in this work for decades after their master's death, basing their teachings as well as their claim to authority on both the BeSHT and the Maggid. Over the years, differences in both personality and ideology colored their works, mostly published near the end of their lives or posthumously, creating an interesting diversity within the emerging Hasidic movement. Levi Yitsḥak outlived Dov Baer by thirty-seven years, always referring reverentially to him as "my master and teacher," even when some of his own views seemed to diverge from those of his master. Other members of the group also lived on into the opening decade of the nineteenth century. The end of this so-called third generation of Hasidic leadership and the waning of its influence are generally depicted as having taken place between 1809 and 1815.

Dov Baer of Mezritch is a complex religious figure, one about whose life very little is known. The tales say that he was already a learned scholar of Kabbalah before he encountered the BeSHT, but that his life was completely transformed by their meeting. One version of their first encounter says that the BeSHT healed him from an affliction of his legs, one possibly caused by excessive devotion to ascetic practices. The healing was effected by something of a magic ritual, the BeSHT circling him with his staff. Another speaks of the master explaining a text, one that the Maggid thought he had already understood, in a way that caused fiery angels to appear around the page.[3] Dov Baer has been described as an introverted religious personality, one who was overwhelmed by the highly extroverted and miracle-filled life of the BeSHT.[4] His main work was within the circle of his disciples, where he seems to have exercised a kind of quiet charisma that allowed each of them to develop his own path of integrating and carrying forward his powerful and transformative teachings. While some early sources claim that the BeSHT transferred his supernatural powers of perception to the Maggid,[5] in fact these played little if any role in that which he chose to pass on to his own disciples.

What was the nature of the shared Hasidic faith that formed the bond among the members of this diverse and highly creative circle? Terms like "popular mysticism" and "revivalism," while appropriate descriptions of Hasidism, do not in themselves tell us very much. Devotion to the personal figure at its center, as well as to the memory of the BeSHT, along with their teachings, is another way to define this group. But the intense bonds that constituted this circle were more than either personal loyalty or intellectual commitment. They were based on a degree of shared religious experience, the memory of deep and sometimes transformative spiritual impressions made upon them by their visits to Mezritch and their contact with the Maggid.[6] These experiences, only seldom talked about in direct terms, reverberate through their teachings, often spoken and then recorded in writing decades after the times "around the Maggid's table" had turned into memory. While expressed in the language of theological speculation and homiletical flourish, it is not hard to see evidence of the mystical experience that underlies them.

Writing in the mid-nineteenth century, the Hasidic bibliographer Aaron Walden offers a list of thirty-one figures whom he describes as Dov Baer's disciples, based mostly on quotations from the Maggid as "my teacher" in their writings. We do not know how close the discipleship of each was, nor do we have any idea how frequently each of them visited the Maggid's court or how long each stayed.[7]

The Maggid's circle included a wide range of personality types, religious attitudes, and degrees of traditional learning. A few of them were ordained rabbis and served in the professional capacity of city or town rabbinates. In addition to Levi Yitsḥak, these included R. Shmelke Horowitz, whom we have already met, and his brother R. Pinḥas. These two were to leave the Hasidic heartland altogether and serve in the rabbinates of the distinguished central European communities of Frankfurt and Nikolsburg.[8] R. Shne'ur Zalman of Liadi, the founder of the ḤaBaD school, clearly had the erudition and reputation to have served as a town rabbi but chose not to do so in order to devote himself fully to the spread of Hasidism.[9] The same is true of R. Elimelekh of Lezajsk, as mentioned above. Most, however, were learned in the aggadic and mystical traditions but less so in Talmudic law and thus followed their master's example and served as *maggidim* or communally appointed preachers. Still others, to whom almost no learned teachings are attributed, were more like folk figures, known in the Hasidic tales as personal exemplars of great piety but not as preachers. Best known among these are R. Zusya of Anipol and R. Leib Sarah's.[10]

Despite our lack of certainty about how central each of these was to the Maggid's court, there is good reason to assume that Levi Yitsḥak, thirty-two years old at the Maggid's death, played a pivotal role in this group. There are three reasons for making such a claim.

The first fact to be considered is that Levi Yitsḥak was a key object of attack in the persecutions of early Hasidism.[11] As we have seen, he was driven from the rabbinate of Zelechow in central Poland and from Pinsk in Polesia, apparently for the "crime" of using his rabbinic post to spread Hasidic teachings and customs, before accepting the position in Berdychiv in 1785. He was also the Hasidic spokesman in the most famous Hasidic-Mitnaggedic debate, indicating that he was probably the most respectable spokesman that the Hasidic forces could muster.

Second, of all the disciples who remained in Hasidism's expanding heartland, he was the one who held the most prestigious posts and hence was most publicly noticeable, both by supporters and enemies of Hasidism, as discussed above. The fact that the rabbi of these communities preached the new Hasidic doctrine, largely that of the Maggid, had to be noticed both by would-be *ḥasidim* and by their enemies.

Third, there is an unusually high degree of overlap of both content and style between teachings attributed to Dov Baer and Levi Yitsḥak, master and disciple.[12] The abstract mystical teachings attributed to the Maggid, centered mostly around the possibility of attaining self-negation (*bittul*) by entering into the divine *ayin*, are found almost unchanged in the sermons of Levi Yitsḥak. This central but highly abstruse part of Dov Baer's oeuvre is not found to nearly the same degree in the writings of several other members of the circle.[13] Another key item, both doctrinal and practical, is the role of the *tsaddik* and his relationship to the divine will. In this matter, Levi Yitsḥak proceeds to expand on his master's teaching, expressing it in even more radical language. But at root his ideas on this subject are very much those of his teacher and are expressed in similar language, more so than is the case with most others.

Since the turn of the twentieth century, it has been claimed that Levi Yitsḥak was to some degree the scribe of the Maggid, or at least a key recorder of his teachings. This claim began with the 1899 publication of a work called *Or ha-Emet*,[14] a partially new (though much overlapping with three prior collections) group of teachings belonging to the Maggid or his immediate school. The editor of the volume introduces it with a complicated tale of his grandfather, supposedly a disciple of Levi Yitsḥak (though his name is not one we know from elsewhere), who had preserved a precious manuscript of the Maggid's teachings partially copied from a text handwritten by Levi Yitsḥak himself. Current scholarship has no way of confirming or disestablishing this claim.

Scribe or not, Levi Yitsḥak sought out and achieved a place of leadership within this group of seekers and teachers who had gravitated toward the Maggid and were suddenly bereft at his passing in 1772. There are a number of passages within his writings, both early and late, that reveal the theme of leadership as central to his self-understanding. Before turning to these, however, we need to look more broadly at questions of leadership and the ways they shaped the emerging Hasidic movement.

No issue was more central to the emerging Hasidic communities of the late eighteenth century than that of leadership. Hasidism was conceived in the midst of both a Jewish community and a larger Polish society beset by failures in this area. On the Jewish side, both rabbinic and lay communal leaders were depicted as corrupt and self-centered by an array of preachers in the century and a quarter between the Khmielnitsky uprising of 1648/49 and the first partition of Poland in 1772.[15] Responsible leaders, it was said, either fled or were martyred, and those who took their place were of a lesser order. No one expressed this critique more sharply than R. Ya'akov Yosef of Polonnoye, disciple of the Ba'al Shem Tov and a key figure in the literary propagation of Hasidism.[16] The broader Polish political context was one of a constitutionally weak political structure of elected monarchy in which the nobility held outsized powers, crippling any sort of reform. Corruption and favoritism were constant issues, and the level of trust in the central authority of the kingdom was extremely low.[17] The 1764 shutdown by Polish authorities of the Council of Four Lands took place in the same year as the election of the final Polish king, one seen by many as a pawn of Tsarina Catherine II of Russia (he was, in fact, one of her former lovers). The late 1760s was a period of great unrest in Polish history, leading up to the first partition of Poland in 1772. That was the same year in which Hasidism first appeared on the stage of history with the bans against it pronounced in Vilna and Brody.[18] In the face of all this, the phenomenon that was to be called Hasidism may in significant part be seen as a response to the challenge to leadership that the times had brought forth.

Ashkenazic Jewish communities in the centuries prior to Hasidism did not have strong traditions defining the roles and responsibilities of leadership or organized pathways for the training of religious leaders. Overarching regional bodies of governance, such as the Council of Four Lands, were the exception rather than the rule. Its collapse may have helped open the way for Hasidism's new models of leadership and communal organization to emerge. Local communities had been essentially run by an oligarchy of the wealthy and the learned, who were often members of interrelated distinguished families. The sort of Talmudic learning in which potential rabbis were made to "show their stuff" often degenerated into a sort of castles in the air intellectual gymnastics known as *pilpul*, widely denounced by preachers of the age.[19] There was a widespread perception that the rabbinate was both ivory-towered and corrupt, distant from awareness and concern for the lives of ordinary Jews and overly influenced by the dictates of the wealthy.[20] Levi Yitsḥak, himself a product of that elite rabbinic culture, shared much with Ya'akov Yosef's critical views, though voicing them with a less angry mien, preferring instead to propagate an alternate model of Jewish leadership.

Hasidism bore this new model at its very heart, an image of master and disciples bound together by bonds at once sacred and lovingly interpersonal. This image was meant to stand out in relief against those disappointments in leadership that had caused many to come to a sense of distrust and revulsion toward those who stood at the head of conventional communities, both lay leaders and rabbis. It was in fact participation in this new sort of leader-and-follower relationship that has defined one's sense of belonging to the Hasidic movement from its early heyday until the present. For that movement, the term *ḥasid* (unlike all of its many prior usages) implies the question, *Ḥasid* of whom? The term here functionally means "disciple" in addition to its prior meanings as "pious one" or "lover of God." The disciple stands in relation to the *tsaddik*, or righteous one, also commonly referred to as *rebbe*, master or teacher. The nature and powers of the *tsaddik*, centered around his relationships with God, his disciples, and the broader Jewish community, are a key theme throughout the theoretical literature of early Hasidism, including the writings of Levi Yitsḥak, where certain aspects of this take a decidedly original turn. To be sure, one may see in this relationship a spiritualization of the old feudal model, one in which the master goes to battle (even against heavenly forces!) and defends his loyal and dependent flock. Existing as it does, however, on the edge of modernity, one may also depict it as a new, charismatically driven model of leadership bringing in its wake a new social order: the Hasidic community around the *tsaddik*. This came to supplant an older institution, the local Jewish *kahal*, which had seen better days.[21]

That alternate model, the figure of the *tsaddik* as a fitting leader for Jewry, was a key part of the spread and popularization of the Hasidic movement. There is no *ḥasid* without a *tsaddik*,[22] and there would have been no Hasidic movement without *tsaddikim*. But whence the authority for such innovation? Here, emerging in part through the inspiration of the Ba'al Shem Tov, was a group of potential leaders anxious to spread a message that was soon to show itself of tremendous power to attract a following. But in what terms might the role claimed by such figures be legitimated? Authority to lead the community has, by all the canons of Jewish tradition, only one legitimate source: the word of God. That source, in turn, might be invoked in one of two ways, either through a claim of direct revelation of God's will or by means of the normative chain of tradition, the legitimacy of rabbinic ordination and transmission.[23] While the founders of Hasidism would lay claim to both of these, neither could be invoked with full force.

The Ba'al Shem Tov and others in the early Hasidic circles were surely motivated, in fact, by some aura of divine call. The religion of spiritual revival that they taught by its very nature fosters charismatic leaders who are likely to experience a deep sense of personally appointed mission. The BeSHT spoke rather openly about out-of-body "ascents" and messages from heavenly sources, as may be seen from the most significant document that survives from him, his letter to R. Gershon of Kitev.[24] In a late-recorded source, transmitted by his grandson, the BeSHT allegedly spoke about why "I had come into the world," surely a claim of pneumatic leadership.[25] There are numerous passages in Hasidic teachings where we are told that "the *shekhinah* spoke from within his throat," referring to the *tsaddik*.[26] But to claim legitimacy on the basis of divine voices or heavenly journeys alone was a highly dubious business. Formally speaking, prophecy had ended with the destruction of the Temple; prophetic voice had been "taken from the prophets and given" either to the sages or to "fools and children"—depending on which version of the ancient saying one chooses.[27] Since then, again in a formal sense, we "pay no attention to heavenly voices."[28] Moreover, such dreams and "prophecies" were the stuff of which the recent and well-remembered Sabbatian claims had been made; they had a dangerous association with the very sort of mystical heresy from which Hasidism was at pains to dissociate itself.[29]

The normative claim to authority already belonged to the rabbinate, the bastion of learning that in the early years stood opposed to Hasidism. No one could claim on purely Talmudic/halakhic grounds that the rabbis loyal to Hasidism in the early days were the greatest scholarly luminaries or halakhic authorities of their time. Though Hasidism was far from being the movement of the unlettered masses that later romantics made it out to be, its leadership surely was mostly unable to battle the rabbinate on the latter's own turf. Levi Yitsḥak's debate with the rabbi of Brisk in 1781 is a notable exception, but it was precisely its unusual quality that rendered it so famous.

Hasidism found its way out of this dilemma by proposing another sort of claim for its leaders, one that was highly innovative in its usage, though having the needed venerable associations in the earlier history of Judaism. It was not as bearer of either revelation or tradition but rather as *tsaddik* that the Hasidic leader was to claim his mantle. His authority was of a different order, one that bypassed the controversial matter of the word of God and went directly to another cosmological line, one that had ever existed in Judaism side by side with the centrality of Torah, though previously always in a somewhat secondary way.

The *tsaddik*, "righteous one" or holy man, was known to the Talmudic sources as one who stood at the very center of the cosmos and could, by virtue of his meritorious deeds, intervene to reverse the decrees of heaven. For such figures (often called both *ḥasid* and *tsaddik* in the early sources) it had always been the virtue of meritorious living rather than learning or traditional authority that had lain at the core of their powers to attract a following.[30] Such well-known figures as Ḥanina ben Dosa or Ḥoni the Circle-maker, from the early rabbinic era, served as exemplars of a type who continued to exist through the Middle Ages. The *tsaddik*'s merit sustains the universe: what greater claim than this need be made for the leadership of a religious community? The authority of the *tsaddik* was not opposed to that of Torah either in earlier or in Hasidic times but rather stood side by side with it, exemplifying another aspect of Jewish religious ideals. While not in conflict with the values of Torah, the *tsaddik*'s authority was of a different order and of different historic lineage as well.

Since the appearance of the Zohar in the thirteenth century, this ancient figure of both piety and power was associated with the aspect of divinity called *yesod* by the adherents of Kabbalah.[31] *Yesod* (literally "foundation") is the ninth of the ten *sefirot* or aspects of the divine self, the one that gathers together all the forces from above and causes them to flow into the feminine *shekhinah* or "Community of Israel." As such, *yesod* is identified with the male procreative organ, with the "covenant" of sexual purity, and with Joseph, the original *tsaddik* who became such by resisting Madame Potiphar's wiles. As cosmic phallus, the *tsaddik* represents both fecundity, with all its power and blessings, and purity, with all its restraint. The deeds of the earthly *tsaddikim*, or Kabbalists, are essential in empowering the *tsaddik* above to continue that flow of life that sustains the universe. This cosmic figure was incarnate on earth, especially in the figure of Rabbi Shim'on ben Yohai, the central hero/teacher of the Zohar and the paradigm for many later Jewish spiritual leaders, including the Hasidic masters.[32] This Kabbalistic association tended to highlight the term *tsaddik* among the various appellations of the pious and directly affected its choice to designate the Hasidic leader.

The theoretical underpinnings of the term *tsaddik* as a designation of this charismatic Hasidic leader were developed particularly within the school of the Maggid, especially by the master himself, Levi Yitsḥak, and his close associate R. Elimelekh of Lezajsk. Its usage as such is complicated by the fact that it also has a more normative meaning: being a *tsaddik*, a righteous person, is a goal toward which every Jew should strive. This derives from the usage of this term in a forensic sense; a court (especially the heavenly one) may find the accused before it to be either *tsaddik* or *rasha'*, roughly "innocent" or "guilty." For some author/preachers of the circle,[33] that is its more general meaning. But for Levi Yitsḥak and Elimelekh, it almost always indicates the figure of a Hasidic leader, legitimized as such by his own constant quest for righteousness as a way of living and rewarded by God with the ability to serve as a channel for receipt and dispersal of divine blessing.[34]

3

FIRST STEPS

The Evidence of *Shemu'ah Tovah*

An important document regarding Levi Yitsḥak's early views on many matters, including questions of leadership, was published in Warsaw in 1938, on the eve of Polish Jewry's destruction, under the title *Shemu'ah Tovah*, attributed to both the Maggid and to Levi Yitsḥak. It was primarily copied, its editor tells us, from a manuscript that was included in the library of the *tsaddikim* of Kozienice, a collection that was lost during the ensuing catastrophe. Supposedly only five damaged copies of the book survived the great destruction.[1] From one of these, it was reprinted in 1972.

The short teachings that comprise the bulk of this volume are parallel versions to texts previously published in collections attributed to the Maggid and belonging to the corpus of his writings.[2] But *Shemu'ah Tovah* includes two other items, published for the first time. One is a group of longer sermons, most of them dated to 1773 and 1774, the two years following the Maggid's death. It also contains a page of questions and answers, mostly on Kabbalistic subjects. These are each headed with "I asked our lord and master," a typical way of referring to a Hasidic rebbe.[3] In two places, the question-and-answer texts are signed by the initials "LY," leaving little reason to doubt their origin.

The sermons cover most of the Torah portions from *Be-Midbar* and *Devarim* tied to passages from Pirkey Avot, which means that they were delivered in the summer months of those two years. They are written in a florid and repetitive rabbinic prose and are marked by lengthy and highly detailed parables. They give the impression, unlike most Hasidic sermons, of having been written out in detail by their creator, perhaps in preparation for their oral delivery. What we seem to have here are sermons by a young rabbi, not yet confident enough to rely on his rhetorical skills, needing to write out every word prior to their oral delivery. These sermons too are quite clearly by Levi Yitsḥak, as is evidenced by a comparison of both themes and specific biblical and rabbinic quotations repeated in later (and shorter) versions of them to be found in the *Kedushat Levi*.[4]

The very unusual fact that these sermons are dated makes them an extremely important historical source, one unnoticed by scholars until now. They represent the earliest stages in the development of both Levi Yitsḥak's thought and his style of expression. But they also show what concerned him in these crucial years at the very beginning of Hasidism's spread. When read with an eye toward history, they show us a young rabbi who stood before questions vexing the emerging movement, one faced by challenges coming from both without and within.

We turn first to two sermons that are directed toward inner developments within the recently bereft circle of disciples. One is dated to *parashat be-ha'alotekha* in 5533, May or June of 1773, about five months after the Maggid's death. The second was written a year later for *parashat Koraḥ* in the summer of 1774.[5] In this period, Levi Yitsḥak was rabbi in Zelechow, but there is no indication of where—or whether—these sermons were actually delivered. My sense is that these were addressed to the group of Levi's Yitsḥak's friends in the Mezritch circle, struggling to come to terms with what was to happen in the wake of their master's passing. Whether they were preached orally or were prepared primarily for written distribution is unclear.

In the first of these sermons, he speaks of a matter we know from his later homilies as well: the importance of spreading the Hasidic message to others rather than devoting oneself to the cultivation of private piety alone:

> Hillel says, "Do not separate yourself from the community, do not believe in yourself until the day you die, and do not judge your fellow until you reach his place. Do not say anything that cannot be heard [in public], for in the end it will be heard . . ." (Avot 2:5).

> In a simple sense, this seems to be a warning for those who seek to partake of God's holiness and to purify themselves, to step up to Torah and God's service. Such a person should not say, "Peace upon you [i.e., "Rest

easy"], my soul! I read scripture; I study the teachings. These suffice to fulfill my obligation."[6] Such a one does not place it as his goal to turn toward the community of YHWH, bringing the many back from sin. He declines to teach them the ways of God in which they should walk, to be earnest in His worship, with awe, love, and attachment [*devekut*]. To these, Hillel says, "Such is not the way in which the light of wholeness shines. This is not how you awaken the spirit of holiness and purity upon yourself, as was truly intended."

A person who serves his Creator fully out of love, with no intent of receiving reward but only to bring pleasure to the Creator, will never stop or rest with his own service alone but will work constantly toward the goal of "If only all the people of YHWH were prophets, as He places His spirit upon them!" (Num. 11:29). In this way, the Creator's joy and pleasure will surely be increased and His glory made abundant. This one is acting like a faithful and clever servant of the king. He loves his master so much, with whole heart and longing soul, that he wants all the king's servants to serve him faithfully. . . .

Scripture addresses such a servant when it says: "If you bring the precious forth from the unseemly" (Jer. 15:19).[7] This is what Hillel means by "Do not separate yourself from the community." *Do not separate yourself from showing them the way they should walk in serving their Creator. Those are the paths of awe, love, and attachment.* He then lays out the reason for this. In addition to this being the proper thing to do out of loving God, it will also bring great benefit to your own self. We know what the sages said: "Whoever brings merit to the public will not be the cause of sin."[8]

But perhaps you will say that you have no need for such benefit, having already attained the highest of rungs, worshipping with a great sense of attachment to God. [You think that] "Your heart has attained the heights in the ways of YHWH" (II Chron. 17:16). Your heart is already hollow within you,[9] and no sin will come your way. Hillel (continuing the passage from Avot) tells you that this is not the case. "Do not believe in yourself until your dying day."[10]

This issue, that of serving as an example and reprover (but always in a positive spirit) for others was crucial to Hasidism's vision for the transformation of Jewish life. In pre-Hasidic Ashkenazic culture, the *tsaddik* was generally understood as one seeking pious anonymity. Certainly, self-proclamation as a "righteous one" would have violated all the norms of modesty. There was a strong folk belief in hidden *tsaddikim*, sometimes numbered thirty-six, by whose merit the world continued to exist.[11] *Tsaddikim* who were already gone from this world could indeed intercede on behalf of the living, and supplication at their graves was an established practice, especially in the post-Safed generations. But living *tsaddikim* were not easily to be sought out.

Hasidism represents a transformation of this norm, the call to which is found in the Maggid's own writings and in those of his disciples. This particular text is significant because of its date, indicating that the preacher was urging efforts at outreach immediately after the Maggid's death. The words "to teach them the ways of God in which they should walk, to be earnest in His worship, with awe, love, and attachment" are precisely a call to build the Hasidic movement, to carry its message out to the broader public. I am suggesting that Levi Yitsḥak is addressing himself directly to his colleagues, fellow members of the Maggid's circle, though he never says so explicitly. There were those in the group, including the Maggid's only son, R. Avraham "the Angel," who were inwardly focused. They would have been content to have allowed Mezritch to have remained another *kloiz* on the earlier proto-Hasidic model, a place where intense piety and new religious insight were to be cultivated for a small group, but not serving as the font of a broader movement. Levi Yitsḥak is speaking for the other side of this argument. "We cannot separate ourselves from the broader community of Jews. We need to teach them the ways *of yir'ah, ahavah*, and *devekut*"—which is the essence of the Hasidic revivalist message. This sermon is a call to his fellow disciples to spread the message of religious revival that they acquired at the table of their master.

The idea of spreading Hasidic teachings among the masses was not new in 1773. Several of the Maggid's disciples had been engaged in this work already for several years. These included those who had turned northward, arousing the ire of the Lithuanian rabbinate and the bans against Hasidism that had been declared several months before the Maggid's death. But now, in the face of both of those events, the disciples must have felt a sense of crisis. What are we to do now that our master has departed? Levi Yitsḥak is here asserting a strong claim of leadership for moving forward and continuing to spread the teachings.

The choice of Numbers 11:29, the verse where Moses reproves Joshua for his concern over the unchecked spread of prophecy (the case of Eldad and Medad), is also quite significant. Levi Yitsḥak could easily have chosen a scripture that dealt with the fear of God or some other more innocent religious emotion. This verse says that the task of the one who takes on this role of leading the community is to encourage religious enthusiasm or "prophecy," precisely of the sort that early Hasidism sought to inspire and was also the source of much controversy.[12] The dispute between Moses and Joshua here may be read as saying that one should not hold back, following Moses' view that it is more important to spread this spirit of "prophecy" than it is to restrict it. Note how *devekut*, mystical "attachment" to God, has casually slipped in along with the well-known pair of *ahavah* and *yir'ah*, love and awe, and that something akin to prophecy is to be spread among the masses as well, "*all* of God's people."

The final statement in Levi Yitsḥak's argument is that one's own merit depends on this. This is no time for merely cultivating one's own inner religious life. He uses Hillel's words in a strong and demanding way, claiming that one who does not reach out to others has to worry about the status of his own soul as well.

No less interesting, however, is the central section of this same sermon (partly passed over above for the sake of order). Here Levi Yitsḥak takes a stand against competition for piety, a typical problem among younger devotees in enthusiastic religious groups, and also against backbiting, people sniping against one another by saying things they would not dare to express in public:

> If one's companions [fellow servants of the master mentioned above] are more competent and attentive in their devotion than he is, attaining higher rank and greater glory than his, he should not resent them out of jealousy. He should take great pleasure and joy in the delight that his master has from their service. He should rather reprove himself for his own shortcomings, feeling shame that he has served less well than his fellows. When he sees other servants fall short, he should reprove them directly, showing them the way to get back on track toward more wholehearted service. . . .
>
> He [Hillel] then goes on to warn the person never to turn away from the fear of God, even for a moment, but rather to practice "I place YHWH ever before me" (Ps. 16:8), as R. Moshe Isserles says in the *Oraḥ Ḥayyim*

> (1:1), in the name of Maimonides, as is known. On the verse "He tells a person what he speaks" (Amos 4:13), our sages taught, "Even in lighthearted conversation." This is the meaning of [Hillel's] "Do not say anything that cannot be heard, for in the end it will be." Anything you would be embarrassed to say publicly [literally "into people's ears"] do not say even in your innermost chamber. Scripture says, "[Even] of the one who lies in your bosom, take care" (Mic. 7:5). The reason is that it will come out in the end. Not only is it the case that you are removing yourself from fear and shame before the One whose "glory fills all the earth" (Is. 6:3), but at the time of judgment you will be told what you have said. Woe for that shame and disgrace! That thing you would not say publicly before those who, like you, dwell in earthly darkness is now revealed in heaven as your sin. It will be proclaimed before the assembly above and all the righteous! So be careful about everything you say and every move you make. Never turn aside from the awe and shame you feel before your Creator, and it will be well with you.[13]

Of course, it is possible that Levi Yitsḥak is addressing some *other* group in which competition and backbiting are taking place. It is also theoretically possible to say that these admonitions are to be read as nothing more than good moral advice. Indeed, if we were to come across them in a more general collection, such as the author's *Kedushat Levi* on the Torah, that is how we might read them. But the dating of this sermon suggests otherwise. The Maggid is dead less than half a year, and these are the issues on young Levi Yitsḥak's mind. It seems entirely likely that he is addressing concerns within the circle of disciples (to whom he refers as *ḥaverekha*), struggling among themselves to find leadership and direction in the period following their master's passing and stumbling into conflict with one another and competition for demonstrations of piety, leading to some shameful secret tale-telling. Some bit of nastiness—the details of which we will never know—has broken out within the group, and Levi Yitsḥak is speaking out against it.

We do not know where or whether this sermon was preached. But it is clear that pronouncing or circulating these words was an act of taking on the mantle and the risk of leadership within the group. Either Levi Yitsḥak already *had* that role of leader in the year following the master's death or these statements of warning and reproof are evidence of his attempt to *assert* such a role within the now bereft and leaderless circle.

A year later, in the summer of 1774, he again preached a sermon that most likely had a clear "address" within the emerging Hasidic community. The Torah portion was Koraḥ, where the question of rivalry over leadership is the key theme. As in all these summer-season sermons, he begins by quoting from Avot, which is publicly read on Shabbat afternoons:

> "Be warmed by the fire of the sages, but be careful of their coals, lest you be burned" (Avot 2:1). We should first take note that Moses our Teacher, peace be upon him, said, "If they [Korah and his followers] descend alive into Sheol, [you shall know that these people have rejected YHWH]" (Num. 16:30). . . .[14]
>
> Our sages taught that "Korah was a clever person. [They asked] what, then, he saw in this folly [of rising up against Moses? They replied that] "It was his eye that led him astray."
>
> Korah's controversy with Moses did not come about because he was a fool. He wanted to become high priest in order to bring forth the flow of divine bounty [*shefa*'] instead of Aaron. He too was a great man, but he wanted to bring forth the *shefa*' in a different manner, as has been explained elsewhere. But [if he was] such a great person, one in whom intellect shone, how could he not have understood that he should not sin against Moses and against the blessed Creator?
>
> The fact is that the intellect he possessed was not due to his own self. "He rather saw a great dynasty proceeding from himself."[15] The source from which his soul was drawn was [also] great and powerful. But when a person like this wants to rise up to that source and is unable to do so because he does not know the order of such ascents, he is uprooted from the world. . . .
>
> The sage is called "wood" [literally "a tree of the field"] and the holy Torah within him is the fire attached to that wood or coal, of which scripture says, "the Torah is light [= 'fire']."

> . . .In matters of Torah, opposing views are good, when the intent is to come to the true conclusion. The heat [of argument] makes for increased learning. But if the opposition to a sage becomes personal, the one opposing will get burned by the sage's coal. This is the meaning of "Be warmed by the fire [of the sages]." Stand up to the fire within them, their Torah. But of the coal, which is the sage's own person, be wary, lest you be burned.[16]

Once again, it seems likely that there is a contemporary situation in the background here. Levi Yitsḥak is a preacher, not a biblical interpreter; there is a reason why he chooses to read *parashat koraḥ* this way. Someone is coming forth to make a rival claim of leadership, and the fight has gotten nastily personal. Levi Yitsḥak is speaking out, here perhaps as a defender of the Maggid's school, against someone he sees as a usurper. He is being somewhat nasty himself, saying that the claimant is less great than his illustrious ancestors and than he hopes his offspring might be. While one cannot say for sure toward whom this barb is being turned, I believe there is a most likely candidate. I want to suggest—for that is all one can do—that he is referring to R. Yeḥiel Mikhl of Zloczow, a leading figure of Hasidic literature who stood outside the Mezritch circle.

Yeḥiel Mikhl (1726?–1781), and he alone, fits the description offered here exceptionally well.[17] He was a person of distinguished lineage, the son of the well-known R. Yitsḥak of Drohobycz, a contemporary of the BeSHT involved in the emerging proto-Hasidic circles.[18] Meshullam Feibush Heller refers to his teacher R. Yeḥiel Mikhl as "a *tsaddik* and the son of a *tsaddik*, of holy descent."[19] The family was descended from an old Prague-connected clan, one that claimed descent from RaSHI and hence from the Davidic dynasty (as did the family of the BeSHT). Yeḥiel Mikhl also had five sons, each of whom became a Hasidic *tsaddik*. They were younger contemporaries of Levi Yitsḥak and perhaps were already acting as future Hasidic leaders or being groomed to do so.[20] R. Yeḥiel Mikhl's approach to Hasidism was quite different from that of the Maggid. He was indeed one who might well have sought to become "high priest" in order "to bring forth the *shefa*ʿ in a different manner." His father was well known as something of a magician, an expert in holy names.[21] It is likely that the son continued in this path, especially as a dispenser of blessings, a sort of Hasidism closer to that of R. Barukh of Miedzybozh, who would clash with the Maggid's school later on.[22] The Karlin tradition tells that R. Shlomo of Karlin, after the Maggid's death, sought out R. Yeḥiel Mikhl in order to gain access to aspects of the Ba'al Shem Tov's teachings—those that stemmed more directly from his career as a *ba'al shem*—that the Maggid had not passed on.[23] These "ways of bringing forth the *shefa*" were recognizably different from the more intellectualist school of Mezritch, where the divine presence was most often to be heard through the preacher's clever reinterpretations of the Torah text. Read this way, our text is also the earliest usage of the term *shalshelet*, or "dynasty," (although taken from the Midrash) to be found in Hasidic sources. In 1774, it is hard to think of any family other than that of the Zloczover to whom it might refer.

Both of these sermons show something of the atmosphere that surrounded the Mezritch circle in the period immediately following the Maggid's death. Not surprisingly, both inner and outer forces threatened the bonds that were beginning to create a sense of shared purpose, the spreading of a doctrine and religious style that was at the earliest fragile stage of becoming a great religious movement. Levi Yitsḥak, in calling for leadership and dedication in spreading the movement's message, in seeking to smooth out inner conflicts, and in protecting the Maggid's circle's turf against a rival claimant, is asserting his own leadership within that circle, announcing himself as a central figure in the spread of Hasidism in its very earliest stage.

But the year 1772 was a critical one, as we have mentioned, not only due to the Maggid's passing. A few months earlier, the first great denunciations of Hasidism had been pronounced by the rabbinic courts of Vilna and Brody after at least two years of growing opposition. These had been published in a special booklet called *Cutting Down the Haughty: Knives of Flint*.[24] In the political history of the lands where Hasidism arose, 1772 also marked the crucial first partition of Poland, a significant part of the territory most occupied by Poland's Jews coming under the rule of Russia's Catherine II. The sermons of *Shemu'ah Tovah* reflect concern with both of these as well as with internal concerns of the emerging movement. We turn next to the very first sermon within the collection, which needs to be understood as a direct response to the anti-Hasidic denunciations. The greatest challenge to the Maggid's disciples' attempt to spread Hasidism was the fiercely negative rhetoric of the authorities, both rabbinic and communal, now clearly articulated in the bans.[25] Like the other sermons in this volume, it opens with a passage from Pirkey Avot, indicating that it was delivered during the summer months, when that text is read in the synagogue on Shabbat afternoons.[26] Here Levi Yitsḥak chooses Avot 2:4: "An ignoramus cannot fear sin, nor can a peasant [*'am ha-arets*] be a *ḥasid*." In 1773, less than a year following the original bans against Hasidism, this was a way of stepping directly into the controversy. The bans had used the claim that the members of what they regularly called "the sect" represented *'amey ha-arets*, an ignorant rabble, and therefore could not be true *ḥasidim*. Indeed, they sometimes denounced the nascent movement by referring to it as one of *mitḥassedim*, "self-proclaimed pietists." Levi Yitsḥak, whom no one could describe as an *'am ha-arets*, takes them on head-to-head. He begins, however, with an equally interesting typologization of the difference between a *tsaddik* and a *ḥasid*:

> With regard to the essential meaning of the term *ḥasidut:* The difference between *tsaddik* and *ḥasid* lies rooted in the following distinction. A person called a *tsaddik* is one who makes a constant effort to justify [*le-hatsdik*] himself before his blessed Creator. He is careful not to transgress even a single one of the prohibitions or negative commandments and fulfills the 248 positive commandments in every condition and detail. This is the whole of humanity, to perfect one's soul in every limb and sinew, totaling 613. That is why he is called *tsaddik*, because he is justified in arguing [his case] as he stands before the King who loves justice. All his deeds are just and upright, with no admixture of sin. But he does not act with lovingkindness [*lo nitḥassed*] to do things that are beyond the letter of the law. Thus he is to be considered a servant, one who fulfills the command of his Owner.
>
> The title *ḥasid* applies to one who does act with lovingkindness toward his Owner. His goal in all he does is to bring pleasure to his Creator. Taking care to fulfill his Creator's commands does not suffice for him. In everything he attains, [he seeks out] some possible device to draw pleasure to his Creator. He will hold fast to this and not let go of it, even though he hasn't been warned or commanded concerning this matter. This one is to be called a son; he is like a son who loves his father greatly, even wondrously, and tries constantly to seek out ways to bring his father pleasure and happiness.[27]

This typology is entirely pre-Hasidic, based on the older rabbinic usages.[28] *Ḥasid* is clearly superior to *tsaddik*, which is to say that there is no evidence at all that a *tsaddik* is to be seen as the leader of the Hasidic community, even as one who commands the will of God, as is widespread in Levi Yitsḥak's later writings. This old typology exists elsewhere as well in the very earliest of post-BeSHTian Hasidic sources. We do not know exactly when *tsaddik* came to mean Hasidic leader and *ḥasid* began to designate the follower of a *tsaddik*.[29] The opposition of "son" versus "servant" is also widely found in the writings of the Maggid's circle, including later sermons by Levi Yitsḥak.[30]

Then he goes on to make his key interpretive point:

> This is the meaning of "an *'am ha-arets* is not a *ḥasid*." The rung of *ḥasidut* can only be attained by one who has achieved rule over his worldly desires, separating from them and cleaving to the intellects alone. From there he rises into the secret level of knowing a bit of God's exalted greatness. Then he is lit afire and desires passionately to bring pleasure to his Creator. [Only] then he can reach the rung of *ḥasid* that I have mentioned. This is not true of one who has not yet detached himself from his material and earthly [*artsit*] desires. He cannot be a *ḥasid*. This is the meaning of *lo 'am ha-arets ḥasid*: no one who is attached to *artsiyyut*, earthliness, can be a *ḥasid*.[31]

Here Levi Yitsḥak has turned the tables on those who have just denounced the emerging new movement, using the rabbinic canon that he and Hasidism's detractors so fully share. Being a true *ḥasid* does not depend upon scholarly knowledge but upon one's ability to become detached from things of this world. It is not the followers of the Maggid who are the true *'amey ha-arets*, but the worldly and prosperous leaders who denounce them!

But it is not only toward Jewish authorities that the young Levi Yitsḥak takes an aggressive stance in these early preachings. Although most of his focus is on inward-looking Jewish communal and spiritual issues, there is one sermon in *Shemu'ah Tovah* that provides a possible exception to this rule. Levi Yitsḥak's words for *parashat ki tavo*, preached in the late summer of 1773, could be read as the young rabbi's response to the first partition of Poland in the previous year. True, Zelechow was still safely in the rump Kingdom of Poland that would limp along and survive for another twenty-some years. But the strong hand of Catherine II's Russia must have been very obvious and threatening. It was well-known that the tsarist empire, with its longstanding ban on permitting residence to Jews altogether, was not friendly toward Jews. How is it, then, the preacher asks, that a good God who rules the world would allow them so much power? Here we see a bit of what might well be called the political philosophy of an emerging Jewish leader in the early modern world:

> Scripture says, "God enters into judgment with the elders of His people and His princes [*sarav*]. 'You have ravaged the vineyard, robbing the poor within your houses. How dare you crush My people and grind the faces of the poor?'" (Is. 3:14–15).[32] We know what our sages say, famously in the Zohar and among interpreters of scripture, that the blessed Creator, in His great mercy and compassion, constantly seeks to do good for His creatures, causing blessing to flow to them, especially to His chosen people Israel. . . . But when sins form a curtain between those creatures and their Creator, . . . when Israel do not do the will of their Creator, the bounty that is set to flow forth from above is given over to the princes [*sarey*] of the nations.[33] Then we, Israel, are sustained by a reduced essence of this flow, our livelihood coming to us via those princes.

Levi Yitsḥak then goes on to offer a lengthy parable to illustrate his meaning, elaborated in full detail, as is typical of the style in this collection.

> A certain king had a single son, beloved to him as the apple of his eye. Once, however, when he transgressed his father's command, the king became angry with him, sending him forth from his palace, exiling him from his table. He was to wander in a foreign land until he completed restitution for his sin.

> Within that time, the king came to regret what he had done to his son. But the set term after which he could be restored to his palace had not yet come. Nevertheless, the king wanted to do some good for him. He therefore called upon one of his officials [*sarey*], a courtier, handing him the key to his treasuries, with their abundant delights. Regarding his son, he commanded, "Should my beloved son come and abide by my doorways, day after day, in weepful regret, bemoaning his past and pleading for the future, give him this treasure. But if he does not, and turns a cold shoulder toward returning to his father and regretting his deeds, this treasure will be yours."

> Now when this servant heard the king's words, he fixed his eyes on that treasure. He desired it and tried to set things in motion so that the treasure become his. He acted cleverly, plotting in various ways to keep the son from returning to his father. He commanded his own servants, guards at the royal entranceway, that whenever the king's son showed up to abide by the palace entrance, they were to push him away and hurriedly get him out of there. This they did. Whenever the king's son approached the gateway, the servants shouted at him and disgraced him. He went away in despair, empty-handed of the goods of that treasury.
>
> This was the result of his own folly. Had he been wise and considered the matter, he would have understood that he was the son of the great and mighty king, ruler of the entire world, who certainly also ruled over this servant who was keeping this good from him. He should have called aloud until the king himself heard him. Surely the king would have had a father's mercy upon his son! He would have restored him to his place and given him rule over all the princes [*sarim*] and royal servants. He would have placed all the delights of those royal treasures in his hands. To whom more than him would the king seek to give greatness and honor?

This parable, its language replete with echoes of the book of Esther, is then applied to Israel's situation in exile. *Ki Tavo* is read a week before Rosh Hashanah, and the son's outcry is connected to the sounding of the shofar, a link already made in sermons of the Maggid. But here we should pay attention to some part of Levi Yitsḥak's unpacking of the parable's meaning:

> This very thing has happened to us, the Children of Israel, the close children of YHWH our God, Creator of all. We are the people of God, gone forth from His land and distanced from His soil. But even though we are in the lands of our enemies, the eye of His providence remains upon us, giving us of His blessing and His abundant goodness by means of those *sarim* who are appointed over the lands of the nations. It is of that which belongs to our father that they have fashioned all their glory!
>
> . . . This is how the universal King arranged matters. If we do not arouse ourselves to abide by His doorways, as said above, the bounty will remain

> in the hands of the *sarim* of the nations. Those *sarim* want it that way. Therefore, they desire to cause us holy folk to sin. When one of us, or the whole people, goes forth to pray and plead for our souls before our Father in Heaven, engaging in good deeds and Torah, they lock the door before those penitents. . . .
>
> Understand that the blessed God is the King, Lord of all the upper worlds and their hosts, above and below. Kingship belongs only to Him! Besides Him there is no kingship or rule!

As the sermon comes to a close, the focus switches from the wicked princes to the evil urge as the force that keeps us from doing good. Experienced readers of these sermons know that these identities are somewhat fluid. But this switch allows him some safety in going on toward his especially powerful conclusion:

> But (returning to the original verse) "[God enters into] judgment. . . . How dare you crush My people?" He commanded only that you tempt them, not that you push away those who seek to repent, keeping them from doing so! This is like the parable of those servants who do not want to let the king's son come to his father. He (the wicked servant, who is also the evil urge) added this on his own! Therefore, his judgment is that he be slaughtered in the future. May it come speedily, in our days! Amen!

This good rabbinic sermon, calling on God to one day slaughter the evil urge as the Talmud promises was written carefully so as not to get its preacher in trouble with the authorities. But if we ask what it might have sounded like to Jews listening to it when preached in 1773, we may hear a much more contemporary echo only lightly veiled within it. What are we to do, Jews are asking, in the face of this threatening power that appears on our horizon, more ominous than the weak and chaotic Polish kingdom to which we are so accustomed? Just remember, says the preacher, that the *tsar* is just another *sar*! In the biblical verse with which he opened the sermon, God is saying to *sarav*, to those human princes who are ultimately just His servants, "How dare you oppress My children!" All their grandeur and power are really our Father's, usurped from us. The time set for our redemption has not yet come, and the nations and their *sarim* still have power over us. Only by standing faithful, not being distracted, and truly calling out to God will we be redeemed and see all these *sarim* (or *tsarim* or *tsarot*, "troubles" or "enemies" or . . . tsars?) brought down!

It would have been unthinkably dangerous for a rabbi to preach openly against the tsar. But a sermon finally directed against the wiles of the evil urge, dressed in the language of rabbinic discussion of the heavenly *sarim*, might just have passed muster.

4

THE HASIDIC TSADDIK AND THE QUEST FOR MODELS

As we have now seen from the earliest evidence of his career, Levi Yitsḥak sought to play a major role in the leadership of the emerging Hasidic movement, and history shows that he succeeded in doing so. Following the Maggid's teaching, his writings offer a very strong presentation of the figure of the *tsaddik* as the proper leader for the Jewish people.[1] He presents this by means of a set of twin binaries, using them to define both the *tsaddik*'s role and the way he is to go about fulfilling it. First, he insists that a truly righteous person is one who takes upon himself the role of public figure, as we have seen above. Hasidism was defined by a willingness on the part of its leaders to set aside the values of humility and hiddenness, creating a new type of *tsaddik mefursam*, the righteous one as public figure who would stand as the central pillar upon which the new religious movement was to be built.[2] In order to justify claims they were making for this new class of charismatic leaders and the shaping of a movement around them, Levi Yitsḥak and others continued to promulgate a binary of "*tsaddik* for oneself" versus "*tsaddik* for (oneself and) others," in which the hidden or overly humble *tsaddik* was considered too weak or insecure to step forward into the public role that needed him.

> "The *tsaddik* blossoms like a palm tree, tall as a cedar in Lebanon" (Ps. 92:1). There are two types of *tsaddikim*, both of them completely righteous. The difference between them is as follows: One is ever attached to God, blessed be He, doing the task that has been placed upon him. He is a *tsaddik* only for himself, but for no other. He does not cause his righteousness to flow forth to others. Thus he is compared to the cedar,

> which, as our sages noted, does not bear fruit. He is a *tsaddik* only within himself, not bearing the fruit of bringing others back to the good, so that *tsaddikim* might multiply in the world. This one does only for himself, reaching high and adding to his reward. The second *tsaddik* is rather likened to the palm tree, one that bears fruit or "blossoms." He brings forth the precious from the cheap, causing good to blossom and increase in the world. Of this our sages spoke when they said, "In the place where penitents [*ba'aley teshuvah*, literally 'masters of penitence'] stand, absolute *tsaddikim* cannot stand." They meant to speak of the second *tsaddik*, the one who is called "*master* of penitence," for he is master and lord over repentance as he brings others back to the good. "He brings many back from sin" (Mal 2:6) as he makes for penitence in the world. Surely his reward is greatly redoubled over that of the first *tsaddik*, even though he too is completely righteous.[3]

The first *tsaddik* here is likened to the cedar, its branches reaching upward, but not out. The palm, by contrast, is a tree on which each branch grows from its very heart but then reaches out horizontally as the tree grows as well as bearing fruit. The cedar is worthy of admiration, growing tall and straight, but it is of no value to others. Levi Yitsḥak applies this dichotomy to the figure of Noah versus that of Abraham, a contrast already found in early Midrashic sources.

> It appears that there are two types of *tsaddikim* who serve the Creator. One may serve with great enthusiasm but wholly on his own, not drawing near the wicked, so that they too might serve God. He serves alone. The other type serves the Creator, but [also] turns the wicked back [to God], so that they too might serve. This is like Abraham, who was making converts. It is taught in the Lurianic writings that Noah was punished for not having preached to his generation, and needed to be reincarnated in Moses. Moses was able to repair [Noah's soul], since he was constantly preaching to Israel.[4]

Here Levi Yitsḥak turns the traditional preference for Abraham over Noah to his own use. It is not only that Noah did not pray for God to serve his generation, nor did he argue to save them, as Abraham did for the sinners of Sodom. Noah should have "drawn near the wicked, so that they too might serve God." This sounds very like the Levi Yitsḥak we have seen trying to get his colleagues to work at spreading the Hasidic message of "love, awe, and *devekut*." Noah was just a "*tsaddik* for himself," unlike Abraham, who was not afraid of getting involved with wandering strangers in order to bring them the message. Levi Yitsḥak's friend Elimelekh of Lezajsk quotes the Maggid's particularly pungent remark on this question. He reinterprets the Talmud's claim of the miracle that "holy flesh never turned rotten," originally referring to sacrificial animals awaiting slaughter in the ancient Temple, to mean, "If a *tsaddik* is truly 'holy flesh,' he will never turn rotten, nor be corrupted by having contact with ordinary folk."[5]

The call to bring others back to goodness or to preach to the wicked rather than living a life of quiet and learned piety is identical with the call to build the Hasidic movement. Spreading Hasidic doctrine and practice was their way of "causing the good to blossom and increase in the world." The untutored masses whom Hasidism sought out were bereft of any real understanding of their routinized religious behavior. They retained a vague sense, due to the influence of Kabbalah on the broader Jewish culture of the seventeenth and eighteenth centuries, that Jewish ritual practice was fraught with mysterious power, but the esoteric details eluded them. The Maggid's circle and others around them saw themselves as forming an enlightened core, willing to take on the task of modeling and teaching a highly simplified mystical Judaism, one of accessible yet profound spiritual content, structured around the *tsaddik*. Those who had seen the great light that shone through in their period of intense study and personal communion with the Maggid wanted to offer a version of it that could attract the masses to a new birth of religious enthusiasm.

To this binary of hidden versus public *tsaddik*, Levi Yitsḥak adds a second, reflecting both his own personality and a growing norm within the emerging movement, reaching back to the temperament of the Ba'al Shem Tov himself.[6] Here he is addressing the question of proper and improper ways of going about the working of preaching and building what would come to known, after his day, as "a Hasidic community."

> There are two sorts of preachers who address Israel to get them to do the Creator's will. One speaks to them in a positive tone, telling each one of Israel what a high rung is his, how the souls of Israel are truly hewn from beneath the Throne of Glory. [He reminds them] of the Creator's great pleasure in a *mitsvah* performed by any Jew, how all the worlds are joy-

> ous at seeing God's command fulfilled. This kind of preaching bends the heart of Jews to do God's bidding and to accept the yoke of God's kingdom. But other preachers reprove Israel with harsh language, shaming them until they are forced to do God's will.
>
> The difference is that the one who approaches them with goodness uplifts their souls to great heights. He speaks constantly of the righteousness and greatness of Israel, saying how great their power is above. This one is a fitting leader for Israel. Not so the one who speaks harshly.[7]

This text, commenting on the qualification needed to succeed Moses (who has failed in this moment of striking the rock), is probably also addressed to his fellow preachers within the Mezritch circle as well as to the hearers of such preaching. Its message, partly through Levi Yitsḥak's influence, came to belong to the essential teachings of Hasidism, one that derived its name from *ḥesed*, the divine attribute of compassion.[8] The movement's literature is replete with calls to seek the spark of good in others and to fan its flames to make it grow. This approach of encouraging listeners to follow their own instinctive goodness (along with the demands of *halakhah*, to be sure) had much to do with Hasidism's success. With rather little change, we could imagine Levi Yitsḥak's charge being given to campus-outreach workers today, either at a Hillel conference or at a training session for some of the Orthodox *kiruv* ("outreach") centers. The one who preaches to Israel has to come at the task from a place of loving concern for his flock rather than one of harsh judgment. Build people up rather than tear them down; you will get them to open their hearts if you tell them how good rather than how bad they really are.[9]

But Levi Yitsḥak's description of the proper preacher, one who always emphasizes the essential goodness of his flock rather than berating them for their sins, is not simply instrumental. The *tsaddik* is also defined by what he sees in those around him. To have a "good eye," or a righteous gaze, means that one sees only the good in people.[10] The *tsaddik* who devotes so much energy to gazing upon God is transformed in the way he looks at people as well. The view of the person that the *tsaddik* shares in preaching corresponds to his own perception of the human other. In Levi Yitsḥak, more than in any other figure within early Hasidism, this "good eye," or generosity of spirit, is described in forensic terms, the *tsaddik* taking upon himself the task of *limmud zekhut*, declaring the merit of

Jews as they are judged before God. Probably because Levi Yitsḥak was himself a judge, presiding regularly over the rabbinic court in the various cities where he served as communal rabbi, he was attracted by the notion of the *tsaddik* as one whose role it was to proclaim the merits of Israel in the hour of judgment. Here, again, is his description of the ideal Jewish leader:

> "May YHWH, God of spirits of all flesh, appoint a person over the community" (Num. 27:16). The point is that one must speak out for Israel's merit. The reason they do not constantly engage in serving their Creator, as do the angels, is because they are preoccupied earning their livelihoods. That is why Abraham, being a man of compassion, always looking to speak of merit, fed the angels (who do not need to eat). He wanted to show them the needs of flesh and blood so they would not speak out against them. That is why Moses here calls God "God of spirits of all *flesh*." It is because people are flesh and blood, needing to earn a living, that they do not serve God constantly. "Appoint . . ." calls for a judge and leader who will always speak out for the merits of Israel, just as You do for people, even those who are not always serving You.[11]

The proper leader of Israel is one who imitates the ever-compassionate God, always looking toward the good side of people. But it is also fair to say that this image of God is a reflection of Levi Yitsḥak himself and the particular sort of Hasidic leader image he sought to cultivate. In fact, the reverse may also be true. He seeks to arouse divine compassion for Israel by treating Israel with compassion himself, showing God, as it were, how to do it.

> The blessed Holy One judges the community of Israel on the Day of Judgment with His great mercy and compassion. But there needs to be an arousal from below, awakening [the force of] mercy above. . . . When we down here act with compassion, pointing out the merits of every Jew and judging them on the side of merit, that same quality is awakened above. Then he too [the earthly judge] and all the seed of Israel are treated with compassion. . . . This is "Place judges and officers at all your gates, to judge the people righteously" (Deut. 16:18): A person who points out the righteousness and merit of all the seed of Israel awakens that gate above. Thus he too will come forth from divine judgment and be found righteous. "A person is treated in accord with his own qualities."[12]

The *tsaddik*'s job is to find the good in Jews then, to point out those merits, both to God and to them. In part, this is to convince God to forgive them, and the *tsaddik* is loved for that intermediary function, appealing to God for Israel, even demanding of Him that He forgive. But the *tsaddik* understands this show of goodness also has a profound effect on his flock psychologically. Showing them their goodness rather than pointing out their sins is the best way of causing them to live up to the rosy picture the *tsaddik* paints of them.[13]

By the last two quarters of the eighteenth century, wandering *tsaddikim* were becoming an ever more common, if somewhat controversial, part of the Eastern European Jewish landscape. Many of them struggled to earn a livelihood and suffered a good deal of public rebuke and humiliation along the way. Some of these memories are recorded later in Hasidism through the tales of R. Zusha, but they surely represent a more widespread phenomenon during the years when Hasidism was struggling to assert itself. In the following text, we see Levi Yitsḥak rising in defense of that phenomenon. Although recorded in Levi Yitsḥak's name in an early secondary source rather than in his own writings,[14] both its homiletic setting (a Talmudic version of a dispute between king and prophet) and the reality it describes lend to it a strong sense of authenticity:

> "Hezekiah (king of ancient Judea) said, 'Let Isaiah come to me. Even though he is a prophet, I am the king.' Isaiah said, 'Let Hezekiah come to me. He may be king, but I am a prophet.'"[15]
>
> This seems most surprising. How could righteous folk like these be so casual about the issue of [holding onto their] pride, which is really tantamount to idolatry!
>
> The matter is like this. Truly faith and trust in God is the most essential (religious) quality. It sustains life, both physical and spiritual, life of body and soul. Our sages taught that Habakkuk reduced all the commandments to one: "The righteous one lives by his faith."
>
> But if that is the case, how and why do we see great *tsaddikim* leaving their homes and travelling about so much? On the face of things, it appears they are doing so for their own needs, in order to earn their livelihood. But could it be said that this is the intent of such righteous ones? Do they not have faith and trust in blessed YHWH, who can sustain

them fully, even as they sit in their own houses? Blessed YHWH can do anything!

The truth is that these *tsaddikim* see the strength of Israel, the holy people, diminished and weakened due to our many sins. [Israel are unable] to be heroes in the battle of Torah, that of overcoming the evil urge, each in his own way. They require healing of soul through moral teaching and fear of heaven, good counsels in the service of blessed YHWH. That is why the *tsaddikim* of the generation, the eyes of the community, leaders of their people, trouble themselves so greatly to travel the roads, wandering from place to place through the world. [They seek to] bring merit to Israel, the holy people, causing them to return to God in a complete way, through such moral teachings and fear of heaven, goodly counsels that will bring them close to blessed YHWH, each on one's own level and in one's own way. This is their main intent and purpose. [Fulfillment of] their own needs and livelihood come to them incidentally, from YHWH, so that they can sustain themselves and their households as well as perform acts of charity and good deeds.

But if someone should whisper to you, "Couldn't the *tsaddikim* arrange that people come to them, so that they wouldn't have to make the effort of travelling around to others?" know that there is [another] deep meaning to this [travel]. They seek to effect powerful and awesome mystical unifications. Masters of secret lore know that when a greater one goes to a lesser one, such an awesome union is performed. This is referred to as the bowing down [of the letter *heh* to the letter *vav*],[16] as is known. That is why great *tsaddikim* trouble themselves to travel out to the common folk [scattered] around the world, to bring about many such unifications. This is their main task in this world, by means of [teaching] Torah and [fulfilling the] commandments, bringing great pleasure and joy to blessed YHWH.

This was the intent of those righteous and humble *tsaddikim* Hezekiah and Isaiah. Each of them thought of himself as nothing and without value, when compared to the other. Each wanted to bring about divine glory, performing these unifications for God's pleasure and joy. That is

> why Isaiah said, "Let Hezekiah come to me," for I am less than he. . . . All this was to increase and glorify Torah. "May His great name be made great and holy [*yitgadal ve-yitkadash shmey rabba*]. Amen."[17]

This sermon is an important historical document when viewed in the context of Hasidism's early spread. The wandering *tsaddik* was a new phenomenon, something that had to be explained and justified. Here we have Levi Yitsḥak describing the situation as it was in the 1770s or '80s, not in the later and more established era of Hasidic dominance. Then the people indeed did travel to the *tsaddikim*. In the early days, before they were established, the would-be *tsaddikim* of emerging Hasidism did precisely this: wandered from town to town, offering blessings, spreading the message, hoping to be rewarded with both disciples and donations to the cause (i.e., their livelihoods).[18] "What are these people doing out there on the roads?" he asks, going to preach and effect healings among rural Jews in small and remote communities. Wouldn't they be better off staying home, engaging in full-time prayer and Torah study, as *tsaddikim* are supposed to do? Surely that is what the famous hidden *tsaddikim* of former generations used to do! It must be (as opponents of Hasidism were saying loudly) that they are just some sort of peddlers, out there trying to make a living.[19]

Levi Yitsḥak was the right person to reply to this critique. He, after all, was *not* one of those wandering *tsaddikim*; he had a most respectable livelihood as rabbi of a major town. His twofold answer is strong and unequivocal, even though typically wrapped in homiletic garb. They are out there not for themselves but to strengthen the faith of Israel, to bring them closer to God through repentance and good deeds. Once again that reply may readily be translated, from the historian's point of view, into, "They are engaged in building the Hasidic movement." That was precisely how Hasidism saw itself, as the effort of enlightened teachers to transform the religious lives of the masses, bringing them closer to God. But they are also, in the course of humbling themselves before the masses—and the wandering *tsaddik* surely did suffer the risk of humiliation and more—engaging in mystical acts that unify the upper worlds.

What we may see here is another example of Levi Yitsḥak's assertion of leadership within the emerging movement. As the most securely established figure among the Maggid's disciples, he is spreading his protection over those of his colleagues who are still out "on the roads," doing the precise thing he said they ought to do in one of the texts quoted above from *Shemu'ah Tovah*. Perhaps not surprisingly, in a parallel text,[20] Levi Yitsḥak turns to those wandering preachers themselves, warning them to do their work only for the glory of God, to make whole His broken throne by returning His wayward children to Him in repentance, and *not* to be overly concerned with seeking out their own livelihoods by being on the road. These two sources together attest to Levi Yitsḥak's voice as a shaper of the movement's spread, defending the new crop of wandering *maggidim* as they spread the word among small-town and rural Jews, but also trying to exercise influence over their conduct. In a movement characterized by spontaneous growth, having no formal standards of ordination or means of quality control, Levi Yitsḥak, perhaps Hasidism's most respectable spokesman, is trying to make sure that the emerging *tsaddikim*—including some self-proclaimed as such—embody the Hasidic message at its best. As we will see below, this was a great concern of his.

Since Levi Yitsḥak's teachings are preserved primarily in the context of homilies woven around the weekly Torah portions, it is to the Torah text that we see him most often turn for models of the *tsaddik*'s behavior, including his relationships both with God and with his flock. As he preaches on Genesis, such biblical figures as Noah, Abraham, Isaac, Jacob, and Joseph each play a role in this quest for precedents and paradigms. Noah, as we have seen, is usually a model of failed or inadequate leadership. His failure to plead with God for his generation's salvation, or even to warn them, as the prophets were later to do in the face of imminent destruction, served to condemn him.[21] For that reason, Levi Yitsḥak tells us, Noah's soul had to be reincarnated in that of Moses, in order to allow for the fulfillment of his earthly mission.[22]

Abraham plays a very large role in Levi Yitsḥak's view of the devotee and his relationship with God. But Abraham is largely a lone seeker rather than a leader, both in the Torah text and in the Hasidic imagination. For the latter, he is the embodiment of faith and trust in God. His introspective faith leads him to discover the entire Torah from within himself, fulfilling it long before it was given at Sinai.[23] His relationships are largely those with God and with his family, but Levi Yitsḥak constantly portrays him as concerned for the fate of his future progeny, making him the first among the lovers of Israel and a key role model for the sort of fatherly rabbinate that would constitute his own lifelong calling.

Abraham also interacts with three royal personages: Pharaoh, Abimelech, and Melchizedek, and each of these is developed in Levi Yitsḥak's sermons. We will have occasion to return to Abraham and Melchizedek below when we discuss Levi Yitsḥak's attitude toward the *mitsvot.*

It is largely around his Kabbalistic association with *ḥesed*, or the quality of divine compassion, that Abraham takes on great importance for Levi Yitsḥak. But he also makes a most interesting and surprising claim regarding Abraham's birth. In very strong and unequivocal language, he claims that Abraham is not truly the son of Terah and his wife but a unique being brought to birth by the mind of God.

> The power that caused Abraham to be born, bringing his soul into the world, was not Terah, for he was not deserving to bring such a holy soul into the world. Rather, the power that birthed Abraham our Father was the thought that arose before our blessed Creator . . . and that thought is considered the father of Abraham, not Terah. . . . There was no part of his father Terah's or his mother's soul in Abraham; their coupling left no imprint upon him. . . . Their red and white body fluids [i.e., blood and semen] produced the lifeless body of Abraham, but the red and white [*gevurah* and *ḥesed*] within Abraham derived from the thought of the blessed Creator.[24]

The sermon goes on to suggest that this divine thought is to be linked with one particular divine *middah (=sefirah).* It is *shekhinah*, Mother of Israel, that births Abraham. It is because of his link to Her (called "Land") that he inherits the Land of Israel. Levi Yitsḥak also makes it clear that the patriarch is disconnected from his birth parents because he is considered the first among proselytes (*rishon la-gerim*),[25] the convert to Judaism is considered like a newborn babe. Reading this today, however, one cannot avoid noticing within it an air of soul-based racism.

Abraham's journey of self-discovery, in which he will discover the entire Torah from within himself, is the original story of conversion. His journeying through the Land of Israel is a journey of faith. On Gen. 12:9, "Abraham journeyed back and forth to the Negev," Levi Yitsḥak comments, "He journeyed out of his own self, stripping off [his corporeal self] as he walked toward the love of his Creator."[26]

Abraham is thus a model of private, inward piety, a key exemplar of a prime value in a movement of religious revival. To some extent he thus perforce remains a model of the first type, a "*tsaddik* for himself," working at the development of his own inner life. Of course, his argument with God for the sinners of Sodom becomes a paradigm for Levi Yitsḥak's understanding of his own rabbinic role, as we shall see. Abraham, however, has no real community to lead. When it comes to the matter of communal leadership, there is no model in the Torah to rival that of Moses, as we have already begun to see. His entire story, from his call at the burning bush until his death, is built around leadership of the Israelite people in the most trying of circumstances. In this matter, all other biblical heroes pale in comparison with him. It is therefore to Levi Yitsḥak's interpretations and struggles with the figure of Moses as leader that we must turn, as he sought within them his own understandings of the *tsaddik*'s role as intermediary between God and His people.[27]

Moshe Rabbenu, Moses our teacher, both in the biblical text and as reimagined by countless generations of preachers and interpreters, embodied all the elements that made up Levi Yitsḥak's own role as *tsaddik* and leader. Moses is depicted as a mystical prophet; he is the only human who was able to remain in an uninterrupted state of *devekut* with God. The devotee in Levi Yitsḥak certainly aspired to that side of Moses, including his humility and extreme self-transcendence. There is a strong pull within all the Maggid's circle to want to be with God alone, to seek out a life of worship and spiritual intimacy, leaving the world behind. One has a sense that they experienced a significant taste of this in the Mezritch years and that they never lost their thirst for it. The image of Moses, either atop the mountain or alone with God in the tent of meeting, plays to this element in their shared spiritual longings.

Moses is also both teacher and lawgiver. The teachings that Levi Yitsḥak shared with his disciples, including the strict legal code alongside the more free-flowing homiletical interpretations, were all part of the Torah of Moses. As head of the rabbinic court in a major community and as teacher of Talmud and legal codes to a *yeshivah* there, he felt a strong responsibility for the law and its upholding.[28] Surely the ongoing tension between the qualities of justice and mercy, love of the law and compassion for the people who had to follow it, ever a characteristic of the rabbinate (so much so that God was depicted in its light), was one that Levi Yitsḥak must have felt to a high degree. His love for common people and his forgiving nature were part of what made him such a unique and much-beloved figure. But these must have existed in some tension with his role as a figure of legal authority, responsible for the upholding of law in his community, as they did with his inner pull toward a life of mystical detachment from the world.

Pieces of this inner conflict are seen in the preacher's understanding of Moses in various contexts. At the burning bush (Ex. 3), his first encounter with God,

> Moses sought kingship, but it was not given to him, except while the generation of the wilderness endured. The role of the king is that of raising up sparks, causing them to be attached to the Creator. . . . Why was kingship not given to Moses? Because Moses' mind was constantly turned upward; he was not thinking at all about the lower world and how to raise it up. . . .
>
> God said to him, "Remove your shoes [*na'alekha*] from off your feet [*raglekha*], for the place where you stand is holy soil" (Ex. 3:5). *Na'alekha* [can also] refer to a locked door, that of your being constantly linked [i.e., "locked in"] to that which is above. You have got to break that habit [*ragil, hergel*], "because the place where you stand is holy soil." "Holy" refers to wisdom and the raising of sparks, which are below.[29]

The leader's work is in this world. You cannot be a ruler if your glance is already turned upward, away from it. Levi Yitsḥak hears Moses given the same message at Sinai in perhaps even stronger terms:

> "Moses rose up to God. YHWH called to him from the mountain, saying 'Thus shall you say to the House of Jacob and tell the Children of Israel'" (Ex. 19:3). This appears to me to be the meaning. The Midrash says that when Moses rose up above, he came to a certain firmament where he saw thousands and tens of thousands of angels. Groups of holy seraphim were standing in fear and awe, in holiness and purity. A great fear and trembling fell upon him, [thinking of] the One with whom he was about to speak. . . .
>
> Moses had prepared himself in intense ways to have the blessed Holy One speak with him on a high level, things that no person could understand. But YHWH said to him, "Do not make all those preparations that you seek to do. [On that level] you will not be able to teach the Children of Israel."

> This is the meaning of "Moses rose up to God," preparing himself to reach that high level of speaking "to God." But the blessed Holy One did not want that, in order that he be able to teach Israel. [Therefore] "YHWH called out to him from the mountain," a lower rung, for the sake of "saying" to Israel, to people to whom He is near. . . . That is why it also says, "Behold I come to you in a thick cloud, so that the people will hear when I speak to you." This refers to the lowly rung on which I will approach you, so that the people understand when I speak to you.[30]

The prophet—or the *tsaddik*—exists in order to communicate his message. He does God no good by seeking to stand on that high rung of self-negation for which his own soul might long. That would allow him only to be "a *tsaddik* for himself," rather than a leader of the people or an emissary of a new religious movement. Levi Yitsḥak, in these passages, is calling upon himself—and perhaps his colleagues—to overcome the solipsistic temptations of the mystical life and to develop the other crucial relationship required of the *tsaddik*, that with the human community he is also there to serve.

The ongoing struggle to turn the prophet as mystic, longing ever to be with God and seeking no other reward, into the prophet or *tsaddik* as leader, ever seeking divine favor for God's people and bringing His blessing to earth, has ancient echoes. One thinks of Plato's *Republic* and the effort to get the philosopher, drawn to a life of contemplation, to turn to the realm of politics and this-worldly concerns. This struggle, while discussed around the figure of Moses, was a live one for the early Hasidic leadership. It is perhaps the central tension running through all his writings, as we shall see below. While the lack of clear contemporary references in the sermons allows only for speculation, it could well be that concrete persons and historical situations underlie some of this discussion. Could the fact that Moses' "kingship" did not last beyond *dor ha-midbar*, the "wilderness generation" that Levi Yitsḥak describes elsewhere as "the generation of words," be a reference to his own teacher, the Moses of his day? Only in a generation when the message of Hasidism could be passed on by heady verbal teachings could the way of the Maggid survive. The next generation, which we shall hear Levi Yitsḥak describe as *dor ha-arets*, meaning "a worldly generation," required a different sort of leadership, one that was wholly turned toward the people and its needs.[31]

The *tsaddik* functions as an intermediary between God and the people of

Israel. The charism by which he leads is born of his two relationships, those with God and with his flock. In the case of Levi Yitsḥak, that "flock" came to include the entire community of Berdychiv and the surrounding area due to the overlap between his roles as communal rabbi and Hasidic *rebbe*. The tension between these two relationships, the *tsaddik* with God and the *tsaddik* amid his people, is often quite apparent, as we have seen. Levi Yitsḥak's need to turn to it so repeatedly clearly shows that this conflict is his own, not only that of the colleagues or future *tsaddikim* he is trying to direct. Striving toward higher spiritual realms, the *tsaddik* wants to maintain a sense of personal purity. Despite the Maggid's claim (or perhaps witnessed by his need to have said it), contact with the folk always bears the possibility of contamination, diverting one from the spiritual goal. Levi Yitsḥak's message to such a *tsaddik*, including himself, is spoken through God's mouth in addressing Moses: the commitment to the people is to take primacy. Commenting on Exodus 25:2, the beginning of the commandment to erect the tabernacle (traditionally understood as following the incident of the Golden Calf), he comments,

> This is the first time after the giving of the Torah [and the worship of the Calf] that Scripture says, "Speak to the Children of Israel." . . . The *tsaddik* has to take great care in conversing with the masses. Speaking with them can interrupt one's attachment to blessed YHWH. The *tsaddik* is only permitted to speak with such people if they might be uplifted by his words. Speaking from within a state of attachment to God makes an impression that could bring such a person along into holiness. . . .
>
> When Israel sinned with the Calf, they were cut off from their holiness, returning to their prior defiled state.[32] Moses was then afraid to speak with them. In response to this, the command came directly from God: "Speak to the Children of Israel." They are the seed of Israel, the children of Abraham, Isaac, and Jacob. By speaking with them, you will surely uplift them and raise them into holiness, causing them to cleave to Me.[33]

In the sermonic context, Moses here is clearly a stand-in for the Hasidic *tsaddik*, perhaps even for Levi Yitsḥak himself. He seeks in the verse a divine imperative that tells him not to be disheartened or frightened off by the sinfulness of those he is to serve. As "the seed of Israel," they have the inherent potential to respond to the *tsaddik*'s words and through them to renew their relationship with the holy. This fits with the descriptions of complaints we find in some accounts of Levi Yitsḥak spending too much of his time in the company of what one might call "publicans and sinners." Here he is responding, claiming that this is precisely the task of the *tsaddik*, a viewpoint with which the Baʿal Shem Tov himself surely would have agreed.

The *tsaddik*'s role as intermediary between God and the people lay at the heart of Hasidism's great success in winning the hearts of the Eastern European Jewish masses. It is no surprise that the figure of Moses should stand right at the center of this claim. The Torah locates him in this intermediary role, for which he becomes the classic example throughout all later generations. In the narratives of Exodus 33–34, following the Golden Calf, and again in Numbers 14, following the report of the twelve spies, Moses talks God down from His threat to destroy Israel altogether. One of Levi Yitsḥak's most powerful invocations of this theme comes, as might be expected, immediately following the Golden Calf incident itself. This reading of the biblical text reaches back into his youthful sermons in *Shemuʿah Tovah*, indicating that this concern for defending Israel was with him quite early.

> We seem able to interpret the verses of *parashat Ki Tissa* concerning the sin of the Calf [in this way]: God said, "I have seen this people, and it is a stiff-necked one. Now leave Me and let My anger blaze against them, so I may destroy them" (Ex. 32:9–10). But Moses our Teacher, as he hurried to bow down and prostrate to pray for Israel as God passed before him, saying "YHWH! YHWH . . ." (34:6), also said in his own prayer that "they are a stiff-necked people. But forgive our sin . . ." (34:8). All the commentators have struggled over the question of why Moses should have mentioned that Israel are stiff-necked while praying for them. Isn't this a lowly quality, one that brings to mind their sin? After all, God Himself had said this when He had sought to destroy them!
>
> The matter is like this. The effect of holiness is permanent. That is why, even after holiness departs from a place where it had dwelt, that disappearance is not total; some imprint of it remains. This is familiar from the secret of "the *shekhinah* has never departed from the Western Wall." Perhaps that is why, even in the case of totally wicked people, we see

> that intimations of repentance come to them nearly every day. It is only because they are so very drawn after their evil desires that these good thoughts just pass them by. But it sometimes can happen that these intimations grow stronger, bit by bit, until that heart turns toward total repentance. All of this comes about due to that imprint that the holiness had left behind, before it disappeared due to sin. . . .
>
> Now we can understand these verses in a meaningful way. God said, "I have seen this people, that it is stiff-necked," meaning that they have a tough character. It is hard for them to separate from anything toward which they have turned. Now that they have turned their backs to Me, and not their faces, it will be hard to transform them. Therefore, "Leave Me . . . so I may destroy them." What use do I have of them?
>
> But Moses, in his prayer, said, "May YHWH walk in our midst, for this is a stiff-necked people!" meaning that this tough people has held fast to His essence, the impression that His holiness has left behind [even after He departed]. They are so tough that they will in no way be separated from [that impression], even when they turn their necks away from facing the holy. Even as they sin and it disappears from them, that deep impression stays in its place, in all its full-strength power. Therefore, they remain close to repenting and returning to the path of goodness.[34]

Levi Yitsḥak sees that it is the very toughness of Israel, that which has brought God to the edge of a violent rampage, that makes for the likelihood of their repentance. As sinful as they seem to be, he assures the Creator they have never given up on Him. It is not in their nature to do so. Here the preacher is not just interpreting scripture, of course. In part he is indeed addressing God, serving as Israel's intermediary, entreating Him not to destroy them, just as Moses had. But by way of doing so, the preacher is also inspiring his congregation, assuring them that even in their most sinful moments, the imprint of holiness remains strong in them, if only they will open themselves to seeing it.

It may also be that there is yet another message here, one that we have already noted in analyzing the sermon immediately following this one in *Shemu'ah Tovah*. We recall that the year 1773, to which this sermon is dated, was a threatening time for Jews.[35] The first breakup of the Polish kingdom had just taken place.

While Zelechow, as we have noted, was still in the rump Polish state that would limp along in quasi-independence for another two decades, the writing was on the wall. It was the tsarist empire that had all the power, and that was a force that had never looked kindly upon the Jews. The preacher is reminding his flock that they are indeed a stiff-necked or "tough" people, meaning one that knows how to resist pressures and remain faithful, no matter what may come, to the holy presence that is impressed so deeply within them.

In several others passages as well, beginning even before the Exodus itself, Moses cries out to God in frustration over his role as leader of a stubborn and ungrateful people, asking God why He has put him in such an untenable position. The Talmud describes Moses as one of the two main biblical figures (alongside Hannah, the mother of Samuel) who "cast words upward," meaning that they spoke out against God harshly, challenging divine justice.[36] As the ultimate human *tsaddik* figure,[37] Moses has the credibility, understood as actual power, to stand up to God in order to save His people. Seeing himself in the same role, Levi Yitsḥak frequently turns toward the example of Moses.

Here the Hasidic master is following in the well-trodden footsteps of tradition. We have already seen that Noah is the failed leader, neither warning his contemporaries to repent nor crying out for mercy on their behalf. Ten generations later, when God tells Abraham of His impending destruction of Sodom, the patriarch responds with a moral challenge: "Will the Judge of the whole earth not do justice?" He then bargains with God, convincing Him not to destroy the city if He finds ten righteous (*tsaddikim*) within it. At that point, Abraham's moral daring seems to buckle, and the city is destroyed. When God comes to Moses following the Golden Calf and threatens to obliterate the Israelites, making a new nation out of Moses' seed, the prophet replies, "If [You will not lead this people], wipe me out of the book that You have written." If You are going to kill Israel, he is understood to be saying, you'll have to be willing to kill me as well.

Following the incident of the spies, Moses again calls upon God to forgive Israel and not destroy them for the sake of His own reputation among the nations. "Because He was unable to bring them to the land He had sworn to their ancestors, He slaughtered them in the wilderness" (Num. 14:16). "What sort of argument is this?" asks Levi Yitsḥak. Couldn't an all-powerful God find a way to protect His reputation? Indeed, He could have, is the answer, until Moses had said it. Once the *tsaddik* gives utterance to such a possibility, he argues, it has standing on its own, and even God cannot dismiss it.[38]

There are passages in *Kedushat Levi* where God's love of the *tsaddik* and the *tsaddik*'s identification with God converge, creating something that comes very close to an incarnational theology.[39] Here, too, the figure of Moses is right at the center of the stage.

> On the verse "A prayer of Moses, a man of God" (Ps. 90:1):
>
> The only intent of the *tsaddik*, all the days of his life, is to cause the flow of blessing. . . . When the *tsaddik* prays to bring mercy and compassion upon Israel, the blessed Creator is "garbed," as it were, in the *tsaddik*, and is thus, as it were, called a "man." The *tsaddik* is, for his generation, in the role of Moses. Therefore, they said, in the Talmud [referring to one of the rabbis], "Moses, you have spoken well." Every *tsaddik* is called Moses. This is the meaning of "a prayer of Moses" (Ps. 90:1). When the *tsaddik* prays to bring mercy and compassion upon Israel, he is "a man of God." God is "garbed" in that *tsaddik*; hence He is a man.[40]

Here the biblical "model" has been totally absorbed within the figure of the *tsaddik*. The Kabbalists had long taught that "Moses is spread forth [and found] in every generation."[41] The sense that Moses was something more than an ordinary human being—a view that we have seen Levi Yitsḥak struggling against—is also an old part of the tradition. On that same verse, "A prayer of Moses, the man of God," the Midrash rather shockingly comments, "Moses was half man, half God."[42] If the *tsaddik* attains a state of self-negation within the divine oneness, he has attained that moment of apotheosis. Yet he is not permitted to strive for that alone. The point is that he is to do so while bearing with him the prayers of Israel! In Buddhist language, one might say that he is forced to become a *bodhisattva*, returning to the world in order to serve others. Then the ultimate goal of prayer will have been achieved, both for the *tsaddik* himself and for those who see him as their emissary before the divine throne.

5

THE MEZRITCH CIRCLE

A Later Look

The disciples of the Maggid outlived him by years and decades. We know them primarily through their writings, most of them posthumous to their authors, all of them appearing long after their shared teacher was gone and the closeness of the Mezritch and Rovno years had faded into memory. As we meet them through the pages of their works, where their master is referred to always with great affection and respect, we see both those elements that make them a single school and the ways in which they have diverged from one another. Let us take a moment to follow some key dates in their careers and the appearance of their works.

We begin with those disciples who turned northward, bringing the Hasidic message of revival to the region that was called Reisin in the contemporary sources, corresponding to present-day northern and eastern Belarus and Lithuania, which extended as far south as Pinsk and Brisk, where it incurred such great resistance. The earliest active figures in this area were Aharon of Karlin, Ḥayyim Ḥaykl of Amdur, and Menaḥem Mendel of Vitebsk. Aharon was the one disciple to predecease the Maggid in 1772; his place was taken by his follower Shlomo, who was also a disciple of the Maggid. Pushed out of Reisin in 1784 by the enemies of Hasidism, he fled to Vladymir Volynsk (Ludmir) in Ukraine, where he died in 1792, a victim of the Russo-Polish war.[1] The *ḥasidut* of Karlin was only reestablished near its original home by Aharon's grandson in 1801. In Amdur also, the anti-Hasidic forces were triumphant, and R. Ḥayyim Ḥaykl's small community, which at his death in 1787 passed on to his son Shmuel, was eliminated by opposition. Nothing was heard of it after the early 1790s.

In 1777, after suffering from significant persecution for his Hasidic faith and practice, R. Menaḥem Mendel of Vitebsk, accompanied by his follower R. Avraham of Kalisk, decided to emigrate to Erets Israel, leading a small band of followers.[2] It is not clear how much this was a flight from the opposition they faced and to what degree it was an attempt to create an intense Hasidic community on a smaller scale, away from the masses seeking to join them as well as from those who sought their harm. They settled first in Safed, but partly due to opposition that had followed them there as well, they moved their center to Tiberias between 1781 and 1784. R. Menaḥem Mendel led the group until his own passing in 1788, when R. Avraham inherited his place, surviving until 1810. The Hasidic community in the Holy Land suffered great poverty, and efforts were organized back home to help support them. This fundraising effort, conducted by emissaries who frequently travelled back and forth, was supported by all of the major *tsaddikim* in Eastern Europe and was perhaps the most significant shared effort that continued to bind them to one another. Much of their surviving correspondence concerns this fundraising collaboration (and sometimes competition).

The departure of R. Menaḥem Mendel and R. Avraham to the Holy Land left their younger disciple R. Shne'ur Zalman of Liadi in charge of their remaining disciples in Reisin. He was also put in charge of the fundraising in that region.[3] Shne'ur Zalman was clearly an ambitious and highly disciplined young leader. He took the disparate and very loosely linked circles of *ḥasidim* and organized them into a highly structured single community throughout the region, eventually known as ḤaBaD Hasidism.[4] There was certainly a difference—and probably some tension—between the Hasidism of Karlin and that of ḤaBaD since their followers occupied and spread their teachings through the same district.

Aside from Shne'ur Zalman, none of the abovementioned figures had his teaching published until quite late and posthumously; the first of these was *Pri ha-Arets* by R. Menaḥem Mendel, appearing in 1814. Others were printed much later. Very different was the fate of the emerging leader of ḤaBaD. His *Tanya* or *Likkutey Amarim*, the first systematic presentation of Hasidic theology, was an instant success upon its publication in 1796, going through five more editions by 1810. His highly disciplined cadre of followers had great success in establishing themselves as the dominant force in the Reisin area. They saw themselves as an intellectual and spiritual elite, tending to look down on the more popular and faith-based Hasidism that was exemplified in their area by Karlin but also included much of what they came to call "Polish Hasidism" (which was actually mostly Ukrainian). The fact that R. Shne'ur Zalman was twice imprisoned in St. Petersburg due to pressure from anti-Hasidic forces greatly enhanced his reputation across a wide swath of Eastern Europe, and he began to have groups of followers even far beyond his original area of influence.[5]

Hasidism was carried into Poland and Galicia by R. Elimelekh of Lesajsk and his disciples. As mentioned above, he avoided any public employment, devoting himself entirely to the cultivation of a next generation of Hasidic leaders, apparently supported by them. Among the eldest of the Maggid's circle, he died in 1786, and his collected sermons, *No'am Elimelekh*, appeared in 1787. This was the first major Hasidic work to appear after the writings of R. Ya'akov Yosef and the first collection of teachings by the Maggid himself (1781), and this too was a great success, immediately generating several reprints. His tradition was carried on by his follower, among the youngest of the Maggid's disciples, R. Ya'akov Yitsḥak Horowitz, the "Seer" of Lublin (1745–1815). Another key figure, R. Israel Hapstein of Kozienice, was both a scholar and a popular teacher, active in the area called Little Poland until his death in 1814. His *'Avodat Yisra'el* was only published in 1842, long after his passing.

In the Ukrainian heartland of Hasidism, the area safest from rabbinic opposition, R. Menaḥem Naḥum came to establish Chernobyl, where he served as preacher, as a major Hasidic center. Thanks partly to efforts by his son, Chernobyl gained a reputation perhaps second only to that of Miedzybosh, where the Ba'al Shem Tov was buried.[6] Menaḥem Naḥum and Ze'ev Wolf of Zhitomir, another popular preacher, both died in 1797. Their books, *Me'or 'Eynayim* and *Or ha-Me'ir*, were published a year later. Levi Yitsḥak, as we know, was rabbi of Berdychiv from 1785 until 1809. He published the first part of *Kedushat Levi* in that same year, 1798; the larger collection of his sermons appeared shortly after his death.

We have some small bits of surviving correspondence among members of this circle from the 1780s and '90s, much of it having to do with their charitable efforts for the community in Safed and Tiberias. We also have approbations for books as they were published, indicating mutual support for one another's literary efforts. We have seen the support offered to Levi Yitsḥak by Elimelekh and his son, perhaps after the Praga debate in 1781 or possibly earlier. We have also seen the members of the Maggid's circle listed together with Levi Yitsḥak at their head, along with several others, in a catalogue of "sinners" included in *Shever Poshe'im* (*Breaking the Sinners*), a treatise published by the fierce anti-Hasidic polemicist R. David of Makow in 1798.[7] All of these seem to show evidence of a low-burner joint effort to help one another in the crucial decades of Hasidism's original spread. Whatever differences there were between them, whether in matters of theology or personal style, did not come out into the open in any way that is known to us.

All of this changed dramatically, however, after the appearance of the *Tanya* in 1796.[8] In that year, R. Avraham of Kalisk wrote Shne'ur Zalman a sharply worded letter from Tiberias, accusing him of several matters, including creating division among the *ḥasidim* of Reisen as well as promoting his own son into a position of leadership before his time. But the ideological heart of the dispute he was raising had to do with the *Tanya* itself. R. Avraham expressed himself in these words, accusing R. Shne'ur Zalman of

> placing the sun in its case [i.e. hiding the light],[9] garbing the words of our holy master of Mezritch, which are the very words of our master the BeSHT, in the words of the holy ARI [R. Yitsḥak Luria], of blessed memory. Even though they all lead to the same place, "the language of Torah and the language of the sages are distinct from one another."[10] This is especially dangerous because, due to our many sins, "rain" falls and pierces,[11] and the generation is not adequate to it. Therefore, "you should choose to speak subtly,"[12] [referring to] matters that are revealed among us, the ways of awe and love, purifying the body and the emotions, so that they belong only to YHWH. . . .
>
> I have seen the *Sefer shel Beynonim* [= *Tanya*] that your learned self has published, and I find not much value in it for the saving of souls. They [i.e., its words] are [overly] learned, full of counsels, "learned commands of people.". . .[13] For those who receive it, one spark will suffice, dividing into various meanings. That is the way of Torah. Too much oil in the lamp, God forbid, extinguishes [the light].[14]

There is much that stands behind this letter. Surely it did not appear out of nowhere, a sudden reaction to the *Tanya*. There was conflict brewing for some years between those elements within the growing Hasidic communities in Reisin that remained faithful to the Tiberias leadership and those who joined into the very disciplined and loyalty-demanding cadres that supported the new leader on the ground, who had been building that loyalty since 1784.

Where did Levi Yitsḥak stand with regard to this dispute? We have evidence of his support for Shne'ur Zalman at a later date, as we shall see. But it is notable that the *Tanya* appeared with letters of approbation from two less prominent members of the Mezritch circle, R. Zusya and R. Yehudah Leib, both of Anipol, but without a letter from Levi Yitsḥak. Given the latter's high status within the circle, as well as his rabbinate in the important town of Berdychiv, the absence is somewhat glaring and has been noted by scholars.[15] Berdychiv is just a day's journey from Anipol by horse and cart; an emissary's continuing on to there to obtain the letter would not have been too difficult. In fact there is a later ḤaBaD tradition to the effect that Shne'ur Zalman specifically asked the printer Israel Yaffe to avoid Berdychiv when he went out in quest of approbations for the book.[16] It may be that Shne'ur Zalman was worried at what Levi Yitsḥak's feelings about the book might be and chose not to put their relationship to the test by asking.

ḤaBaD sources also record a comment by Levi Yitsḥak when the book appeared. "What a wonder," he supposedly said, "to insert [*araynshteln*] such a big God in such a little book!"[17] Those sources proudly record it as a compliment, but I am less sure than they are about its intent. The Maggid's teachings, as well as Levi Yitsḥak's own, were always presented in the expansive and evocative form of *drash*, or homiletics. Here that expanse is reduced into ordered chapters, systematically presenting Hasidism as a *doctrine* for the first time. In that context, the notion that "one spark will suffice" might well be taken to refer to the surprising power of a new homiletic reading of a verse, enlightening hearers or readers to open their minds and think in multiple news ways, as the Kalisker suggests. One could imagine that a Levi Yitsḥak, too, might have had some concern with "too much oil in the lamp" in the spelled-out, systematic ways in which the *Tanya* presents Hasidic teachings, "extinguishing the light" of spontaneity that was present in the Hasidic *drash*.

The controversy went through several rounds, details of which lie beyond the scope of our concern here. In the opening years of the nineteenth century, several other Hasidic leaders became openly involved on the Kalisker's side. These included R. Asher of Stolin (recently returned to reestablish his family's "seat" in the Karlin district)[18] and his disciple R. Noah (later of Lechowicz), both of whom operated in territory contiguous with the ḤaBaD area and surely suffered some sense of competition with the growing popularity of R. Shne'ur Zalman and his teachings. But they also had the support of the most prominent Hasidic leader from outside the Maggid's circle, the BeSHT's grandson R. Barukh of Miedzybozh.

R. Barukh represented a rather different sort of Hasidism than that of the Maggid. His reading of his grandfather's legacy was considerably less intellectualist and more fully populist than that of either Shne'ur Zalman or Levi Yitsḥak. He was not a rabbi, and it does not seem that he had a high level of either Talmudic or Kabbalistic learning. The part of the BeSHT's legacy that he best affirmed was the *tsaddik* as a source of blessing and healing, a view lying closer to the *ba'al shem* side of his grandfather than to the mystical teachings that were so central to the Maggid. During the 1780s and '90s, he dwelt mostly in Tulchin, quite far to the east of Miedzybosh and Berdychiv. His voice was little heard in the debates between *ḥasidim* and their opponents. It seems, however, that he maintained a strong popular following in his area, clearly based in part on the power of his ancestry. His closer relations were with *tsaddikim* from outside the Mezritch circle, including R. Yeḥiel Mikhl of Zloczow and his sons, whose Hasidism rather closely resembled his own. There was some ongoing tension or rivalry between him and Levi Yitsḥak.[19] It is also likely that he had long hoped to reclaim the status of the BeSHT's own family as the proper leaders of the now increasingly successful Hasidic movement, taking it back from the followers of Dov Baer of Mezritch. This effort was augmented after he moved to Miedzybosh in 1800, attempting to reestablish it, also the burial place of the Ba'al Shem Tov, as "capital" and chief pilgrimage center of the Hasidic universe.

In the years following 1803, there emerged a new alignment of forces in the Hasidic world, joining R. Barukh, R. Asher, and the Kalisker.[20] They described themselves as believers in a Hasidism built around faith in God and the *tsaddikim*, including their power to bless and heal, simplicity (or "wholeness") as their chief religious message, and loyalty to the traditions of the BeSHT.[21] In part, this may have been a coalition of convenience. Both R. Asher and the Kalisker felt themselves to be the losers in ḤaBaD's great campaign of spiritual "conquest" in the Reisin area. R. Avraham felt that he had lost the support of most of his and his teacher's disciples back home, who had been taken away by the young man they had left in charge after their departure in 1777. This also had much to do with disputes over money, a long series of claims and counterclaims about the collection and distribution of funds that were a pipeline vital to the survival of the little bands of *ḥasidim* settled in both Tiberias and Safed. They too eventually became bitterly divided between loyalists of the two leaders.[22] R. Asher, returning to the Reisin area a decade and a half after his teacher R. Shlomo had left it, found that his simpler Hasidic teaching had fewer takers in that district, which had been so washed over by the influence of Shne'ur Zalman. Both the Kalisker and the Karliner must have had some feelings of jealousy in the face of the great success of R. Shne'ur Zalman in the years following both the publication of the *Tanya* and the fame brought about by his imprisonment and suffering for the Hasidic cause. They teamed up with R. Barukh, also an active participant in the funding effort for the Galilee communities, who had the wealth and large group of followers they needed to support them.

But such a reading would ignore the reality of an old division, now coming more to the surface, within the Mezritch circle itself. As we noted at the outset, those attracted by the Maggid represent a wide range of what might be described as religious seekers among young Jewish men from all over Eastern Europe. People like Shne'ur Zalman, Shmelke Horowitz (later of Nikolsburg), and Levi Yitsḥak came to Mezritch with a strong foundation in Talmudic learning. Although they shared in the BeSHT's critique of a Judaism based on this alone, understanding its dangers, they surely never abandoned their own love of this learning or high estimate of its importance. The other end of the spectrum included people like Shlomo of Karlin, who seems to have rejected his scholarly past more sharply and who offered a very different image of the *tsaddik* to be followed and imitated. It is likely that R. Zusya of Anipol and R. Leib Sarah's also belonged to that end of the spectrum, with such figures as the preachers of Chernobyl and Zhitomir resting somewhere in between. All of these varied types seem to have respected and supported one another, recognizing the multiplicity of *tsaddikim* in their world and realizing that different sorts of souls would be attracted to different masters. That was the ethos of the Mezritch circle, especially with regard to others who had stood within it. This ethos survived for a quarter century after the Maggid's death, until it didn't. The *Tanya*'s publication and success was the occasion for this rupture, but it brought forth tensions that must have existed beneath the surface at least since the Maggid's passing.

In 1805, R. Avraham Kalisker wrote to Levi Yitsḥak laying out his side in the dispute, one that had now led to a complete lack of contact or respect between the two sides, and sought his support.[23] He must have realized that this was something of a "long shot" request. The old friendship of Levi Yitsḥak and Shne'ur Zalman had been reinforced by the betrothal of their grandchildren in 1802, following which Levi Yitsḥak always referred to Shne'ur Zalman as "my in-law."[24]

Amid the exaggerated expressions of politeness and affection that characterized all such letters, Levi Yitsḥak said the following in his response:

> It is most surprising in my sight that it would occur to you to complain about the behavior of our lord and master [R. Shne'ur Zalman]. All of his essential conduct is based upon that of our master the Maggid, all of whose concern was to teach his people Torah and *mitsvot*. That is the essence of service, as we have received it from our master. He [Shne'ur Zalman] also conducts himself in this way. This is the holy path of our holy Torah, the dwelling-place of God's light. If only all of God's people were *tsaddikim*, acting in this manner! In fact, one who does not conduct himself in this way is not following the path of our teacher. Anyone who complains about it is like one who complains about him [the Maggid]. The essence of his holy worship and conduct was just this way. I am thus very surprised that you, who were there together with us in your youth, before our master, would find this to be an object of wonder.
>
> As for that which you say in the name of the late Menaḥem Mendel, who was so very dear in the sight of our master, I have not heard it. But I will attest to this, in an absolute way. My genius of an in-law was very precious in the eyes of our master, beyond measure.

On the face of things, this seems to be a letter of unequivocal support for Shne'ur Zalman and a rebuke of the Kalisker. Read carefully, however, this may be seen as a somewhat evasive letter. He says that Shne'ur Zalman is doing what the Maggid would have wanted, "teach[ing] his people Torah and *mitsvot*," i.e., spreading the Hasidic message. On this score, it was fairly apparent in 1805 that ḤaBaD was the most successful of all Hasidic groups in doing so. We will recall that this is what Levi Yitsḥak had admonished his colleagues to do from the very beginning: Go out and spread the teachings. Bring people to "love, awe, and *devekut*." But note that Levi Yitsḥak says nothing about the key accusations against Shne'ur Zalman, those of combining Lurianic teachings with those of the Maggid or of excessive devotion to intellectual contemplation. The teachings of *Kedushat Levi* are in this sense entirely different than those of his friend Shne'ur Zalman; his never involve the complex symbolism of the Lurianic Kabbalah. This difference must have been obvious to him. Combined with the lack of an approbation of the *Tanya* and the ambiguity of his reported first comment regarding it, there is room to think that here personal friendship and appreciation for Shne'ur Zalman's great success, perhaps as well as respect for his sufferings for the Hasidic cause, forced Levi Yitsḥak to remain silent about whatever intellectual differences may have existed between them. Later Hasidic historiography views Levi Yitsḥak as an unequivocal supporter of R. Shne'ur Zalman. In 1810, after Levi Yitsḥak's passing, Shne'ur Zalman made the long journey to Berdychiv to comfort his family. Several of his well-known sermons were delivered on that occasion.[25]

As history went on, ḤaBaD went very much its own way, creating a Hasidism strongly committed to its own teachings in both learning and praxis, always claiming to be the true fulfillment of the Maggid's teaching but having very little contact with the rest of the Hasidic world. It is not accidental that down to present times, the other leading families of *tsaddikim* continued to intermarry with one another, while marriages of the Schneersohns increasingly took place within their own extended clan. The Deḅarmdigers, the descendants of Levi Yitsḥak, while never creating a dynasty of their own, married into the leading families of the emerging Ukrainian Hasidic elite of the nineteenth century and became part of that community. Memory of the fracture caused by this dispute was mostly forgotten other than insofar as it concerned the Schneersohns, who remained quite separate.

PART II *Mystic Disciple and Teacher*

6

TRANSLATING THE TRANSCENDENT

Levi Yitsḥak was the disciple of a mystical master. Much of the material that we have preserved in the name of Dov Baer of Mezritch deals with the metaphysical ideas and devotional teachings of Hasidic mysticism dressed in homiletic garb. Hasidism's essential message, that God is everywhere present and accessible, that all of life is to be seen as a proper arena of divine service, and that joyful worship of God is the entire purpose of human existence, is a distillation into popular and accessible form of a centuries-old mystical strand within Judaism. Kabbalah, or "tradition," as this form of mystical Judaism is broadly called, consists of vast and highly complex edifices of symbolic language, doctrines, and practices, rereading the entire legacy of rabbinic Judaism through its own multiple lenses. By the late eighteenth century, the tower of Kabbalistic wisdom was beginning to totter, mostly due to forces from within, including overelaboration to the point of utter obfuscation of its meaning. Controversy resulting from both the Sabbatian and Frankist debacles had also served to discredit Kabbalah in some circles and more broadly to call forth caution regarding its study and dissemination. In Central Europe, it was also on the verge of collapse due to the challenge of emerging modern science, but that had not yet reached the areas of Hasidism's growth.

Hasidism emerged in regions and from within circles where faith in Kabbalah remained very strong but where its more intricate teachings were beyond the grasp of all but the most highly trained. The Hasidic masters carefully mined the riches of that tradition, simplifying it radically, in order to make it serve as the basis for their popular revival of Judaism. In doing so, they emphasized its core mystical message, encapsulating it in such oft-repeated key traditional phrases as

"There is no place devoid of Him," "Know Him in all your ways" (Prov. 3:6), or "He is the cosmic Aleph." These were presented and discussed by each Hasidic author in his own distinctive way. Other adages or brief devotional instructions were built around them.

In addition to generally downplaying the complex intellectual structures, including meditational instructions,[1] of the Kabbalists, they largely turned aside from the strict and self-punishing regimen of ascetic practices with which Kabbalah had become associated.[2] Instead, they used selected fragments of its symbolism to put forward a mostly positive and optimistic devotional psychology, viewing the Torah less as a patchwork of mystical secrets pointing toward the upper worlds and more as a manual of instruction for living the inward devotional life in this world. Aware that they were seeking to create a popular movement based on what had once been a body of esoteric teachings designed for a small and learned elite, they used their own communication skills and charismatic personalities as a bridge between the sometimes abstruse teachings and their wider audience. Most significantly, they succeeded in using the mystical teachings in a way that conveyed their love and concern for the inner lives of those who surrounded them, creating communities of loyal followers who reflected and returned that love.

Hasidism's ideal figure was the Ba'al Shem Tov, a natural mystic, shaman, and healer, who related to the Kabbalistic sources, and to Judaism altogether, in an idiosyncratic and creative way. The legend that he spent years wandering in the mountains and only with difficulty was accepted by the more learned townspeople of Miedzybozh, where he eventually settled, probably reflects an awareness that the BeSHT was something of an outsider to the normative world of Jewish piety.[3] He is a historical figure constantly redrawn by romantic folklore, highly popular in his era and the century that followed but inspiring the creative imagination even in our own day.[4] It was in his name, and around his image, that Hasidism was forged.

Dov Baer of Mezritch was the most significant intellectual and spiritual leader of the emerging movement. He took the transformative mystical insights of the BeSHT and set them into a newly simplified metaphysical context. While rigid typologies are never precise when applied to the complex inner life of any individual, it is generally accurate to think of the BeSHT as an *ecstatic* mystic while Dov Baer is more of a *contemplative*. "Ecstatic," in this context, refers to a religious personality given to altered states of mind, including out-of-body experiences in which one feels oneself transported to another dimension of existence. The ecstatic's mystical encounters lead to a high-speed charge of consciousness, sometimes resulting in a "leap" into a higher realm. Visionary elements are part of the ecstatic mindset, occasionally leading to prophetic utterances, either comprehensible to others or emerging in a form that in another cultural context is characterized as "speaking in tongues." The Merkavah literature attests to the great antiquity of this element within the Jewish mystical tradition. The BeSHT's religious life was partially guided by shamanic practices, learned from a variety of sources, through which he came to a pneumatic ("soul-driven" or inspired) rereading of Jewish texts and traditions as he encountered them. The most important document that we have written by the BeSHT, his 1750 letter to his brother-in law,[5] R. Gershon of Kitov, briefly discussed above, clearly illustrates this ecstatic character.

The contemplative mystic is one whose inner life is characterized more by "water" than by "fire." He tends to sink into the depths of a word, scriptural verse, or idea rather than fly to the heavenly heights to catch a glimpse of angels or listen for their words. His experience is one of a reflective *slowing* of ordinary consciousness rather than a speeding up. For the contemplative, *insight* may be seen as the highest goal of religious experience. His "opening of the inner eye" will lead to a deeper understanding of the truth, a breakthrough of boundaries that had restricted perception rather than to a blinding flash of light or ascent to a higher world.

Dov Baer's contemplative life was built around intensive study of and reflection on the Kabbalistic classics of prior ages. The highly poetic and imaginative thirteenth-century Zohar, filtered through the two great sixteenth-century schools of later Kabbalism, those initiated by R. Moshe Cordovero and R. Yitsḥak Luria, constituted his daily regimen of study.[6] Dov Baer's core theology is very much shaped by Cordovero (as transmitted through various intermediaries)[7] while his understanding of Jewish ritual life was indelibly formed by the Lurianic manuals that had come to dominate (still in mostly unpublished manuscript form) in his day. His teachings virtually leave behind both the classical Kabbalistic metaphysic of the ten *sefirot* (these are mostly psychologized, referred to states of the devotee's mind and emotion rather than metaphysical realms) and the five *partsufim* or "faces" of God, ever going through stages of maturation and development, that dominate on the Lurianic side.[8] He uses terminology derived from both, but only as convenience rather than as reflecting a commitment to either system as such. He also invents some new religious language of his own. Rather than getting caught up in the intricacies of Kabbalistic symbolism, he turns directly to the essential mystical questions: the nature of reality and the relationship between God, world, and soul. He ponders the question of being and nothingness, seeking out the hidden divine *ayin* ("naught; *nihil*") that underlies and animates *yesh*, "being," all that exists. That *ayin*, better rendered as "The Nothing," rather than simply "nothing," represents the innermost recesses of the Godhead. God has created the world *ex nihilo*, making that Nothing into being, according to one well-known formulation; the task of the *tsaddik* (but sometimes of all Jews) is to reverse the process, to discover the *ayin* within and behind the "mask" of the *yesh*. In identifying, discovering, and revealing the *ayin*, one cleaves to God and becomes one with the divine. That *ayin* is the true core of existence. Seeming multiplicity, the diverse realm of *yesh*, covers over that truth and must be penetrated in order that it be revealed.[9]

The Kabbalistic notion of *tsimtsum*, the self-reduction or concentration of divinity that allows room for the non-God to exist, is key to understanding this process. Following certain trends within Kabbalah, *tsimtsum* is presented by the Maggid in a mostly psychological way. God has hidden from us the truth that He is present throughout existence so that we will live our lives as the earthly and individual souls we were created to be. But just enough of the deeper truth is present in those souls to stir us to awareness that life is about something more, thus setting us forth on our spiritual quest, seeking out the *ayin* behind the *yesh*, sometimes presented (already by BeSHT) as a "palace" or "wall" of illusion.

Like many within the Jewish mystical tradition, Dov Baer was particularly fascinated by questions of language and its place, both in the cosmos and in the human soul.[10] The ancient rabbinic trope that God "looked into Torah and created the world" is translated into a strong mystical nominalism in which the sacred word stands as the true center of existence. This is combined with a notion of God as a sort of primal Kabbalist. Language is broken down from meaningful speech into letters, both graphic and aural. It is through manipulation of these letters that God both created and sustains the universe. Entering into contemplation of the letters empowers the *tsaddik* to gain entrée into the mind of God, and in this way even to affect the divine will.[11] The divine pairing of a recondite *'Olam ha-Maḥashavah*, "Realm of Thought," and an accessible *'Olam ha-Dibbur*, "Realm of Speech," is also particularly characteristic of the Maggid's teachings. Here the inner divine process of self-articulation is directly parallel to the contemplative's own effort to express his thoughts in language.[12] Although Hasidism in general is a devotional mysticism, focused more on issues of human worship and inward states than on metaphysical realms, the teachings recorded in Dov Baer's name still tend toward abstraction and often seem like they would have been difficult to understand, especially for the noninitiate.[13]

This intellectual abstruseness might have been magnified by a highwire act of homiletics in which he seems to have engaged. We have a unique eyewitness account of a visit to the Maggid's court, probably sometime in the late 1760s, by a young Jewish seeker who was later to become the well-known Berlin philosopher Salomon Maimon. Describing the Maggid's preaching on the Sabbath of his visit, he says,

> After the meal was over, the superior struck up a solemn inspiring melody, held his hand for some time upon his brow, and then began to call out, "Z___ of H___, M___ of R___," and so on. Every newcomer was thus called by his own name and the name of his residence, which excited no little astonishment. Each recited, as he was called, some verse of the Holy Scriptures. Thereupon the superior commenced to deliver a sermon for which the verses served as a text, so that although they were disconnected verses taken from different parts of the Holy Scriptures they were combined with as much skill as if they had formed a single whole. What was still more extraordinary, every one of the newcomers believed that he had discovered, in that part of the sermon which was founded on his verse, something that had reference to the facts of his own spiritual life. At this we were of course greatly astonished.[14]

This practice may well account for some of the seeming diversions or sidetracking that occur regularly in the Maggid's recorded teachings. By the time such sermons were edited from various written recollections, all of them translated from the oral Yiddish into a highly wooden rabbinic Hebrew, it is no wonder that they are often quite difficult to decipher and reflect later layers, including the editor's reinterpretations (as well as many a printer's error) interpolated into the text. The pearls of mystic insight—and they are indeed present in R. Dov Baer's teachings—require a skilled diver to retrieve them and render them accessible.

Levi Yitsḥak became a popularizer of his master's sometimes difficult ideas. His sermons and short teachings, as preserved in the *Kedushat Levi*, are relatively comprehensible, even when dealing with mystical matters. Levi Yitsḥak, more than Dov Baer, was devoted to the spread of Hasidism as a popular movement, as we have already seen. This demanded a version of the teachings that could reach and move ordinary people as well as would-be mystic scholars of the sort who gathered around the Maggid. It is to this work of translation and broadening of appeal that Levi Yitsḥak's sermons are chiefly dedicated. He had to make the message of *ayin*, the mystical Nothing, reach a larger audience, turning his master's often murky abstraction into teachings more accessible and concrete.[15]

Such "translation" took place on multiple levels. It is hard to know, when reading a particular teaching in the *Kedushat Levi* (these range from a single paragraph to several pages in length), for how wide or narrow an audience it was intended. The editors of Hasidic homilies generally made no distinction between things the authors might have taught to their innermost circle of disciples, training to become *tsaddikim* themselves, and sermons they might have preached publicly in the main synagogue of Berdychiv or wherever they dwelt. In creating a religious revival intended for a wide variety of Jews, ranging from the highly learned to the illiterate, how much did they need to convey of the subtle mystical teachings that were the source of their own inspiration? Did generalized calls for *devekut* ("attachment" to God) and *hitlahavut* ("fiery religious enthusiasm") suffice, or did the preacher need to share also the process of how the individual soul could come to be reabsorbed into and again emerge from the divine *ayin*? Levi Yitsḥak, along with others in his circle, often seems to be struggling with these questions. We see in him a great concern for communication. It is likely that he worked at creating concentric circles among those he taught, beginning with a small inner ring of those able to digest and follow the mystical practices, eventually widening out to an audience that included all of Jewry in the Pinsk and then the Berdychiv districts, who would have received them in a significantly diluted form.

This effort at spreading the teachings he had received in Mezritch endured throughout the thirty-seven-year period between the Maggid's passing (1772) and Levi Yitsḥak's own death (1809). In the course of it, the disciple emerged as a teacher much more concerned with human life, personal interactions, and the daily struggles of ordinary Jews than he was with absorption into the secret inner life of God and the goal of mystical self-annihilation. It is sometimes possible to perceive the inward tension he feels between these realms, and occasionally we can see him in argument with his own master's voice, internalized within him.

Tracing this issue of the accessibility and utility of profound mystical teachings in creating a popular movement of religious revival will be a major theme throughout this second section of our study. All this will become clear as we read from the *Kedushat Levi* and try to meet the man behind the sermons. We will thus have to start at the beginning, with Levi Yitsḥak the mystic. The very first teaching in *Kedushat Levi* begins with these words: "the [first] principle is that the blessed Creator created all and is all, His influx never ceasing. In each instant, He sends forth His flow to His creatures, to all the worlds, to all the palaces, all the angels, and all the holy beings."[16]

This is the reason, Levi Yitsḥak goes on to say, that the prophet (Is. 45:7) (and the liturgy following him) refers to the act of creation in the present rather than the past tense: "He *creates* light and *forms* darkness." Levi Yitsḥak continues, "He is whole and includes all. Therefore, when a person comes to *ayin*, realizing that he is naught, that it is only the Creator giving him strength, he is naming blessed YHWH as 'Creator' [*yotser*, a noun formed from the present tense], meaning that now too He is creating."[17]

The strongly panentheistic language here makes for a dramatic opening of the volume, surely intentional.[18] God who "is all" and "includes all" is *eyn sof*, the endless and unknowable One of Kabbalistic teaching, depicted as an ongoing engine of creation, extending the flow of His own self into ever new creatures that are at the same time a part of Him, the single true Being. The goal of devotional life is to realize this, to "come to *ayin*," understanding that you are naught, that God is all. This is the essential mystical teaching of the Maggid's Hasidism: awareness of the overwhelming presence of God that leads to transcendence of the self, a realization that all of one's powers are only due to the unceasing influx of divine energies, the constant renewal of creation.

This realization of one's own smallness, almost to the point of nonexistence, has nothing to do with self-deprecation. The Hasidic preacher, who wants to reach out to people by building them up rather than tearing them down, has to treat himself in the same way.

> It is known that the greatest human attainment is that of realizing your own lowliness. This comes about as you stand before the great and lofty King, seeing how great and exalted He is, how all the heavenly angels stand in awe and trembling before Him. Scripture says (Num. 12:5), "Moses was humbler than any person on the face of the earth." This hints that

> he was humbler than they because they were "on the face of the earth" [facing downward, toward the ground]. Moses' pure and holy mind was always turned upward, seeing the angels above, standing in fear and awe. That is what brought him to humility.

> This is the rung of the perfect and holy *tsaddik*, coming to humility as a result of looking toward our great and blessed Creator. Of this the sages (b. Pes. 8a) taught, "The *tsaddikim* before the *shekhinah* are like a candle in the presence of a torch." Some people might attain humility by becoming aware of their own lowliness and slight value. But the true *tsaddik* does so by gazing upon the greatness of the Creator, as we have said. It is when he beholds the great brightness above that the quality of humility comes to dwell within him. On "like a candle in the presence of a torch," RaSHI commented, "The light of the candle is not visible, because of the torch's brightness."[19]

It is by facing upward, seeing the glory of God, that we are to achieve humility, rather than by facing downward toward our own abasement. This is bedrock Hasidic teaching. Levi Yitsḥak then goes on to delicately tie this insistence on the positive path toward humility to a verse from the Song of Songs (1:5): "I am black but comely, O daughters of Jerusalem, like the tents of Kedar, the curtains of Solomon." It is exposure to the upper light that darkens the *tsaddik*'s countenance, a blackness that makes him more comely, like the bedouin's darkened tents burned by the desert sun. We are humbled not by shame, by thinking that we might be "blackened" by sin, but through gazing upon the light-filled presence of the Divine. Moral self-awareness flows directly from the heart of the *tsaddik*'s personal mystical experience.[20]

The way to attain this state is described as an act of *gazing*, directed both inward and upward. "All creatures have to gaze [*le-histakkel*] at their own *ayin*, namely their root. This is the blessed Endless [*eyn sof*], from which all their energy derives." Gazing upon "their own *ayin*" refers at once to the nonexistence of the individual and to the presence of the divine *nihil*, the only true existent, within the person. This inward gaze leads one away from the physical universe and brings one into consciousness of the singular selfhood of God.[21]

> King David was attached to the quality of *ayin*, aware that his very life-force and all his movements were a part of the divinity within him; this

> was his life. . . . "There is no place devoid of Him," and anything not attached to a part of the divine has no life. That is what we have said concerning the verse "See that I, I am He" (Deut. 32:39). I [alone] am an "I"; no human or angelic being can say of himself "I," a term that denotes substance and reality. One who says "I" needs to examine himself and know of what he is saying it. Since the life-flow within one is the blessed Creator, and of that one may not say "I," implying that it was one's own. . . . This is the meaning of "I, I am He." Only I, the Creator, can legitimately say "I." Besides Me, no creature above or below may properly say "I" of itself. To what would they be referring?[22]

It has not escaped Levi Yitsḥak that *ayin* ("nothingness") and *ani* ("I") are composed of the same letters and therefore the same numeric value. This makes them mystically connected and to some extent synonymous. That had already been noted by his teacher. To attain the state of *ayin* is to transcend the individual self and to become present to the echoing and uniquely ever-present *ani* of God.[23]

This radically mystical view of reality, in which *ayin* is the only true existence, into which one's self is to be subsumed, places Levi Yitsḥak very close to the Maggid's teachings as well as those of his son "the Angel" and another disciple, R. Ḥayyim Ḥaykl of Amdur. Here is Levi Yitsḥak in a passage woven around a Midrashic teaching about bowing and its role at key moments within the Torah:

> When a person comes to *ayin*, cleaving to the Source of Life, life-energy [*ḥiyyut*] flows upon him. Then he comes to the World of Transformation, which raises him up to the Lord of all. Then all is attached to YHWH, living eternally. This is the meaning of "he and his alternate will be holy" (Lev. 27:10). . . .[24]
>
> This is what the sages meant in the Midrash, regarding "We will bow down and return to you" (Gen. 22:5). Rabbi Yehudah said, "All is due to the merit of bowing. Abraham only returned in peace from Mount Moriah due to the merit of bowing." Bowing indicates humility. By gazing upon the greatness of the One before whom he bowed, he understood his own lowliness and came to *ayin*. . . .
>
> So too, the Torah was only given through bowing, by means of *ayin*, attachment to *ayin*. [Only] this enabled [Israel] to receive the Torah, as in "You will bow from afar" (Ex. 24:1). This bowing meant coming to

> *ayin*. "From afar" means that you be distanced and stripped of your own selfhood. Thus were they prepared to receive the Torah. This is also the meaning of "From afar YHWH appears to me" (Jer. 31:2). When I am "afar," when I am not there with myself in thought at all, then "YHWH appears to me."[25]

The divine *ayin* is also linked with the letter *alef*, another association reaching back into earlier Kabbalistic sources.[26] *Ayin* serves as one of the key symbol-terms for the most primal stage of divine self-manifestation: the will to flow forth toward creation. The divine name associated with *ayin* is *ehyeh*, the first and future tense articulation of the divine self, the letters of the Godhead beginning with an *alef*. Here too there is a play of letter reversal, as *alef* spelled backwards is *pele* or "wonder." To gaze into *ayin* is to be in a state of utter wonder since no form of particular existence has yet come to be.[27]

Reflections on such well-known and seemingly simple words as *ayin* or the letter *alef* were ways of making mystical teachings attractive. But their seeming accessibility served as a way of bringing the hearer into the realm of profound ideas. That same *alef*, taken as a word rather than just a Hebrew/Aramaic letter, has the meaning of "instruct." This same homily thus quotes, "I shall instruct you in wisdom" (Job 33:33), also readable as "I shall *alef* you into wisdom." Wisdom or *ḥokhmah* is the highest of the ten inner divine realms, or *sefirot*, according to the Hasidic count. Sometimes it is identified directly with *ayin*; in other sources it is seen as proceeding from *ayin*, which is too elusive to be counted.[28] It is the origin-place of all existent beings, their locus prior to their first stage of individuation before they are "born" out of the womb of *binah*, the next of those realms. This recalls Job 28:1, "Whence [*me-ayin*] does wisdom come?" Kabbalists, beginning in the twelfth century, read this verse as a statement rather than a question, to be rendered as "Wisdom proceeds from *ayin*." *Ḥokhmah*, also called "beginning," is the first stage of emergent *yesh* or thinghood. It derives from *ayin* but also stands in contrast to it.[29]

For the Maggid and young Levi Yitsḥak in his wake, as contemplative mystics, all these seemingly complex and abstract associations are expressions of the inward states of mind that they sought out, standing as metaphysical expressions of their inner contemplative world. Formulae like "*Ḥokhmah* proceeds from *ayin*" or "I shall *alef* you into *ḥokhmah*" are intended as objects of meditation, pathways into the inner contemplative universe. The devotee is meant to wrap his mind around such a phrase in the course of devoted study or as preparation for prayer. The Maggid's homilies toss off such formulae precisely to nourish the souls of his spiritually awake and hungry disciples. In Ḥ aBaD, where everything was systematized, we have evidence of how these phrases were turned into structured contemplative exercises.[30] But surely they constituted a powerful presence elsewhere in the Maggid's circle as well, though in less systematized ways, serving as objects of contemplation to replace the far more complex Lurianic meditations on prayer (*kavvanot*) that had been set aside.

This highly rarified notion of divinity sometimes reminds the reader of formulations found in Maimonides, the great spokesman in the Middle Ages for an abstract and contemplative Jewish theology.[31] The bridge between the philosopher's utterly transcendent and unknowable Cause of Causes and the indwelling One within all of being in these mystical renditions had been forged by many generations of Kabbalistic thought,[32] most prominently that of Cordovero, who offered a great synthesis uniting Kabbalistic and philosophical Judaism.[33] This Cordoveran channeling of Maimonides tended to emphasize more of the contemplative experience than the great philosopher himself had deigned to describe. Some of this is present, cast into homiletic garb, in the writings of Levi Yitsḥak as well. Just as a person cannot properly say "I" of himself, as we have seen, so can one not properly say "You" to God:

> "You, He, are YHWH alone" (Neh. 9:6). "You" is a way of referring to one who is present. But how can a person say "You" [to God]? "He" [in the third person or "hidden" form] is YHWH alone [i.e., God is completely hidden and therefore beyond being addressed in prayer]. But the point is this: in everything a person sees, when the eyes are directed straight toward the ways of YHWH, one is able to see the Cause beyond all Causes, that which cannot be grasped, hidden and elusive to any created being. This much one can grasp. "You, He" means that "You" are the hidden "He." One may grasp that there is a Creator of the universe, though One [of a nature] that is beyond our grasp.[34]

The "You" we address in prayer is indeed the "He" who remains forever hidden. The passage then goes on to explain this insight in terms of the Kabbalistic *sefirot*, but it winds up claiming that a *tsaddik* who attains this insight has reached a state of prophecy, one in which "the *shekhinah* speaks from within his throat."[35]

All of this is redolent with Maimonidean influence. God is so deeply hidden that even the common second-person address of all Jewish prayer is called into question. The fusion of Maimonidean abstraction with Kabbalistic metaphysics that underlies the Maggid's thought pulls one back and forth between them as one goes from one teaching of his to another. In some passages, the utter abstraction of God as *ayin*, beyond will and unconcerned with earthly matters, seems to dominate; in other passages, the *sefirot* take on an important mediating function, as does the earthly *tsaddik* himself.

Generally speaking, Levi Yitsḥak's mystical attention is given to the very highest realms within the Kabbalistic universe of discourse, *keter* and *ḥokhmah*, as we have seen. This is true of the Maggid's own writings as well. A moralist within the group like the author of *Or ha-Me'ir*, for example, will pay much more attention to the lower *middot* and through them to the building up of *shekhinah*'s entire form. Levi Yitsḥak's inner eye is turned higher, to the inner moment of transposition between nothingness and being.

These passages seem to be addressed to Levi Yitsḥak's most serious and devoted followers, those wanting to walk the mystic path of the true *tsaddik*. It was only the mystic who was able to reach beyond the personal, stepping into such deep realms of religious encounter. This demanded *bittul*, or self-negation, a term widely found in the writings attributed to the Maggid and in Levi Yitsḥak's teachings. *Bittul* is the core of mystical experience as described "from below," the goal to be attained by the seeker. It is a complete loss of self in the moment of absorption within the cosmic One. By definition a temporary, perhaps even a momentary, state in the course of life, it is presented as the apex of both *yir'ah*, self-effacing awe, and *ahavah*, passionate love, of God. *Bittul* is nourished by love and longing as well as by brokenheartedness and a sense of desolation. Here is a particularly revealing description of its comings and goings, showing Levi Yitsḥak's awareness of the painful sides of the religious quest:

> It is known that the *tsaddikim* rise, level after level, in their devotion. This takes place in a "back and forth" manner. First, they leap forward in their passionate and sublime awe of YHWH, resulting in the negation of self. Then they come "back," returning to themselves. This means that their heart breaks within them, as they become aware of their own lowly state. The heart is disquieted by this. But the more the heart is broken in this "back" movement, the greater is the [next] rush forward, the soul

> going out of itself in longing to rise up to YHWH and be negated. Then one becomes engulfed in great pleasure, due to the beautiful shining of divine light and vitality than flows upon one.[36]

Here Levi Yitsḥak shows some of the sensibilities displayed so powerfully by his younger colleague R. Naḥman of Bratslav. The broken heart one feels in this description should be distinguished from that resulting from ordinary human disappointment, even discouragement at one's moral progress. Here the return itself, the realization that the glory of *bittul* is only momentary, is enough to break one's heart. "Here I am again," the seeker says to himself, "just an individual human, with all my inadequacies. Ah, but there is another cycle to come! My faith tells me that every such 'fall' is an opportunity to rise yet higher." Consolation for the inconstancy of this state of self-transcendence is found in the widely repeated utterance of the BeSHT: "Constant pleasure is no pleasure at all."[37] One *must* fall, in other words, in order to experience the pleasure of renewal in rising again.

This multitiered approach to religious experience is also reflected in a comment of Levi Yitsḥak's on the *Shema*ʿ ("Hear, O Israel") that stands at the center of daily Jewish worship. The word *Shema*ʿ, he says, is made up of three consonants: *shin, mem*, and *ʿayin* (not to be confused with *ayin*, "naught," which begins with an *alef*). *Shin* and *mem* make up the word for "name," while *ʿayin* represents the eye.

> It is not proper that a person looking at the king should call him by name. When people are speaking to one another directly [literally "mouth to mouth"], they do not call one another by name. But if you are not looking at the king [when you are in a "third-person" situation], it is then fitting to refer to him by name. The same is true of the blessed Creator. There is a mind that grasps the Creator, as it were. This mind then addresses the mind that does not see the Creator.
>
> That is why *shema*ʿ is composed of "name" and "eye."[38] "Name" refers to the mind that does not see [God], but calls out the name. It is derivative from the mind that sees, the "eye." The one who sees does not call out the name.[39]

The higher religious consciousness, that of the *tsaddik*, dwells beyond language. His eye's gaze is fixed upon *maḥashavah*, the realm of divine thought, where there are no words. He *sees*, or perceives, the God who is beyond naming, then conveys that insight to the lower mind, which is in the realm of verbal articulation. It is only there that names, even the name YHWH, become relevant. So too does the *tsaddik* as mystic pass on something of his own mysterious and transformative inner experience to the enthusiastic masses, who worship *hashem*, the *named* God, who responds to their passion by loving them in return.

These brief elliptical references to the core of mystical experience are typical of the *Kedushat Levi*, as they are of the writings collected in the Maggid's own name. They are not easy to decipher, becoming clear only after careful reading and contemplation. One has the impression that the author wanted to include these but chose to do so in such obscure fashion that only one who knew what to look for or had some prior experience in such matters would understand them as such. This quasi-esoteric style of writing has a long history within the Jewish mystical tradition. It reaches back to Moses Naḥmanides's decision in the thirteenth century to include Kabbalistic secrets, called "the way of truth," within his popular Torah commentary but to word them in a way that only those already familiar with Kabbalah's esoteric symbolism would be able to decipher.[40] It is striking to see some of that same duality even within Hasidism, a movement so dedicated to popularization and accessibility. There is still a sense of revealing and hiding at once.

The language of *ayin* and the gaze into it is particularly characteristic of R. Dov Baer. It is prominent in the writings of several members of the Mezritch school but by no means all. In addition to Levi Yitsḥak, it is deeply present in the teachings of R. Menaḥem Mendel of Vitebsk and R. Hayyim Haykl of Amdur. It is present in the background of R. Shne'ur Zalman of Liadi's work as well, although he extends it much farther, creating his own system of thought. While all of the "graduates" of the Mezritch school are imbued with its spirit of devotional piety, speaking frequently of *devekut* (mystical attachment) and love of God, Levi Yitsḥak is among those who most fully preserve the Maggid's mystical metaphysic and his particular way of articulating religious experience.

As we have said earlier, the years of visiting Mezritch made a tremendous impression upon this group of seekers. As seen in these texts, this included moments of mystical experience and elevated consciousness. Generally speaking, however, it is the style of Hasidic preachers to keep accounts of such direct experiences somewhat shrouded, referring to them in the third rather than the first person, and often bringing them up in the context of a homily, sometimes attributing them to a biblical character or a sage of old. The *Kedushat Levi* offers ample evidence that its author is speaking from a place of such experience, though often ascribing it to others. In describing the biblical Oholiav, one of the makers of the wilderness tabernacle, Levi Yitsḥak refers to him as "a sage of silence," meaning a contemplative. He served YHWH not only with his own mind, but he attained divine aid that enabled him to gaze upon the *ayin*. This caused his human mind to be obliterated, rendering him silent. "But when such a person returns to his own mind," Levi Yitsḥak adds, "he is filled with divine influx." Oholiav, the weaver of curtains, is turned into the curtain itself in this illuminated reading. He is "woven of azure and purple, drawn of varied sorts of the goodly flow."[41]

Levi Yitsḥak speaks of this moment of the return from an experience of self-transcendence also in the context of describing the positioning of lights within the candelabrum in the tabernacle: "All the worlds gaze at the blessed Creator with a sublime clarity that lies above them. This great clarity causes them to be in awe and fear, so much so that they are obliterated. The fear and awe are so great that they have no joy at all. Joy is present [only] when they return to themselves. Then that divine clarity contracts itself, dressing in worldly garb, and they are in joy."[42]

This understanding of the return from a mystical state and the sense of bliss or contentment that one feels in such a moment is no mere theory, nor is it something one learns about from books or just invents as a homiletical flourish. Notice again that the word *histakkel*, "gazing," plays a central role. He seems to think of the experience largely in visual terms, even though it is an eyes-closed encounter with the primal Nothing. The higher perception of divine oneness in the *shema*ʿ, we will recall, is that of the eye, reaching beyond what can be named. In one intriguing passage, he even suggests that it is the right eye that performs the actual gaze, followed by the left eye, which is the organ that integrates that gaze and teaches awareness of it to the mind. The two eyes are equal and parallel to one another on the face, however, indicating each of us is only permitted to experience in the gaze as much as we are able to mentally absorb. Raw experience cannot outstrip our vehicle for communicating the nature of that experience to ourselves—a rather surprisingly modern and sophisticated understanding of perception.[43]

There is much in this aspect of Levi Yitsḥak's teaching that will make special sense to today's psychedelic voyagers. The process of "reentry," or return from a period of detachment from self to an ordinary mental state, can be fraught with difficulty. Much of the early Hasidic discourse about the incongruity between the infinite mind of God and the finitude of the human brain may be viewed in this context. Such phrases as "gazing into the *ayin*" or being "filled with the divine influx" will have particular meaning to those who approach them on the basis of some parallel experience.[44]

It is not only the mystic who is engaged in this inward gaze toward oneness or nothingness. The entire cosmos is filled with such yearning. The last passage quoted refers to "all the worlds" taking part in this mystical gaze. This leads them to a state in which all opposition between distinctive and potentially contradictory selves is overcome, the *coincidentia oppositorum* so characteristic of mystical insight across lines of tradition. Such binaries as water and fire, earth and spirit, are revealed to be one.[45] This collapse of difference in the oneness of being includes the most essential of oppositions, that between self and other. This, of course, is the very crux of the mystic's claim. Individual identity is to be set aside in favor of a sense of inclusion within the single selfhood of the One.

In order to attain this state of inner nothingness, both the mystic and the worlds themselves must disdain and transcend their corporeal existence. Levi Yitsḥak seems to prefer this formulation of the spiritual goal over the embrace of corporeal things and the attempt to worship God through them, known by scholars as *'avodah ba-gashmiyyut*. This is a key teaching in some other works of early Hasidism, as we shall discuss in more detail below, and Levi Yitsḥak is notable for standing at some distance from it.

> "His sister stood afar off, to know what would become of him" (Ex. 2:4). Through this, one may also explain the verse "From afar YHWH appears to me" (Jer. 31:2). As long as the worlds hold fast to their corporeality, they are unable to attain service of the blessed Creator. They can do so only when they distance and strip themselves of their physical nature.[46] This is the distance of which the verse speaks; only when a person is far from his own corporeal self does YHWH appear to him. This is the meaning of "his sister [*aḥoto*] stood." The word *aḥot* may be derived from '-*ḥ*-*h*, meaning "to sew together" or to become attached [*devekut*]. One who is attached to the physical realm needs to distance himself from it, in order "to know what would become of him." "Knowing" refers to joining together, like that of "Adam knew his wife Eve" (Gen.

> 4:1). "What" refers to the *ayin* that flows through him constantly, as one continually receives the life force from the blessed Creator. "What" is the naught.[47]

The message of this subtle reading of the verse is that distancing oneself from the material world is a precondition for attachment to God. In this matter as well, Levi Yitsḥak shows himself to be a close follower of his master, the Maggid. Dov Baer had originally gone to the BeSHT, legend recalls, to be healed of afflictions that may have been brought on by excessive devotion to ascetic practices, following the way of most Kabbalists in Eastern Europe of the era. The BeSHT, a person possessed of a healthy appreciation for the physical dimension, sought to wean him away from that path, as he did with his other best-known disciple, R. Ya'akov Yosef of Polonnoye. While supposedly transformed by taking in the BeSHT's sense of God's presence throughout the universe, both of these disciples seemingly did not have an easy time with its practical application. The metaphysical framework into which the Maggid set the BeSHT's insights was one that continued to denigrate corporeal existence, often depicting it either as quasi-illusory or as the outer "husk" one had to break through in order to reach the only true existent, the incorporeal *ayin*. In this and other passages, Levi Yitsḥak shows himself to share this view, in sharp contrast to some other members of the Mezritch fellowship and quite clearly breaking with the BeSHT's own seeming embrace of worldly blessing and the love of simple things.

But how could that work for a mystic who was also actively seeking to create a religious revival for ordinary Jews, people who were attracted to Hasidism precisely because of the "earthiness" or this-worldliness of the Ba'al Shem Tov's original message?

7

THE MYSTIC AND THE RELIGIOUS REVIVAL

It is a long way from this sort of abstract theology of divine nothingness or unknowability to the familiar and highly personal God of popular Hasidic piety. Many a Hasidic tale, including some that involve Levi Yitsḥak, invoke an image of the simple *ḥasid* calling out to his *tate in himl* ("Daddy in Heaven"), in a most personal and intimate way. The paternal and royal metaphors for God, so taken for granted in Judaism, are also ubiquitous in the Maggid's own teachings. Dov Baer was the father of only one son, R. Avraham ha-Mal'akh "the Angel" (1739–1776), who was born after a long period of barrenness in Dov Baer and his wife's marriage. It is clear from his writings, especially his many father-son parables,[1] that he was filled with fatherly affection, which was probably directed toward his disciples as well as to his son. It is likely that this was a contributing factor in the close bonding of the members of the Mezritch circle. The gap between the master's abstruse mystical teachings and this direct, affectionate religious language offered an important challenge to the shapers of the movement, as it does to the contemporary scholar seeking to understand its success. How could the rather sophisticated intellectual mystics who composed the Maggid's circle create a broad-based popular movement, one that would come to embrace and justify the folk religion of ordinary, unlettered Jews? How do you stir religious enthusiasm among the masses with a theology that is all about the abstractions of being and nothingness? This issue is addressed with surprising frankness in a particularly abstruse text that is properly a part of the Maggid's corpus but was copied in manuscripts attributed to Levi Yitsḥak and was undoubtedly well-known to him.[2]

The text is offered as a comment on the open or cracked *alef* that is sometimes found in a Torah scroll, a letter where the parts are not fully connected. The homily ever so subtly describes God, the cosmic *alef,* as being in this situation, but intentionally so. The One is an *alef* cracked open. This *alef* represents *eyn sof,* the utterly transcendent and unknowable God. That primal God, beyond all description and totally self-contained, has let Himself become "cracked" in order to create (*bara'*) a being that would serve as a Father to us, that would bear the qualities of divinity, could love us, derive pleasure from us, and remain in relationship with us. God is called the "Cause of Causes" because He allowed or caused this "cracking" to take place. That God of the primal *alef* is not even mentioned in the Torah, which as a consequence begins with the letter *bet.* To look into that God-beyond-God is to transgress the ancient warning "Do not seek out that which is too wondrous for you."[3]

On one level, this daring teaching may be seen as a simple restatement of a well-known Kabbalistic idea. The notion that *eyn sof,* the endless source of being, is not mentioned in the Torah is found already in thirteenth-century Kabbalah.[4] The God of the Torah is a personal, willful deity, the object of worship and petition. The Zohar actually depicts this personal God, known in rabbinic tradition as the blessed Holy One, as being conceived and *born* of higher and more recondite divine forces. Divine energy flows from the utterly unfathomable wellspring of *eyn sof,* through these hidden "parental" forces, *ḥokhmah* and *binah,* and from them into "God" as we know Him. But the language used here, including the very surprising verb *bara'* ("created"), paints the personal God figure as something more like a demiurge, a lesser divine being, or perhaps even an apparition, projected out of the mysterious One in order to fulfill the emotional needs of human worshippers.[5]

This teaching is restated in somewhat briefer and toned-down form at the beginning of *Kedushat Levi*: "It first arose in the undivided divine will to draw forth from within itself a certain power, out of which the world was to be built up, from which all the worlds were to spread forth. These are love, awe, glory, faith, relationship, and rule [i.e., the seven lower *sefirot*]. After this force had been emanated, it was again activated by that [original] force, so that the matter be revealed, all the worlds becoming manifest. Thus, the first force to be drawn forth is attached and bound to the infinite [*eyn sof*]."[6]

The unknowable Godhead, beyond personal description, brought forth the God who is the font of personality and religious emotion, an intermediary stage in the creation of the human and emotional realm. It then employed that force in the creation of the lower world, including the human mind. This notion serves as a link between the contemplative theology that seems to have attracted this remarkable group of mystical seekers to Mezritch and the vision they were to offer when they went forth to create a Hasidic revival that was brimming with emotionalism and devotion to a highly personified God figure. For the enlightened members of this inner circle, the contemplative path, leading from the ordinary world of self and other back into the *ayin* from which all emerged, was the attractive message. They forged devotional exercises around that faith, a pathway back into the One or the Naught that led them toward spiritual regeneration. But such attainment was not accessible to ordinary householders, nor was it required of them. They could relate better to the God of love and awe, the personified One toward whom they would turn in utterly personal devotion, transcending all desire for reward, seeking "only You." For the mystical initiate, that God of love, relationship, and intimacy was, in turn, "attached and bound" to the One of transcendent mystery.

This passage and others like it may be seen as apologia, offering assurances to the more theologically sophisticated reader or listener that the author does not take the anthropomorphism of his parables literally. Such statements of self-distancing from one's own use of religious imagery have a long tradition in Jewish sources. The anonymous poet who wrote the long-popular *Shir ha-Kavod*, probably in twelfth- or thirteenth-century Rhineland (attributed to R. Yehudah he-Ḥasid), opened with a demurral ("They [the prophets] depicted You not as You are, but by likening You to Your deeds") before going on to write a bold hymn describing the beauty of God's head, hair, beard, and crown, with which he seems quite infatuated.[7] The author of Tikkuney Zohar wards off critics by his theologically careful Prayer of Elijah,[8] but then goes on to compose a work of most daring Kabbalistic imagination, not hesitating to personify even *eyn sof*, the endless Godhead, something that had not previously been done.[9] R. Ḥayyim Vital also warns his readers not to take literally any of the bold Lurianic imagery he is about to convey and then sets himself to doing so with little further hesitation. Here Levi Yitsḥak (or the Maggid) is assuring the reader that he does *not* attribute these human characteristics to *eyn sof* but to a created (his choice of word!) lesser entity.

With this defense in place, the writings of both the Maggid and Levi Yitsḥak abound with parables about fathers and sons, kings and princes. While almost always referring to the love between God and Israel or the *tsaddik*, they also signaled the message of the *tsaddik*'s own love for his hearers and his willingness to serve as an affectionate and forgiving father figure to the community that developed around him. We have already seen one rather elaborate parable of king and prince above, where the *sarim* surrounding the king tried to keep the exiled son from returning to claim his legacy.[10] Stories with that motif of the exiled son are found throughout Levi Yitsḥak's writings; they seem to have been a major vehicle for him in communicating his theology. He used them to convey the complex message of both the nearness and distance of God. In some versions, the son's exile from his father's house is depicted as the result of a past misdeed, while in others it seems possible that the son was sent away without reason, perhaps even as an emissary to a distant province. Whatever the origin of this exile, the emphasis is always on parent and child's abiding love and longing for one another. Here I want to quote two more of these parables used to illuminate two very different moments in the Jewish liturgical year, Rosh Hashanah and Tish'ah be-Av, celebration of the New Year and mourning over the destruction of Jerusalem:

> Regarding the shofar blasts, a fine parable, partly by my holy teacher R. Berish: There was a king who sent his only son away to a distant land, for some reason known only to him. As time passed, the son became accustomed to the ways of the villagers among whom he lived. He became a coarse fellow, forgetting the niceties of life with the king. Even his mind and his most intimate nature grew coarse. In his mind, he came to think ill of the kingdom.
>
> One day the son heard that the king was coming to visit the province where he lived. When the king arrived, the son entered the palace where he was staying and began to shout aloud in a strange voice. He did so with voice alone, since he had forgotten the speech [= language] of the king. When the king heard his son's voice and realized that he had forgotten even how to speak, his heart was filled with compassion. This is the meaning of sounding the shofar.
>
> But once he told it this way. One of the king's servants had a family member of whom the king thought very highly. He loved him so much that he had his form engraved [*toke'a*] on his throne so that he could

> gaze at his lovely form and take pleasure in remembering him. On the day when the king's servants were to be judged, they shouted out to the king, "Just look at that form carved on your throne, and you will be filled with compassion because of your love for us." This is the meaning of sounding [*teki'ah*] the shofar. "The image of Jacob our father is engraved beneath the Throne of Glory."[11]

These two versions, and the presence of a differing account of it recorded by another of the Maggid's disciples,[12] seem to indicate that he recounted this parable regularly, perhaps even annually, before the shofar was sounded.

But here is the same story, now retooled for use on the great day of mourning:

> A certain king had an only son, who went in a path that was not good. What did the king do? He exiled the son to a distant place. He stripped off his festive garments and dressed him in dark black clothes. On the [anniversary of] the day when the king had done this act regarding his son's clothes, he made a point of recalling his son. If the son had shown some regret within that time, he would restore him to his home with great glory. Even if not, he would still recall this day when he had exiled him. On that day he would have those [festive] garments hung out so that they would not molder or be eaten by moths. Perhaps also [he hoped] that the son would pass by in the market and see his former garments. Then he might have regret and come to repent. When that heart-sore [*nilbav*] son saw the garments after such a long time, even though they would no longer fit him due to his great sufferings in his exile, seeing them still caused his heart to be pained and his flesh seared. These clothes used to fit him, back when he was exiled from his father! When he wholly took this to heart, how greatly were [the father's] mercies aroused, seeing his son regret his deeds! Surely the father could fashion for him even better garments than those he had before![13]

The motif of Israel as God's exiled child is an ancient one, well-known in Midrashic sources and particularly from the Zohar. But in the Maggid's circle, and especially in Levi Yitsḥak's writings, it seems to become *the* story that fits all occasions. We will see it yet again, in a darker version, below.[14] There is a quality of desperation in the frequent invoking of this tale that reflects the anomaly of

Israel's situation in the exile. We remember who we really are, or were. The image of being "Israel, my firstborn son" (Ex. 4:22) is not forgotten. We also know how far we are from that situation and what it would take to return. The way of repentance is open before us and our loving Father in heaven awaits our return. It is only what the sources refer to as "the yeast in the dough,"[15] the evil urge—and perhaps the sin of pride in particular—that keeps it all from happening.

Meanwhile, we are to live out a life that combines the celebration of God's presence and a longing over our distance from Him as best we can. If the *ḥasid* is not capable of the spiritual sophistication of his teacher, he does know something about the two basic religious emotions of love and awe. Levi Yitsḥak gives expression to multiple layers of these. Here we see him as a teacher of a more popular piety, trying to bring the passion he discovered within the mystical circle to a broader group of hearers. Detailed discussions of *yir'at hashem*, fear or awe of God, are woven as a leitmotif running through his writings. Throughout Jewish pietistic literature, reaching back to the Zohar and beyond, the twin elements of love and awe are taken to be the basis of inward religious life. The Tikkuney Zohar famously describes them as the "wings" by which prayer flies upward.[16] The need for balance between them is epitomized by the prayerbook's "Unify our hearts to love and fear Your name," recited just before the morning *shema'*. While love seems to be the higher goal in much of the Hasidic discourse, multiple voices in the Maggid's school recall his insistence that *yir'ah* precede it.[17] Love is a spontaneous emotion, something of a divine gift, that comes about as a result of the groundwork laid by one's efforts at *yir'ah*. One can only love something one can see, Levi Yitsḥak says in one place, and we cannot come to see God with the mind's eye until *yir'ah* brings us to it.[18]

Not surprisingly for the typology-loving Levi Yitsḥak, he differentiates between two levels of *yir'ah*, also a trope inherited from the older literature. The ancient term *yir'at ḥet*, literally "fear of sin," is used in *Kedushat Levi* to refer to a sense of awe before divine greatness that results in a sense of personal inadequacy. "You worship God contemplatively, gazing upon His greatness, how He both surrounds and fills all the worlds, and how all worlds, angels, and souls are as naught before Him. As you delve so deeply into contemplating His grandeur, you begin to take account of your own lowliness, of how absolutely far from God you are. This causes a sublime awe to fall upon you, and a fearsome sense of wanting to do His will."

This sort of *yir'ah* is familiar to readers of any sort of Western devotional literature.[19] It is not fear of punishment, which is dismissed by Levi Yitsḥak, as by many others, as simply an outer doorway to it.[20] It is rather a sense of distance or alienation from God caused by the great contrast between divine grandeur and one's own inadequacy to embrace it or to live up to the greatness for which one feels called to strive. It also appears to be dynamic rather than static; the greater one's sense of divine magnificence, the smaller and farther one feels in contrast to it. This *yir'ah* is reminiscent of what one reads in Kierkegaard's *Fear and Trembling* and in many other religious classics of the existential variety, where the devotee ultimately casts himself before God's mercies, seeking to be retrieved from the self-defeat of this overwhelming alienation from the divine world.

But this is only the first and lower level of *yir'ah* in Levi Yitsḥak's lexicon of spiritual states:

> The second category is the higher *yir'ah*, where you gaze upon the exaltedness of the divine Self, endless and utterly simple. "No thought can grasp it at all." You become constantly and utterly attached to the Self of the blessed Creator. Then a great awe, fear, and dread falls upon you, utterly nullifying your existence. You fulfill His will in Torah, *mitsvot*, and good deeds. You serve not because you look at your own lowliness, because you do not encounter your own self at all, which is totally negated. In this self-negated state, you serve only in the presence of the blessed Creator's Self.[21]

The higher *yir'ah* is nothing other than the state of self-transcendence.

The language of love and passionate longing is also widely present in *Kedushat Levi*. Its author is himself known in the later tradition for singing out to God as "You, You, You!" in the familiar Yiddish form, surely addressed to this God of love, the subject of the popular revivalist Judaism he was seeking to preach.[22] That intense and unbridled love language, describing the relationship of God and Israel, is present already in the *Shemu'ah Tovah* sermons and continues through his later works. There he describes the love of God and Israel as that of two intimate friends. The parental metaphor gets set aside and an unusual expression of what can only be described as the eros of friendship takes center stage:

> When a person speaks with his fellow, it may be that his lips open but his mouth lies, that his heart is not with him. But when you do speak from

the very walls of your heart, you muster all your strength to enter those words. The source of all our powers lies in the heart. The voice too dwells in the heart. That is why, in the course of this sort of speech, sometimes a loud sound bursts forth on its own, unintentionally.

That is what they meant by "Words that proceed from the heart enter the heart."[23] You speak from the heart, the place where that sound came from. But [now] it garbs itself in language, clearly pronounced words that emerge from the organs of speech. This will arouse love in the heart of your companion. I mean to say that you want to cause your love to flow toward your friend, [hoping that] this will awaken his love toward yours, receiving it graciously.

This is the kiss. When two people kiss each other, they reveal the love that is in their hearts through that kiss, drawing their loves close to one another, becoming one. This is the cleaving of spirit to spirit, mentioned in the holy Zohar.[24]

That is why an utterance that proceeds only from the speech organs is described as coming "from the lips outward." It doesn't pass the ears and find its way into the heart. But when words proceed from the heart, in love and passion, which is [the source of] that sound, the burning sparks of their flame kindle the fire of love in the heart of one's friend. It too is awakened, coming forth to greet [that love] like a bridegroom going forth to meet his bride.

Levi Yitsḥak is saying all this, of course, about the love of God and Israel, as he goes on to make clear in this description of revelation:

He revealed to them the secret hidden in His heart, that of the innermost Torah and its wholeness, since Torah and the blessed God are one. Then His great love spread forth with its fiery flames, the divine spark. Parallel to that love, so too did ours spring forth from the inner walls of our hearts, ignited by the flame of His love . . . until the very root of our hearts was aflame with love.[25]

Levi Yitsḥak's language here is shaped by the classics of earlier Jewish devotional literature,[26] but he expresses it in ways that were exceptional in his Eastern

European setting. This was a sort of sermon on divine love that could have been appreciated by hearers who were not initiates into the more esoteric language of unity. The joining of two souls in an abundance of love, whether between spouses, intimate friends, or parents and children, rings true to human experience.

But just as the discourse on *yir'ah* leads to a mystical self-transcendence, so too does the talk of love. It is not easy to separate this highly emotional language from the mystical side of Levi Yitsḥak. To try to do so too rigidly would betray the sources, missing the subtle complexity of the religious personality with whom we are dealing.

> But the matter of loving the Creator is thus. When one gazes at and contemplates the blessed Creator's greatness, how He is the essence and root of all the worlds, both filling and surrounding them, that no place is devoid of Him,[27] that all worlds are negated before Him . . . all this conceiving awakens the heart, and the soul is filled with longing. One's passion burns with the fire of true love, seeking to be near to YHWH always, never to be separated, distanced, or cut off from Him, but to be attached to Him constantly, perceiving His greatness and glory.[28]

The *tsaddik*'s disinterest in corporeal things, however, in the interest of turning to God alone seems to stand at odds with the reality of popular Hasidism. It was precisely the *tsaddik*'s involvement with this-worldly matters that made Hasidism controversial and suspicious, first in the eyes of the *mitnaggedim* and later as the object of jibes by the Westernized *maskilim*. There is no question that Hasidism succeeded in gaining such a wide popular following precisely because the common folk did believe in the ability of the *tsaddik* to supplicate God successfully for this-worldly reward and blessing. This included support for one's needs in the worldly realms known as "children, life, and sustenance." These referred to easing childbirth (cures for barrenness play a great role in the blessings offered by Hasidic masters, as they had for the earlier *ba'aley shem*) and parenting, matters of health and longevity, and the ability to earn a livelihood. From the very beginning, Hasidism offered assurances that the *tsaddik*'s blessing mattered in such affairs, that he was able to affect the divine will and bring about the flow of goodness and prosperity. God's special love for the *tsaddikim*, the fact that He "longs to hear their prayers,"[29] meant that having one's own concerns articulated in the prayers of the *tsaddik* gave them an extra chance of receiving a positive divine response. The fact that the movement had been created to reflect the way of the Ba'al Shem Tov, who was reputed to have had extraordinary shamanic powers in the realm of healing, very much shaped the way Hasidic leaders were viewed by the broader public in a world where modern medicine was not yet present. For most Jews, such "corporeal" blessings were precisely the reason for seeking the *tsaddik* out. The *tsaddik* had inherited the former place of the *ba'al shem* in Jewish society, essentially that of a folk healer, and the efficacy of a *tsaddik*'s blessings in all these areas was loudly touted.[30] Many accounts exist of non-Jews as well as Jewish men and women lining up to receive the blessing of good fortune from the hands of these Hasidic holy men. Insofar as we can tell, this was true of Hasidism in its earliest period as it was (and remains) throughout its history. The essential "contractual" relationship between those who visit the *tsaddik* (including, but not limited to, his close disciples), is that they will offer him a gift (*pidyon*)[31] and he will include their prayers, often those for worldly matters, in his own.

Like the Maggid and others in his circle, Levi Yitsḥak was a firm believer in this power.[32] He never tires of quoting the Talmudic dictum to the effect that "the blessed Holy One may issue a decree, but the *tsaddik* negates it,"[33] a source to which we will return for fuller discussion later. Unlike his colleague Shne'ur Zalman, he did not discourage Jews who sought out his blessing in the material realm. On the contrary, it is clear to him that it is proper, even necessary, for the righteous one to worship God in a way that will bring blessing upon those around him.

> We see that there are [some] *tsaddikim* who have the [power to] effect that which they seek in their prayers [and others who do not]. The great[est] *tsaddik* enters the garden of the King's palace and considers what it means to come before the King. He thus forgets what it was that he wanted to ask concerning worldly matters, seeking only to forever be attached to the King. Nothing pleases him other than to worship his Creator, to be a royal servant—and he forgets all his [other] concerns.
>
> But this is not the case for those *tsaddikim* who have not attained that rung. Even though such a [lesser] *tsaddik* stands before the King, he remembers what it is that he wanted to ask. Thus, the [first and higher] *tsaddik*, the one who cannot recall his worldly request, effects nothing.

> The lesser *tsaddik*, who remembers to actually ask, accomplishes his goal. The first *tsaddik* is called "one who offered an incomplete prayer," since it does not have wholeness and did not bring about the flow [of divine blessing]. All he thought of were matters of the World to Come, serving God. The one who kept his request in mind, seeking to bring the flow [of life or blessing] into this world as well, offers "the complete prayer."[34]

Surprisingly, it is the "lesser" *tsaddik* who is better at doing the job of bringing blessing into the world! This is parallel to the instruction to Moses not to "ascend to God" but to stay down on the mountain so that he be able to bring his message to the people. Later we will see the same dichotomy used with regard to the earthbound quality of the *mitsvot* as a way of serving God. The word "flow" in this passage translates the Hebrew *shefa'*, literally "influx," a Kabbalistic term that plays a key role in the theology of early Hasidism, especially that of the Maggid and Levi Yitsḥak. *Shefa'* is the flow of *ḥiyyut*, the life energy that renews existence in each instant. Life itself, both of the individual and of the world as a whole, depends upon the constancy of that flow. When it is constricted—by sin, the forces of evil, the rule of gentiles over the world, Israel's exile, etc.—it is reduced to a trickle that merely allows the world to go on, but amid poverty and suffering. But the prayers and good deeds of Israel, most especially those of the *tsaddik*, bring about an abundance of *shefa'*, which then overflows into a life of blessing, including the material blessings of "children, life, and sustenance." While the *tsaddik*'s good works bring blessing to the world as a whole, it is particularly those close to him, having received his explicit blessing, who are most likely to benefit from this renewal of abundance.

There is a close link in Hasidism, as indeed throughout the Jewish esoteric tradition, between the mystical and magical aspects of the secrets it reveals. The Hasidic belief that the *tsaddik* undertakes a spiritual journey as he prays, one that can also bring benefit to those around him, begins with the Ba'al Shem Tov. In the famous letter mentioned above, he recounts that on the eve of Rosh Hashanah three years earlier, "I performed an adjuration of soul-ascent." This formulation reaches back into the tradition of *merkavah* voyagers in late antiquity, who ascended the heavens and beheld the divine throne, and especially to magical accounts of such journeys. At each rung of ascent, we read in the early medieval *Sefer ha-Razim*, the voyager administers an oath to the angels of that realm not to harm him.[35] "I adjure you, O angels of the third firmament," etc. Those texts are deemed "magical" rather than purely mystical because the journey is being used by the voyager to attain such worldly goals as wealth, favor of the king, or the love of a woman. In the Ba'al Shem Tov's case, the journey is being undertaken for the sake of all Israel as well as for his own shamanic clients as a *ba'al shem*. He meets the messiah in the course of his heavenly ascent, asking when the final redemption will arrive, but he also gains the power to defeat both plagues and enemies that have beset Israel in his day.

Early Hasidic sources are wrought with conflict over the legitimacy of seeking even such seemingly worthy worldly goals in the course of intense prayer experiences. While no one within the Hasidic camp openly denies the *possibility* of such attainments, there is deep division about their *worthiness*, whether their attainment is an appropriate use of the great gift of coming near to God in prayer. The literature includes a number of very touching parables that describe the worshipper as desiring nothing other than to feel the warmth of God's love or to bask in His glory. "Be like the servant who serves God *in order not* to receive a reward," says a Hasidic rereading of a classic rabbinic text.[36] Those who seek rewards are dismissed from God's presence as soon as the rewards are handed out. But the true devotee seeks nothing other than to remain in that presence, "to dwell in God's house forever." There is no more beautiful description of this than that found in Levi Yitsḥak's own comment on the opening words of the Song of Songs. "The kisses of His mouth" means that we are to feel God's kiss as one on the mouth, an expression of pure love, like that of bridegroom and bride, rather than a kiss on the hand, one that comes in anticipation of or gratitude for some gift.[37] We shall see that this question of worldly reward for the devotional life, also formulated as the ability of the *tsaddik* to bring forth blessing, is an essential one throughout Levi Yitsḥak's teachings. The ideal in the Maggid's circle seems to have been that the *tsaddik* is to seek nothing for himself other than God's loving presence. The constancy of his relationship with God, the ability "to dwell in His courts forever," is his only goal. While present in those heavenly courts, however, basking in the light of God's presence, he may indeed seek out blessings for his followers, the Jewish people, and the world. This is what allowed for the bridge between the mystic and the folk, permitting a group of intensely abstract God-seekers to become founders of a popular religious and social movement. In some sources, it is made clear that it is precisely the *tsad-*

dik's own personal selflessness that allows him to be a clear and open channel of divine blessing for others. Faith in the efficacy of that "channel of blessing" was key to Hasidism's success.

If we assume that Levi Yitsḥak himself engaged in this practice that he so boldly defends, we will again be forced to qualify the definition of his role with which this book opened. Here Levi Yitsḥak is clearly functioning as a Hasidic *rebbe*, essentially an alternative designation for *tsaddik*, rather than in the role of *rav*. He is bending the role of *rav* itself, using his communal position not only to spread the *teachings* of Hasidism, as we have discussed earlier, but also to act upon them. He can do so precisely because of his having transcended any neediness on his own behalf. His willingness to take on the prayer needs of others as he enters into the place of absorption into the divine oneness stands as testimony to his effort to love and identify with the needs of the earthbound Jews around him, carrying them with him even as he leaves this world behind.

8

THE QUESTION OF MIRACLES

Both the Maggid and Levi Yitsḥak were unstinting advocates of faith in the *tsaddik*'s powers to bless and heal, suspending the course of nature in doing so. As we have seen, promoting such a belief was essential to the successful spread of Hasidism. We will have occasion below to dwell at length on the question of the interplay between God's will and that of the *tsaddikim*, a key area of innovation within Levi Yitsḥak's teachings. But it is also noteworthy that neither master nor disciple was particularly well-known for actually making use of the supernatural powers they claimed were possessed by the *tsaddikim*. A later ḤaBaD source (grantedly biased against use of the miraculous, in the tradition of its founder, R. Shne'ur Zalman) records that "in Mezritch, miracles lay in heaps under the table, but nobody bothered to pick them up."[1] Of the many tales told later about Levi Yitsḥak, remarkably few reflect involvement with the supernatural.[2] What he "brought back" from his heavenly visits—in which his disciples surely believed—were gifts of compassion and divine forgiveness.

The question of miracles and the supernatural, both theoretically and practically, was never far from the mind of Levi Yitsḥak. We will recall that only the homilies on Hanukkah and Purim, plus some other incidental teachings, constituted the original *Kedushat Levi* as published by him in Slawuta, 1798. A treatise on Hanukkah and Purim, two relatively minor holidays of the Jewish year, is a highly unusual first literary undertaking, especially for a rabbi in a significant position.[3] One might instead have expected a collection of responsa or a volume of novellae on a Talmudic tractate. The only other well-known figure in prior Jewish history to have devoted whole works to these holidays is the great Rabbi

Loew, the MaHaRaL of Prague (d. 1609).[4] It is indeed in his tradition that Levi Yitsḥak seems to want to place himself.

The main theme in Levi Yitsḥak's discussion of both holidays is that of the *nes nistar*, or hidden miracle, or the relationship between revealed and hidden ways in which God acts in history. The rubric of "hidden miracle" is one first developed by R. Moshe ben Naḥman, or Naḥmanides (1194–1270), as part of his antirationalist thrust. The theme is then carried forward by the rabbi of Prague. Levi Yitsḥak quotes copiously from Naḥmanides on this subject.[5] While it is not our purpose here to offer a full history of this idea, it is fair to say that one may trace a line of thinking from Naḥmanides through MaHaRaL and thence to Levi Yitsḥak.[6]

Levi Yitsḥak repeatedly makes it clear that the hidden miracle, that which takes place without seemingly violating the laws of nature, is more impressive to him than such obvious miracles as the plagues in Egypt or the splitting of the Red Sea. The fact that the Creator of the universe could suspend the laws of nature is no particular surprise to the eighteenth-century Jewish believer. After all, the logic usually goes, He who created the world should be able to change the rules by which it operates. But the emphasis on the *hidden* miracle puts the question of faith into sharper focus. The essential Hasidic message is that God is present throughout this world and is accessible to people living in ordinary historic times and in an ordinary state of consciousness (*katnut*). The message of the hidden miracle is that this world as it exists is the scene of constant divine self-revelation accessible even to those simple Jews so loved by Levi Yitsḥak. And such simple Jews themselves are hidden miracles—bearers of the hidden divine presence.

The treatise on Purim and Hanukkah (treated in that order) begins with this notion. Levi Yitsḥak quotes the Talmud's discussion of whether Israel had freely received the Torah at Sinai, given the legend of God's holding the mountain over their heads as a threat against their rejecting the divine word.[7] If the people were given no choice at Sinai, it would hardly be just for their acceptance of Torah to obligate their descendants for all time. The Talmud's resolution of this problem is that "they accepted it again in the days of Mordecai and Esther" (based on a Midrashic reading of Esth. 9:27), and this reacceptance seemingly makes the legitimacy of the Sinaitic covenant a moot point. That rather strange claim, basing religious obligation on the Purim story, is interpreted by Levi Yitsḥak as follows. It is only the discovery that God is present within the seemingly *natural* world that obligates us mere mortals to serve God and follow His commandments. The

Esther story is told without resort to miracle, in fact without any mention of the name of God or any evidence of divine interference in the course of history. The "mountain held over their heads" at Sinai is thus a symbolic representation of what happens in the supernatural moment, when God's hand is so forcefully and miraculously present that those who witness it have no ability to deny God's active role. Accepting the Torah in such circumstance, when the heart is overwhelmed by gratitude for the miraculous liberation from Egypt, as well as all the "bells and whistles" of the obvious divine presence at Sinai itself might not carry over into ordinary time. For Torah to obligate people like us, who live in a world bereft of such obvious miracles, it has to have been accepted by people living in a state similar to our own. Esther and Mordecai lived in such an era; hence it is the Torah as reaccepted then that becomes ours.

This does not mean, of course, that the divine hand was truly absent from history, but only that it acted in a hidden way. Hence the term "hidden miracle." The Esther chronicle demonstrates to us that God is present even when unseen. That is why the story is told in a *megillah*, because it "reveals" (*megalleh*) a this-worldly divine presence that would otherwise be hidden.[8] Similarly, the festival is called Purim, "lots," because it takes place in the natural world, one in which the person has alternatives and therefore free choice about whether to recognize God's presence and to accept the yoke of His service. This can only take place in the mental state called *katnut*, ordinary mind, where most people dwell. When one experiences the state of *gadlut*, or expanded consciousness, one is back at Sinai, as it were, so surrounded by the intense experience of divinity that there remains no alternative but to accept it.

So too does Levi Yitsḥak explain[9] the Talmud's surprising statement that "all the festivals will be canceled in the future, except for Purim."[10] The major festivals of the year are structured around the story of the Exodus and Sinai. Those were supernatural events, which there will be no need to recall in the messianic future. Nature itself will be so transformed—here Levi Yitsḥak quotes the prophet's vision of the wolf lying down with the lamb—that the supernatural will have been rendered superfluous. The messianic era will represent a new state in which the temporary suspension of nature for the effecting of God's will (or the *tsaddik*'s) will no longer be required, since nature itself will be transformed and will itself do what is needed.

There may be no obvious miracles taking place in our era, but there is still the "hidden miracle." The exact quality of the hidden miracle in Levi Yitsḥak's treatise is not entirely clear or consistent. He seems to be looking toward a God who is ever concerned with Israel's welfare and acts in their behalf. In the Hanukkah narrative, God acts behind the screen of military activity, allowing the smaller and weaker army to defeat its enemies, as in the liturgical insertion "You handed the many over into the hands of the few, the strong into the hands of the weak" and so on, recited during the holiday's *ʿamidah*. In the Purim story, God acts within the heart of the king to turn his will toward Israel's benefit.[11] In a particularly impressive passage,[12] Levi Yitsḥak suggests that the order of the Hebrew calendar reflects an increasingly open revelation of God's presence. Hanukkah is the first festival to occur within profane time (i.e., after the fall sacred season). The victory of the Maccabees could be seen as an entirely natural one, the result of military prowess. The hand of God that gave them victory remains almost entirely hidden. Next comes Purim, when Israel did not act in battle to defend themselves (he conveniently ignores the embarrassing concluding chapters of the Book of Esther). Israel relied only on Esther's beauty, her clever machinations, and the king's will.[13] Here humans were less powerful, so the positive result was a greater revelation of divine interference, meaning that the miracle was somewhat less hidden. Only from there does the year proceed to Pesah, an event that took place "without arousal from below," when the hand of God in history was entirely revealed.

In these passages, *nes nistar* seems to mean the active, conscious hand of God in controlling historical events but exercised from behind the scenes.[14] On reflection, however, Levi Yitsḥak tells us that all miracles, but especially these, exist for the purpose of demonstrating to us that life itself is in fact miraculous. That which appears to be natural or ordinary (*hergel*)[15]—the rising and setting of the sun, for example—is in fact an act of divine will. That ties him quite closely to the position articulated clearly by Naḥmanides in his comment to Exodus 13:16:

> When God favors a [particular] community or individual and performs a sign for them in changing ordinary reality [*minhago shel ʿolam*] and its nature . . . the wondrous sign indicates that there is a capable God who creates, knows, and overlooks all . . . and as a result of these great public miracles, a person comes to accept also the hidden miracles that are the basis of the entire Torah. A person has no portion in the Torah of Moses our Teacher until he believes that all our words and all that happens to

us are miracles; there is nothing in them of nature or ordinary reality, whether regarding the many or the individual.

While scholarship has shown that Naḥmanides elsewhere demonstrates a significantly more nuanced view of the role of miracles (in fact one closer to that of Maimonides than is widely thought),[16] it seems that this passage was the crucial one in Levi Yitsḥak's understanding of the medieval sage. "Nature" is but an illusory outer cloak that garbs the hidden activity of the divine will in every moment of existence. If that is the case, however, then "miracle" and "nature" seem to be differentiated primarily by attitudes of the beholder.[17] The same sunrise can clearly be described as either, depending upon the religious consciousness (or lack thereof) in the one who sees it. To be a religious person is to appreciate "Your miracles that are with us daily, evening, morning, and noon." This seems somewhat different from his descriptions of Hanukkah and Purim. While these are hidden miracles, they nevertheless seem to be described as *extraordinary* events of divine interference. But the sunrise is not that. Of course, the banishing of *hergel* means that everything is indeed to be seen as extraordinary. But then there is no "ordinary," no rule to which these events become exceptions. In other words, if *everything* is to be seen as miracle, is *anything* any longer a miracle except in the eye of the beholder?

But we must understand that all this subtle discussion of miracles and the supernatural does not take place in a void. Levi Yitsḥak is taking a leading role in a movement that very much depends on popular faith in the *tsaddik* and his ability to bring about miracles! The *tsaddik*, we recall, replaced the *ba'al shem*, or shaman/magician, as the repository of popular healing. You could count on the *tsaddik*'s prayers to be effective because he was especially beloved of a God who, as we have said, "longs to hear the prayers of the righteous." In general, Levi Yitsḥak was a great believer in the Kabbalistic teachings about "arousal from below," the central role humans play in the fate, indeed in the governance, of this world. The inner *ayin* of divinity, as we have seen, lies beyond worldly concerns. But the cosmic *alef* has cracked itself open, becoming or creating a God of *ḥesed*, or divine love. The act of creation itself could only come about as a result of the flowing forth of divine love. If creation is a constantly ongoing process, so too is the flow of divine *ḥesed* that brings it about. That love is specifically focused on Israel and the *tsaddikim*, the ultimate goal of creation and the ones who will restore the cosmic balance by uplifting and restoring the flow of energy to its Source. Hence their desires are of utmost importance; God's love for them permits them to implant (even "impregnate") a particular desire within the divine mind in their moments of mystical union.[18]

In the Purim story, Mordecai is depicted as such a figure.[19] A mystical devotee in the way of the Maggid's teachings, Mordecai contemplated the origins and purpose of existence itself. He ascended into the place of cosmic nothingness and there was able to direct the flow of a hidden miracle onto the historical plane.[20] A parallel passage depicts him as a sage who knew all seventy human languages, thus having access to the seventy angelic princes, those who rule over each nation, and their workings.[21] Here music enters the scene alongside language. Mordecai was able to sing the proper melody of the angel opposing Israel and thus to overcome its power. Another passage depicts a similar "singing contest" between King David and Nebuchadnezzar, who sought but failed to defeat the power of the Psalmist to arouse and thus shape the divine will in defense of Israel.[22]

Mordecai and David here are prototypes of Hasidic *tsaddikim*. The notion that the righteous leaders of their generations can unite with the mind of God, perhaps in the course of singing the proper *niggun*, implanting within God a desire to help those in need, is given respectability by this "historic" contextualizing.[23] Recent Hebrew editions of the full *Kedushat Levi*, supplied with indices of sources, makes it clear that the Talmudic passage about the power of the *tsaddik* to undo divine decrees, "The blessed Holy One issues a decree, but the *tsaddik* nullifies it,"[24] is Levi Yitsḥak's favorite rabbinic quotation. This passage is quoted by others of the Mezritch circle as well but nowhere as frequently as in *Kedushat Levi*.[25]

What we have here, in effect, is a theological justification for a phenomenon of popular religion that was growing within Hasidism, surely with the tacit support of most of its leaders. At the same time, this was a source of embarrassment in confronting the movement's critics, Levi Yitsḥak's rabbinic peers across the Hasidic/Mitnaggedic divide. Understanding this tension, and the difficult position in which it placed Levi Yitsḥak and others like him, will help explain why it is that this full believer in the *tsaddik*'s supernatural powers almost never seems to resort to them. It also explains why he seeks to place so much emphasis on the superior value of the *hidden* miracle. Hidden miracles, an outsider might say, are not *performed* but only *claimed* ex post facto. If the sick child is healed or the enemy is kept away from the city gates, it is only in retrospect that the *ḥasid* can say that it was the *tsaddik*'s prayers that caused this to happen. By definition, no one sees a hidden miracle in the hour when it is happening. The case of Mordecai, therefore, is a relatively easy one because it took place so long ago. The Jews were saved in otherwise unexplained ways. Retrospectively, it must have been the efforts of the *tsaddik* that caused this to happen.[26]

This seems to be Levi Yitsḥak's answer to the question of miracles as of his thinking in 1798 and the reason for publication of his book on this unusual subject. Can the *tsaddik* perform miracles? Yes, indeed. But we happen to live in non-miraculous times. The biblical era, when the hand of heaven in history was fully seen and when a Moses or an Elijah could perform visible wonders, is long past. We live in a time like that of Mordecai, and the Torah we have received is one that applies to such an era. We have *tsaddikim* like Mordecai, who can rise into the divine mind and who affect divine will and human fate. But the results will not be obvious. Only retrospectively (*bedi-ʿavad*) will we be able to see that their hidden miracles have indeed taken place.

But what of revealed miracles? Is the *tsaddik* called upon to perform these as well? In Levi Yitsḥak's treatise on Hanukkah and Purim, devoted almost entirely to the question of miracles, there is no indication that this is the case. He seems in this sense to be a faithful disciple of the Maggid, not interested in turning the wonderworking potential of being a *tsaddik* into a visible reality. But when we turn to Levi Yitsḥak's better-known work, *Kedushat Levi*, on the Torah, published shortly after his death, we see him continuing to struggle with this question.

His views on this matter are best seen in certain Torah narratives, especially from the book of Numbers, where rebellions against God and miraculous interventions seem to alternate with surprising frequency and regularity. In his sermons on the *Koraḥ* and *Ḥukkat* readings, Levi Yitsḥak refers to the distinction between *dor ha-midbar*, "the generation of the wilderness," and *dor ha-arets*, "the generation [that will inherit] the land." He reads *dor ha-midbar* as "the generation of speech," a generation so affected by the revelation of Sinai that Moses could relate to them through the word alone. The succeeding generation, *dor ha-arets*, are more corporeal, "earthy" people, not responding to the appeal of the word. Without saying so directly, he is pointing to the common Hebrew/Yiddish locution *ʿam ha-arets*: "people of the land," meaning "the ignorant" or "unlettered." For people like these, words do not suffice; one needs *la-ʿasot ʿuvda*, "to do a deed," something impressive like a miracle, in order to convince them. It is Korah, the misguided would-be leader, who thinks that one can go on with words alone. Korah denied that "the teaching of Moses is garbed also in the world of action." Levi Yitsḥak demurs from this view. In a most daring reading, he ascribes to Korah the notion that the coming *dor ha-arets*, those "going into the land" (but really "the generation of the ignorant"), can be approached in the same way as "the generation of speech. "[27]

This, you might say, is an interesting, if somewhat surprising, reading of the biblical narrative. We must again recall, however, that Levi Yitsḥak is a *preacher*, not a biblical interpreter. For the preacher, understanding the text of the Torah portion is a means, not an end. His real interest is not in the text itself but in something going on in the lives and minds of those to whom he is speaking. The debate between Moses and Korah can be read as a thinly veiled internal Hasidic polemic. There are those in Levi Yitsḥak's circle who say that Hasidism's value lies exclusively in its profound teachings. It had been this sort of "generation of speech" Hasidism that had brought him to Mezritch and created the wonderful circle of disciples that sought to carry the Maggid's teachings forward. Some of them, including R. Menaham Mendel of Vitebsk, R. Avraham Kalisker (who had gone off together to the Holy Land in 1777, in part to create a smaller and "purer" strain of Hasidism, uncorrupted by the mass movement), and the Maggid's son R. Avraham "the Angel," wanted to proceed in just this way. Their Hasidism was one of profound teachings and the creation of intense and often emotionally charged religious community around those ideas and devotional practices.[28] These were to remain small communities, uncorrupted by the masses and their demands. R. Shne'ur Zalman (his *Tanya* was published two years before Levi Yitsḥak's treatise) was seeking a way to expand that sort of community. He was doing this by creating a disciplined following based on a distinctive religious regimen and systematic inculcation of values. But the doctrine he was preaching in the *Tanya* and especially in his sermons (published only later) was a highly rarified and intellectualized Hasidism. He too was surely a popularizer, but in a different mode from that of Levi Yitsḥak, perhaps reflecting the different regions in which they lived. R. Shne'ur Zalman was not a personality to turn toward the ordinary people as was Levi Yitsḥak and certainly not one to do "miracles." He was operating in Reisin, a region where the intellectual climate was quite different. He wrote the *Tanya*, after all, to keep people from visiting so much that they would disturb his thinking and writing. All of these, in varying ways, were continuing to operate as in "the generation of speech."

Levi Yitsḥak was trying to push for the growth of Hasidism as a popular movement among mostly unlettered and spiritually unsophisticated Ukrainian Jews. His "ordinary" Jews, those of the market towns, were predominantly people of trade, usually not of great learning. The backbone of the Berdychiv community was made up of pious merchants, people who were believers, who were willing to live within the rules of *halakhah*, but did not have much time or energy to engage deeply in learning or religious questions. Levi Yitsḥak sensed that they were indeed *dor ha-arets*, "earthy" Jews, people whose needs were quite concrete. Like businessmen everywhere, they were quite fully absorbed in pursuit of their livelihood. But Levi Yitsḥak had another concern as well. In his area there were many popular *tsaddikim* who were quite happy to offer the worldly blessings that these people sought. R. Barukh of Miedzybozh, the BeSHT's grandson, was trying to reclaim dynastic leadership of the movement. Such figures as R. Aryeh Leib of Shpola or the sons of R. Yeḥiel Mikhl of Zloczov offered versions of popular Hasidism that were quite "transactional." In exchange for your supporting the *tsaddik* materially, he will see that you are blessed in that same material realm. Generally, they seemed to appeal to a more rural and lower class than a Levi Yitsḥak, who, by dint of his title as communal rabbi as well as his own origins, represented a different sector of the community. In exchange for faith and material support, such popular *tsaddikim* were happy to give out blessings, perhaps even accompanied by amulets or herbal remedies. (The transition from *ba'al shem* to *tsaddik* did not happen overnight.) But these came unencumbered by the more profound teachings that Levi Yitsḥak and others of his ilk saw as the true core of the Hasidic message, the revivalist call for love, awe, and *devekut*. How was the more serious would-be Hasidic leader supposed to act? Should he be willing to offer cures and blessings in order to attract Jews to the teachings that were his own true purpose?

We can see a clear-eyed and daring reflection on this question in a parable offered by another Mezritch figure, also operating in Ukraine at the same period of the movement's initial growth. Listen to how R. Menaḥem Naḥum of Chernobyl describes himself:

> Am I not a sort of peddler, bearing a peddler's potions?[29] I have needles, pins, and knitting needles. I have all kinds of herbs; whoever needs herbs can find them with me! If you require a needle, I have one to stick you! I can also heal the sick and make the barren fruitful. I can restore souls and stir up wars; I can uproot kingdoms and can make for plenty in the

> world. I can end wars and renew pleasure in your love life. I can make plants grow. I can bring about various sorts of blessing and nullify ill decrees. I can implant wisdom and preach like a mighty wellspring. To sum it up: everything is in the *tsaddik*'s hands, following the secret of "*the tsaddik rules by the fear of God*" (II Sam. 23:3).
>
> . . . I both make up these examples and fulfill them.[30] Some people would be embarrassed or ashamed to come to me in order to receive penance for their sins. For that reason, I attribute to myself all these other things,[31] like healing the sick and making the barren fruitful and the rest. Then when someone sees a person coming to me, he might say, "He must have some need regarding sickness or childbearing." In this way people won't be ashamed at all; whoever has sin or transgression on his hands will come to me, and with God's help I will heal his spirit.[32]

This is both a very poignant and highly revealing text. The real task of the *tsaddik* is that of healing the spirit; that is what he is trying to accomplish. All the rest is a sort of window dressing, an array of claimed powers that make it easier for people to turn to the *tsaddik*. These very claims, on the other hand, the "potions" in the *tsaddik*'s bag of tricks—matters in which we know that R. Menaḥem Naḥum himself engaged—are what is making the movement grow!

For Levi Yitsḥak, the divide between the inner work of Hasidism and the needs of the masses is even more acute. A leading figure in the spread of the Hasidic message, he was also rabbi of a large and prosperous community. Already a controversial figure, having been chased out of both Zelechow and Pinsk for advocacy of Hasidism, he could not afford to "degrade" his office by being seen as a *bal moifes*, a wonderworker, something beneath the dignity of a learned communal rabbi. This accounts for the surprising fact that we have almost no miracle tales about Levi Yitsḥak. He believed both in the power of the *tsaddik* to change the decree of heaven and the importance of demonstrating that power. Only this will show the *tsaddik* as reaching out to ordinary Jews, caring about their worldly needs. Yet he continued to hold back from doing so. The influence of the Maggid remained very strong. Perhaps so too did his disdain for wonderworkers when he saw them in action. The tales about him, written and published in an era when there was no shyness about accounts of *tsaddikim* and their miracles, are primarily recollections of personal piety and the love of

Israel. Levi Yitsḥak regularly defied the seeming will of heaven in arguing with God to see the merits of Israel, but he did not engage in miracles—at least not in open, obvious ones—to bring about their salvation. Our age, he had come to realize—and not entirely with regret—is a time of only *hidden* miracles. That is why he chose to publish a book about them.

9

AN EMERGING RELIGIOUS PERSONALITY

The essentially anti-worldly mysticism of the Maggid eventually had to come into conflict with the people-centered and embracing personality of Levi Yitsḥak. It was one thing to say that this world was one of illusion and that the only true value was that which led to *devekut*, or intimate union with God. It would have been quite another, unimaginable for Levi Yitsḥak, to be indifferent to people and their fate. The Maggid was clearly a loving teacher, but that love seems to have mainly been focused on his own circle of disciples. If he had any aim to transform the religious life of Jewry, it would take place through the leadership and personal examples these leaders would provide. Levi Yitsḥak, while imbibing his master's teachings, showed a greater concern for simple people, such as would never be able to fathom the Maggid's profound teachings. The characteristic for which he is best known is his forgiving and compassionate attitude toward ordinary Jews, including the sinners among them. Such an attitude was by no means to be taken for granted in a person of Levi Yitsḥak's origins and stature. A rabbi's son, he arose from among the educated elite and was clearly sufficiently learned to be accepted to rabbinic posts in four significant Jewish communities. He was also a leading disciple of a mystic teacher who made great demands on those who constituted his inner circle. It would be easy to imagine that this combination of factors would lead him to stand at a certain distance from the semi-educated merchants, tradesmen, and even paupers who constituted the broader edges of his rabbinic flock.

But such was not the case. Both the later legends surrounding Levi Yitsḥak and numerous references within his own writings portray him as one ever concerned with supporting the concerns, both spiritual and material, of ordinary people, of making Hasidic teachings accessible to them, and of defending them against all accusers, be they in heaven or on earth. This is a distinctive feature of his personality and his conduct as a rabbi. It stands out as such among the other members of the Mezritch circle from which he emerged, and we can even find passages in his writings where he seems to be arguing the case for this attitude, giving the impression that it encountered some opposition.

Was Levi Yitsḥak always this way, or was the love of ordinary Jews and appreciation for their struggles something he learned in the course of his rabbinate? We should remember that his rabbinic duties began quite early in his life, when he was in his early twenties. We have seen above that he was rabbi in Ryczywol during the lifetime of the Maggid, which means that he was the fervent mystic disciple while at the same time needing to minister to the needs of his community. Indeed, that is what got him in trouble in more than one rabbinic post, as we have seen. But here we need to listen to a surprising reading that young Levi Yitsḥak offers of a passage in tractate Avot in one of his early sermons:

> ["In a place where there are no men, try to be a man" (m. Avot 2:5).] The sage comes to indicate the true and proper path that a person should walk. In saying "where there are no men," he is referring to the upper worlds, where there are no men, only angels, spiritual personages, seraphim. *There* "try to be a man," one to be considered significant by them. This rung can only be attained by one who serves God in love, being careful about His commandments and studying Torah for its own sake, as stated above. But to be an important and famous person in "a place where there are men," namely in this dark and lowly world, one of delusions and lies, is vain and empty, a complete error. Try rather to be a man in that "place where there aren't men," as I have said.[1]

This voice is strikingly different than the Levi Yitsḥak we meet in the pages of *Kedushat Levi* as well as in the later legends. As with most Hasidic writings (the *Shemu'ah Tovah* sermons are a great exception), individual teachings and sermons in the *Kedushat Levi 'al ha-Torah* are undated; there we have no way of knowing when particular statements were made or sermons preached. But here we see the young spiritual elitist in Levi Yitsḥak. It is amid the community of angels that you need to stand up and take your place! Perhaps this community of "angels" is none other than the small circle of devotees in Mezritch, just now mourning their leader.

Comparing this with the later Levi Yitsḥak is indeed striking. But are we witnessing the long evolution of a mystic scholar, at first wanting to dwell among the angels, learning about people in the course of his career, slowly growing toward a more worldly stance? Or is this a conflict that existed within Levi Yitsḥak from the beginning of his way, his own natural affinity for people struggling from the outset with his master's otherworldliness, a worldview that he was trying to follow? Such a question is not easy to resolve. It comes into sharpest focus around the personality of Levi Yitsḥak, but it goes back to the broader question of a group of mystics trying to create a broad popular religious revival.

One window into this question of elitism and popular leadership in the Hasidic sources has to do with understandings of the important value of *bitaḥon*, or trust in God. Jewish pietism in all its historical forms, reaching back into the biblical Psalter, has placed great importance on this sense of trust, often used as a synonym for *emunah*, "faith."[2] It plays a major role in all the writings of early Hasidism. The Maggid displays what has been called an "elitist" notion of *bitaḥon*, linking it to utter negation of personal will and a sense of indifferent acceptance of one's worldly fate.[3] Its classical expression may be seen in the well-known verses of Psalm 27: "One thing I ask of YHWH. That is what I seek: to dwell in the house of YHWH all the days of my life, to gaze upon the beauty of YHWH and to visit His temple." The devotee seeks nothing other than to remain in God's presence.

There are passages like that in Levi Yitsḥak, reflecting what may be considered Western religion at its most sublime. But this is more an ideal to be venerated in accounts of the *tsaddikim* than it is a standard to be upheld in a popular religious movement. Therefore, it is not surprising that we find, alongside this highly refined view of *bitaḥon*, a more worldly and optimistic one as well:

> Thus, if a person trusts in YHWH to act upon all his needs, everything he asks for will be granted from above. One who worries constantly about his sustenance and that of his household will bring about a [parallel] lack in sustenance above. Therefore, blessed is the person who does not forget You and who places his trust in YHWH. Then "YHWH is your shadow" (Ps. 121:5), providing one's sustenance. . . .
>
> We have explained that the miracles at the Reed Sea were brought

> about by [such] an arousal from below, Israel's faith in YHWH. Naḥshon jumped into the sea out of faith in YHWH, that God would perform a miracle and split it. This awakening of faith *caused God to perform that miracle for them.*[4]

This is *bitaḥon* of a different sort; there is nothing passive about it. There is indeed an outcome that I need to help make come to pass, and my trust takes the form of hope that it will indeed happen. But there is more than hope here. Human trust awakens divine compassion because our need becomes (or reflects) a divine need. Our *bitaḥon,* which involves seeing this truth, *causes* God to perform the miracle we need. This is the sort of faith that Levi Yitsḥak could hope to stir in the Jewish masses toward whom he was turning. You pray that the lack within God be fulfilled, but you understand that this parallels the specific worldly lack you are praying over. This then becomes a way of justifying the ordinary Jew, who prays out of personal need. As one dedicated to building a popular movement, Levi Yitsḥak does not hesitate to say that such *bitaḥon* is rewarded.

We have seen that Levi Yitsḥak commends the Hasidic preacher to ever seek out the good in Jews, constantly arguing in their favor, convincing them of their goodness as he also tries to convince their Creator. This is also the way Levi Yitsḥak wants to conduct himself as rabbi and judge of his community. The same quality he sought in the preacher applies to the rabbi or judge as well. There is a specific Hebrew term for this sort of leadership, one that is frequently used regarding Levi Yitsḥak, distinguishing him in this way from other Hasidic masters. The term is *melits tov* or *melits yosher*, one who "intervenes" (or "speaks out") in search of goodness or righteousness. He takes the role of the defending angel in the heavenly courtroom, ever speaking of Israel's goodness and thus saving them from punishment. It is most interesting to note that this term was used concerning Levi Yitsḥak in his lifetime, appearing even prior to the publication of his major works. In 1794, the first book by Levi Yitsḥak appeared in print, his brief *Commentary on the Six Remembrances*, six things a person is supposed to call to memory each day. In the introduction to that little volume, Levi Yitsḥak is described by the editor, clearly a resident of Berdychiv, in words that we have partially quoted above.[5]

But now we turn to the concluding lines of that little encomium: "As we have heard with our own ears, all his words are the words of the living God, each day speaking out for the goodness [*le-hamlits tov*] of his people, the house of Israel."[6]

Immediately following this description is the editor's report of a sermon he heard delivered by Levi Yitsḥak on the holiday of Sukkot. Commenting on the emphasis on "the first day" of the holiday in the biblical verse (Lev. 23:40), the Talmud refers to it as "the first day for the counting of sins." This seems to mean that after the slate has been wiped clear on Yom Kippur, God again begins to keep track of the sins of Israel. But such a reading is impossible for Levi Yitsḥak! He does not want a God who counts sins! He therefore links it to another Talmudic passage to the effect that when one repents out of fear, sins become demoted to misdemeanors, but when one repents out of love, sins are transformed into actual merits.[7] During the Days of Awe, says Levi Yitsḥak, we repent out of fear of judgment. But once Sukkot, "the season of our rejoicing," comes upon us, our return to God is out of love. Then the sins are transformed into merits, and it is only those "sins" that God wants to count, ever seeking out the merit of His beloved children![8]

Here we have a picture of God behaving exactly as Levi Yitsḥak seeks to do, counting only the merits of Israel, not their sins. Levi Yitsḥak would read this in reverse, of course. The *tsaddik* is to act just like God, who is described in the Torah as merciful and compassionate, best defined by His thirteen Attributes of Mercy, by which He forgave Israel after the sin of the Golden Calf. But we might also view this as Levi Yitsḥak's hopeful view of God as one who views Israel and acts with the same compassion as does the *tsaddik*. "Who is imitating whom?" remains an open question. We shall have occasion to return to it yet again.

The presence of the *melits tov* epithet and the recounting of this sermon at the head of the very first publication by Levi Yitsḥak make it clear that he was well-known for this characteristic already at this midpoint in his rabbinic career. This leads us to think that whatever tension might exist between the otherworldliness of there being no truth but *ayin* and the very earthly concerns of Jews struggling to make a living coexisted in Levi Yitsḥak's soul for a long time, perhaps even from the earliest years of his quest for leadership.

This definition of *tsaddik* as *melits tov* is prominent throughout Levi Yitsḥak's writings as well as in the tales told about him. Consideration of it leads to another conclusion as well. Levi Yitsḥak exhibits a greater interest in the fate of the Jewish people and their earthly situation than do others within the circle from which he emerged. The concern for *klal yisra'el*, including efforts to improve their situation by means either inspirational (affecting their behavior) or mystical/magical (affecting the divine will) were a part of Hasidism's legacy from the Ba'al Shem

Tov. Indeed, the BeSHT differed from prior *ba'aley shem* in part by exhibiting a sense of responsibility for entire communities, as well as for the people as a whole, rather than just the specific petitioners who had come to him. This is displayed clearly in the final portion of his letter to R. Gershon Kitover, where such concerns are directly articulated. They are also integral to his treatment in the legendary tradition as presented in *Shivḥey ha-BeSHT* and elsewhere.

Dov Baer of Mezritch is less identified with this commitment to the broader Jewish community, and especially with concern for its this-worldly fate. He is, as we have seen, a mystic who seeks to lead his followers toward an indifference to "external" matters. Cultivation of the inner life is his singular goal. This includes the "uplifting" of worldly concerns and a willingness to cast one's burden onto God, the ultimate act of faith. His turn away from the *ba'al shem*-like aspects of his master's legacy seems to have lessened his involvement with broader "healing" of Israel's ailments, alongside those of the individual.

While the term "neutralization of messianism," which Gershom Scholem applied to the Maggid's school, has been questioned by more recent scholarship, certain attitudes that led him to that conclusion cannot be denied.[9] Scholem's argument, briefly stated, is that for more radically mystical figures like the Maggid, the historic fate of Israel, and hence the need for redemption from it, mattered little since they were already "redeemed" by being in the presence of both God and the *tsaddik*. Critics, beginning with Scholem's student Isaiah Tishby, have pointed out that there is messianism to be found in many early Hasidic sources, including texts emerging from the Maggid's circle. A careful reading of these, however, will show that their primary focus is on *spiritual* redemption, the ending of *galut ha-da'at*, the "exile" of mind or awareness. In the *Me'or 'Eynayim*, the end of Israel's exile will be a universal awareness that "knowledge of YHWH fills the earth as water covers the sea" (Is. 11:9); that is why *galut* needs to come to an end. For the *Or ha-Me'ir*, every move undertaken toward Israel's redemption is another step in the "building of *shekhinah*'s form," the completion of which is the ultimate redemptive goal. The same, in one version or another, is true of most members of the Mezritch circle.[10]

But not Levi Yitsḥak. As we have seen, beginning with his early sermons included in *Shemu'ah Tovah* and through the *Kedushat Levi*, the Father/child love affair of God and Israel lies at the very heart of his teaching. Yes, this applies to the individual as well as the people as a whole, and Levi Yitsḥak is very much interested in bringing his disciples in toward the self-negating mystical goals of the Maggid. But it all begins with the unique love between God and His chosen people, those for whom He created the world.[11]

The text of Levi Yitsḥak's commentary on the Six Remembrances is as instructive as is the little introduction to it. There is almost no trace of the Maggid's mysticism in this treatise; it is clearly written for a popular rather than a spiritually enlightened audience. No matter which of the six he is discussing, the topic rather quickly reverts to that of God's love for Israel, the real message he is seeking to deliver. The first remembrance is that of Shabbat, meaning that one is to recall and anticipate the seventh day throughout the days of the week. Here is a portion of Levi Yitsḥak's comment:

> The commandment to remember Shabbat: The activity emerging from this remembrance is clear to every enlightened person. Shabbat is an awakener, rousing every human heart to know that blessed YHWH is Creator of the world, renewing that creation in each moment in order to do good for His creatures and causing His goodness to flow upon all the worlds. Thus [the sages] have said [commenting on the concluding verse of the Psalter], "Praise YH for every single breath."[12] It arose in the divine mind to create the world in order to benefit His creatures and to demonstrate His love and goodness toward His people, the Children of Israel. If any sorrow dwells over Israel, "In all their suffering, He suffers" (Is. 63:9); that suffering extends upward [to God]. So too the opposite: When Israel are doing well, He derives pleasure from our happiness. Therefore . . . blessed YHWH does not deduct from the goodness hidden away for Israel in the world to come, in accord with the good they consume in this world. The faith is firmly set in our hearts that God derives pleasure from the flow of goodness He pours upon Israel, including material goodness, in this world. Why, then, should YHWH deduct from our reward, since He is happy about this? All our merits are preserved for life eternal.

Shabbat, going back to creation, bears a universalist message, reflecting God's concern for all creatures. But notice how quickly he moves on from that. Actually, Shabbat serves merely as an introduction to announcing His special care for the Children of Israel and seeing to it that they thrive, both in this world and the next!

Next, he turns to the obligation to recall the exodus from Egypt every day. Rather than viewing the biblical use of recalled Egyptian bondage as a spur toward treating strangers in a kindly manner (as the Torah itself does so frequently), Levi Yitsḥak sees it as a reminder of God's choosing Israel, calling them "My firstborn son" (Ex. 4:22). Remembering the Exodus is a way of recalling God's special love for them. Here we find the first reference to Levi Yitsḥak's famous quip that we call our great national holiday Pesah, expressing our gratitude to God for having "passed over" or protected the houses of Israel in Egypt, while God's Torah refers to it as "the festival of *matsot*," attesting to Israel's love for God in faithfully keeping His commandment. Each of us thus bears witness to the love of the other. He then goes on to discuss the Talmud's tale of God's *tefillin*,[13] which contains verses praising Israel as "a unique people in the world." He winds up with, "It is forbidden for a person to be idle, even for a moment, in all his days. How much more so should one never speak ill of an Israelite! All your days, either be praising God or be speaking in praise of all Israel. . . . All their days, [our sages] engaged in no idle conversation. Either they were thanking or praising [God] or were commending [*le-hamlits*] the goodness of His people, that they find grace in the eyes of God, so that goodness and blessing flow into them."[14]

Of course, neither the election of Israel nor God's love for them is an invention of Levi Yitsḥak. But the constant emphasis on this theme, a sense that seeking Israel's good should be one's primary activity in life, makes him stand out, even within the Mezritch circle. One simply would not find it preached to this uncritical extent in other prominent authors of the school. Levi Yitsḥak's fellow Ukrainian *tsaddikim*, the preachers in Chernobyl and nearby Zhitomir, would have turned the subject toward *tikkun ha-middot*, improvement of Israel's behavior, in order to uplift sparks and rebuild the wholeness of *shekhinah*. Shne'ur Zalman of Liadi would quickly have us back in the inner divine worlds that are the source of Israel's soul, making various subtle distinctions among them. Elimelekh, who is close to Levi Yitsḥak in several ways, would have turned to the special role of the *tsaddikim* in uplifting Israel and the great burden of purity required to engage in that work. So too would the Maggid himself; in this way, R. Elimelekh is very much a faithful renderer of his teaching.[15] For Levi Yitsḥak, it is always about Israel, God's unending love for them, and the commitment of both God and the *tsaddik* to seek out and defend their goodness.[16] It is no accident that Levi Yitsḥak remained—or was even resurrected as—a folk hero among Jews who were to stand very far from his theological views.

The defense of Israel and the recounting of their goodness is a theme that runs throughout the sermons and short teachings collected in *Kedushat Levi 'al ha-Torah.* "Because God chose only Israel, no person is permitted to speak ill of them, but only to proclaim their merit. . . . The mouth was created only for the study of Torah and to declare the merit of Israel."[17] God redeemed Israel from Egypt because He heard their outcry as a desire to serve Him. The Song of Songs is a hymn to Israel's devotion. Even as they wander "through the markets and streets, seeking that which their soul loves," their entire intent is toward heaven. If they earn any money, they give it to charity or use it to celebrate Sabbaths and holy days. On the day of judgment, God "uplifts sin" (taking *nosei* as "lifts" rather than "bears"), removing it from the scales of justice so that merits will weigh the scales to their side and win the day.[18] God does that which any merchant or customer in the marketplace knows is cheating: He lightens the scales in order to find Israel innocent!

The book of Numbers, the fourth book of the Torah, begins with a detailed census of the Israelite people undertaken by Moses at God's command. The command to do so concludes with the verse "As YHWH commanded Moses, so did he count them in the Wilderness of Sinai" (Num. 1:19). "Isn't the verse in reverse order?" asks Levi Yitsḥak. Wouldn't it be better to say that Moses counted them as YHWH had commanded?

His answer to this question takes us to the very heart of Levi Yitsḥak's teaching: "God gave the Torah to Israel. The souls of Israel constitute the body of Torah. Israel *are* the 600,000 letters of Torah. Israel are Torah; each one of them is a letter. Therefore, in his counting of Israel, Moses was studying Torah. This is hinted at by [the order of the verse]. 'As God commanded Moses' means that the Torah YHWH commanded to Moses was *itself* the counting of Israel."[19]

For Levi Yitsḥak, love of Torah and love for Jews are one and the same. The mouth "that was created only for the study of Torah and to declare the merit of Israel" in fact has but one task, expressed in acting upon these two aspects of a single love.

In another teaching, Levi Yitsḥak comments on the words of the daily evening prayer "Remove Satan from before us and behind us." "Why do we need those words of direction?" he asks. Wouldn't it be enough to say, "Remove Satan from us?" To answer, he turns to a well-rehearsed Hasidic trope, the parallel between Yom Kippur (always called *yom ha-kippurim* in the Torah, in the plural form) and Purim. On Purim, he says, Jews are busy with merrymaking and drinking. Satan comes down, has a look, and tries to condemn them before God. "But look what they were doing just yesterday!" he is told. They were fasting and reciting hymns of penitence on the Fast of Esther! On the day preceding Yom Kippur, Jews are supposed to eat a lot, enjoying the blessing of this world before the great day of fasting and self-affliction. On that day too, Satan registers his complaint. "Yes," says God, "They are feasting and overdoing it. But just look at what they'll be doing tomorrow!" Of this the prayer says, "Remove Satan from [looking] before us and behind us"—one for Purim, one for the eve of Yom Kippur.[20]

Here, again, we have God in the role of *tsaddik*—loving Israel, defending them, seeing only the good, and conspiring with Levi Yitsḥak to outwit the Accuser. God sees that their ascetic devotion to Him is intact, even in the hour of their merrymaking.

There are occasions when Levi Yitsḥak's description of God as seeking only the good in Jews, and therefore responding to their prayers, takes the form of a call to Him to do so. God *must* make His compassion and love for Israel manifest in the world. How could He do otherwise? This is particularly true in the face of Israel's suffering in this world, when both they and the non-Jews who oppress them might not understand God's love for Israel to be the case. Here we touch the edge of the *tsaddik* challenging God, *insisting* that He do good, fulfilling His own compassionate nature. This theme is very much emphasized in the later folk tradition around Levi Yitsḥak, but it is found only in somewhat muted fashion in his own writings and early accounts of his behavior.[21]

> "Not for us, Lord, not for us. But give glory to Your name" (Ps. 115:1). To explain the repetition of "not for us": Our sages taught that Jacob separated himself from Esau. Esau took this world, and Jacob the World to Come. Yet we ask God for goodness in this world as well, [seeking blessings for] livelihood and so forth. Even though Jacob has no portion in this world, those requests are still proper. . . . If the nations of the world did not curse and vilify Israel, seeing our lowly status in this world, but believed that [our ill fortune was because] Israel has no place in this world's goods, it would not be necessary to give those to us. But since they do not believe this, and constantly curse us . . . saying, "Where is their God?" (115:2), we ask You for worldly goods . . . so that Your name not be disgraced.[22]

It is not for *our* sake that we seek these blessings but for Yours! Here the Hasidic master may be seen as arguing with God, trying to convince Him to bless

His people for the sake of His own reputation. The reader (surely as well as the original hearers of this sermon) is reminded of Moses' arguments with God (Ex. 34 and Num. 11, et al.) when He threatened to destroy Israel. Here, interestingly, Levi Yitsḥak abandons any reliance on the merits of Israel. The question of merit becomes irrelevant since all their rewards belong to the next world, not to this world. "Save us for Your name's sake!" It is only to protect Your own reputation that it is *necessary* to save us here as well.

One year, when the first day of Rosh Hashanah fell out on the Sabbath, Levi Yitsḥak took to reminding God that He, too, was obligated to observe His own law. On Rosh Hashanah God is said to have the books of life and death open before Him. But this is the holy Sabbath, admonished Levi Yitsḥak. You are permitted to violate it (and writing is such a violation) only for the purpose of saving a life! Therefore, You have no choice but to inscribe us all in the Book of Life![23]

In another passage, which may be called a complaint against God rather than a challenge to divine authority, Levi Yitsḥak asks why humans were created with a will to do evil: "The essential desire of the human soul is to serve YHWH. It is only the body that has earthly desires. But both soul and body are made by God! Just as He made the soul to serve Him, surely, He could have done the same with the body as well. We therefore have a claim (*te'anah*, a legal argument) against the blessed Holy One to forgive our sins. He had the power to make the body subservient to His blessed service."[24]

The role of the *tsaddik* is to love Israel, to see only the good in them, and to defend them against all accusers. These include both earthly enemies and heavenly forces, whether depicted as prosecuting angels or as God Himself as judge. But Levi Yitsḥak's defenses of human frailty are also addressed, perhaps even primarily so, toward pangs of conscience and feelings of religious or moral failure that so much burden the human psyche. Here we need to place Levi Yitsḥak within the broader framework of the spiritual transformation that Hasidism set forth to bring about. Israel Ba'al Shem Tov first became a popular figure largely because of a significant deviation he offered from the moral universe of Jewish preachers and spiritual guides in eighteenth-century Poland. He was opposed to the rigorous ascetic demands that had become part and parcel of what was called Kabbalah in his day. In a well-known letter to a leading disciple,[25] R. Ya'akov Yosef, he urges him most strongly to reject the way of self-punishment: "Do not turn aside from your own flesh!" he called out to him, using the words of the prophet Isaiah. But the ancient prophet had been referring to fellow humans in using that phrase. The BeSHT takes it to refer to the disciple's own bodily self. "Do not reject or punish your body!" is what he is saying. Elsewhere, teachings in the original master's name speak out against excessive worry about sins, which will keep one far from God, the pathway blocked by a sense of guilt. If you transgress, he taught, resolve never to do it again—and then return immediately to serving God in joy and exultation.[26]

Levi Yitsḥak is a learned rabbi very much committed to the law and its fulfillment, as we shall see in more detail below. His Hasidism, two generations after the Ba'al Shem Tov's, was acquired in the respectable study hall of Mezritch, not learned from or inspired by shamans—perhaps even including non-Jews—in the Carpathian mountains.[27] Nevertheless, he has gotten the BeSHT's message. The Hasidic approach to moral growth is one of gentleness and joy, not ferocity or condemnation. For Levi Yitsḥak, this takes the form of serving as the much-needed defending angel for Jews, for whoever stands before the court of God's judgment as well as their own. In an especially revealing passage devoted to the theme of self-judgment, Levi Yitsḥak makes the psychological—one might even call it "therapeutic"—nature of his call for God's mercy abundantly clear:

> "Do not enter into judgment with us, for no living being can be justified before You."[28] This may be explained by a parable. A king's servant has transgressed against him, and the king desires to make that sin pass away [i.e., to let it be forgiven]. He therefore commands, "You be your own judge. Whatever outcome you find, thus will it be." The servant's spirit was deeply disturbed, and he cried out bitterly, "Do not do this to me," knowing that he would have to find himself guilty. Judging himself, he could not go more lightly than the penalty prescribed by law. He therefore begged that the king himself judge him, knowing that he was a compassionate and merciful ruler. He was all-powerful, and it was within his hand to be generous and forgive the sin.
>
> Thus we ask, "Do not enter into judgment *with* us," in such a way that we too would have to judge ourselves. . . . We know that by law we are guilty . . . but You are merciful, compassionate, and repeatedly forgive.[29]

The all-forgiving and compassionate God exists as counterweight to our own self-punishing instincts. Levi Yitsḥak, the *rebbe* in the role of defending angel, is there to rescue us from the burden of our own castigations, entrusting us into the hands of a loving God.

There is, however, a "flip side" to Levi Yitsḥak's great and all-embracing love of Jews. His compassion did not extend to the other side of the religious/ethnic fence that was a daily presence in the Eastern European *shtetl*. Levi Yitsḥak's attitude toward non-Jews was hardly one we could call enlightened. The great love for humanity that he seemed to demonstrate toward Jews did not extend beyond the limits of the Jewish community. Although some of his pronouncements against the gentiles can be taken as simply belonging to the historical baggage of his era, Levi Yitsḥak is unusually outspoken and somewhat extreme in this matter even within that context.

This disdain for the non-Jewish world came to him early and cannot be dismissed as a result of negative experiences in the course of his rabbinate in Pinsk and Berdychiv. In a sermon preached in the summer of 1773 or '74,[30] when he was probably still in Ryczywol, young Levi Yitsḥak took up the question of Israel's election, an important theme in Jewish preaching. What sort of special love can God have for Israel, he asks, following a well-known Midrashic trope, if He first offered the Torah to the other nations? Edom and Ishmael, representing the Christians and the Muslims, first had to turn the Torah down before God offered it to the Jews. Doesn't that make Israel God's third choice, demonstrating that they are of a lower rather than higher status in God's eyes?

He responds with what is the longest (and indeed somewhat overwritten) parable in this collection of early sermons. Once again, we return to the world of king, son, and servants. There was a king who had great wealth, invested in collections of many sorts of treasures, each kept in a separate treasure house. (One wonders whether he might have seen treasuries like this, as still exist in some once-royal museums in Europe.) One chamber had gold and silver, another contained the royal library, still another a collection of weapons and armaments, and so forth. There was a unique key fitted to open each chamber. The king also had a single and much-beloved legitimate son, to whom he intended to leave all these treasures. To make the son's life easier, the king hired a skilled locksmith to design a master key that would unlock all the treasuries.

It turns out, however, that the king had a number of other children, born of concubines rather than of the queen. He feared that these would one day become deadly rivals to his son. To prevent that, he called one of them aside and offered him that master key. He did not tell him, however, that it would open any of the chambers he chose. "Because you are so dear to me," he said to him, "I want you to have this key to my collections." The fact was, however, that this son had been stealing from the king for a long time. He was so racked with guilt that when he saw the key, he immediately thought he was being asked to open the roomful of armaments and would be forced to choose the weapon with which he would be punished. Without trying the key in any lock, he gave it back, saying that he was not worthy of this parental gift. Each of the other illegitimate sons did the same (in other words, they were *all* stealing from the king) until finally the king could give it to his only true son without fear of competition or complaint.

The meaning of the parable is obvious. God had no real interest in giving Torah to anyone but Israel. When each of the other nations asked what was in it, God intentionally mentioned that thing He knew would make them reject it, as recounted in the Midrashic source. The nations, in other words, have a relationship with God that is solely based on guilt and fear. But when God then offered the Torah to Israel, He showed them the nature of the special key. In contrast to his attempt to somewhat deceive the others, he spoke to this true son with his heart fully open, without any attempt at deceit. The passion of the true love then awakened between them, like that of friends who exchange intimate kisses, has been quoted above.

The Midrashic story that originally served as an apologetic for the election of Israel—God did indeed offer His Torah to the nations, but only we accepted it—has now been turned around to serve the very opposite purpose, showing that God never had the slightest intent of truly offering it to anyone but His only true son. Had God spoken to the Gentiles at Sinai, Levi Yitsḥak suggests elsewhere, they would have stood as still and unmoved as trees or rocks since they have "not a drop of holiness within them," while Israel were so agitated they felt their souls would depart from them.[31] Jews have within them an imprint of holiness that cannot be erased, but "the Gentiles have no relationship to anything that is holy, only to superficial things." This makes them fickle in their loyalties, as he says, "Even when one of them acts well and directs himself to become attached to something holy, as soon as he backslides, he will be cut off from it entirely. The holy will make no impression on him. The gentiles have no essential or true relationship to holiness, only one that can come about by chance."[32]

Living in a society as filled with deep piety as was small-town eighteenth-century Catholic Poland or Orthodox Christian Ukraine, one could say that it took an extra strong set of blinders to be as seemingly unaware of it as was Levi

Yitsḥak. This is especially notable in one who took such special care to seek out even the slightest sign of religious merit among his Jewish brethren.

Several complete sermons of Levi Yitsḥak are found in a section of his 1798 volumes called *Kelalot ha-Nisim*, the *Principles of Miracles*. The first of these is a response to the question of why God punishes those enemies of Israel who seem to be doing His bidding in oppressing them. Pharoah's enslavement of the Israelites, after all, was in fulfillment of a prophecy already revealed to Abraham. Nebuchadnezzar destroyed the Temple as God's agent in response to Israel's sins. Why should they be held liable?

Here the parable is one of wicked tutors hired by a well-meaning father who wants someone who will discipline his beloved child for the sake of his own growth. The tutors turn out to be sadists who whip the poor child for their own pleasure. Rather than using their power to bring him to fulfill his father's desire, they do everything they can to keep him from it, meanwhile keeping up their harsh rule over him.

He concludes the sermon this way, speaking out in direct terms against the enemies of Israel:

> [God says of Israel in Egypt,] "For I know his pain" (Ex. 3:7). Blessed YHWH knows the pain of the Children of Israel. It was not to fulfill His decrees that the Egyptians acted, but the malice in their hearts caused them to hate God and His people Israel. That is why God sent forth His wrath against them, gladly and joyously redeeming us from slavery to freedom. Now, in this bitter exile, may He again bring us forth from slavery to freedom, fulfilling "As in the days when you came forth from Egypt, I will show wonders" (Mic. 7:15). May He enlighten our eyes with the sweetness of His Torah. Amen Selah.

Jews living in the time and place occupied by Levi Yitsḥak certainly saw themselves as an oppressed people. Although there were great variations in their relationships with both the gentile authorities and the local populace from time to time and one locality to another, they saw themselves as suffering under the twin burdens of exile and oppression. It is no surprise that such populations bear resentment, even hatred, toward those they view as their oppressors. It is also no surprise that they see the God they worship sharing in those feelings:

> It appears that the Creator's love for the Children of Israel, the people near to Him, is truly great. One who loves his son, out of that powerful love and affection, will hate, destroy, break down, and demolish all those who oppress that child. This is due to his love for his son. This is what the holy lamp, our teacher Dov Baer, referred to as *ḥesed shebi-gevurah*, the divine rigor within compassion. Because of God's great love for the Children of Israel, they are called His sons, and He breaks down, demolishes, uproots, and takes recompense against those who oppress and despotize them. Sometimes blessed YHWH takes vengeance on the wicked because of their own wickedness, the fact that they sin before the blessed Holy One. This is called *gevurah shebi-gevurah*, pure rigor. But at other times, blessed YHWH takes vengeance upon the nations of the world because He loves us, His people the Children of Israel. That causes Him to hate the nations that oppress us.[33]

The ultimate punishment of Israel's oppressors is important to Levi Yitsḥak. God sends His blessing into this world somewhat indiscriminately. All the living enjoy His gifts without attention to their moral failings. That is why the *tsaddikim* need to become involved in the channeling of divine blessings. They are the ones who know who is deserving of them and who is not. If blessing comes about only from above, it will be entirely a gift of divine love. If directed by the righteous, it will be specifically turned toward Israel and away from their enemies.[34]

10

PLEASURES SUBLIME AND WORLDLY IN THE RELIGIOUS LIFE

Hasidism is a movement of devotional mysticism. This means that its teachings are concentrated largely on cultivating the inner life of the individual. In contrast to the medieval Kabbalist, who sought out *derekh ha-emet*, "the true way," in reading the Torah, referring to the secrets of the upper universe hidden within it, the Hasidic authors read it *'al derekh ha-'avodah*, as a guide to religious service or devotion. Questions of faith, religious experience, and proper attitudes fill a large portion of their writings, including *Kedushat Levi*.

Two interrelated issues take on particular importance among the followers of the BeSHT and the Maggid, matters that were clearly much discussed among the disciples who emerged from the circle in Mezritch. One is the question of pleasure or delight in acts of worship. Is it proper to *enjoy* the life of prayer, study, and the fulfilling of divine commandments? Should one cultivate such a sense of pleasure or is it a distraction from the wholehearted act of giving? Does pleasure belong to God, to the worshipper, or to both? The other is the question of worldly goods and the pleasure one might take in them. If divinity is to be found everywhere, may one enjoy the things of this world as one undertakes uplifting the sparks of holiness within them? Or is that too a dangerous distraction from *'avodat hashem*, the effort of constantly serving God? Both of these issues become extremely fraught in the sources of early Hasidism, not least because both touch on delicate questions of eros and sexuality and their place within a non-celibate life that seeks to be wholly devoted to God's service.

In our preceding chapters, we dealt with the ability of the *tsaddik* to bring about worldly blessing and the important role it played in Hasidism's growth. But this belief has to be seen in the broader context of the place of both power and pleasure in all aspects of the divine/human relationship.[1] Following an old rabbinic trope that "Israel add power and strength above" through their faithfulness to God's Torah,[2] the Kabbalists had come to broadly understand Jewish religious life and praxis as a closed circuit of energy flowing between the Creator and His chosen community of human devotees, mutually empowering one another. God gives life and blessing to Israel; they return that blessing and strengthen, or even enliven, God by the energy of their devotion. Since God created the world for the sake of Israel, especially for the righteous among them—and Levi Yitsḥak makes no bones about his commitment to this belief—it is natural that He has placed the keys to its very survival and daily regeneration in their hands.

The human empowerment of God and the desire to cause God pleasure are deeply bound together. A God who is pleased by, or delights in, human deeds will bless the world, His blessing falling especially on those who have brought about such divine delight. Three terms are used for divine pleasure in the ancient Jewish sources: *naḥat*, *ta'anug*, and *sha'ashu'a*. They represent differing degrees within a hierarchy of intensity. *Naḥat* reflects a general sense of contentment; it is a term often used in Yiddish (pronounced *nakhes*) as well as in Hebrew to refer to the pleasure adults take in beloved children. *Sha'ashu'a* often refers to sexual pleasure, especially in Kabbalistic contexts, and *ta'anug*, the most common term, lies somewhere in between.[3] The charge of energy that human deeds bring to God may be seen as bearing both power and pleasure. The Hasidic sources tend to focus more on the latter, but the two remain inseparable.

This understanding of the universe was by no means entirely new when articulated by the medieval Kabbalists. Some aspects of it reached into the mythic worldview of ancient rabbinic sources and in turn are rooted in even earlier forms of religious teaching. Ancient Israelite beliefs about the cosmos-sustaining power of the daily Temple sacrifice—beliefs that surely reached back much farther than the biblical text itself—were transferred, in postexilic Judaism, to daily prayers, study of Torah, and life in accord with the divine commandments. "The blessed Holy One set forth a condition to the work of creation. 'If Israel accept My Torah, it will be well. But, if not, I will return you to primal chaos.'"[4] Many passages attest to the belief that the religious activities of Israel are vital to the continuity of the cosmic order. For the Kabbalists, this came to include the very existence of the divine as manifest in the *sefirot*, or at least their inner balance. Without them, existence would not proceed from one moment to the next. In the words of the famous thirteenth-century commentator Naḥmanides, one of the first to include the teachings of Kabbalah in a written work intended for a broad audience, the commandments fulfill a "divine need," not merely one of mortals.[5]

This classic form of Kabbalistic piety is alive and well in the thought of Levi Yitsḥak. Here he is commenting on a well-known Talmudic story:

> "Rabbi Yishmaʿel said, I once came into the innermost place . . . and saw Akatriel. . . . He said to me, 'Yishmaʿel, My son, bless Me.'"[6] There exist both preordained and newly created sources of grace. The preordained are those of which [it is said,] "You have sworn since days of yore" (Micah 7:20). By these, God created His world as an act of grace. But the newly created are those through which God, as it were, crowns Himself in the glory of Israel by means of their good deeds. Through these, He causes grace to flow into them. Therefore, the more Israel do the Creator's will, the more God crowns Himself in their glory. . . . This is the meaning of "Yishmaʿel, My son, bless Me," following the secret meaning of "Give power to God" (Ps. 68:35). "Israel add strength to the heavenly retinue." This is "Bless Me," adding to the glory of Israel above by means of their good deeds and goodly words of Torah and prayer. Thus is much grace added below [as well].[7]

This Kabbalistic worldview is profoundly anthropocentric and theocentric at once. Human deeds are of ultimate importance, freighted with cosmic energy. In contrast to the austere and self-contained God of Maimonides, who by definition stands beyond any possibility of need (implying imperfection), the Kabbalists and Hasidic preachers took quite literally the rabbinic claim that God longs for, desires, and even allows Himself to *need* Israel's prayers and acts of devotion.[8]

God's desire, even passionate longing, for the pleasure wrought by human devotion also takes us back to the most ancient and profound reaches of religion's history, a history that repeats itself in the inner lives of devotees throughout the ages. The gods of the ancient world created humans to bring them pleasure. Sacrifices were placed on the altar to feed the gods, to keep them from the effort of having to do their own hunting and cooking. The gods took pleasure in these offerings and hopefully would bless their devotees in exchange for such gifts.

An echo of this ancient (I mean the word in its historical and psychological sense) aspect of religious devotion is found in Genesis 8:21, Noah's offering: "YHWH smelled the sweet savor and YHWH said in His heart 'I will no longer curse the land because of humans.'" Nowhere else in scripture are we given this glimpse into divine enjoyment of sacrificial offerings, just as it appears in the Gilgamesh epic. Leviticus (called *torat kohanim*, the "Priestly Teaching," in early Jewish sources) describes each offering with the carefully worded phrase "a pleasant aroma for YHWH," which can be read either as a worldly delight offered *in God's honor* or as pleasing to God Himself. The prophetic tradition (see especially Psalm 50 and Jer. 7:21–28) makes it completely clear that God is beyond such needs or desires and that religious devotion is not to be seen as "transactional."

But the *human* need behind such teachings does not disappear. Acts of empowering (or "crowning") divinity and offerings that bring pleasure to God continue in postbiblical Judaism. The religious mind wants to do that which is pleasing to the deity. In rabbinic tradition, *torah* and *mitsvot* take the place of sacrifices in sustaining the world and drawing forth God's blessing. Prayer, especially that of the assembled community, is viewed partly as a rite of divine coronation.[9] This desire of God and Israel to offer gifts of love to one another is most boldly expressed in the eroticizing of Israel's devotion through the allegorical reading of the Song of Songs. God and the Community of Israel are lovers, bridegroom and bride, seeking and finding fulfillment in one another's love. Their acts of love include Israel's redemption from Egypt and her acceptance of God's Torah, the heart of Judaism's sacred narrative.

Kabbalah adapts and expands upon these elements of the earlier rabbinic tradition. "Community of Israel" becomes a name for *shekhinah*, the inner divine bride, the Consort of the blessed Holy One. Earthly Israel are Her devoted troops. It is their "arousal from below" that awakens the exiled *shekhinah* to in turn stir the passion of Her beloved Spouse, restoring the *zivvuga kaddisha*, the holy coupling that is the source of all blessing, both above and below. This cosmic act of love sends forth an overflow of *shefa'*, the constantly renewed flow of life upon which existence itself depends. Here we have indeed moved from *naḥat* to *sha'ashu'a*.

In this way, eros and the transmission of power, itself perhaps experienced as a surge of erotic energy, may be seen as the twin summits of Kabbalistic spirituality. The theurgic act of empowering divinity, which is the core of the Kabbalistic view of the *mitsvot*, is at the same time an arousing of "sexual" desire within God so that the holy union may take place and blessing flow from it. This Midrashic reading of the Song of Songs, transformed from the mystical courtship and marriage of God and the Jewish people to a mating of male and female energies within God, provides much of the passion that animates Jewish religious life in the Kabbalistic imagination. Every ritual act is performed "for the sake of uniting the blessed Holy One and His *shekhinah*," the active/receptive or male/female nodes of energy within the inner divine realm. The worshipper is to see himself as awakening those forces of cosmic love and longing, "adorning the Bride" to make her beloved by Her spouse. In doing so, he gives unstintingly of his own spiritual energies, present in the form of *kavvanah*, or intensity of devotion.[10]

The sexualizing of this empowerment God receives from humans, particularly from the *tsaddikim*, who worship with such intensity, means that power and pleasure are fully united within divinity. The energizing of divinity comes about in the form of an erotic charge, a source of divine pleasure. Formally, the blessed Holy One desires *shekhinah*, His feminine counterpart. We are the arousers of that desire, both Hers and His. But behind the veil of this symbolic structure, perhaps there in part to preserve a needed heterosexual appearance, God's love for the *tsaddikim* and for Israel, including His desire and need for them, is quite clear.

Devotion thus bears within it a strong erotic element from the human side as well. Even so sober a figure as Maimonides, after all, had prescribed that our love of God should be analogous to a nearly maddening love for a woman.[11] Although Kabbalistic spirituality theoretically focused upon the inner divine act of mating to take place in the upper worlds, the passion and intensity with which the worshipper is to arouse himself toward that goal clearly colored his own religious life as well. This is by no means hidden in the vast Kabbalistic corpus. Upper and lower worlds are parallel to one another. Humans were created male and female with a strong built-in desire to unite in order to awaken within them a passion that would lead them to bring about the cosmic coupling as well.[12]

With Hasidism's devotional focus, the question of the legitimacy of feeling, or even intentionally arousing, such pleasure comes front and center. Is it legitimate to seek pleasure in acts of religious devotion? Does the experience of such pleasure either verify or delegitimate the value of one's service to God? There are expressions found in both later Kabbalistic (including, but not limited to, Sabbatian) and early Hasidic sources that speak of *'avodat hashem be-ever ḥai*, "devotion with a living limb," meaning a spiritual erection.[13] The *tsaddik*, for the Kabbalist, is an earthly representation of *yesod*, the phallic element within the divine symbol system. His role in providing pleasure for his Maker is seemingly inseparable from his own somewhat spiritualized erotic arousal.

But just how fully "spiritualized" does this need to be, and how exactly does one going about measuring such things within the emotional life of religious devotion? *Tsaddik* as *yesod* is supposed to represent sexual *purity* as well as *potency*. How does one keep such eroticized devotion pure? Generations of Kabbalists struggled with these questions, especially during the seventeenth and eighteenth centuries. Various Manuals of Repentance, *Tikkuney Teshuvah*, were published, often including extreme ascetic regimens to purify one's thoughts and deeds in the course of devotion. In the public mind, Kabbalah came to be identified more with a rigidly anti-sexual asceticism than with the truly eroticized message that lay at its heart.

As mentioned earlier, the Baʿal Shem Tov, around whose image the Hasidic movement was created, was distinguished amid the many Kabbalistic teachers of his era by dint of his firm rejection of such ascetic practice and the values that supported it. He seems to have had what we would call a rather healthy appreciation for human sexuality and an acceptance of its delights.[14] In his letter to his brother-in-law, considered the most important surviving document from his own hand, he describes the delight of prayer by an a fortiori argument from the delights of union between bridegroom and bride.[15] This clearly refers to human delight, not just that which is created within God.

But the degree to which Hasidism actually followed the BeSHT in this matter is quite checkered. The Maggid, like R. Jacob Joseph, supposedly had come to the Baʿal Shem Tov after a period of asceticism and never entirely got over it. Issues related to it were quite hotly debated among his own followers. Levi Yitsḥak and his friend R. Elimelekh of Lezajsk had some surprisingly strong leanings toward the ascetic side, at least with regard to what they expected of their own closest disciples.

The question is not whether there are sparks of holiness to be found within the physical realm, even within human sexuality. That is taken for granted throughout the school. It is one of taking pleasure while engaged in the spiritual life. There are numerous passages in *Kedushat Levi* showing that Levi Yitsḥak took a somewhat conservative position in this regard. The issue comes up specifically with regard to marital relations. Levi Yitsḥak was quite strict regarding the *mitsvah* of *ʿonah*, performing one's conjugal duties, since it inevitably required arousal of one's own pleasure. Here we find Levi Yitsḥak expressing a rather extreme view.

The reason that seminal emissions are ritually defiling,[16] he writes, even within the context of fulfilling God's commandment,[17] is that it is impossible to bring them about for God's sake alone, without thinking of one's own pleasure. Rather realistically, he says that one might imagine fulfilling any other commandment purely for the sake of God, but not *mitsvat 'onah*, the obligation to have sexual relations with one's wife. He then brings a parable of two servants of the king who perform precisely the same labors for their ruler. One does them to fulfill the king's will while the other does them for his own pleasure. Only the former can be considered the king's true servant. In the case of carrying out God's command to have relations with one's wife, such pure and completely selfless service is impossible because sexual arousal is a necessary part of it. Therefore, even the fulfillment of the *mitsvah* requires purification afterwards, acknowledging that some thought of personal pleasure has inevitably crept in.[18] Ideally, then, the *mitsvot* should be fulfilled for the sake of divine pleasure alone.

But there are numerous passages in which he insists that other commandments as well should be observed only to awaken pleasure in God. We are here to serve, not to take pleasure.[19] Otherwise, the religious person winds up in a cycle of self-worship, performing the *mitsvot* in order to receive pleasure. This is one of the very rare places where he records a view that openly differs from that of the Maggid, going beyond him in the demand of selfless piety.

> This is the meaning of the verse "I rejoice, rejoice in YHWH" (Is. 61:10). A person is happy because he brings joy to the blessed Holy One by his deeds.[20] This is the meaning of "I rejoice." I am happy and rejoice because I bring joy to the blessed Creator. . . . My master and teacher, the holy lamp Dov Berish, of blessed memory, said something in the same style on this verse: I rejoice in the fact that I find joy in the commandments of the blessed Creator. *But we say*, I rejoice because I cause joy for the blessed Creator.[21]

There is a subtle but important distinction here, explaining this daring and rare "but we say" following his master's teaching. The Maggid's reading of the verse allows for the legitimacy of personal pleasure in performing the commandments. I rejoice in the fact that I find pleasure in serving God rather than in less worthy matters. That leaves the door open for a great deal of popular Hasidic piety, with its great emphasis on *hiddur mitsvah*, beautifying and rejoicing in the way the *mitsvot* are carried out. Levi Yitsḥak's standard is higher. I may take pleasure not in the fact that I am so blessed as to be doing God's will rather than pursuing my own interests. The only pleasure permitted is my rejoicing in the fact that I am *bringing pleasure to God.* He repeats this sentiment quite strongly in the following interpretation of the priestly blessing as recited in the synagogue service. Even here, where the point is that Israel be blessed, he is insistent:

> A person who stands up to pray before his Creator, whether *shemoneh ʿesrey* or some other supplication, *has to pray only so that the blessed Creator get pleasure from it* . . . [*In Torah study as well,*] *the human deed should take place only so that God get pleasure.* We know that when a person prays for himself, wanting to receive something, the back of his hand is down and his open palm is facing upward. But when a person prays in order to influence, bringing the flow to the Creator, as it were, the back of that influencer's hand is upward and his palm is turned down. In the priestly blessing, the priests lift their hands so that the back of the hand is parallel to their faces, like one poised to give . . . *they should be blessing Israel so that God derive pleasure.* You will be influencing the Creator, and afterwards He will send blessing and goodness to Israel for your sake.[22]

It is no great stretch to understand that this comment refers to the *tsaddik*'s blessings, not just those of the priest. Great power to bless lies in the *tsaddik*'s hands, like those of the priest, but only if he cares about nothing other than giving pleasure to God.

The human role in providing pleasure to God is spoken of quite blatantly and without embarrassment. Who, in the divine-human love relationship, is providing pleasure for the other? Does the role of *mashpiʿa,* source of the influx, not make one the provider of pleasure, hence the "male" in the relationship? Is it possible to imagine a relationship with God in which we humans are "male," the givers of pleasure, and God is receptive and "female?" Interestingly, this is the case in a number of these homilies. The Maggid startlingly read a well-known Hallel verse (Ps. 118:23), *me'et YHWH haytah zot,* to mean, "YHWH has turned into a female; that is wondrous in our sight!"[23] In the text attributed to the Maggid, this claim is quickly muted, tied back into the parabolic language of parent and child. But Levi Yitsḥak quotes it much more boldly:

> As I heard from my teacher and master Rabbi Dov Baer of Mezritch: "This was from YHWH; it is wondrous in our eyes" (Ps. 118:23). The word *zot* indicates the female, as is known.[24] As we said earlier, the essence of worship is causing pleasure [*taʿanug*] that reaches the blessed Creator. Then the Creator is called a receiver. This is the meaning of our verse: The blessed Holy One enters the category of the female, as a *zot*. . . . That is indeed a great wonder in our eyes.[25]

Levi Yitsḥak applies this reasoning particularly to the act of Torah study, probably having in mind the creation or bringing to birth *ḥiddushey Torah*, novel interpretations, which is essential to the early Hasidic understanding of the commandment to study Torah, underlying all the texts we are reading. Note again the bold erotic language all directed to the question of giving and receiving pleasure:

> "A concubine stands at your right side, with a diadem of fine gold" (Ps. 45:10). The Midrash applies this verse to Torah, saying, "If Torah is beloved by Israel, they will merit Torah that is like a diadem of fine gold." This Midrash demands explanation. Why should Torah be likened to a concubine, to whom one turns out of sexual desire, and not to some other [or less demeaning] passion?
>
> We can explain it this way. Everything God created in the world was created male and female. This applies to the physical realm but also to the service of God. . . . This means the following. When a person loves something of this world, whether money, food, drink, or anything else, that thing causes pleasure to flow into him, making it [the source of pleasure] the "male" and the person, the one who receives that pleasure, "female." . . . All worldly pleasures work that way . . . except for sexual desire, which is different. While there may be some of that in it at first [i.e., the man being needy to receive pleasure], ultimately the husband is the male, and he is the one who is the source of the flow. It is his wife who is the female, the recipient [of his seed].
>
> *The same is true in serving the Creator*. Fear and love of God both exist in higher and lower forms. There are those who fear and love God for the

> sake of their children's lives, or to seek wealth, or to avoid being stricken. But that is not true fear or love [of God], merely a lower form. The true root of loving and fearing God is [to recognize that] God is the all-powerful Ruler, and to bring God pleasure. . . . *One who truly serves God with this higher fear and love is in a state completely like that of sexual arousal, in which the person is male, causing pleasure to flow into his Creator*. God is in the position of the female, receiving gratification and pleasure.[26]

Imagine how this passage must have sounded to both the *mitnaggedim* and the *maskilim* and how easily they might have used it to condemn or mock Hasidism! But Levi Yitsḥak and his colleagues were undeterred. They had inherited the use of such bold sexual metaphors from the Kabbalah, and they readily psychologized these, as they did with most Kabbalistic symbolism. Service for the sake of God's pleasure alone is a key theme in the *Kedushat Levi*, one to which he returns with great frequency. Even with regard to the Sabbath, where allowing for bodily delights at the Shabbat table was so widely encouraged and praised within Judaism, especially Hasidism, Levi Yitsḥak gives us a surprisingly stern warning:

> There are two aspects to observing Shabbat, those of *zakhor* and *shamor*.[27] *Zakhor* is "male"; *shamor* is "female." This means that there are people who observe the Sabbath for the sake of God's pleasure [*ta'anug hashem yitbarakh*]. By means of the Sabbath day, they attach their soul to a bond above. They are thus able to serve His blessed name with expanded mind, to bring about a flow through all the upper worlds. This is *zakhor*.[28] There are also those who serve for their own good . . . but this is not the proper way, intending to do our God's *mitsvah* for one's own benefit, for the reward that comes about from it, even if that is a spiritual reward. This is remaining "female" [= *shamor*], seeking to receive from God. The essence of human service should be to bring about that flow by means of your deeds, as Scripture says (Ps. 68:35): "Give power to God."[29]

This is a very austere vision of Shabbat, much more so than is found in many a Hasidic source. The Ba'al Shem Tov famously taught that the physical pleasures of Shabbat were indeed ordained by God so that the body would rejoice along with the soul, thus not holding it back.[30] Levi Yitsḥak, at least in this passage, seems to want a Shabbat of soul alone. Note also that the identification of "pleasure" and "power" is here made particularly clear. But the main point is that worship must be utterly selfless and the self-conscious enjoyment of spiritual pursuit is, at the very least, a dangerous distraction. In order to be *zokher shabbat*, to give to God as a male gives, you need to be entirely beyond seeking your own pleasure.

The pursuit of pleasure in fulfilling God's command was the reason why Aaron's sons Nadav and Avihu were consumed by fire at the dedication of the tabernacle. The Midrash says that they entered the sanctuary "drunk on wine." Levi Yitsḥak was incapable of taking this literally, given the sanctity of the moment and of Aaron's family. Instead, he suggests, they were "drunk" on the spiritual pleasure of this elevated moment.[31] The only pleasure one may take in worship is that which one feels as a result of giving pleasure to God.

> King Solomon said, "A wise son makes his father rejoice" (Prov. 10:1). We are called sons of the Ever-present. When the *tsaddik* serves, God, as it were, derives pleasure from it. By way of parable, a father has a son and that son lacks for nothing. His home is filled with the possessions of the wealthy. The father takes pleasure in the fact that the son's life is going just as his heart desires. But the son, to whom God has given all that good and blessing, *takes pleasure only in the fact that his father takes pleasure in him. This* [*alone*] *is his joy and pleasure*. The *tsaddik*, serving God with a whole heart, takes no pleasure in the fact that he serves God, or in the fact that he is in line to receive much good in the future. He exults and delights only in the fact that God takes pleasure in his service.[32]

The only letup in Levi Yitsḥak's potentially dour demand that we think of God alone comes from God's side. Here we see the affectionate Father God whom Levi Yitsḥak, like the Maggid before him, knows so well. You may serve God for the sake of reward if you are thinking about how much pleasure it will give God to reward you! Two sons proudly wear new suits of clothes that their father has given them. The younger son, here representing *katnut*, the lesser state of mind, walks about in the suit because he takes pride in wearing it. But the mature son, with the mind of *gadlut*, wears the suit because he knows it gives his father pride to see him in it.[33] That sort of pleasure is permitted. You may enjoy the fruits of this world but only to please God, who gets parental *nakhes* ("pleasure") in seeing you enjoy them.

Indeed, there are many sources in which the passionate love between God and the *ḥasid* is described as the passion to be found in the parent-child relationship rather than in images of courtship and romance between men and women. A contemporary of Levi Yitsḥak's, R. Ḥayyim of Chernovtsy, writes, "[Sometimes] even the fulfillment of Torah is irrelevant, because the passion is so great. This is like a father and his much-beloved son who have not seen each other for many years. When they see one another face to face, they embrace and kiss one another with a love that is as strong as death, their souls going out to one another. All their senses cease to exist, as in the moment of death. This is the love that the children of Israel should have for their Creator . . . since they are a part of him."[34] For the Hasidic preacher, it is Jeremiah's "Ephraim is my beloved son, child of delight; whenever I speak of him, my loins long for him" (Jer. 31:19) rather than the Song of Songs' "My beloved is mine and I am his" (Song of Songs 2:16) that takes center stage. That passionate intensity of the parent-child relationship sometimes serves to mask, or even replace, the erotic language of Kabbalah.

There are various possible reasons for this shift and the great emphasis on father/son parables in the Hasidic corpus, as we have seen so much exemplified by Levi Yitsḥak. Despite the boldness we have seen in a few passages above, it may be that certain fear about erotic language still accompanied the popularizing of mysticism. The Hasidic authors, themselves mostly of the educated elites, did not fully trust their hearers to protect their message from vulgarization. This reticence may have increased due to the recent negative example of Frankism and the fierce reaction to it, a point raised regularly in the bans and denunciations against Hasidism. But it may also be that in a society of very young arranged marriages, followed by multiple births and child-rearing experiences, the experience of loving parenthood was both better known and more legitimate than to speak of God as bridegroom in an act of love with *shekhinah* as His beautiful bride. The Castilian *romancero* background of the Zohar's bridal spirituality that survived so well in the postexilic Sephardic culture of the Near East did not seem to thrive as comfortably in Eastern Europe, where ascetic views of sexuality were the order of the day among religious elites, both Jewish and Christian. Here the young Levi Yitsḥak, quoting and explaining the Maggid, speaks quite clearly about the issues of giving both power and pleasure to God:[35]

> As our master and teacher, the late *ḥasid* and man of God Berish said regarding the Zohar's statement that "Israel sustain their Father in heaven": It is His will to cause His goodness to flow upon us. This flow is

> impossible unless we arouse it from earth, down below. It is aroused by the power of Torah, prayer, and good deeds. Through these, we cause the emptying out [of the channels] and draw this holy flow upon us. Our receiving this flow gives Him pleasure and delight [*ta'anug ve-naḥat ruaḥ*]. Thus He receives pleasure and gratification [*ta'anug ve-sha'ashu'a*] from us, the holy people, as in "More than the calf wants to suckle, [the cow wants to nurse]." This is that "sustenance," as explained in his writings at length.[36]

Note how utterly desexualized the language of arousal, flow, and gratification have become here. The fluid of life that is stimulated by our arousal, so clearly the semen of the divine male throughout the Zoharic tradition, is now the "safer" and more *heimishe* fluid of mother's milk. The child, by demonstrating wisdom or righteous living, brings about this flow of blessing, giving pleasure to the parent as well, who longs to give.[37] Both of these transmissions are sometimes described as "lifegiving"; the pleasure derived from the child is *meḥayyeh* to the divine Parent, and the gift received in response is one of *ḥiyyut*, the energy that constitutes the core of life.[38]

Both the Maggid and Levi Yitsḥak's teachings overflow with this sort of talk. It is not just the royal father and the exiled son but simply the loving householder father teaching his child to walk or to read whom we encounter on page after page of their teachings. Their descriptions become particularly poignant when talking about the divine Parent's need for the child and the pleasure that he (the child is always assumed to be male) alone can provide. The Talmudic dictum that we have just seen Levi Yitsḥak quote, "the cow wants to nurse more than the calf wants to suckle" (Pes. 112a) is marshalled to say that God desires to give at a more intense and constant pace than we humans have the ability to absorb and therefore becomes the needy or "poor" partner in this relationship. We, by receiving His (Her?—since God is the milk-giving cow!) blessing thus become givers of life to God.[39]

In this context, Levi Yitsḥak offers a remarkable rereading of a saying of the Ba'al Shem Tov, "Constant pleasure is no pleasure." Rather than referring to *human* pleasure in divine service, as seems to be its obvious meaning, widely quoted as such in other Hasidic sources, he applies it to God's own quest for pleasure. Sometimes God chooses to push a worshipper away, he suggests, because He will get greater pleasure out of watching the effort that person makes to get back to Him, "breaking through barriers to become attached to God."[40] Sometimes this loving parent is almost willing to fool himself in the pleasure to be received from the child. Levi Yitsḥak quotes the following from the Maggid:

> A father is testing his son, asking him some difficult question. When the son doesn't quite get it on his own, his father helps him to understand it. [The father] then takes pleasure [in the son's accomplishment], even though he hadn't attained it by his own mental powers, and he himself had helped him. Still, he enjoys the fact that his son came to understand it.
>
> So it is with YHWH. He is our Father. Even though everything we do is with His help, without which we could do nothing . . . He wants it to be called ours, something we have done—in order to draw forth His flow of goodness.[41]

There is a subtle bit of parent-child psychology here. The loving parent wants to reward the child, so much so that He sets up a situation where the child seems to "earn" that reward. But here too there is no utter consistency. This act of parental generosity cannot go unchecked. The loving parent will go a long way to please a beloved child, arranging things according to his desire. But when the parent's role doubles as that of teacher, there cannot always be coddling. The time comes when the child must be challenged to raise his mind to the level of the parent.

> I am YHWH your God (Ex. 20:2). RaSHI here quotes a Midrash that says, "At the sea He appeared to them as a youth; when giving the Torah He appeared as an elder." This can be understood by a parable.
>
> There is a father who loves his son. Whatever the father does, the son says, "Do it this way for me." Because he loves the child so much, he does as requested. This means that out of love he makes himself somehow like the son, as the son desires him to be. But if he is teaching him some intellectual matter, he has to do it in accord with his own mind, so that the son will [come to] understand. He should not do [i.e., simplify] as the son desires.
>
> So it is with our blessed Creator, who created everything, including the sea. But Israel said that they wanted the sea to turn into dry land. The

> Creator, blessed be He and His name, had to show Himself in a son-like manner, doing as His son desired. This is what they meant by saying that "He appeared as a youth," in that son-like state [i.e., acting like a child].[42] But at Mount Sinai, where Israel stood to receive the Torah, the Creator had to give them Torah as He wanted. That was the "elder"; he appeared as an elder sitting and teaching.[43]

It is not hard here to picture the rabbi of Zhelichow or Pinsk and his son, the parent leaning over into child's play with him, allowing him a world that accorded with his own fantasy or dreams until it came time for the father to act as teacher. Then the rules changed, and seriousness or maturity of mind was a demand not to be compromised.

While this insistence on utter selflessness in the religious act, offering pleasure to God alone, may seem unsurprising in a Jewish devotional work, Levi Yitsḥak's repeated insistence on this theme leads one to suspect that this must have been a live question in the minds of those he was addressing. It has to be read within the context of a widespread discussion of the valuing of pleasure, particularly spiritual pleasure, in the teachings of early Hasidism.

The legacy of the Ba'al Shem Tov gave strong legitimacy to enjoying the delights and pleasures of the spiritual life. Here are the words of R. Ya'akov Yosef, the reformed ascetic: "The quality of *yesod* is that of having pleasure [*ta'anug*] in the service of YHWH, greater than all other pleasures. 'From my flesh I see God' (Job 19:26): In the sex organ lies the choicest of pleasures, the oneness that unites male and female. And from the physical, one can understand the spiritual pleasure, that of attaching oneself to God's blessed oneness, the root of all pleasures."[44]

This sense that God is the source of all pleasure and that attachment to God is therefore the greatest of all pleasures, *ta'anug kol ha-ta'anugim*, is widespread in early Hasidic writings. The pleasure of uniting with God is *analogous to but greater than* that of physical union, as the BeSHT had also taught in his letter to R. Gershon. The more usual reading of "Constant pleasure is no pleasure" is that the ebb and flow of our own enthusiasm for worship takes place so that we will experience fresh pleasure as we return to it, "so that there will be pleasure, which is essential to the service of YHWH."[45] The passage referred to above concerning the "living limb" says clearly that there can be no proper service of God without the arousal of pleasure and desire. To say that this pleasure is *analogous to* sexual love is not to say that it involves sexual stimulation itself. But in the psychology of the individual the distinction remains a subtle one and sorting them out is by no means easy.

Within the Maggid's circle, the BeSHT's most loyal follower in this sort of language was R. Menaḥem Naḥum of Chernobyl (1729/30–1797), author of *Me'or 'Eynayim*. By the time Levi Yitsḥak arrived in Berdychiv in 1785, R. Menaḥem Naḥum was making quite a name for himself as a Hasidic master in a district to his north, midway between Pinsk and Berdychiv. When the *Me'or 'Eynayim* appeared in print, in the same year and place as the original *Kedushat Levi*, the rabbi of Berdychiv offered it an exceptionally warm and generous letter of approbation.[46] But a careful reading of these two works shows a good deal of difference in their approaches. It may well be that Levi Yitsḥak had a chance in the eleven years he lived after that 1798 publication, to read it more closely and felt a need to express dismay at some of the things he saw there.

In order to fully unpack the divergence between them, an important fault line within early Hasidic teaching, we have to get to the second of our two related issues, that of serving God by means of corporeal things, referred to by modern scholars as *'avodah be-gashmiyyut*.[47] Among those who created the Hasidic movement, some saw in the BeSHT's teachings a sharp rejection of the radical anti-materialism that was the regnant view of most contemporary preachers. Instead, they viewed the material world and the possibility of pleasure in it as potential avenues toward the service of God. The notion that sparks of divinity could be found within physical things and that engagement with the physical world was a way of releasing those sparks to return to their Source itself implied a degree of embrace of the corporeal world and a certain legitimation of taking pleasure in it.[48] There is ongoing debate about how fully the embrace of corporeality was meant, but there certainly are sources that speak in that tone.

The Chernobyler took a strong and relatively consistent position with regard to serving God through the material world, equalizing "our Torah-study and prayer, our eating and drinking" as avenues of religious devotion.[49] This did not refer to stringencies regarding laws of *kashrut*, as some latter-day *ḥasidim* might choose to read it, but was a way of saying that all of life, including the most ordinary human acts, was to be treated as an avenue of devotion, equal to, and sometimes even posed as superior to, study and prayer.

Strictly speaking, rabbinic tradition prescribes that God is served by *torah u-mitsvot*, study and observance of the specific commandments. This leaves a vast realm of the anomian, a realm not governed by tradition. To be sure, moral treatises (*sifrey mussar*) composed over many generations discussed how to conduct all of daily life in holiness and very much shaped normative behavior. Hasidism went further, however, in declaring that *everything* one did or encountered in life was to become part of the sacred path. The scripture most often quoted to defend this view was Proverbs 3:6: "Know Him in all your ways."

It was not only eating and drinking that the preacher of Chernobyl had in mind in seeking out holiness in the physical realm. The *Me'or 'Eynayim* quotes six times a teaching of the BeSHT regarding a Torah verse that reads, "If a man take his sister and reveal her nakedness, that is *ḥesed*" (Lev. 20:17). Biblical scholars called that use of *ḥesed* a contronym, a word meaning its opposite, and it is usually translated "disgrace." The BeSHT insisted that *ḥesed* here should be taken at face value, meaning that even in this forbidden love, there is a trace of fallen divine love, capable of being uplifted. This teaching is found only in a single brief reference in the voluminous writings of R. Ya'akov Yosef,[50] and the fact that the Chernobyler quotes it repeatedly is significant.

Note the utterly different spirit in Levi Yitsḥak's comment on a similar Leviticus verse regarding sexual taboos:

> "No man shall approach his close relative to reveal her nakedness [i.e., for sexual purposes]; I am YHWH" (Lev. 18:6). Let us explain this. Well-known is the statement of King David,[51] of blessed memory, *"Know Him in all your ways" (Prov. 3:6). This means that your intent in all your preoccupations and deeds should be toward bringing pleasure to our blessed Creator. One should marry a woman not out of desire, but only because YHWH has commanded us to take a wife. We should think of this always, not approaching her, God forbid, for the sake of pleasure.* One should approach her only because of the blessed Creator's command. This is the meaning of "No man shall approach his close relative"—*this refers to his own wife, who is a close relation.* Do not approach her only "to reveal her nakedness"—but rather because of the command of God.[52]

Again, we see that sexuality, and the dangers involved in the pursuit of sexual pleasure, even within marriage, is a matter of concern to Levi Yitsḥak. The "close relative" here is one's own wife! He has taken a biblical text originally referring to the prohibition of incest and completely changed its meaning, finding a much greater stricture in it, while the BeSHT and the Chernobyler had taken a parallel verse and reread it in the opposite direction. Here Levi Yitsḥak seems to be urging his hearer to strive for what we saw above is the impossible: marital relations for the sake of the *mitsvah* alone. In the course of doing this, he has made sure to include his own interpretation of "Know Him in all your ways." For Levi Yitsḥak, the meaning is very different, almost opposite: God can and should be served through everything one does, but the point is to do so *for the sake of His pleasure alone.*

In order to get a sense of the radicalism of R. Menaḥem Naḥum's stance regarding enjoyment of the material world, we need to quote at some length a teaching of his regarding the biblical Nazirite, who takes a vow to abstain from intoxicating drink for a set period of time. When that period is over, he must bring a sin offering to the Temple. Here is R. Menaḥem Naḥum's comment on that passage:

> "Moses spoke to the heads of the Israelite tribes, saying . . . 'If a person utters a vow . . . forbidding a certain matter to himself, his word may not be profaned; he shall do all that he has said'" [Num. 30:2–3].
>
> We must first consider our sages' teaching regarding the Nazirite. On the verse "[The priest] will offer him atonement for his sin against the soul" [Num. 6:11], they asked, "Against what soul has [the Nazirite] sinned?" They replied: "His sin is that of distressing himself by abstaining from wine."
>
> To understand this matter: *The world and everything within it, both great and small, was created by the word of God.* "By the word of the Lord the heavens were made, by the breath of His mouth, all their host" [Ps. 33:6]. That word also sustains them and gives them life. "You keep them all alive" [Neh. 9:6]. Were it not for the life force within each thing, it would vanish from existence. But [external] things are in a broken state in this lowly world, having come about through the sin of Adam and the generations that followed. Sparks of fallen souls became encased in things of this world, including food, drink, and all other worldly things. There is

nothing in this world that does not have a holy spark within it, proceeding from the word of the blessed Holy One, making it alive.

That divine spark is the taste within the thing, that which is sweet to the palate. "Taste and see that YHWH is good" [Ps. 34:9]. *This means that when you taste or see something good, it is YHWH, the holy spark garbed within that thing.*[53] Our eyes see that after a person partakes of food, the sustenance remains within, while the waste, which does not give life, is expelled. That is something worthless and negative, since the main purpose of food is that the person be sustained and given strength. *The good taste one enjoys in that food or drink is a spark of the Divine.* Therefore, when you eat something, the spark within it is joined to your own life-energy, and you become strengthened by it.

When you have whole and complete faith that this spiritual sustenance is indeed God's presence hidden within that thing, you will turn your mind and heart entirely inward. Linking both of those aspects of yourself [i.e. the physical and the spiritual] to the sustenance coming from that spark, you will join them all to the Root of all, that One from whom all life flows. Then you will bring that broken, exiled spark before God, causing great delight. The whole purpose of our religious life is to bring those holy sparks out from under the "shells," those broken places, into the realm of the holy. Thus is holiness raised from its broken state. . . .

Therefore, anyone who distresses and punishes himself by refraining from taking pleasure in this world is called a sinner, following the Talmudic opinion that one who engages in fasting is called a sinner. [*Eating,*] *too, is serving the Lord, like Torah, prayer,* tefillin [*phylacteries*], *and all the commandments!* The blessed Holy One created and conducts the world through Torah, meaning that there is Torah in everything. *Every believer must have faith that there is nothing that stands outside God's service, so long as it is in accord with Torah, that which Torah permits us to eat and drink.* He must just make sure to do these for the sake of their Maker, not for his own pleasure. In this way, they are all considered perfect devotion. That is why [the one who refrains from them] is called a sinner; he has prevented the rising up of the holy sparks dressed in that particular food from which he has abstained.[54]

Levi Yitsḥak will have none of it. Despite this last line, Menaḥem Naḥum is clearly finding God in enjoying the pleasures of this world. It is sinful to avoid or deny such pleasures; that is why the *nazir* must bring an offering to atone! Serving God through enjoying the pleasures of this world is of no interest to Levi Yitsḥak. The only *ta'anug* that is legitimate within a life dedicated to God's service is God's pleasure, not our own. We humans, and we Israelites in particular, exist for the sake of giving pleasure to God. Anything else is at very least a distraction, and maybe worse.

In subtle but significant contrast to Menaḥem Naḥum, we have seen that he suggests God has given us commandments that involve physical pleasure—such as conjugal relations and Sabbath eating—so that we will learn to *break down* any desires we might have in doing them. But the sharpest articulation of Levi Yitsḥak's disagreement with the path of his colleague in Chernobyl is to be seen in the following bold passage in *Kedushat Levi* regarding the sin of Eve, one that should be seen as standing in direct opposition to the views we have just seen expressed by Menaḥem Naḥum, perhaps even as an outright polemic against him and those of his ilk.

> He [the serpent] said to the woman, "Even though God said not to eat of it . . . lest you die." The serpent said, "You shall not die" (Gen. 3:1–4.). . . . One needs to understand the trick by which the snake seduced the woman to violate the command of God. The snake's argument went this way: Were not "the heavens made by the word of God" (Ps. 33:6)? It is known that all the world and every creature were created by the word and speech-act of God, as in the "ten utterances," including "Let there be light!" Their life force and their very existence are derived from the light and life-energy that come from the [ongoing] divine utterance and speech-act. He is the Source, the Life of life, and His words are living and vital. In that case, how is it possible that the Tree of Knowledge, which was also created by divine utterance, could be harmful or deadly? Was not it too created by the Source and Root, the Life of life?
>
> "Therefore," said the serpent, "even though God said, 'You shall not eat,' how is that relevant? . . . Who says that you should listen to that divine utterance? Why shouldn't you listen instead to His first utterance, the word by which it was created?"[55]

The serpent is expressing precisely the view of the *Me'or 'Eynayim*, just going one crucial step farther! Since everything was created by God, holiness can surely be found in it. Never mind the specific divine commandments. Rather see godliness everywhere! Here it is the serpent who quotes the same verse in Psalm 33:6 that Menaḥem Naḥum used in condemning the Nazirite for not taking pleasure in this God-created world. Beware, says Levi Yitsḥak, of "the devil quoting Scripture!"

This goes along with the very different ways in which the Chernobyler and the Berdychiver *tsaddikim* use the verse "Know Him in all your ways." For Levi Yitsḥak, it is a warning. Even if you have to engage in a base physical activity like sex, be sure to be doing it only because of God's command. The verse does not offer license to "broaden the bounds of the holy," a favorite phrase of the Chernobyler, worshipping God through all the things of this world. Whatever you do in this world, reads Levi Yitsḥak, make sure to seek no pleasure in it, but do it only out of loyalty to the divine command. The Maggid's ascetic worldview is here alive and well in his disciple. The *Me'or 'Eynayim* would say—and does in several places—that God gave us bodily desires to arouse feelings of love in us so that we then might use that same love to worship God, that we should use the desires aroused by such activities as fuel to energize our religious lives.[56] It is likely that Levi Yitsḥak felt there was a danger in such a welcoming embrace of worldly pleasure.

If there remains any doubt about Levi Yitsḥak's rather dim view of the great emphasis placed by others on the high value of serving God through corporeal things, he expresses it quite unequivocally in his opening comment on the Song of Songs: "It is correct that true *tsaddikim* can serve their Creator through eating, drinking, and sleeping—but this is not complete service. Only by attaching all three rungs of our souls to His blessed Self in prayer, song, and praises [does one serve completely]. Its name [*tefillah*] proves this, as it is derived from a word meaning "attachment," as is known. . . . This is complete service, which is not the case with eating, drinking, or sleeping."[57]

In the *Me'or 'Eynayim* and elsewhere, one can find statements precisely to the contrary: the highest form of service is that of *'avodah be-gashmiyyut* since only that involves the essential work of uplifting and transforming the material world, the essential task for which humans (chiefly meaning Israel) were created.

We are faced here with the complex question of Levi Yitsḥak's attitude toward this world and those who live within it. We recall God's voice telling him not to seek to go too high, that his task as a *tsaddik* was to bring blessing down to others, not to seek the lone piety of detachment at the top of the mountain. Yet when it comes to the *pleasures* of this lower world, the ascetic voice within him is the one that seems to speak most loudly. We can best depict what I believe must be seen as an inner conflict by going back to a teaching we looked at earlier but now viewing it as preserved in two opposing versions. The setting is the Torah's description of Moses' encounter with the Burning Bush and God's instruction to him. "Moses turned aside to see," we are told. There God said to him (Ex. 3:5), "Take your shoes off your feet." In *Kedushat Levi*,[58] we read that Moses' attention was turned entirely upward, "not paying attention at all to the uplifting of this lower world." God told him to remove his *na'al*, which can mean "lock" as well as "shoe." "You are too locked away in the upper worlds," is the message. "The ground you are standing upon is also holy," waiting to be uplifted. Unlock yourself, as it were, and discover that "the place where you are standing is holy ground." This message indeed sounds closer to the view of the *Me'or 'Eynayim*. But R. Binyamin of Zalozhtsy, another member of the Maggid's circle, quotes this same remark in Levi Yitsḥak's name but bearing an entirely different message. It was Moses who wanted "to turn aside" from his constant attachment to God in order to look at the bush. "Remove your shoes," God tells him, meaning that he should stop paying attention to such corporeal things![59]

Which of these is the real Levi Yitsḥak? we might ask, and which the distortion of a hearer or recorder? Is there a way of explaining how both of these might preserve authentic memory of Levi Yitsḥak speaking? Haven't we seen him as the forgiving, accepting *tsaddik*, ever seeking God's pardon for the sins of Israel, apparently also ready himself to accept their foibles? How can he also be so very demanding in his views on the nature of divine service, turning away from any physical pleasure or enjoyment of this world? How can he hope to build a popular movement if he is so austere, demanding the absolute negation of pleasure?

Perhaps here we have to go back to the question of audience.[60] As we have noted, the editing of *Kedushat Levi* does not offer us any distinction between sermons he offered in the synagogue and teachings he shared only with his innermost circle. But that gap is surely there. Levi Yitsḥak wants to maintain the very highest standards for his circle of disciples, those whom he saw, and who saw themselves, as potential *tsaddikim* in training.[61] For them, some of the Maggid's ascetic strain was definitely thought to be appropriate, and their master demanded it of them. They had to learn to "remove their shoes," to stop paying any attention to the corporeal world, including the rewards of success and popularity, always striving to rise higher and to uplift the world along with them. Otherwise, Hasidism would be corrupted, becoming too easy a path. He fears an "eat, drink, and be merry!" message that might emerge from popular Hasidism and that would be as far as imaginable from the Maggid's message. He must keep his disciples distant from such a path. On the other hand, they had to remember that it was *this* world, including that of ordinary Jews, that they were there to uplift. If they disdained that, they would accomplish nothing. That is never an easy balance to strike, as spiritual teachers around the world will attest.

For the broader community, Levi Yitsḥak did indeed show a face of Hasidism that was loving, kind, and forgiving. He understood the weaknesses of ordinary people and portrayed a God who was as forgiving as he was. But when it came to the training of *tsaddikim*, he was utterly demanding. In this regard, he is very like his friend R. Elimelekh, whose book *No'am Elimelekh* is mostly a manual for the training of future *tsaddikim*.[62] There, too, the ascetic side of the Maggid's legacy is in full view, and the demands are quite severe.

What we see in these rather ascetic and demanding readings of the tradition is Levi Yitsḥak addressing the increasingly crowded field of would-be *tsaddikim*, who were sprouting like mushrooms in the last two decades of the eighteenth century. With the rapid success of Hasidism, *tsaddik* or *guter yid* was fast becoming a professional designation, replacing the *ba'al shem* of decades earlier. There existed nothing like formal training courses or accepted standards in this role; there was no "ordination" of *tsaddikim*. Levi Yitsḥak represents the Hasidic *tsaddik* in its elitist manifestation. He is the disciple of a well-known master, has extensive rabbinic learning, and stays away from tricks and miracles. In these matters, he is probably closest to R. Shne'ur Zalman of Liadi within the Mezritch circle. He is trying to maintain those high standards as the movement grows. If you want to be my disciple or a *tsaddik* of my sort, he is saying in these passages, rejection of worldly pleasures is part of what it takes.

11

DEFENDING THE COMMANDMENTS

Hasidism is a form of classical Jewish pietism. While the movement was born on the cusp of the modern era in Jewish history, its creators were entirely rooted in the medieval and postmedieval consensus of Jewish self-definition. The Jews are God's chosen people, to whom He gave the Torah. The authority of divine authorship and command stands behind it. Scripture is literally true while at the same time subject to endless reinterpretation. The juxtaposition of various biblical verses and snippets of rabbinic dialogue, even taken entirely out of context, may be used to prove a point. The sages, meaning the rabbis of the Talmudic era and their successors, established how divine law is to be carried out in practice, leading to the great legal codes that came to be seen as authoritative. Formally speaking, one was never to diverge from them, although in reality much discretion was left in the hands of each generation's legal decisors.[1] *Aggadah*, the storehouse of rabbinic wisdom and narrative, is a source of truth, alongside the normative *halakhah*. Prior generations of mystical scholars, including the Zohar and the Lurianic writings,[2] have explained the inner meaning of all these truths, sometimes shaping praxis as well, and their words are to be revered, though sometimes read selectively.

All this seems as though it might leave rather little room for ongoing religious creativity. But nothing could be farther from the truth. The early generations of Hasidism may be said to represent a renaissance of the Midrashic art.[3] New and often daring readings are offered to biblical and rabbinic sources, presented in such a way as to shock the original hearer of the oral sermon or the reader of the page in a Hasidic book. The Ba'al Shem Tov himself seems to have been a master of this, and it was successfully conveyed through several generations.[4]

This creative reading of verses, narratives, and even legal formulae (while barely changing the law in practice!) was a tool of "shock therapy" for awakening the hearts and minds of the preacher's audience but also served as a vehicle for the internalization or spiritualization of Judaism, the major goal of early Hasidic teaching.[5] All of the Torah, from the patriarchal narratives through the enslavement of Israel and their liberation from Egyptian bondage, to Sinai, the tabernacle, and the wanderings through the wilderness, are there to teach the *ḥasid* about his own spiritual journey, to make him aware of the reality and sacred character of his own inner life. Hasidic literature is a repository of tremendously varied and original interpretations of traditional sources, often leading in quite radical directions. Levi Yitsḥak's writings, as we have seen and will see still further, are a font of such interpretations.

There are thus two sides present in Levi Yitsḥak's attitude toward tradition, values which he surely did not perceive as contradicting one another. As rabbi of major communities throughout his career, he was a figure of authority for Jewish practice. The *rav*, as head of the local rabbinic court, was to see that the discipline of *halakhah* was carefully followed within the area of his jurisdiction, and we have every sense that Levi Yitsḥak was quite fully committed to this task. At least in Berdychiv, and probably in Pinsk as well, he conducted a *yeshivah*, as we have seen, where students came to him to study Talmud and the codes of Jewish praxis.[6] As we shall presently see, within the circle of Mezritch there was a strong tendency toward an emphasis on *kavvanah*, or inwardness, as the most important element within both Torah study and fulfillment of the *mitsvot*. Love and awe were seen as the "wings" that would make one's learning or praxis fly heavenward;[7] without these, they were something of a "dead letter." There are occasional sources that portray the necessity for *kavvanah,* or a reaching inward toward the secret Torah, over against excessive concern over details of practice.[8] On this matter, Levi Yitsḥak was a conservative voice, pulling back against any such potentially contranomian tendencies. On the other hand, when it came to speculation around the nature of Torah's ultimate truth, what it looked like in times before Sinai or what it might look like after the arrival of messiah ("speedily, in our day. Amen!"), he stands in the front row of the radical thinkers—or dreamers—within the movement. The same is true of some of his views regarding the *tsaddik*'s ability, even obligation, to reinterpret Torah for each generation, even within the period of the Law's authority.

He seems to have accomplished this remarkable pairing by drawing a significant line between Torah and *mitsvot*, the two essential components of Jewish religious living. The *mitsvot*, as embodiments of the divine will, are to be followed in their entirety, as outlined by the Talmudic and post-Talmudic sages. The original meaning of *mitsvah* is "commandment," and that was not to be forgotten. True, Hasidism had inherited from the earlier mystical tradition two alternative readings of the term, both of which are found widely quoted in Hasidic works, including in Levi Yitsḥak's sermons. One (presently to be quoted) sees the word *mitsvah* as secretly embodying the name of God; to perform the *mitsvot* is thus to engage with divinity.[9] The other derives the word *mitsvah* from an Aramaic root that means "together"; performing the *mitsvah* is a way of joining oneself together with God, an occasion for spiritual intimacy.[10] Both of these were offered as ways of deepening and internalizing the experience of religious practice, but neither was thought of as displacing the unswerving commitment to fulfilling what was literally believed to be the divine command.

When it came to *Torah*, however, here meaning the fulfillment of the command to study and engage with Torah, there were rather few limitations that defined just how, or with what texts, one was to engage. Classically, at least in the Eastern European context, it meant what was called *GeFeT* (= *Gemara, Perush, Tosafot*), study of the Talmud's legal discussions and engagement with issues that arose from them. We find significant criticism in the Hasidic sources of *pilpul*, or overinterpretation of the Talmudic tradition, as a way of self-aggrandizement or grandstanding. There are some texts, coming from circles close to the BeSHT, that by way of attacking the *mitnaggedim* and their values seem to devalue Talmud study altogether.[11] There was no clear norm that enforced engagement in *nigleh*, the revealed Torah, over *nistar*, the Torah's secret meanings. Studying the Zohar or the writings of other Kabbalists was a form of engagement with Torah, one that had become highly respectable after the sixteenth-century Kabbalistic revival and was prized within the circles out of which Hasidism emerged. So was the sort of careful and creative reading of Torah texts themselves, leading to the highly original comments the Hasidic master was expected to offer on each week's reading.[12] Among the *ḥasidim*, much of the time and effort allotted to Torah study was devoted to these, rather than to hard-nosed Talmud study, to the consternation of the anti-Hasidic rabbinic elite.

As a rabbi, Levi Yitsḥak surely engaged regularly with the legal sources, both to deal with questions that presented themselves in his community and as teacher to students in his *yeshivah*. But the breadth of the notion of *talmud torah* also gave him the opportunity to engage freely and often radically in spiritualized readings of the texts, as we shall see, without violating any norms. From the subject matter of his published works, it seems quite clear that this was his major interest.[13]

As mentioned above, contemporary scholarship around the inner life of Hasidism in its earliest generations is much indebted to the insights of the late Rivka Schatz-Uffenheimer in her book *Hasidism as Mysticism*.[14] Although her comparison of Hasidic teachings with those of Christian Quietists of the seventeenth century has been criticized in more recent scholarly discussions,[15] her formulations remain the basis of much of the current conversation. Schatz opens her chapter "The Status of the *Mitsvot*" by noting that the Hasidic authors broke ranks with many generations of prior Kabbalistic authorities in not offering mystical rationales for individual ritual commandments. Instead, she claimed, their emphasis was on the twin pillars of contemplative prayer and the notion of serving God through ordinary human deeds, *'avodah be-gashmiyyut*. The latter effectively transformed all of daily life into an endless series of *mitsvot*, or opportunities for religious devotion.[16] In the face of this, she argued, the specifically prescribed *mitsvot* of the Torah, while faithfully observed, tended to fade somewhat into the background of the Hasidic spiritual agenda.

We have already noted, however, that Levi Yitsḥak stands at some distance from this notion.[17] God is served, he seems to believe, in good rabbinic fashion, primarily through Torah study and fulfillment of the commandments. Still, he too seems to devote rather little attention to mystical interpretations of individual commandments. Perhaps this task had already been undertaken by the Lurianic Kabbalists in such great detail that the Hasidic masters found no need (or little room) to innovate within it. While it is true that the complex Lurianic instructions for prayer were mostly ignored within Hasidism, the power of Shmuel Vital's *Peri 'Ets Ḥayyim*, where each detail of ritual performance was assigned a specific Kabbalistic meaning, was still very much present in early Hasidic circles. It is rather the edifice of the *mitsvot* as a whole, the enterprise of worshipping God through fulfilling His commandments—as opposed to a purely formless outpouring of love and awe—which Levi Yitsḥak seems very much at pains to defend. Here, again, we shall attempt to seek out the context of his concern.

Based on a single well-known passage in the Talmud,[18] the Kabbalists had made much of the notion that the 613 commandments of the Torah, comprised of 248 positive commands and 365 prohibitions, paralleled the number of limbs and sinews of the human body.[19] The devotional point is that "All my bones shall proclaim: YHWH, who is like You!"[20] This parallel structure of person and Torah is a commonplace of later Kabbalistic homilies and is repeated frequently in Isaiah Horowitz's *Two Tablets of the Covenant*, a work that widely influenced Hasidism. Like the Maggid, Levi Yitsḥak makes frequent reference to this idea, assuming also that each person (or Israelite) has an inner structure of spiritual "limbs" and "sinews," corresponding to those of the bodily self. Each of these cries out for the fulfillment of its own particular commandment, just as the body's limbs call out for the fulfillment of their corporeal needs.

Levi Yitsḥak even goes so far as to make the unusual claim that this structure of limbs and sinews extends beyond the parallel of person and Torah, embracing the natural world as well. In the first teaching on this matter in *Kedushat Levi* on the Torah, he says,

> God created the world through Torah. Thus, everything in the world contains the letters of Torah, and the holy sparks encased within them. The human is comprised of 248 limbs, parallel to the 248 positive *mitsvot*, and 365 sinews, parallel to the 365 prohibitions. They constitute the life force of those limbs and sinews.
>
> But earth also has 248 limbs. Thus [Scripture] speaks of the "heart" of the earth, as well as its "mouth" and "eye." They too embody the life force of the *mitsvot*. When a person performs a *mitsvah*, the whole earth is his. That is how Joshua conquered seven lands [the lands of the seven Canaanite kings]. He knew the life force of each and every city, and which *mitsvah* belonged to it. In fulfilling those, he conquered them all. . . .
>
> This is "He told His people the power of His deeds" (Ps. 111:6). . . . May God give us a pure heart to know the *mitsvah* of each thing.[21]

The biblical warrior Joshua is here seen as a sort of mystical conjuror, conquering the land by dint of his esoteric knowledge of the secrets of the *mitsvot*. Here again we see the role of power in the Kabbalistic worldview. Throughout *Kedushat Levi*, the *mitsvot* are depicted as supernatural entities, sacraments enshrouded in mystery. This secret meaning of the *mitsvot* was revealed to Moses; he understood the *sekhel*, the inner meaning of each commandment, even prior to fulfilling it. For Israel, however, only their actual performance revealed their secret truth.[22] While he says this about the generations of the wilderness and those who entered the Land, he probably intends it to refer to his hearers as well. The *tsaddik* may indeed be a Moses or a Joshua, understanding the secrets, but ordinary Jews can experience that only in the deed. In the stories told about him, Levi Yitsḥak seems to display a particular affection for the observance of particular *mitsvot*.[23] Here the Kabbalistic background of Hasidic thought is fully present, even if little discussed. In another section of the work's opening teaching, part of which we have quoted above, he speaks of the word *mitsvah* itself as a combination of the hidden and the revealed.

> *Ayin*, or Nothingness, refers to that which is beyond nature, while *yesh*, or being, is within the natural world. We link the two of them by Torah and the *mitsvot*, as Scripture says: "The life force ebbs and flows" (Ezek. 1:14). This is why the Zohar teaches that the *mitsvah* and Torah are both hidden and revealed, referring to both Nothingness and Being, constituting a link between the two. The word *mitsvah*, in its first two letters *mem* and *tsade*, refers to the divine name *yod heh*, but in a reverse alphabet. This is the Naught [the name of God in hiding] while the concluding *vav heh* of the word refers to being.
>
> Let us explain what are the hidden and revealed aspects of the *mitsvah*. The fact that we bring pleasure to blessed YHWH by performing the *mitsvah* is hidden from us, not appearing. But the good we do for ourselves is indeed apparent. This is the meaning of "The hidden things are for YHWH our God; the revealed are for us and our offspring, forever" (Deut. 29:28). "Hidden" is that aspect within the *mitsvah* that we do "for YHWH our God," since it remains hidden from us. "The revealed" is indeed for us and our offspring, as we bring about the influx [of worldly blessing] that is revealed to us.[24]

Levi Yitsḥak, as a great popularizer of Hasidic teaching, needs to underscore for his broader audience the worldly benefit of living in accord with God's commandments. Just as the *tsaddik* can bring forth blessing, so does living in accord with God's will. He follows the general Hasidic rubric of always insisting that the *mitsvot* must be performed selflessly, thinking only of the pleasure they will bring to the One who commanded them. God even does the righteous the favor of hiding from them the fact that *mitsvot* are to be rewarded, either in this world or the next, in order to enable them to live their religious lives in pure devotion.

Mother Rachel is used as a paradigm for such selfless devotion.[25] In what were probably his more popular sermons, he frequently mentions that earthly reward will, in fact, not be far behind. For his more enlightened followers, however, his teaching is clearly that the *mitsvot* are their own reward, following an ancient rubric to that effect.[26] The devotion with which you perform a *mitsvah* will bring about the only reward sought by the true devotee: the ability to perform it with still greater passion in the future:

> When a person performs a *mitsvah* with great passion and enthusiasm, he brings glory to our blessed Creator. The Creator is glorified amid all the angels on that day, [saying], "See how much that one loves the commandments and the great joy with which he does his Creator's will!" God takes so much pride in that person that He desires to cause even greater consciousness [*sekhel gadol yoter*] to flow out to His creatures than previously. The next time that person performs that commandment, he will do it with greater consciousness than before.[27]

In this context, it is especially interesting to look at one particular strategy of Levi Yitsḥak's for defending the *mitsvot*, a series of homilies in which he insists that service of God by means of the *mitsvot* is superior to what might seem like a more purely mystical form of worship, the inward devotion of the contemplative soul alone, without any form of expression in the physical realm. If YHWH is utter abstraction, after all, the *ayin* or Naught that lies behind every *yesh* or outward form of being, why not worship Him in this formless way as well?

> There are two types who worship the Creator. One worships by means of dedication [*mesirut nefesh*], the other by means of *mitsvot* and good deeds. The difference is that the one who worships the Creator through dedication [alone], without *mitsvot* or good deeds, is truly in the Naught [*ayin*]. The other, who worships through the *mitsvot*, is serving by means of actuality [*yesh*, i.e., by means of material things], since the *mitsvot* are actual. Therefore, the one who serves through the dedication of *ayin* cannot bring the influx [of blessing] upon himself because he is nothing, attached entirely to YHWH. But the one who serves by means of *mitsvot* and good deeds, since they are actual, can indeed draw divine blessing forth upon himself.[28]

He then goes on to discuss the structure of the 613 limbs and sinews. When the Talmud claims that Abraham observed all the commandments, says Levi Yitsḥak, it means that he transcended his own physical self and thus discovered all the *mitsvot,* corresponding to his spiritual limbs and sinews, within himself.[29] His journey toward God was a journey inward, identical with discovery of his own truest self. As long as he lived outside the Land of Israel, however, he could not fulfill those *mitsvot* that apply only there.[30] Thus his inner Torah could not yet be complete. Because of that lack, he chose to serve God by dedication alone. Levi Yitsḥak goes on to say,

> Therefore, outside the land, Abraham was not able to serve God through the *mitsvot*. . . . That is why we find that he acted with such dedication that he cast himself into [Nimrod's] fiery furnace, along with various other trials. All this was outside the Land. . . . Therefore, outside the Land, he was truly attached to the Naught, and he could not bring the influx [of divine blessing] upon himself. But in the Land of Israel, serving through the actuality of the *mitsvot*, he could bring about the flow from the Creator. That is why, on the verse "Get yourself forth from your land," RaSHI comments: "For your own benefit, for your own good." Go to the Land of Israel for the sake of your own good, because there you will worship through the *mitsvot*, and thus will be able to bring forth that flow.

Abraham, however, is concerned once he sees that this change has come about.

> The person who serves the Creator by means of the Naught sees God with his very eye, while the one who serves through *mitsvot* and good deeds sees YHWH [only] by means of an instrument [*aspeklaria*, literally "speculum"], since he is serving by means of actual things [in a mediated way]. This is the meaning of "After these things, the word of YHWH came to Abraham in a vision, saying" (Gen. 15:1). Now that Abraham was serving through the *mitsvot*, the word of God came to him [only] in a "vision"; he saw God through an instrument. But YHWH said to him, "Do not fear, Abram." Do not fear the fact that you are now serving through *mitsvot* rather than through [pure] dedication. "Your reward is very great"—through this service of *mitsvot*, you will be able bring forth the influx, which indeed is "very great."

Abraham realizes that he is now serving God on a *lower* level of devotion than he had previously.[31] His worship is now conducted through the "instrument" of corporeal things, subject to measure and limitation, rather than the limitless soaring of the soul! He is no longer in the Naught, no longer able to see God "with his very eye." God has to reassure him that he has not "fallen" from a higher rung of worship and does so by the promise that this type of service has its own reward. Yes, his direct experience of God will be lessened, coming only in a "vision." But earthly rewards will now become his. Since he is serving by means of *yesh*, by concrete means, he himself will exist on the level of actuality as well, and thus will be able to draw forth the flow of divine blessing. This is parallel to the two types of *tsaddikim* we met earlier. The higher type of *tsaddik* forgets that he has earthbound concerns when he enters the divine presence. It is only the "lower" *tsaddik*, like the one serving God through the earthbound *mitsvot*, that can bring blessing down to earth.

It is particularly fascinating that this treatment is placed in the context of the encounter between Abraham and Melchizedek, king and priest of Shalem (later Jerusalem), based on a reading of Genesis 14:18: "Melchizedek, king of Shalem, brought forth bread and wine; he was priest of the exalted God." Levi Yitsḥak quotes RaSHI on this verse, based on an old rabbinic debate about whether Melchizedek revealed to Abram the secret of Torah or of high priesthood.

Was Levi Yitsḥak aware that Christian priesthood, beginning in the New Testament,[32] sees itself as descended from the priesthood of Melchizedek? Surely, he was aware that the name Melchizedek is one that was and still is commonly adopted by Russian priests upon ordination.[33] In Levi Yitsḥak's day as in ours, there are many Russian priests, and especially bishops, bearing that name, one never used among Jews. Is there a subtle reference to someone in particular embedded in this teaching? Could such a figure have been seeking converts among Jews, leading to a sermonic "debate" between the two of them as representatives of their respective religions? More significantly, is he aware that classical tropes of the Christian side in the ancient polemics between the two faiths accused Judaism precisely of serving God by worldly, material means and of being insufficiently "spiritual?" If so, Levi Yitsḥak offers a very clear Kabbalistically inflected answer. Yes, we serve God by means of the *yesh*. It may indeed seem a less pure and rarified way of worship. But it highlights our attachment to the world of concrete reality and our commitment to bringing divine blessing down into it. Christianity, one might say, preserved both the "high priest" legacy of the two traditions' shared biblical heritage and what it considered to be an "Abrahamic" version of Torah, expressed in the Pauline reading of Gen. 15:6:[34] "He [Abraham] had faith in God, and He considered it justification." Justification "by faith alone" is a Christian innovation. Judaism, Levi Yitsḥak reminds his reader, insists upon "works," and only they can bring God's blessing into this world.

Such questions, of course, remain in the realm of speculation. Any such intent would have been carefully hidden, beyond our ability at retrieval. But there is an even closer question of "address" regarding this teaching and others like it. The goal of "seeing the Creator with one's very eye" must have sounded quite attractive in the context of a circle of mystics like the one from which Levi Yitsḥak emerged. The admission that there is a higher spiritual experience, one offering a more intimate encounter with God, than that of service through the *mitsvot*, is particularly intriguing here. This reflects the praxis of "gazing" that we discussed earlier, where one's inner eye became focused on God alone. Despite that reality, Levi Yitsḥak insists, this more concrete form of worship is the better one, for it alone can bring forth divine blessing. Since most hearers of Levi Yitsḥak's sermons presumably favored such an outcome, they would accept this highly original championing of life with the *mitsvot* over one devoted to a purely contemplative piety.

Who would be the Jewish targets of the need our preacher felt to speak in defense of the commandments in this way? Most likely we would turn to some of the more radically contemplative types within the Mezritch circle. Hayyim Haykel of Amdur and Abraham the "Angel," the Maggid's own son, come to mind. No one claims that actual observance of the commandments was neglected by these early leaders of Hasidism. While there are some dark hints in this direction found in the anti-Hasidic polemics of the early years, there is no evidence to support them. But the theoretical sense that access to a higher or more "ancient" form of Torah (*torah kedumah*), or a more direct experience of divinity, than that offered through the mediation of *mitsvot* might be possible—even in post-Abrahamic and pre-messianic times—might itself have been seen as sufficiently threatening to call forth such a defense. Here Levi Yitsḥak is expressing a view close to that expressed more drastically by his friend R. Shne'ur Zalman: it is the actual physical performance of the *mitsvah*, more than the *kavvanah* accompanying it, that renders it effective.[35]

This teaching, too, should be seen through the lens of Levi Yitsḥak as movement-builder. Just as we saw him, in an early teaching, encouraging others not to dwell in their private piety but to bring the message of "love, fear, and attachment" to others, here too we see him engaged in a later version of the same message, addressed to colleagues or disciples who had tasted of a profound inner spirituality. Yes, you as a mystic might find the possibility of greater closeness to God in serving through inward contemplation alone, living your own private spiritual life. But that is not your purpose. As a *tsaddik*, you are here for others, needing to bring the flow of blessing into the world and to those around you. Levi Yitsḥak understands that this is the true function of the Hasidic leaders, fulfilling the needs of the increasing number of Jews who are looking toward them, bringing them God's blessing.

The notion that Abraham observed the entire Torah before it was given seems to have had great importance for Levi Yitsḥak. We first find it mentioned in his little book on the Six Remembrances, published in 1794. When speaking of the obligation to remember the day Torah was given, he turns to a brief discussion of the patriarch. Abraham was able to discover the commandments "because he powerfully steeled himself against the evil urge, purifying himself until he attained transcendence of his corporeal self. He was so intensely attached to YHWH that he attained every *mitsvah*." Four years later, in his treatise on Hanukkah and Purim, he expands on this theme in his opening homily. Abraham knew the entire Torah because he was able to look deep within his physical self, discovering the spiritual "limb" or "sinew" that lay behind each material one. These all received their life force from the 613 *mitsvot* and are essentially identical with them. The ability to discover and fulfill the Torah was an extension of the patriarch's journey of self-discovery. In the three days of preparation for Sinai, Levi Yitsḥak goes on to claim, all Israel reached the same state that Abraham had achieved. The Torah is given by God at Sinai, despite the fact that the people had already discovered it from within, only to serve as a sort of legal "backup," requiring them to observe the commandments even when not living on such a high level of spiritual self-understanding.[36]

The theme occurs several more times in the posthumously published *Kedushat Levi*.[37] Each time it does, it is accompanied by a reference to the full apparatus of the correspondence between the 613 commandments and the inner limbs and sinews. Once again, Levi Yitsḥak may be seen as defending the *mitsvot*, even in this theoretical context, against some of the more radical notions that were afloat in early Hasidic circles. In the writings of several of his peers,[38] we hear that Abraham's "observance" of the *mitsvot* was really a matter of inward intent, *kavvanah*, rather than actual deed. R. Menaḥem Naḥum claims that Abraham knew the entire Torah as it had been in its primordial state within divine wisdom, *preceding its division* into specific commandments.[39] It only needed to be given in this form to the generation emerging from Egyptian bondage because they were no longer on the high rung that Abraham had attained. Some said that Abraham poured the devotional intensity of all the Torah into fulfilling a single divine command, that of leaving his land or the act of circumcision. Others suggest that the patriarchs, through other sorts of deeds, including Isaac's digging of the well and Jacob's marking the speckled sheep, accomplished the same devotional tasks that we do through our particular forms of devotion, the *mitsvot*. Levi Yitsḥak seems wary of this, a notion coming close to that of *'avodah be-gashmiyyut*, the possibility of serving God by means other than those specified by the Torah. The mystical correspondences of limbs and sinews seemed to assure that it was the full list of commandments, just as we know them, that Abraham observed. He comes into the land in order to fulfill a portion of the prescribed list of *mitsvot*, those applying only to one who dwells within it.

Levi Yitsḥak's calling on the figure of Abraham as defender of religious authority may come to its sharpest point in his discussion of the binding of Isaac, the ultimate test of the patriarch's willingness to follow the divine command. He interprets the events of Genesis 22 in the context of a fully Midrashic/Hasidic understanding of Israel's progenitor. Abraham had known his Creator from the time he was three years old. He already observed all the commandments of the Torah, including the [purely rabbinic] rule of preparing Sabbath food on the festival. He did this all out of pure motivation, "for the sake of God's glorious and awesome name." He was guided along this path

> because it is known that each of our *mitsvot* [embodies] sublime, awesome, and wondrous lights . . . endless radiance. These lights within the *mitsvot* bring satiety, delight, and fulfillment, sweetness like that of the honeycomb, to the souls of Israel, the holy people, as they fulfill them. . . . As the *tsaddikim* peer [into them] and attain a taste of that brilliant radiance . . . their souls nearly pass out of them from the unimaginable pleasure and sweetness. They burn with the flame of ecstatic and passionate love, longing to fulfill each holy *mitsvah*, along with every general and specific detail it contains, with perfect precision and mystical intent. They rejoice in doing the will of their Creator!

> Abraham our father, having grasped all the holy commandments, tasted of their brilliant light and sweetness. . . . Yet one might have said of him that he had not fulfilled the commandments of His Blessed Name out of the higher *yir'ah* [because they were not yet actually commanded], which is the great fundament and root of His worship. Of this Scripture says, "Now, O Israel, what does YHWH ask of you other than to fear Him?" (Deut. 10:12). So too in our oral teaching: "The blessed Holy One has nothing in His world but the treasury of the fear of YHWH."[40] One might say that Abraham's righteousness was due to the great delight he took in those lights that are attached to the holy *mitsvot* [i.e., he fulfilled them out of love alone]. . . .
>
> Thus it might be said that when God commanded him to slaughter his son, there were no holy lights present in the upper worlds. This was not truly a divine commandment but only a test. He derived no pleasure from the great lights, because there was none to be had. Nevertheless, we see that Abraham still wanted to fulfill the word of the King. . . . He rose early in the morning to slaughter his son, refusing to listen to any of Satan's arguments or delays along the way. He did this only because of his great awe before the King, the blessed Holy One . . . Ruler and Master, Essence and Root of all the worlds.[41]

It is hard not to see this exaggeratedly lavish description (some of the excess in the original has been trimmed down here) in a polemical context. Abraham is like one of those enthusiastic *ḥasidim*, fulfilling the *mitsvot* out of ecstatic devotion, overflowing with the pleasures of love. He discovers all the *mitsvot* from within himself and he does them because they help to kindle all the inner light that he is constantly seeking. But that does not suffice for Levi Yitsḥak. He wants to be assured that when the delights and pleasures of devotion disappear, the fear of God will still stand firm and keep the worshipper loyal to fulfilling the divine will. Abraham fulfilled the commandment of God even when he felt none of that inner "juice"—and so should you.

Of course, there is another possible reading of this passage as well. Who is the great promulgator of this vision of loving the commandments, anticipating them eagerly as they come along, and feeling the great joy of their fulfillment, if not Levi Yitsḥak of Berdychiv himself? Might we be witness here to a polemic directed internally, a warning addressed to his own soul as well as to others? Is he worried that he himself might love the *mitsvot* so much that his love eclipses the proper fear of God in doing them? Does he find a need to remind himself that he needs enough of *yir'ah* to keep the discipline of the *halakhah* even in those moments when enthusiasm fades?

Thinking about the question this way opens us to yet a broader possibility of interpreting Levi Yitsḥak as giving expression throughout his writings to his own inner conflict rather than arguing only with others. He had been drawn to Mezritch, after all, by the mystical insights of the Maggid, which he never left behind, and which we have seen echoing through his teachings. Could it be a voice he hears within himself that would rather serve God by devotion alone, without the forms, one who wants to cleave to the One and forget all those needy people "below," to whom he finds such an urgent need to provide sustenance, both spiritual and material? Might his whole Torah be a response to that inner voice?

12

INTERPRETING TORAH

This complete loyalty to the *mitsvot* as the proper way of serving God did not stand in contradiction to the theme to which we now turn our attention, one also found widely in Levi Yitsḥak's writings: the ability, even the obligation, of sages and *tsaddikim* to interpret the Torah anew in every generation.[1] This notion, too, is present in the writings of multiple authors within early Hasidic circles. But Levi Yitsḥak's pronouncement of it is particularly bold and all the more surprising from one who held a respected rabbinic position and who was so strict regarding the commandments.

The authority of the rabbis to reinterpret Torah, even when seemingly against the will of heaven, has a long and well-documented history within Jewish sources. It is usually epitomized around the Talmudic tale of Rabbis Yehoshua and Eliezer's argument about the ritual purity of the oven of Akhnai, a debate that would have taken place in the early second century between two of the leading *tannaim*, or early rabbinic sages.[2] Rabbi Eliezer sought to defend his view with heavenly portents and voices while Yehoshua insisted on the power of reason and the majority voice among the sages. R. Yehoshua's victory was greeted by a heavenly smile and an acknowledgment that "My children have defeated me!" The view from this aggadic tale, even regarding a matter of *halakhah*, where the rules were stricter, generally prevailed in the tradition. In the mystical sources, however, it was often explained in ways that viewed the rabbis' own opinions to be nothing other than echoes of the resounding and unceasing voice of divine revelation.[3] This in effect undercuts the Talmudic story, taking the power of decision back out of the hands of the majority of sages and returning it to the divine voice that guides them and speaks through them.

The right of preachers and biblical interpreters to offer innovative interpretations of Scripture was widely respected throughout Jewish history. While the great deference that Jewish legal processes showed to precedent significantly narrowed the later rabbis' options with regard to religious praxis, the same did not hold true in the realms of *aggadah* and biblical interpretation. The principle that "Torah has seventy faces,"[4] meaning it can be read in a multiplicity of ways, was given a wide berth.

In Hasidism, however, this liberty to reinterpret scripture was transformed in two significant ways. First, it was widely proclaimed to be *obligatory*. Each generation *needs* a new reading of the Torah, and its leaders must respond to that need. Second, the authority to offer such reinterpretation is shifted from the sages to the *tsaddikim*. It is no longer their body of knowledge and sober judgment or their standing in the majority that legitimates contemporary rabbis' rereadings of Torah but rather personal piety and closeness to God, virtues of the *tsaddik* or *rebbe* more than those of the *rav*. Here are the words of R. Ephraim of Sudilkow, the grandson of the Ba'al Shem Tov:

> "*Moses diligently sought out the goat for the sin-offering*" (Lev. 10:16). The *Masorah* notes that these words, "diligently sought" [*darosh darash*] are the midpoint in a letter count of the Torah. One needs to understand what is meant by this, what difference it makes. In my humble opinion, [it is as follows]: We know that the written and oral Torahs are all one, that neither can be separated from the other. Neither is indeed possible without the other, since the written Torah reveals its secrets through oral interpretation. The written Torah without the oral Torah is incomplete. It was like half a book until the Sages came and interpreted Torah, enlightening our eyes and revealing its hidden secrets. Sometimes they would uproot something from the Torah, as is the case regarding the [punishment by] lashes. The Torah says, "He shall be struck by forty lashes" (Deut. 25:3), but the sages reduced them by one.[5] They did all this through the manifestation of their holy spirit, because blessed YHWH appeared over them. [This enabled them] to see the root of everything written in the Torah in its true state, empowering them to do this. The wholeness of the written Torah is thus dependent upon the oral. . . . Everything depends upon the sages' interpretations; they constitute the wholeness of the written Torah. . . .

> *This is true of each generation and its interpreters. They make the Torah complete. Torah is interpreted in each generation according to what that generation needs. God enlightens the eyes of each generation's sages [to interpret] His holy Torah in accord with the soul-root of that generation. One who denies this is like one who denies Torah, God forbid.*[6]

Hasidism may be seen here as having some traits of a movement of the youth, a younger generation rebelling against what it sees as the hidebound ways of its elders. When the proto-Hasidic figure R. Naḥman of Kossov was told that he should not turn aside from the customs of our forefathers (*ovos* in Yiddish-inflected Hebrew), he answered with the Torah verse "Do not turn toward ghostly spirits" (*ovos*; Lev. 19:31)![7] Do not turn our ancestors into false gods. This follows the spirit of a well-known older quip that *minhag*, "custom," had the same consonants as *gehinom*, "hell."[8] Torah may formally be one and unchanging, but each generation has to read it in its own way, according to "the soul-root of that generation," a phrase that sounds very like "the spirit of the times."

This obligation to reinterpret in the spirit of each new generation is one that Levi Yitsḥak treats with great seriousness. In commenting on the traditional explanation of the Talmud's term for an irresolvable dispute, *TeYKU* (literally "it shall stand"), said to be an abbreviation for "the Tishbite [= Elijah] will resolve challenges and difficulties," he asks why Elijah, rather than Moses, is to be the source of such answers: "To render legal decisions, one needs to discern by what quality the world needs to be conducted. For this, one has to be alive and of this world. Someone who is not alive cannot know this at all . . . Elijah is fully alive, never having tasted death. He is always in this world. That is why he will respond to all the questions."[9]

It takes a living leader to provide the proper interpretation of Torah for the current generation. Moses, who was subject to death, can no longer do that.[10] This is a daring idea for Levi Yitsḥak to express, especially given his great regard for Moses as his model for leadership. However great the leader, his power to speak for the current generation passes with his death. (Might Moses here be a stand-in for the Maggid, in an argument with others about doing something in a way that the master would not have wanted?) Only Elijah, who "rose in a whirlwind to heaven" and never actually died, can resolve questions for all time.

The same idea of each generation's need to understand Torah in its own way is also expressed in unusually bold fashion in this comment on God's instructions to Moses in building the tabernacle:

> "Like all that I show you—the structure of the tabernacle and that of all of its vessels—and thus shall you do" (Ex. 25:9). On "and thus shall you do," RaSHI comments "for all generations." But the *Tosafot* object: the altar Moses made was not identical to that made by Solomon! RaMBaN raises a similar question.
>
> But following our method, we can readily understand that "and thus shall you do" refers to something else. Really, the structure of the tabernacle and all its vessels . . . followed the prophetic vision that Moses had on Mount Sinai. . . .
>
> But we also know the rabbinic statement that "no two prophets prophesy in the same style."[11] Each does so in accord with his own categories, in accord with his own way of worshipping God; in that very way does the holy spirit appear to him. This means that Moses and the generation of the wilderness, following the qualities of worship and prophecy they attained at Sinai, had to construct this particular form of tabernacle, structuring its vessels in just this way. . . .
>
> Then Scripture adds "and thus shall you do"—[and RaSHI comments:] "for all generations." This means that *in each generation, when you want to build the Temple, the structure should accord with the prophecy attained at that time*. That should determine the form of the Temple and its vessels. Solomon did it in accord with his own worship and his own prophetic spirit. The form he made followed that which he had understood.
>
> Thus, RaMBaN's objection can easily be dismissed; of course, his altar was different! That was the commandment—that they not do it always in one particular form, but in accord with the flow of prophecy that takes place at that time. That should determine the form of the earthly vessels.[12]

The "building of the Temple" in each generation is an easy stand-in for the conduct of one's religious life, as we live in an age of exile when "prayer stands in place of sacrifice."[13] One could easily imagine Levi Yitsḥak using this line of argument to defend the innovative practices of Hasidism with regard to prayer, which were among the chief objections listed in the denunciations by the *mit-*

naggedim. The life of piety today had to follow the dictates of the prophetic spirit as manifest in the leaders of our own age. The "prophets" of this age are clearly the *tsaddikim* rather than the normative halakhic authorities (though it is important to recall that Levi Yitsḥak represented both of those). These are the same "prophets" whose presence in Israel the young Levi Yitsḥak had sought to encourage.[14]

A variant approach to the ability of Israel or the righteous to affect the divine will derives not from the view that each generation has the authority to reinterpret in accord with its time, but from something like its opposite. The time in which God reveals His will is in fact endless. Here Levi Yitsḥak is playing on an older reading of Pesaḥ as *peh saḥ*, "the speaking mouth":[15]

> When a king of flesh and blood commands his servants to do a certain thing, so long as they are still speaking with him, they have a chance to change his command. But once he has spoken and they have departed from him, there is no such opportunity. But the way of the blessed Holy One is not like that of flesh and blood. Even though the words have flowed forth, been created, formed, and fashioned,[16] their emanation reaching into this lowly world, [indicating] that one should do thus-and-so, they can [still] be changed by the *tsaddikim*. Or, if His children repent, they will immediately be transformed into another permutation [of divine speech-letters], doing good for His people. This is like the king speaking to his people while they are yet before him. "The whole world is filled with His glory" and "there is no place devoid of Him." His power now is just as it was then. This is "the speaking mouth": the [divine] mouth that speaks, even though all the worlds have already been created, is still addressing His servants as they stand before Him.[17]

Because God is beyond time, so too is the moment of His revelation. God is ever speaking the Torah in the present tense, while His servants stand before Him. Therefore, the *tsaddikim*, those who hear Him best, still have the power to convince Him to change His mind, before the command becomes final, which it never quite does![18]

This faith in the ability of the *tsaddikim* not only to reinterpret, but actually to change the Torah, is made clear by a remarkable usage Levi Yitsḥak makes of one of his favorite quotations from rabbinic literature: "The blessed Holy One issues a decree, but the *tsaddik* cancels it."[19] We have already referred to this notion above, and will have occasion to visit it yet again in our further discussion. The usual reading of this passage in Levi Yitsḥak as well as throughout Jewish literature understands the *gezerah*, "decree," to be some bit of importune fate that may befall an individual or a community. That is the usual meaning of this Hebrew term. The Talmudic passage can be heard either bearing a magical tone—the *tsaddik* has the *power* to rescind divine decrees, such as sickness, plague, war, the ill intent of one's king or landlord, or with a more devotional tone: he *has the ear* of God, who will surely hear his prayers and annul the decree. But watch Levi Yitsḥak apply this passage in an entirely different way:

> "I am YHWH your God, who brought you forth from the Land of Egypt, from the house of bondage" (Ex. 20:2).
>
> . . . The most basic premise [*kelal gadol*] in serving our blessed Creator is that we Children of Israel are obliged to have faith in two Torahs, the written and the oral, all given by a single shepherd. The written Torah God passed to us by the hand of Moses, His faithful servant, inscribed on the tablets in black fire on white fire. The oral Torah was handed to Moses in accord with its [ongoing] interpretation, that which every faithful student would ever say anew.
>
> This means that the Oral Torah was given to us in this way: *as the tsaddikim of the generation interpret it, so shall it stand.* This is the great power that the blessed Holy One has passed on to us, out of His love in choosing Israel, His people. All the worlds are conducted according to the Torah *as they will it. This is what the sages said in "The blessed Holy One issues a decree, but the tsaddik cancels it."* This applies to one who serves the Creator, blessed be He and His name, recognizing His total power.[20]

Here the "decree" that the *tsaddik* has the power to rescind is nothing other than the commandment of the written Torah itself! The *tsaddikim* have the authority to interpret, and as they do, so goes the Torah, including its influence in the upper and hidden worlds. The actual meaning of the Torah will change in each generation according to the ongoing interpretations of that generation's *tsaddikim*. This power was included within God's election of Israel and the gift to them of His Torah. Elsewhere, Levi Yitsḥak says that Israel were at first reluctant to accept this condition and resisted receiving the Oral Torah; they feared that the idea of an ever-changing Torah was more than they could handle. This was why they had to reaccept Torah in the days of Mordecai and Esther, realizing that a Torah for the real world (called *erets*, referring to the non-supernatural realm) would demand that flexibility.[21]

This extreme empowering of each generation and its leaders is all the more remarkable in a figure whom we have also seen as a conservative defender of the *mitsvot* as the only proper way of serving God. No wonder that he says that Israel was at first unwilling to accept the Oral Torah. The notion that a new understanding of Torah would need to take place in each generation was more responsibility and flexibility than the community gathered at Sinai was prepared to take upon itself. (Perhaps this means that it was more responsibility than young Levi Yitsḥak was willing to take on in the beginning of his career and that he too had to grow into it.) It was this burden that Israel accepted only in the days of Mordecai and Esther, of which the Talmud says, "They again accepted it." Living in the natural world rather than the age of miracles, he seems to be saying, they realized that in fact such changing ways of understanding Torah would be inevitable—a remarkably modern-sounding insight!

It is not clear whether Levi Yitsḥak experienced these disparate positions regarding the authority of *mitsvot* and the freedom to reinterpret Torah as a tension or polarity in his thinking or whether these views dwelt together quite naturally within him. We do not have even the slightest evidence that he was radical or innovative in his application of *halakhah* within the communities where he served.[22] Yet, conservative in praxis as he was, he shared with others in the Mezritch circle a firm belief that Torah was infinitely more than that which was manifest in the words of the text and that these greater secrets would be revealed in messianic times. He also understood that some foretaste of that deeper revelation was accessible, at least to the *tsaddikim*, in this unredeemed world as well. It was this affinity with the deeper Torah that allowed them to reinterpret, even to "nullify the decree" of the written Torah, while still remaining faithful to its deeper truth.

Let us examine this theme through the imagery of Torah inscribed "in black fire on white fire," as Levi Yitsḥak described the written Torah in the passage we have just quoted. The phrase originally occurs in an early rabbinic source to explain how Torah could have existed with God before the creation of the world, when there was neither the parchment nor the ink required for its writing.[23] Fire, apparently as a heavenly entity, could somehow have existed before there was an earth. Levi Yitsḥak's treatment of this motif is found in several versions. The two most important ones both have to do with the traditional ways in which the two great poems within the Torah—the Song of the Sea (Ex. 15) and Moses' final warning to Israel (Deut. 32)—are written in the Torah scroll. As we will see, the two homilies, possibly two versions of an original oral teaching, shed light upon one another.

> In the tractate Megillah 16b: "All poems are to be written space over brick and brick over space."[24]
>
> The verse "a new Torah will go forth from Me" (Is. 51:4) is surprising.[25] Isn't one of the thirteen principles[26] that this Torah will never be exchanged and that there will never be another?
>
> The matter is thus. The letters of Torah are known to represent inward lights, revealed in the course of the emanation of the worlds. The white spaces that surround the letters represent surrounding lights, those remaining hidden, not yet revealed. In this way, we may understand that the surrounding white spaces are also letters, but they are hidden letters, higher than those revealed. For this reason, it is forbidden to touch a Torah scroll [on its face, with one's hand], because in that touching one would be negating or covering some white space, which is a hidden letter.
>
> At the crossing of the sea, however, a great supernatural miracle occurred. The divine life force and light were revealed to a degree far, far beyond [the regular order of] emanation. This was that which transcends, the "surrounding" light. That is why this song is written space over brick and brick over space. The two of them [the black letters and white spaces or hidden letters] were joined together. The white of the hidden letters came to be revealed, like the revealed [black] letters. That is why the sages said, "A handmaiden at the sea saw more than the prophet Ezekiel."[27] There was such abundant divine revelation that she too was able to see it.
>
> This is the meaning of the verse "A new Torah will go forth from Me." In the future, there will be a [new] divine revelation. "The glory of YHWH will be revealed, and all flesh will see" (Is. 40:5). That which surrounds [or "transcends"] will be revealed, the white space, the hidden letters that surround the revealed letters of the Torah. This is the "new Torah from Me."[28]

The unique way that the Song of the Sea is written in the Torah scroll represents the faith that in that moment the "white letters" were revealed along with the black ones, and the two of them fully integrated. This (one might say "poetic") view of reality was accessible to all in the miraculous moment. Such will be the case again in the future, when the "new" Torah will be revealed from within the one which already exists, visible to all humanity, as is clear from the (revised) verse in Isaiah.[29]

The other version of this teaching, recorded by Pinḥas of Dinowitz, ascribes the description to the Deuteronomy rather than the Exodus poem, but the effect is the same.[30] Most interesting is the explanation appended to this discussion, all supposedly quoted from Levi Yitsḥak:

> The white space on the parchment contains holiness and great light. That is why the Torah scroll is considered unfit when two letters are attached: the light within the white space has been covered over. It is not possible in this world to attain that light, but only after the coming of our messiah (speedily and soon!). Since the *Ha'azinu* poem points toward the future, it is written brick over brick [i.e., in two parallel columns], for then the light within the white space will be revealed and night will shine like day. "The *tsaddikim* will be seated with crowns upon their heads [*be-rosham*]."[31]
>
> There are three spaces within the brain: that between the brain itself and the membrane, between one membrane and another, and between the [outermost] membrane and the skull. This refers to the higher and lower fear [of God].[32] We know that the [outermost] membrane and the space around it, that between the skull and the cranium over it, on which hair grows, are unknowable, beyond conception. This is a fear of God of which we in this world cannot conceive at all. When our righteous messiah arrives, we will attain this level of fear as well.
>
> This is the meaning of "their crowns upon their heads" [read as "*in* their heads"]. They will attain the fear that dwells within their crania.[33]

From this text it is clear that the "new" Torah to be revealed is a new level of human understanding, one that already exists, hidden within the recesses of the human mind, but remaining beyond our ability to access in the unredeemed world. The first version, connecting the teaching to the Song at the Sea, offered an exception in the moment of that miracle. The shifting of the teaching to *Ha'azinu* locates it entirely in the future. Still, it is significant that the difference between this world and the messianic era is now located in the depths of self-knowledge, the opening to levels of consciousness that are already present within the mind. (There is something remarkably prescient about the way he almost says that diverse levels of understanding seem connected to distinct regions within the brain! Once again, the psychedelically experienced reader will take special notice.) This is the same self-knowledge that Abraham had, allowing him to know and fulfill the Torah before it was given, the same self-knowledge glimpsed again by all Israel as they stood before the mountain. While there is no direct claim here that this understanding can be reached again in pre-messianic times, there seems to be some possibility that the *tsaddikim*, including the one who has just revealed this truth, know something about it.[34]

This combination of relative conservatism with regard to the *mitsvot* and openness to radical thinking around Torah and its ultimate meaning was well suited to the needs of Levi Yitsḥak and others in his circle. In their battle with the rabbinic authorities who fought Hasidism so fiercely, they were looking for an inward rather than an outwardly directed sense of freedom. It was not the outside world, either intellectually or materially, that drew them. Lightening the burden of the law was not their goal; neither was any greater openness to cultural influences from without. They sought a deeper truth *within* Torah, one that might nourish the soul that was not sated within the realm of normative or legal discourse. Conformity in the realm of deed—with the exception of a few "trademark" expressions of special piety—offered them the freedom to stay within the community and explore the inner depths the tradition had to offer. It also gave them the legitimacy and credibility to bring their message of spiritual revival to ever-broader swaths of the Jewish population.

13

LOOKING INTO THE FUTURE?

This power of the *tsaddik* to reinterpret Torah, thus transforming the divine will, leads us directly into what may be the most interesting and surprising innovation of Levi Yitsḥak's theology. In quite a number of passages throughout *Kedushat Levi*, he asserts definitively that God has turned His authority in governing the world entirely over to Israel and to the *tsaddikim*. God has chosen to absent Himself from His divine rule, taking no part in the determination of human fate or history, in order to allow Israel's will to entirely supplant His own. We shall need to examine this startling notion from several points of view and seek to explain it. We begin, however, with another key passage that uses the reinterpretation of Torah as its point of departure. Here we return to Akhnai and his famous oven, now looking at Levi Yitsḥak's reading of the passage:

> It is known that we have two Torahs, the written and the oral. The written Torah was given to us at Sinai, while the oral is referred to as "*our*" Torah . . . it is called that because the power exists in the Jewish people [*ba-umah ha-yisre'elit*], namely in the Tannaim, Amoraim, and later sages, to interpret and explicate the written Torah in accord with their will and opinion, even if this is not heaven's [original] intent. The Talmud tells of the incident of Rabbi Eliezer and R. Joshua, when R. Joshua stood up on his feet and said, "We pay no attention to heavenly voices," referring to such a voice that had spoken for the view of R. Eliezer.[1] The *tsaddikim* of this time also have that power to interpret the Torah as is their will. *Even if it is not so in heaven, they change the will above, as it were, to their own, following their interpretation of Torah.*

> So too with other matters. They have the power to transform the will above from an ill decree, God forbid, to good. "The *tsaddik* rules over the fear of God" (II Sam. 23:3), [on which the Talmud says,] "'Who rules over Me? The *tsaddik*.' The blessed Holy One issues a decree and the *tsaddik* nullifies it." They change the will above to their own.[2]

Here we see spelled out the notion we encountered above, placing Torah as the "decree" that the *tsaddik* can rescind. It is not just halakhic authority that is in the hands of humans rather than remaining with God. Torah represents the divine will. If the law changes by means of the proper tools of rabbinic innovation, so too does the will of heaven. Here and elsewhere, Levi Yitsḥak connects this power to the giving of the Torah itself. Sinai was a "descent" for God, who came down from His all-powerful position and handed His Torah over to humans.[3] The opening word of the decalogue, *anokhi*, is read (through reinterpreting a Talmudic acronym)[4] as indicting that "I have given you My will." Until Sinai, Torah could have multiple meanings. Thus, Abraham observed the entire Torah in his way, and the angels were undisturbed, having their own understanding alongside his. But at Sinai, God "*gave* us His Torah," which meant that our human understanding, that of the *tsaddikim*, would supplant any other, becoming the only possible true meaning.[5]

These accounts of God's abdicating His own will in favor of Israel or the *tsaddik* are not entirely original to Levi Yitsḥak. Their roots lie in the complex and essentially unresolved paradoxes of the Maggid's theology. As we have seen, the Maggid had a lofty and abstract notion of divinity, often identified with the divine *ayin*. This mystical view, we have noted, is paradoxically quite far from the affectionate paternal images of which he was so fond. He uses the term *eyn sof* as a name for God more than is usual.[6] His mystical reflection is much concentrated on the inner identity and reversibility of being and nothingness, *yesh* and *ayin*, which are symbolically represented by *ḥokhmah* and *malkhut*, upper and lower wisdom.[7] But when *ḥokhmah* becomes *ayin* rather than deriving from *ayin* and pointing toward it, as it had in classic Zoharic Kabbalah, there is no place for the phenomenon of divine will.[8] All the Maggid's God has of will is His love for Israel and the *tsaddikim*, for whose sake He created the world, according to old rabbinic teachings. God allows them to shape a will that is essentially alien to His own true being, which remains indifferent to the small outcomes of individual lives and human fate in this lower, half-illusory, world. Levi Yitsḥak reads Ps.

145:19, "He does the will of those who fear Him," rather as, "Will—it is made by those who fear Him," meaning that the *tsaddikim* themselves create the will of God: "Will does not apply to the *eyn sof*. But 'those who fear Him' *make it*; they are the righteous [*tsaddikim*]. This follows in the way of "'He consulted the souls of the righteous [before creating humans].'"[9]

On this precise theme, Levi Yitsḥak cites a fuller teaching of the Maggid, directly connected to the passage we have just quoted regarding the two Torahs:

> I heard from our teacher Dov Baer, regarding the Talmudic statement that "When Israel do [*'osin*] God's will, they are called [His] 'children,' but when they do not do His will, they are 'servants.'"[10] This is strange. How could they be considered God's servants when they are not doing His will? The Talmud explained this by a parable of a king who had an only son. Because he loved his son so much, he would set aside his own will in favor of the son's. If he had a beautiful table or lamp sitting in one corner, and the son wanted it in another, he would do the son's will, taking great pleasure in doing so. The son was thus creating a new will in the father, transforming his former will.
>
> This is what our sages meant by "When Israel are *'osin* [read as '*making*'] God's will." When they are on such a high rung that they can make a new will in the blessed Creator, they are called "children" of God. But "when they are not making God's will," not on such a high rung as to create such a new will, even though they are still *tsaddikim*, they are [only] "servants" of YHWH, not "children."[11]

To be a true child of God, the *tsaddik*—or "Israel"—has to be able to implant a new will in God, who loves him so much that He will do his bidding.[12] Otherwise one is merely a servant, following the will of God as it already exists. The surprising point here seems to be that God is so utterly transcendent that He remains indifferent to the fate of individuals. This amounts to a certain lack of worldly discernment. It is only the *tsaddikim*, because they are so intimately linked both to God and to real life, bound up with this-worldly situations, who are able to bring about some sense of moral differentiation within the divine will as they "create" it. This view is utterly remote from the biblical God, who is all about moral discernment and the rewards and punishments that derive from it.

Here Levi Yitsḥak discourses on another favorite Talmudic story, the account of Rabbi Akiva and his three friends' ascent into Paradise, the result of a mystical "journey."

> The Talmud tells of four who entered the *pardes* [literally "orchard" but of the same origin as "Paradise"], of whom [only] R. Akiva emerged in peace.[13] He said to them, "When you reach the pure marble pillars, do not say, 'Water, water . . .'"
>
> The principle is that each holy spark must have faith that the blessed Creator created all the world, including every creature, above and below. He sustains them, causing all they need to flow into them, out of His great mercy and compassion. [This includes] even the enemies of Israel, because it is the way of the Creator to be good to them [despite their wickedness].
>
> But the *tsaddikim* of the generation have the power to draw that flow in accord with their will, so that it flows only toward those who truly serve YHWH. The wicked will not receive any of that bounty, because they are not doing the blessed Creator's will. By their good deeds, the *tsaddikim* arouse the Creator to don the garb of pride. Pride causes God to rise up high above the lower creatures, so that no flow goes out to the wicked, who are not doing His will. It goes instead only to the righteous, who are serving Him in truth. The wicked one is too despised by God to be given His bounty. Because they do not receive it, the wicked suffer a great fall.[14]

The text goes on at much greater length to explain the mechanism of the *tsaddik*'s influence, using a very interesting musical metaphor and then turning to the familiar theme of letters and their power. But the homily never comes back to explain the Talmudic tale more fully. It seems that "Water, water" refers to divine indifference, the flow of *shefa*ʿ to all equally, regardless of their deeds. To God, it is all just water! R. Akiva is telling his fellow *tsaddikim* not to be accepting of that divine moral indifference but to use their own influence in the upper world to direct divine blessing so that it flows properly, reaching the righteous alone.

Even beyond its roots in the Maggid's abstract notion of the deity, one might say that Levi Yitsḥak's view is a result of one of the major innovations of later Kabbalah as a whole, the notion of *tsimtsum*. Once one says that God needs to empty Himself out of a primal space, creating a void to make room for the existence of the other, an implication is created that earthly existence thrives on the absence of God as much as it requires His presence. In the nonliteral reading of *tsimtsum* that came to dominate in the Hasidic circles,[15] this absence of God was applied specifically to an absence of God from human awareness. This is well-known from the widely quoted parable of the Ba'al Shem Tov about the father teaching his child to walk, ever stepping farther away from him in order to build the child's confidence in his own ability.[16] But here that confidence seems to have grown exponentially, the child growing up and declaring the father powerless, ready to take the reins and rule the world on his own.

Levi Yitsḥak is remarkably bold in his declarations of the *tsaddik*'s authority over God. "Mordecai came out from before the king" (Esth. 8:15) is read to mean that Mordecai, as *tsaddik*, is "*before*," higher in authority, than the divine King, following the Midrashic and Zoharic precedent of reading the royal courts of Persia in the Esther story as pointing toward the heavenly courts above.[17] But it is also made clear that this power is limited to its use for good, Levi Yitsḥak's sort of good. The *tsaddik* may only exercise power over divine decrees to bring about greater compassion for Israel, never to buttress the forces of stern judgment. Thus he reads the Exodus 19:6 charge to Israel just before the revelation at Sinai, "You are to be unto Me a kingdom of priests." "Unto Me a kingdom" means that Israel do indeed rule over God! But they may do so only as "priests," since *kohen* in Kabbalistic symbolism represents *ḥesed*, divine compassion.[18]

Extreme formulations of the *tsaddik*'s power over God are frequent in the *Kedushat Levi*; one has the sense that its author realizes how new and powerful this idea is and is trying especially hard to make the point or to impress it upon his hearers/readers.

> "The staff [*mateh*] of God is in my hand" (Ex. 17:9). The way God causes the world to turn [*mateh*], exercising His will over the world, is in my hands! I can turn the world in the direction I want. As our sages said: "Who rules over Me? The *tsaddik*." This is "the staff of God"—the way that God can turn the world, is "in my hand." This power has been handed over to me, so that the Creator obeys me.[19]

There is power in the hands of the *tsaddikim* of each generation to transform the thought of the Creator, as it were. The Creator does not conduct Himself just according to His own will, and all things are not conducted following His will.

God is rather conducted (or "led") by the *tsaddikim* of each generation. Their will is done, even insofar as it changes the thought of God.[20]

An almost unimaginably daring version of this idea is quoted by R. Pinḥas of Dinovitz in the name of Levi Yitsḥak. The blessing a Jew recites before drinking a glass of water concludes with "for all was made according to His word." If the *tsaddik* truly drinks up the waters of Torah, this teaching proclaims, God Himself declares, speaking of the *tsaddik*, that "all is made according to *his* word."[21]

Did anyone in the Maggid's circle or the early Hasidic world notice and protest the radical view of the *tsaddik*'s power that Levi Yitsḥak was articulating? There is no clear evidence to that effect, but a possibility emerges from an unexplained remark recorded in the name of his friend R. Shne'ur Zalman. When their grandchildren were married in Zlabin in 1807, Shne'ur Zalman is supposed to have said, "The blessed Holy One is the *tsaddik* above and R. Levi Yitsḥak Berdychiver is the *tsaddik* below."[22] Might it just be possible that there is a raised eyebrow that went along with this statement of praise? Might this comment stand as a parallel to Levi Yitsḥak's comment on the *Tanya*, indicating a buried awareness of some bit of ideological tension that existed between the two of them?

Was there anyone else in this group who shared these very extreme views of the *tsaddik*'s power over the will of God? The most obvious candidate would be Levi Yitsḥak's friend and close colleague R. Elimelekh of Lezajsk. Here is his version of the same idea, also couched in intentionally provocative language:

> We have written several times that the *tsaddik* is called "a man of God," as in "Moses, the man of God" [*Elohim*; Deut. 33:1; Ps. 90:1]. [He is thus called] because the *tsaddik* is *ish*, "master" or "husband," of judging forces [*dinim*= *Elohim*]; they are in his hands to be turned any way he wants, to defeat or "sweeten" them. The *tsaddik* is the judge [*dayyan*], because judges are referred to as *elohim* (compare Ex. 22:8). As he judges and decrees below, so it will be, for when there is judgment below, there is no judgment above. Therefore, in this way he can nullify all judgment forces and decrees from Israel. That is why the *tsaddik* is called *ish ha-elohim*, meaning master [or "husband"] of *Elohim*. This is what the Talmud means by "God issues a decree and the *tsaddik* nullifies it," as it says, "You speak a decree and it is fulfilled" (Job 22:28). But how

> does this verse prove that the *tsaddik* can nullify divine judgments and decrees? Doesn't the verse mean that the *tsaddik* decrees and the blessed Holy One fulfills? But now we understand it correctly: When the *tsaddik* judges below and decrees, there is no judgment above. Thus [the decrees] are nullified on their own.[23]

This is not quite the same as the *tsaddik judging* God, as in the later literary uses of Levi Yitsḥak, especially in the post-Holocaust generation, to which we alluded in the introduction to this study. Here human judgment has *replaced* that of heaven, but God Himself is not the accused. It is not hard to see, however, how these sources opened the door for such a later reading in a generation that needed to find it.

The question to be answered is what motivates Levi Yitsḥak and Elimelekh to move so radically in this direction, taking up a thread from within the Maggid's abstract theology but pushing it so much farther, both in tone and frequency of his comments. It is hard to imagine that the rabbi of Berdychiv has been influenced by the Deist thought that was quite the rage among English, French, and American intellectuals of his day. But this claim of the abdication of divine authority leads in a direction close to theirs. There would seem to be no more point in turning to God for mercy or for sustenance since it is the *tsaddikim* who now rule in such areas.

Of course, one could simply give this view the label of "extreme *tsaddikim*," to revive a term used by an earlier generation of scholars. Indeed, one might say that these are simply raw assertions of power, meant to justify the claims of these Hasidic leaders to be the ultimate authorities in Jewish life, claiming a power that even surpasses that of God or His Torah. Occasionally, Levi Yitsḥak seeks to make it clear that God has chosen this situation of self-subjugation to the *tsaddikim*, but most often this view is presented without apology. But this longtime reader of Levi Yitsḥak suspects that there is something more than a quest to assert power behind these wildly exaggerated claims.

The question of supernaturalism and the ability to effect miracles is a great concern of Levi Yitsḥak's throughout his life. Of course, he believes the Torah narrative quite literally, and it is completely clear that there God suspended nature at His will, particularly in the grandest miracles of the plagues in Egypt and the dividing of the Reed Sea. The giving of the Torah was also an entirely supernatural act, we will recall, so much so that Torah had to be reaccepted in the time of Mordecai and Esther, when miracles were no longer apparent.

"Why," Levi Yitsḥak keeps asking himself, "are such miracles not taking place today?" Surely God loves Israel as much today as He did back then. Israel have been oppressed in exile for nearly two millennia, and there appears to be no saving hand. His first answer was that of the hidden miracle. Once the Torah has been given, human freedom to follow or reject it is of the essence. If Sinai was too obviously miraculous to allow Israel any real choice in accepting the Torah, and it therefore had to be accepted again, God needs to hold back, acting only behind the scenes of history to bring about Israel's redemption. The *tsaddikim* are those who have the eyes to see that *hergel*, or "the ordinary," is simply a mask behind which divine activism is hidden, the supernatural "hidden miracle" lying within the bounds of the seemingly natural.

At some point, or to some degree, this resolution fails to satisfy Levi Yitsḥak. He looks for that hidden divine hand but cannot find it. It is becoming clear in his day that the collapse of Poland and the imposition of tsarist rule over his district (1793) is likely to make things worse for the Jews. By the first decade of the nineteenth century, that suspicion was being well confirmed. Where was the hand of God? Perhaps Levi Yitsḥak's faith in the hidden miracle had begun to wane.

There is no salvation on the horizon, no messiah about to save Israel from exile and oppression. At the same time, the influence of Hasidism is growing. In his district, very little opposition to the *tsaddikim* is left in his last decade of life. Could this be the answer? Might we *tsaddikim*, with our growing power, be the "Esther" of our generation, the ones through whom divine influence is to radiate, leading to the salvation of Israel? Has God decided to act through us? If that is the case, the notion that "God has stepped aside and given His power to the *tsaddikim* and to Israel" is just one step beyond the theology of the hidden miracle. We *tsaddikim are* the hidden miracle of our day, and we have to act to govern God's world! Now it is no longer God but Israel and their true leaders who stand at the center of the universe. Of course, this itself has come about by divine decree, but it reflects a different picture of reality, one in which God is willfully eclipsed.

What we have here might be called a theology of human empowerment still wrapped in a blanket of passionate devotion both to God and to Torah. But it is also not hard to see here the moment of early modernity in which Hasidism came to be. All the claims and authority of the tradition are still unchallenged, and yet the absence of the divine hand from human affairs and the need for bold leaders to step into that space are becoming ever more apparent. If R. Naḥman of Bratslav, Levi Yitsḥak's younger contemporary, is to be seen as peering over into the coming modern era and its challenge to faith,[24] Levi Yitsḥak is finding a way to act in face of the reality that we live in a world seemingly not guided by divine intervention, either hidden or revealed.

This understanding of Levi Yitsḥak's theology also ties him directly into the figure of Levi Yitsḥak that was to dominate in the great body of legends and literary recreations emerging in the century following his death. Israel are an independent body, standing over against God. The task of the *tsaddik*, like that of the ancient prophet, is that of two-way intermediary between the people and their God. If he is to gently reprimand the people and urge them to improve their ways, he needs to be much less gentle with the Master of the Universe, who has now stepped aside in his favor. He demands of God that Israel be saved, but he himself is the vehicle of that salvation, needing to take control of a world that God has abandoned!

How much gap is there between that view of reality and the claim of the earliest Zionist or Bundist leaders, less than a century in the future, who saw themselves living in a Godless universe but still loving Israel? Hardly *tsaddikim*, they too felt that God had abandoned His world, leading them to step in and act in His place, taking history into their own hands. The distance between Levi Yitsḥak's faith and their denial is a wide one, to be sure. Levi Yitsḥak's God is everywhere present, ever speaking the commandments—yet has decided to no longer govern the world. But might Levi Yitsḥak, both the man and his teachings, have served as a bridge—intentionally or not—between two eras, with their very different views of how to replace the absent divine hand and bring about Israel's—or the world's—redemption?

ABBREVIATIONS USED IN THE NOTES

b.	Talmud Bavli
BeSHT	Ba'al Shem Tov
DME	*Degel Maḥaneh Efrayim*
KL	*Kedushat Levi*
m.	Mishna
MDL	*Maggid Devarav le-Ya'akov*
ME	*Me'or Eynayim*
NE	*Noam Elimelekh*
LY	Levi Yitsḥak
ST	*Shemu'ah Tovah*
TYY	*Toldot Ya'akov Yosef*
y.	Talmud Yerushalmi

NOTES

INTRODUCTION

1. Levi Yitsḥak plays a relatively modest role in the collections of Hasidic tales collected by Rodkinson and Bodek, published in the 1860s and '70s. In the early decades of the twentieth century, there were several entire chapbooks devoted to Levi Yitsḥak stories, including many in which his name seems to be simply inserted into a generic miracle tale. See further discussion below, especially around chapter 9, n. 20. The growing enhancement of the figure of Levi Yitsḥak in the modern era is the subject of an important and lengthy study by Zvi Mark in the *Levi Yitsḥak* volume, which he also coedited, 292–396.

2. See Bereishit Rabbah 39:1. This midrash is widely quoted in both Hasidic and modern Jewish writings.

3. The 1811 edition was published in Berdychiv by Levi Yitsḥak's son Dov Baer. The first complete *Kedushat Levi*, combining the two parts, was published there in 1816 by Yosef, the son of Levi Yitsḥak's deceased son Meir. This became the basis of a great many future editions. A final section, Levi Yitsḥak's comments on the tractate Avot, was published from a manuscript in 1862. The twenty-first century has already seen three new editions of *Kedushat Levi* with commentaries plus several unadorned reprints. The best of the new editions, referred to throughout this volume, is that edited by Michael Rand and published by *Hadrat Ḥen* in Ashdod in 2005.

4. See extended discussion in Green, *The Hasidic Homily*, as well as in the introduction to my translation of *The Light of the Eyes*.

5. This pattern was set by the publication of Elimelekh of Lezajsk's *No'am Elimelekh* in 1788. Other examples include *Me'or 'Eynayim* and *Or ha-Me'ir*, both published in 1798.

6. See *Toledot ha-Meḥabber* in the Munkacz edition of *Kedushat Levi*, #95.

7. Mezirov, 1794. This little work will also be given our attention below.

8. The short teachings (undated) comprising the rest of that volume belong to the complicated corpus of the Maggid. Some are also attributed to the Ba'al Shem Tov.

9. A recent work called *Yalkuṭ Kedushat Levi*, edited by descendant Michael Derbarmdiger and published by Mekhon Kedushat *Levi* in 2004, is a fairly complete compendium of these quotations. Special mention should also be made of two early collections of Hasidic teachings, both containing some important Levi Yitsḥak materials. *Ge'ulat Yis-*

ra'el, edited by Yehoshu'a Avraham ben Yisra'el, was published in Ostrog in 1821. *Siftey Tsaddikim*, composed by Pinḥas of Dinovitz before 1825, appeared in Lvov in 1865.

10. See Levi Cooper's exhaustive survey of Levi Yitsḥak as a halakhist, "Rabbanut, Halakha, Lamdanut," in Mark, ed., *Levi Yitsḥak*. The author of *Tif'eret Beyt Levi* (#28) quotes a family tradition to the effect that Levi Yitsḥak also composed works on *halakhah*, but these remained unpublished and the manuscripts were lost in a great fire that later engulfed Berdychiv.

11. G. Nigal, the most important scholar of the Hasidic tale, offers a very thorough listing of these various collectors and editors in his *Melaktey ha-Sippur ha-Ḥasidi* (Jerusalem: Carmel, 1995), but he does little to characterize the obviously varying genres among them.

12. The best-known among these is Simḥah Raz, *Ohev ve-Ahuv* (Jerusalem: Feldheim, 2008).

13. The great exceptions to this pattern are ḤaBaD and Bratslav, which have long traditions of study and commentary on works by their own masters.

14. See especially Margolin, *Mikdash Adam*; Kauffman, *Be-khol Derakhekha*; and Green, "Around the Maggid's Table."

1. THE LIFE AND TIMES OF AN EIGHTEENTH-CENTURY RABBI

1. While it was possible for a Jew to go over the head of the rabbinic court and appeal to secular authorities (this would usually mean a magistrate appointed by the nobleman who owned the particular town and countryside surrounding it, or possibly the nobleman himself in extreme cases), such behavior was frowned upon within the Jewish community. Only in disputes involving non-Jews or in capital or other serious criminal cases did the non-Jewish authorities have to be brought in.

2. The *Pinkas Va'ad Arba' Aratsot* was published many years ago by Israel Halpern. On its decline and disbanding, see Polonsky, *The Jews in Poland and Russia*, v. 1, 205–9.

3. See my article "The Hasidic Tzaddik and the Charism of Leadership" in *Essays in Honor of Moshe Idel* (also available, as are my other articles, on my website artgreen26.com) and the sources quoted there.

4. Well-known *maggidim* in early Hasidism included R. Menaḥem Mendel of Vitebsk, R. Aharon of Karlin, R. Menaḥem Naḥum of Chernobyl, and R. Ze'ev Wolf of Zhitomir.

5. See Immanuel Etkes's biography *Rabbi Shneur Zalman of Liady: The Origins of Chabad Hasidism.*

6. At the time it was technically the Halicz district in the old Polish kingdom. The designation "Galicia" was an Austrian rendition of that Polish name, beginning with the partition of 1772.

7. The four Peretz brothers are mentioned by Rabbi Yosef Teomim, author of the well-known halakhic treatise *Pri Megadim*, in his introduction to his father Meir's *Rav Peninim*,

as generous supporters of scholars in Lubartow, where he served as preacher. Quoted in *Tif'eret Bet Levi*, 3. *Shemen ha-Tov* (see n. 11 below) names Levi Yitsḥak's father-in-law as Shmu'el Peretz, as does R. Joseph Levinstein in his letter to Dubnov, included in Wilensky, *Ḥasidim*, v. 2, 355. Levinstein was an important informant of Dubnov's in the first writing of Hasidic history. *Tif'eret Bet Levi*, 3, mentions several others with whom Levi Yitsḥak was associated in Lubartow, including the *Pri Megadim* himself, but that is not confirmed.

8. For a later Hasidic tale reflecting Levi Yitsḥak's father-in-law's impatience with this arrangement, see *Shivḥey Tsaddikim*, 53–55.

9. This exposure may underlie the following legend: Once Levi Yitsḥak had to judge a major financial dispute between two lumber merchants. When one of them saw that he was losing the case, he sought a way out of his situation, which was going to cost him a lot of money. He said to Levi Yitsḥak, "Maybe the rabbi of Berdychiv doesn't understand the lumber business very well." Smiling, the rabbi replied, "If you were talking about some heavenly matter, perhaps regarding Torah learning, you might say that you know it better than I. Surely you have more piety than I do. But in business I am at home; I understand it better than you do." Included in *Toledot ha-Meḥabber* in the 1939 Munkacz edition of *Kedushat Levi* #19.

10. Ryczywol is the name of several locations in Poland. This Ryczywol is in the Mazovia province. It would have been on the road between Lubartow and Warsaw, hence a road well-trodden by Jewish merchants, such as members of the Peretz family.

11. There is a small volume of Hasidic counsels for daily living attributed to R. Shmelke published under the title *Darkhey Yesharim* by one of the small Russian-Polish Hebrew printing houses around 1820. *Shemen ha-Tov* is a collection of Hasidic teaching by R. Shmelke combined with legends about him and collected by Avraham Michelson, the son of Zvi Yehezkel Michelson, rabbi of Plonsk and a well-known source of Hasidic oral history. It was published in Piotrkow, 1905. #18 (page 64) and #33 (page 70) report that it was members of the Peretz family who first connected Levi Yitsḥak with R. Shmelke. The latter source mentions that Yisra'el of Kozienice and Ya'akov Yitsḥak of Lublin were also part of the circle around R. Shmelke. A document copied from the Pinkas of Ryczywol community and printed in #36 (page 71) testifies that R. Shmelke was serving as rabbi there already in 1754. For a more fanciful account of Levi Yitsḥak's first visit to Ryczywol, see #46 (page 75).

12. The view of young Levi Yitsḥak as a disciple of R. Shmelke is reinforced by an approbation he wrote for an edition of R. Baḥya's *Ḥovot ha-Levavot* published in 1774 in Frankfurt-am-Oder. The publisher of that volume lists the *haskamot* as being by "R. Shmelke . . . chief rabbi and *rosh yeshivah* of the holy community of Nikolsburg and the province of Moravia . . . and seconded by his outstanding disciple, one like him in his ways . . . Levi Yitsḥak, chief rabbi and *rosh yeshivah* of Zelechow and the district." This important testimony was rediscovered by Gershon Kitzis and is mentioned by Mark in his

essay "Din Torah" in Mark and Horen, eds., *Levi Yitsḥak*, 368. Levi Yitsḥak's role within the Mezritch circle following the Maggid's death will be the subject of much discussion below.

13. There were many cases—unlike that of Levi Yitsḥak—where the purchase was the more important cause of such appointments. Evidence of the corruption in the rabbinic appointment process is widespread in both Hebrew homiletic literature of the age and in Russian archival sources. It has been discussed by Adam Teller in "Tradition and Crisis?" On the purchase of the rabbinic office in Pinsk by Levi Yitsḥak's successor (and fierce opponent of Hasidism), R. Avigdor, see Nadav, *Pinsk*, 304–8.

14. The letter is included in Wilensky, *Ḥasidim*, v. 2, 355. It is not unlikely that Perl, as the daughter of a wealthy family, would have been literate in Polish, while her rabbinically trained husband was not. Ryczywol was a small community but apparently of some economic significance. See the remark by Levinstein, ibid., 357.

15. Some confusion existed in the earlier scholarly literature about the order of LY's positions. Ḥayyim Lieberman's article *Seder Ha-Rabbanut Shel Rabbi Levi Yitsḥak* proves that Zelechow preceded Pinsk. This is found in volume 1 of his collection *Ohel RaḤeL*. Lieberman's view is supported by Mordechai Wilensky in *Tarbiz*, 30, based on a letter written in 1895 from Joseph Levinstein to Dubnov. See also n. 17 below.

16. This was not his brother Pinḥas, who later became famous as rabbi of Frankfurt-am-Main, but another, possibly named Naḥum. *Tif'eret Bet Levi*, 4, however, lists R. Naftali Hertz Margulies as Levi Yitsḥak's immediate predecessor in Zelechow.

17. *Shemen ha-Tov*, 70, tells of his having brought his three disciples (see n. 11 above) to R. Dov Baer in Rowno, where he moved only in 1770. This would mean that Levi Yitsḥak knew his master only during the final two years of Dov Baer's life. More likely is the testimony of anti-Hasidic polemicist R. David of Makow, who records that in 1778 Levi Yitsḥak told him that he had known the Maggid for twelve years, since 1766 (Wilensky, "The Polemic," 151). There are some accounts saying that Levi Yitsḥak took on these practices already when in Ryczywol and was persecuted for them there as well. See *Toledot ha-Meḥabber* #11.

18. *Tif'eret Bet Levi*, 4. The Talmudic reference is to b. Berakhot 31a. This description of extreme behavior by Levi Yitsḥak, especially at prayer, is confirmed both in anti-Hasidic documents and in the memoirs of the *maskil* Avraham Baer Gottlober, composed in the 1870s but containing much important and generally reliable information about earlier times. See the original 1880 edition, 383. The relevant passage is quoted by Lederberg in his "Misḥak ve-Theatraliut" in Mark and Horen, eds., *Levi Yitsḥak*, 264–65.

19. Note that this description is all about the young rabbi's conducting himself as a *ḥasid*, but not as a *rebbe*. There is no talk of his offering blessings, effecting healings, or the like. Descriptions of Levi Yitsḥak's unusual behavior during prayer and in moments of spontaneous ecstasy, including shouting out in Polish or Yiddish, jumping up on the

table or crouching beneath it, etc., are so widespread in the later literature that they most likely reflect a remembered reality.

20. Wolf Yasny, ed., *Yizkor-bukh fun der Zhelekhover Yidisher Kehile.*

21. See Schorr in LY volume, Mark and Horen, eds., 47, n. 5, and sources cited there.

22. On R. Uziel Maisels and on physical attacks against LY in Zelechow, see Wilensky, *Ḥasidim*, v. 2, 357. On this whole period, as well as on Levi Yitsḥak's ongoing relationship to the community of Żelechów, see Avraham Abish Schorr, "Rabbi Levi Yitsḥak mi-Berdichev Beyn Tsaddikey Doro." See also the remarks by R. Joseph Levinstein in his letter to Dubnov in Wilensky, *Ḥasidim*, v. 2, 357.

23. Details here concerning Levi Yitsḥak's children are copied from a *kvitl*, or prayer petition, allegedly given by Levi Yitsḥak to his friend/student R. Ḥayyim Krasner, who set out for the land of Israel, asking him to pray for them at the holy places there. A facsimile of the petition is printed in *Kedushat Levi ha-Shalem* (Jerusalem, 1978), edited by his descendant Ze'ev Derbarmdiger. The original is apparently in the family's possession. The document is undated, but all the children were already married, and all but the youngest had offspring. It is clearly from the Berdychiv period but prior to Meir's death in 1806.

24. Berdychiv, 1811. It is known by two titles, *Likkutey MaHaRIN* and *Toldot Yitsḥak ben Levi.*

25. *Keter Torah* (Mezirow, 1803); part two in Zhitomir, 1806.

26. The rest of the family order included three daughters, named Mitl, Esther, and Golda, a son named Dov Baer, and a youngest daughter named Liba Tirtsah.

27. Based on details found in *haskamot*, R. Hayyim Lieberman was able to fix Levi Yitsḥak's departure from Zelechow between May 1775 and August 1776. See his article in the *Alexander Marx Jubilee Volume*, reprinted in his *Ohel RaḤeL.*

28. The leading historian of Pinsk Jewry is Mordecai Nadav. See his *The Jews of Pinsk, 1506 to 1880.*

29. Avraham Rubenstein had tried to identify references in anti-Hasidic documents from 1774 as referring to Levi Yitsḥak, then rabbi of Zelechow, but Wilensky disagreed, finding him first mentioned only in the second round of bans in 1781, by which time he was a key figure. See Rubenstein, "Notes," and Wilensky, *Ḥasidim*, v. 1, 77, 79, 82.

30. A gold mine of information about Karlin Hasidism, as well as about the development of Hasidism in this period and region as a whole, is to be found in the collected writings of Avraham Abish Schorr, *Ketavim.*

31. On Rabbi Raphael's attitude toward Hasidism, see Nadav, *Pinsk*, 295–97.

32. See Nadav, *Pinsk*, 242–93.

33. This matter became a subject of controversy between him and R. Asher, later of Stolin, the third *rebbe* in the Karlin tradition (the son of its founder, R. Aharon). He settled in Zelechow around 1793 and lived there for eight years. Although Levi Yitsḥak was by then happily ensconced in rather distant Berdychiv, there were still *ḥasidim* in

Zelechow who retained a loyalty to him and resisted the new leadership of R. Asher. On this, see Schorr, *Ketavim*, 475–82.

34. Published in Wilensky, *Ḥasidim*, v. 1, 122–31.

35. This includes works like *Tsava'at RYVaSH* (published 1793), *Alpha Beta* (1799), and *Likkutim Yekarim* (1792). The most important studies of this genre are those of Ze'ev Gries, such as his *Conduct Literature*.

36. The public performance of somersaults, well-known in the circles of R. Avraham Kalisker and R. Ḥayyim Ḥaykl of Amdur, were specifically designated as weapons against pride, as they would lead one to be humiliated. See Rubenstein, "Notes." This sort of stoical Hasidic response to denunciation and persecution surely did not exist in the third round of controversy in 1798, when the *ḥasidim* as well as their opponents turned to the tsarist authorities to denounce the doings of the other side. LY's response by silence is suggested in *Tif'eret Bet Levi*, 5–6.

37. It first appeared as a pamphlet, as discussed by Wolf in *Iggeret ve-Sefer*. See the discussion by Cooper in *Levi Yitsḥak*, Mark and Horen, eds., 65, n. 4. It is reprinted in Wilensky, *Ḥasidim*, v. 1, 168–76.

38. See discussion in Wilensky, *Ḥasidim*, v. 1, 168–69.

39. This is a standard and formal statement of humility, implying no sense of guilt or responsibility for the conflict.

40. Although Levi Yitsḥak had already occupied the rabbinate of Pinsk for nine years, he is still referred to here, and even later when he was already ensconced in Berdychiv, as the rabbi of Zelechow. It was not unheard of for rabbis to retain earlier titles in this way despite having moved onward. This practice continues even today. In this case, however, it may be that he considered his deposition from that town illegitimate and continued to insist on his authority there by retaining the title. See discussion in A. A. Schorr, *Ketavim*, 476–81.

41. This is meant to justify Hasidic bodily movement during prayer, an accusation already raised against Levi Yitsḥak in Zelechow, as we have seen.

42. To stave off angelic insinuations that God is showing favoritism toward His beloved *tsaddikim*, God must send His love in the form of trials that the *tsaddik* will then confront and overcome. This may be seen as a sort of theodicy, explaining why the righteous suffer in this world.

43. This is a typically clever reread of a legal principle taken from an entirely different context (See b. Shabbat 25a), understood here to mean that the accusers are themselves sinners.

44. A proverb first found in the Alphabet of R. Akiva, beginning, and in Tikkuney Zohar 22 (66b).

45. R. Elimelekh's remarks on this subject apparently conclude here.

46. This is an understated but particularly bombastic accusation against the rabbi of

Brisk, and perhaps those behind him. He is indeed a leader, distinguished by both his ancestry and his learning. His role as accuser against a true *tsaddik* must be the result of some unatoned sin in his past. The phrase "sins of youth" usually applies to masturbation or other acts resulting from sexual temptation. In the next line, R. Eleazar takes responsibility and apologizes for the harshness of this language. Wilensky (*Ḥasidim*, v.1, 171, n. 19) quotes Dubnov in suggesting that this "leader of his generation" may refer to the Vilna Gaon.

47. This is, of course, a response to the claims of the anti-Hasidic forces that the charismatic leadership of Hasidism amounted to a sort of forbidden prophecy.

48. b. Yoma 69b.

49. See Wilensky, *Ḥasidim*, v.1, 132ff, 135, n. 9.

50. See discussion by Nadav, *Pinsk*, 301–4.

51. These documents have recently been discovered by Professor Yohanan Petrovsky-Shtern, and we look forward to their publication. I thank Professor Petrovsky-Shtern for having shared with me something of their important contents.

52. This is by no means to claim that the rabbinic courts themselves were always above corruption. Levi Yitsḥak's particular concern for judicial integrity in his rabbinic court is confirmed by various tales/reports in *Tif'eret Bet Levi*, 10. This is a significant theme in the tales about him, particularly when the victims are poor and the corruptors wealthy.

53. Lieberman, *Ohel RaḤeL* (New York, 1980), v. 1, 67.

54. Nadav, *The Jews of Pinsk*, 303–4, based on his article "R. Avigdor ben Haim's Struggle against Hasidism," in *Zion* 36 (1971), 201. R. Avigdor, a fierce enemy of Hasidism, and a relatively unqualified candidate for this distinguished post, succeeded Levi Yitsḥak, paying a large amount of money to acquire that privilege. The *ḥasidim* suffered under his rabbinate until 1793, when they succeeded in ousting him.

55. Among latter-day *ḥasidim*, down to the present, there is a belief that just pronouncing the word "Berdychiv" is a device that helps one attain the fear of heaven. See *Sippurey Tsaddikim he-Ḥadash*, part II, 9–10.

56. It is noteworthy that on the title page of the portion of *Kedushat Levi* that Levi Yitsḥak had printed in 1798, he refers to himself as rabbi of Berdychiv, Zelechow, and Ryczywol, but does not mention Pinsk. It seems that stop on his itinerary might have been a bad memory for him.

57. Petrovksy-Shtern, "The Drama of Berdichev," quoting Ignaz Schiper, a well-known interwar historian of Polish Jewry.

58. Though, interestingly, the cases Cooper brings are more about divorce and ritual matters than they are about business disputes. Perhaps a lesser *dayyan* dealt with those matters in Berdychiv.

59. See discussion by Cooper, *Levi Yitsḥak*, 93–94.

60. For details, see Cooper, *Levi Yitsḥak*, 97.

61. KL 2:402, *perushey aggadot*. The remark is included in the 1798 volume. This intention is noted also on the title page of that initial publication. On a manuscript of Levi Yitsḥak's Talmudic commentary lost in a later fire, see Cooper, *Levi Yitsḥak*, 109–10. On recent attempts to reconstruct and publish the minor Talmudic/halakhic legacy of Levi Yitsḥak, see the same work, 112–16.

62. In a large community like Berdychiv, there were probably several *maggidim* preaching in various synagogues. For the sermons of a Berdychiv *maggid*, clearly not a *ḥasid*, who served while Levi Yitsḥak was the town's rabbi, see *Imrei Binyamin*, printed in Tarnopol in 1814. The printing in Tarnopol makes it clear that this was a non-Hasidic work. Tarnopol was the one printing press in the Ukraine during those years that was controlled by the *maskilim*.

63. See *Zikhron Tov* 12, #4, as well as the important information on him gathered by Schorr in his *Ketavim*, 460–61, n. 30.

64. For a reference to a particular halakhic view of Levi Yitsḥak passed on by Wahrman, see Cooper, *Levi Yitsḥak*, 87. Wahrman also offers the interesting detail that he went to Berdychiv partly in hope of learning healings and cures from Levi Yitsḥak but did not succeed in doing so. Did Levi Yitsḥak, like the Maggid, have access to such traditions but refuse to pass them on? Or might Wahrmann's expectations simply have been misguided?

65. See the explanation of this controversy offered by Zvi Mark in *Cathedra* 64 (2004), 487–500.

66. *Zikhron Tov* 12, #1. "Singing very lovely tunes" is my best rendition of the obscure ויצאו מפיו תנועות יפות מאד.

67. *Zikhron Tov* 16, #15. Although this collection was printed quite late, these statements read like actual memories passed down rather than legendary recreations.

68. *Sippurey Tsaddikim he-Ḥadash*, part II, 10. It should be noted that R. Elimelekh died in 1786, a year after Levi Yitsḥak moved to Berdychiv. This incident comes into clearer focus if we imagine that when the already famous Levi Yitsḥak moved to Berdychiv from much more distant Pinsk, would-be disciples from Galicia indeed came to visit him.

69. Petrovsky-Shtern, "The Drama of Berdichev."

70. On this period in Jewish history, see the full treatment by John Klier in *Russia Gathers Her Jews: The Origin of the "Jewish Question" in Russia, 1772–1825* and the more general discussion in Polonsky, *The Jews*, v. 1, 322–54.

71. *Heikhal Berakhah, be-midbar*, introduction. Komarno tradition (*Otsar ha-Ḥayyim*): חלישות הדעת שנפל ממדריגתו בענין מ״ש [מורא שמים? מרה שחורה?] והיה מתפלל מתוך סידור קטן במהירות וניתק מעט דעתו. The source says that his longstanding friend (from back in the Zelechow years), R. Israel of Kozienice, was very helpful to him that year. This is reported by the Komarner's father-in-law, R. Avraham Mordechai of Pinczow, who was with Levi Yitsḥak in Berdychiv for the course of the following year, 1794.

See also Schorr, "Rabbi Levi Yitsḥak mi'Berdychiv Beyn Tzadikei Doro," in Mark and

Horen, eds., *Levi Yitsḥak*, 50–51. On such "falls" in the life of the *tsaddik*, see Levi Yitsḥak's own reflection in KL 1:419, *shir ha-shirim*, s.v. *le-reaḥ*.

72. The account of this incident recorded in Berger's *'Eser Orot*, 50, #23 seems to confirm this reading. It attributes the fall to his great struggle with the heavenly "princes" in that year, mentioned already in the Komarno source. But these "princes," as we shall see below in Levi Yitsḥak's own words, represent the interests of their earthly subjects, and the struggle with Count Radziwill could certainly have been read that way. A. A. Schorr (*Ketavim*, 479, n. 138–39) suggests that this "fall" of Levi Yitsḥak's may also have had to do with his conflict with R. Asher of Stolin when the latter settled in Zelechow in that year, a place where the local *ḥasidim* had maintained loyalty to Levi Yitsḥak from the time he had lived there. I suspect he may be attributing too much importance to that conflict.

73. It in fact serves as the title of Paweł Maciejko's masterful history of the Frankist movement, *The Mixed Multitude: Jacob Frank and the Frankist Movement, 1755–1816*.

74. For tales (possibly later) of Levi Yitsḥak's interchanges with *maskilim*, see *Tif'eret Bet Levi*, 11. It is also possible that *'erev rav* simply refers to the coarse merchants and leaseholders who were part of the system that so oppressed the Jews of Berdychiv.

75. On Levi Yitsḥak's relationship to the publishing industry, see Cooper, *Levi Yitsḥak*, 73–76. His conclusions are partially built on those of Grossberger in "Le-Hagdil Torah ule-Ha'adirah."

76. A full history of Hebrew printing in Berdychiv is Ya'ari's *Ha-Defus ha-'Ivri be-Berdychiv*.

77. See Halpern, "Rabbi Levi Yiẓhaq of Berdichew," 90–93.

78. Halpern, op. cit., 93–98. This Halpern essay is the major source for Levi Yitsḥak's communal activities. See also treatment by Cooper, *Levi Yitsḥak*, 68–73.

79. KL 2:52, *balak*.

80. The decree was the formal iteration of a process that had been taking shape for several years. See discussion in Polonsky, *The Jews*, v. 1, 334–37.

81. Although there is much murkiness about the origins and intent of the original heresies, they are attributed to the influence of a Jew named Zacharias of Koffa around 1480. A group of his followers, originally in Novgorod, arrived in Moscow that year and created something of a scandal. Zacharias was executed, along with some of his followers, in 1491. In 1550, Ivan the Terrible refused entry into Russia to Polish Jewish merchants because of the fear that they would influence further conversions or Judaizing tendencies. Later groups of Subbotniks, or Sabbath observers, among Russian Christians, well-known down to the nineteenth century, were at least culturally descended from these groups. For a recent treatment of the original heresies, see Goldfrank, "The 'Judaic-Reasoning Novgorod Heretics' and Some Echoes of Spain in Late Medieval Russia." See also the discussion in Klier, *Russia Gathers Her Jews*, 25–32.

82. This reading is confirmed by a longer sermon of Levi Yitsḥak's recorded in *Ge'ulat*

Yisra'el (#9 in the Levi Yitsḥak section). Here he names the country as Edom rather than Moab. Commenting on Num. 20:14 ("Moses sent messages from Kadesh to the king of Edom, saying 'Let me pass through your land . . .'"), he says that the Edomite ruler feared that the Israelites would uplift all the holy sparks that existed in his country as they walked through it, leaving behind none of the divine life force that makes existence possible. Even though Moses assured him that Israel would remain passive (*be-shev ve-'al ta'aseh*), he feared to let them in.

83. KL 2:329–30, *kedushat purim* #2.

84. A major point was made in the proposed Russian reforms of the Jews' status in 1804 of the requirement that rabbis learn to read and write Russian. See Klier, *Russia Gathers*, 136. As rabbi of such an important commercial center, this certainly was an ability expected of Levi Yitsḥak. We have no record, except possibly this reference, of how he felt about it.

85. See Schorr in *Levi Yitsḥak*, Mark and Horen, eds., 55, n. 33. See also his remarks in *Ketavim*, 461, n. 30.

86. R. Asher, the future *rebbe* of Stolin, lived in Zelechow for some period in the earliest years of the nineteenth century, and there was some conflict between him and Levi Yitsḥak as to the loyalty of the Ḥasidim in that town. See notes 40 and 71 above.

87. KL 2:5, *shavu'ot*.

88. Gutmann, *Tif'eret Bet Levi*, 10.

89. Levi Yitsḥak refers to him by that title already in 1798 in a teaching of his included in his original edition of *Kedushat Levi*. KL 2:431, *ḥiddushey torah*.

90. Gutmann, *Tif'eret Bet Levi*, 30. There is a surviving letter, seemingly authentic, by R. Yisra'el Hofstein of Kozienice addressed to Yisra'el in Berdychiv in summer (5 Elul) of 1814 (first published in *Siftey Kodesh* [Lodz: Mesorah, 1929] and reprinted at the front of the 1960 Jerusalem edition of *Likkutey MaHaRYN*). It contains an unusual introduction addressed to the people of Berdychiv, telling them how fortunate they are to have this great *tsaddik* in their midst. It seems likely that this was a statement of support, perhaps coming shortly after he ascended to that position.

91. Rabbi Avraham Abele Gombiner, a seventeenth-century Polish rabbi who was orphaned during the infamous Khmielnitsky massacre of 1648, is known by the name of his most influential work of scholarship. The *Magen Avraham* is a famous commentary on the *Oraḥ Ḥayyim* of Rabbi Yosef Karo's *Shulḥan 'Arukh*, which notably describes common practices of Polish Jewry, including Kabbalistic customs as transmitted by Rabbi Isaiah Horowitz in his *Shney Luḥot ha-Berit*.

92. On the question of rabbinic leadership passing by inheritance in an earlier era, see Avraham Grossman, "From Father to Son."

2. LEVI YITSḤAK IN THE MAGGID'S CIRCLE: THE CHALLENGE OF LEADERSHIP

1. Such non-Mezritch-based figures as R. Ya'akov Yosef of Polonnoye and R. Mikhl of Zlochow are denounced in the bans, to be sure, but their "crimes" are either publication or local activities, not large-scale movement building. For discussion of the early spread of Hasidism, see Rapoport-Albert, "Hasidism after 1772," and Green, "Around the Maggid's Table." My own view differs slightly from that of Rapoport-Albert. While I agree that there was no center of authority in the spread of Hasidism, I place greater emphasis on the closeness and mutual support of those who saw themselves as disciples of the Maggid and on their key role in the movement's spread and success. I also see an ongoing rivalry between the Mezritch circle, as a loosely defined group, and other, mostly less intellectual, Hasidic circles. Eventually (around 1800), that lineup changed, and such Mezritch disciples as Avraham Kalisker and Shlomo Karliner joined with the latter group, which came to be led by Barukh of Miedzybozh. See chapter 5.

2. We know of this "court" from the vivid and widely discussed account in the diary of Salomon Maimon. A convenient version of the relevant chapter is to be found in Hundert, *Essential Papers on Hasidism*. See also the new translation of Maimon's autobiography by Yitsḥak Melamed and Avraham Socher (2018). A brief portion of Maimon's account is reproduced below in chapter 6. See the important discussion of this source by Assaf in "He-Ḥasid ke-Adam Meṣaḥeq," and prior literature quoted there. The Maggid's court and its formative influence on this unique Hasidic institution is discussed in Etkes, "The Early Hasidic Court."

3. These appear in combined form in *Shivḥey ha-BeSHT*, 126–29. See *In Praise of the Ba'al Shem Tov*, 81–84.

4. Pedaya, "The Ba'al Shem Tov." In chapter 6, below, I will refer to them as "ecstatic" and "contemplative" mystics, my own preferred terms to describe the same differences that Pedaya has noted here.

5. See R. Shlomo Lutzker's introduction to the 1781 edition of *Maggid Devaraw le-Ya'akov*.

6. They also visited Rivne (Rovno), where the Maggid moved two years prior to his death.

7. *Shem ha-Gedolim he-Ḥadash*, 29–30. Israel Berger in *'Eser Orot*, 34–35, lists thirty-nine. Attempts to identify the key figures in this group as it existed before the Maggid's death are also problematic. Often, they rely either on the success of the disciple's reputation for written texts, collections of sermons published only decades later, or on his role in the later growth and spread of Hasidism, either through disciples or descendants who themselves became *rebbes* in the early nineteenth century. Neither the frequency with which the Maggid is quoted nor the precise way of referring to him ("my teacher," "our

master and teacher," etc.) in their writings is a good indicator. These matters are largely the work of editors, not the original preachers. Regarding one on the list, R. Meshullam Feibush Heller of Zbarash, we know from his testimony that he visited the Maggid's court only once and was more closely linked to the group around R. Yeḥiel Mikhl of Zloczow.

8. On R. Shmelke, see above in chapter 1. Others include R. Yissachar Ber of Zloczow, who was close to Levi Yitsḥak from their youth, and R. Uziel Meisels, also mentioned above, who served as rabbi of Satanov and authored several halakhic works in addition to his Hasidic *Tif'eret 'Uzi'el*.

9. ḤaBaD sources say that he turned down the rabbinate of Mogilev-Podolsk in 1777 and that he briefly served as rabbi of his native Liozna shortly afterwards. Heilman, *Bet Rabbi*, 12, n. 2.

10. There is no early book of Zusya's teachings, and there are famous Hasidic tales accounting for that. *Menorat Zahav*, a brief collation of teachings in his name gathered from other sources, was first published in Warsaw, 1904 (*Bet 'Eked Sefarim* lists 1902). But I note that he was regularly sought out for *haskamot* (unlike R. Leib Sarah's and R. Barukh of Miedzybozh, for example), including by R. Shne'ur Zalman for the *Tanya*. This makes me wonder whether the image of him as unlettered might be exaggerated. On R. Zusya, see Kauffman, "On the Portrait of a *Saddiq*: R. Zusha of Annipol."

11. R. David of Makow, the fiercest of Hasidism's denouncers, puts Levi Yitsḥak at the head of his list of sixteen "sinners" serving as leaders of the sect. See his *Zot Torat ha-Kena'ot* in Wilensky in *Ḥasidim*, v. 2, 196, and again in his testament, 244. R. David knew Levi Yitsḥak personally from his days in Zelechow. The fact that he had *ḥasidim* whom he visited in Makow itself must have been particularly irritating to R. David. From the Hasidic side, Heilman's account in *Bet Rabbi*, 9, of the origins of the Hasidic-Mitnaggedic conflict, while inaccurate in some details, identifies the insults against Levi Yitsḥak to have been the starting point.

12. I leave aside here the problematics of defining the Maggid's corpus itself, distinguishing it from the larger body of early anonymous Hasidic teachings. I am thus tentatively assuming such works as *Maggid Devarav le-Ya'aqov* (1781) and *Or Torah* (1804) to belong to "*kitvey ha-maggid*." For initial discussion of the problematics of establishing the Maggid's corpus, see Mayse, *Speaking Infinities* and *Beyond the Letters*.

13. It is largely absent, for example, from the *Me'or 'Eynayim* and the *Or ha-M'eir*. In the writings of R. Shne'ur Zalman of Liadi, it is indeed present but significantly reworked. In this matter (though not in some others), Levi Yitsḥak is closest to R. Avraham, the Maggid's son, and R. Menaḥem Mendel of Vitebsk. A later ḤaBaD tradition describes four close disciples listening to the more intense mystical teachings of the Maggid, referred to here as the "entire" teaching of the Maggid: "R. Shlomo of Karlin became ill with bloody stools, the [future] rabbi of Berdychiv went out of his mind [היה יוצא מגדר הכלים] amid tremendous mystical devotion and excitement [דבקות והתפעלות] [they were

therefore unable to hear all of it], and only our great rabbi [i.e., R. Shne'ur Zalman] and the Wolper received it [in full]." Reported by R. Shalom Ber Schneersohn, as recorded by his son R. Yosef Yizhak Schneersohn in *Sefer ha-Siḥot, Torat Shalom*, 82. Quoted by Schorr in *Ketavim*, 328, n. 52. This seems to be a description of a particular event, a moment when the Maggid revealed some great mystical secret. While these later ḤaBaD sources are to be treated with some suspicion (see Rapoport-Albert, "Hagiography with Footnotes"), the depiction here of Levi Yitsḥak as part of this innermost group of mystic hearers within Mezritch seems accurate. His very demonstrative response also fits with other descriptions of him that we have seen. On the mysterious Wolper (R. Ḥayyim of Wolpa), see Schorr, *Ketavim*, 368–85. Schorr disputes as calumny the ḤaBaD tradition that he later became a wandering alcoholic.

14. Sometimes also referred to as *Imrey Tsaddikim*.

15. See discussion by Piekarz, *Bi-Yemey Tsemiḥat ha-Ḥasidut*, 96–172, and many sources quoted there.

16. See Dresner, *The Zaddik*, 75–110. There is no question that R. Ya'akov Yosef's way of writing as a highly learned rabbi who was nevertheless so attracted to the BeSHT as to constantly refer to him as "my teacher" gave to the latter a certain respectability. Attributing that legitimacy to BeSHTian Hasidism was a major goal of his books. It may even be that he chose to write in an intentionally exaggerated rabbinic style, following the complex sermon pattern so identified with R. Moshe Alshekh, precisely in order to give this impression.

17. See discussion in Polonsky, *The Jews*, v. 1, especially 191–200.

18. The bans are published and fully discussed in Wilensky, *Ḥasidim*.

19. On this controversy, see Dov Raffel, *Ha-Vikuaḥ 'al ha-Pilpul*.

20. See discussion by Teller in "Tradition and Crisis?"

21. The *kahal* was under attack from without as well as facing decline in authority from within. The new tsarist authority, seeking greater control over the lives of its Jewish subjects, saw the *kahal* as an obstacle in its way. See Polonsky, *The Jews*, v. 1, 292–93, 365, 371–72.

22. *Tsaddik* is the more technical and theological term for the Hasidic leader used throughout the literature. In common parlance, especially in Yiddish, he is more generally referred to as *rebbe*. Only in the late twentieth century, largely as a result of the ravages of the Holocaust, do there emerge significant groups of Jews, especially in Israel, who define themselves as Hasidic by practice and family tradition without attachment to a particular *rebbe*.

23. See Scholem, "Revelation and Tradition."

24. Translation of the letter, as well as discussion of its various versions, can be found in Etkes, *The Besht*, 272–81.

25. *Butsina Di-Nehora*, 37. When questioned about the value of ascetic practices, he

said, "I came into this world to show a different way. A person should draw three things upon himself: Love of God, Love of Israel, and Love of Torah." These are often taken to be the starting point of Hasidic teaching.

26. See Green, "The Hasidic Homily," 261, n. 26, for extensive documentation. Salomon Maimon, in his account of his visit to "M," (= Mezritch) already mentions that the Hasidic masters claim to be invested with the holy spirit when they preach.

27. See the Talmudic sources as discussed by Glatzer, "Talmudic-Midrashic Interpretation of Prophecy," and Urbach, "*Halachah* and Prophecy."

28. b. Berakhot 52b; ʿEruvin 7a, etc.

29. Already in the earliest bans against Hasidism, issued in Vilna in 1772, suggestions of false prophecy are included. See Wilensky, *Ḥasidim*, v. 1, 37, n.7.

30. See Green, "*Zaddik* as Axis Mundi," as well as Scholem's earlier "Three Types of Jewish Piety." See also Mach, *Der Zaddik*.

31. On *tsaddik* in the Kabbalah, see Scholem, *On the Mystical Shape of the Godhead*, 88–139, and Liebes, "The Messiah of the Zohar." On the issue of piety and power in the figure of the *tsaddik*, see J. Garb, *Manifestations of Power*, and the extensive discussion below.

32. See Liebes, "The Messiah of the Zohar."

33. See discussion in my introduction to *The Light of the Eyes*, section 7, "The *Tsaddik* in *Me'or ʿEynayim*."

34. In the writings of R. Yaʿakov Yosef and others of his generation, the new sort of leader is still usually called by the old term *talmid ḥakham*, although its meaning has been transformed in the emerging Hasidic spirit. See discussion in Dresner, *The Zaddik*. In the writings of some other members of the Maggid's circle, the term is used sometimes to designate the emerging Hasidic leader but often to refer simply to a righteous person. This ambiguity of usage can often lead one astray in understanding the intent of a particular passage.

3. FIRST STEPS: THE EVIDENCE OF *SHEMU'AH TOVAH*

1. According to the title page of the 1972 edition.

2. Prior printings of the Maggid's teachings include *Maggid Devaraw le-Yaʿakov* (1781), *Or Torah* (1804), *Kitvey Kodesh* (1862), and *Or ha-Emet* (1899). The relationship among these works, plus unattributed early Hasidic teachings and quotations from the Maggid elsewhere, is extremely complex. To these must be added a work called *Likkutey Amarim*, first published in Lvov, 1911, and attributed to R. Menaḥem Mendel of Vitebsk but recently shown to be another collection of the Maggid's teachings. It is not clear, for example, whether the teachings of the Maggid in *Shemuʿah Tovah* were derived from the same manuscript(s), as were prior publications, or from an independent source. See Mayse, "Beyond the Letters," and his "Speaking Infinities," 238–44.

3. Levi Yitsḥak refers to the Maggid in this way in various pages of the *Kedushat Levi* on Hanukkah and Purim, which he published in 1798. See, for example, 2:288, *ḥannukah*; 349–50; 366, *purim*. The Zoharic phrase *butsina kadisha*, "holy lamp," is often added. That appellation in the Zohar literature refers specifically to R. Shim'on ben Yoḥai, but it is widely used in hasidic works to refer to the *tsaddikim*.

4. The overlap between the *Shemu'ah Tovah* homilies and material found in *Kedushat Levi* is extensive. The *Parashat Devarim* sermon in *Shemu'ah Tovah* is found in abbreviated form in KL 2:262–63, *likkutim,* linked to the same Avot passage. The second sermon on *va-etḥanan*, beginning with *atah hor'eyta*, is found in KL 2:182, *ve-zot ha-berakhah,* though with a sharper anti-Gentile tone, perhaps caused by LY's experiences in the course of his career. The lengthy sermon on *yir'ah* in *'ekev* is repeated in shorter form in KL 2:121–25, *'ekev*. The theme of giving pleasure to God, strongly stated in connection with the passage from Pesaḥim 112a ("More than the cow wants to nurse…") is a major theme in *Kedushat Levi,* witnessed, for example, in 1:67, *va-yera*; 2:130, *re'eh*; 2:257–58, *likkutim*. The intimacy of kissing between friends, described quite passionately in *Shemu'ah Tovah,* 23b, *'ekev*, is strongly echoed in KL 2:418, *perushey aggadot*. Further parallels are likely to emerge through close comparative study.

5. These two sermons plus one other are printed near the end of *Shemu'ah Tovah* 84a–87, not in the order of the others. The reason for this is not indicated. They are not as elaborately written out as are those printed at the head of the volume. My guess is that they were intended for a different audience, delivered in a more informal setting.

6. *Shalom 'alayikh nafshi*, in connection with separating from the community's needs, is found in b. Ta'anit 11a.

7. I.e., "Work to bring out the best in people."

8. m. Avot 5:21.

9. I.e., you are already in a state of deep spiritual devotion, based on Ps. 109:22.

10. הלל אומר אל תפרוש מן הצבור ואל תאמין בעצמך וכו׳ [עד יום מותך] ואל תדין את חברך וכו׳ [עד שתגיע למקומו] ואל תאמר דבר שא״א לשמוע וכו׳ [שסופו להשמע . . .] ע״ד הפשוט יראה כי בא להזהיר האיש הישראלי הבא להתקדש בקדושתו ית׳ ולהטהר לעמוד על התורה ועל העבודה. לבל יאמר שלום עליך נפשי לדידי קראי לדידי תנאי ודיינו להפקיע א״ע. ולא ישים מגמתו אל עדת ד׳ להשיב רבים מעון. וימנע מלהורותם דרך ד׳ ילכו בה להזדרז בעבודתו ביראה ואהבה ודביקות. ע״ז אמר כי לא זו הוא הדרך ישכון בה אור השלימות ולא זו העיר רוח קדושה וטהרה על עצמו כפי שלימות התכלית האמיתי הנרצה. כי הנה העובד את בוראו מאהבה שלימה שלא ע״מ לקבל פרס. רק לעשות נחת רוח ליוצרו לא ישקוט ולא ינוח לו במעשי עבודתו את הבורא ית׳ לבד. אבל ישים כל מגמתו תמיד לאמר מי יתן והיו כל עם ד׳ נביאים כי יתן ד׳ את רוחו עליהם שבזה יתגדל ויתרבה הנחת והשעשוע להבורא ב״ה ויתעצם כבודו. כעבד מלך הנאמן המשכיל אשר לאהבתו את אדוניו בלב שלם ונפש חפיצה יחפוץ שכך עבדי אדוניו יעבדוהו באמונה[. . .] וסיפר הכתוב במעלת העבד הזה. אם תוציא יקר מזולל כפי תהי׳. וז״ש אל תפרוש מן הצבור ר״ל אל תפרוש מהם מלהורותם הדרך ילכו בה בעבודת הבורא ב״ה הם דרכי היראה והאהבה והדביקות וביאר טעם הדבר. כי זולת שהדבר ראוי ונכון מצד האהבה לבורא ית׳ כנ״ל, עוד ימשוך מזה תועלת גדול אל עצמותך. כי נודע מ״ש רז״ל כל המזכה את הרבים אין חטא בא ע״י. ושמא תאמר שאינך צריך

לזאת התועלת. כי כבר הגעת אל ראש המעלות הרמות בעבודתו ודביקותו ית׳ וגבה לבך בדרכי ה׳ וכבר לבך חלל בקרבך ולא יאונה לך כל עון אשר חטא. לזה אמר לא כן הדבר שלא תאמין בעצמך וכו׳. (Emphasis added.)

11. See Green, "*Zaddiq* as Axis Mundi in Later Judaism," and Scholem, "The Legend of the Thirty-Six Righteous."

12. The question of "prophesying," without any clear definition, was around even prior to Hasidism in the circle of R. Naḥman of Kossov. R. Naḥman was capable of prophecy (the term is not clearly defined), but the members of the circle had agreed to avoid it, most likely as a reaction to the widespread phenomenon of prophecy in Sabbatian circles, where both the act and the term were welcomed without hesitation. On Sabbatian prophecy, see Rapoport-Albert, *Women and the Messianic Heresy of Sabbatai Zevi 1666–1816*. On the Hasidic hesitancy, see Heschel, *Circle,* 116. The later conflict between R. Shne'ur Zalman of Liadi and R. Avraham Kalisker, where the latter was accused of having stirred up the first opposition to Hasidism, may also relate to the place of prophet-like forms of extreme behavior. See discussion below in chapter 5.

13. *Shemu'ah Tovah* 84–85. ואם חבריו יעבדו עבודתם בחריצות ושקידה רבה יותר ממנו. אשר בזה יגיעו למעלה רמה ונשגבה יותר ממנו. לא ישנא אותם מקנאתו בהם. אבל יהי׳ לו זאת לשעשוע ועונג גדול הנחת אשר אדוניו מקבל מעבודתם. רק שיוכיח את נפשו ויכלמנה על קיצורו בעבודה מחבריו. ולעבדי המלך המקצרים בעבודה, יוכיחם על פניהם ויורם את הדרך אשר בה ישובו להזדרז בעבודה על תכלית השלימות[. . .] עוד בא להזהיר את האדם לבל יסור יראת ד׳ מעל פניו אף רגע אחת, אבל יעשה כמש״ה שויתי ה׳ לנגדי תמיד וכמ״ש הרמ״א ז״ל בא״ח (סי׳ א׳) בשם הרמב״ם כנודע. ואמרו רז״ל מגיד לאדם מה שיחו אפי׳ שיחה קלה וכו׳ וז״ש ואל תאמר דבר שא״א לשמוע. ר״ל דבר שהיית בוש מלהשמיעו לאזני בני אדם אל תאמרהו אפי׳ בחדרי חדרים. וכמש״ה משכבת חיקך שמור וכו׳ וטעם הדבר שסופו להשמע. ר״ל זולת זאת שהוא ית׳ מלא כל הארץ כבודו ואתה מסלק בזה המורא והבשת מעליך. עוד גם שבשעת הדין יגיעו לך שיחתך זאת ואוי לאותו בושה וכלימה אשר יגיעך אז שהדבר אשר לא היית מדברו בפני בני אדם יושבי חושך כמותך שוכני בתי חומר גלו שמים עוונך ויפרסמוהו לעיניך בפני פמליא של מעלה וכל הצדיקים ולכן תהי׳ נזהר בכל דבורך ותנועותיך ותמיד על יזוז מורא בוראך ובושתך ממנו מעליך וטוב לך.

14. Here follows a lengthy digression concerning the judgment of body and soul.

15. All this, including the word *shalshelet*, is taken directly from Tanḥuma, *koraḥ* 5.

16. *Shemu'ah Tovah* 85–86. והוי מתחמם נגד אורן של חכמים והוי זהיר בגחלתן וכו׳ [שלא תכוה]. נקדים לשום לב אל מ״ש משה רבע״ה וירדו חיים שאולה [וידעתם כי נאצו האנשים האלה את ה׳. . .] והנה ארז״ל קרח שפקח הי׳ מה ראה לשטות זה. עינו הטעתו וכו׳ כי הנה ענין מחלוקת קרח שחלק על מרע״ה לא שהי׳ שוטה רק שרצה להיות כה״ג שסבור שהוא יוריד השפע הקדוש ויהי׳ במקום אהרן. כי הי׳ ג״כ אדם גדול. רק שהי׳ רוצה להביא השפע באופן אחר כמבואר במקום אחר. אך הנה אדם גדול כזה שהשכל מאיר בו קשה עליו איך לא הבין שלא יחטא נגד משה והבורא ב״ה אך הענין שהשכל שהי׳ לו (בו) לא הי׳ בו מצד עצמיותו רק שראה שלשלת גדולה יוצאה ממנו ומקום מחצב נשמתו הי׳ רב ועצום ואדם כזה כשהוא רוצה לעלות למקום מחצבו ואינו יכול מחמת שאינו יודע סדר העליות הוא נעקר מן העולם[. . .] והנה הת״ח נקרא עץ השדה וגחלת והתורה הקדושה שבו הוא האור הנאחז בהעץ הוא הגחלת כמ״ש ותורה אור[. . .] בד״ת ההתנגדות הוא טוב כשהכוונה הוא לעמוד על אמיתת הדין שמהחימום ההוא רווחא שמעתתא כנ״ל. אבל אם ההתנגדות הוא לעצמות גופו של הת״ח יכווה המתנגד בגחלתו כנ״ל. וזהו והוי מתחמם כנגד אורן וכו׳ ר״ל הוי מתנגד להאור שבו זו התורה ומהגחלת הוא עצמיותו הזהר שלא תכווה כנ״ל.

17. On R. Yeḥiel Mikhl, see Altshuler, *Rabbi Meshulam Feibush Heller*, 30ff. While I do

not agree with all of Altshuler's conclusions, there is much to be learned from a careful reading of her work. Without saying so directly, she points to an ongoing rivalry between these two *maggidim* and their followers.

18. On R. Yitsḥak, see Heschel, *Circle,* 162–81.

19. *Likkutim Yekarim,* 110a. Cited by Altshuler, 30.

20. R. Yosef of Yampole was the eldest of the five sons. Alfasi, in *Sefer ha-Admorim,* does not list a birth date for him but does list his brothers Yitsḥak of Radziwill as born in 1741 and Mordechai of Kremnitz in 1746. This contradicts Altshuler's assertion (page 41) that R. Yosef was born only in the late 1750s, based on a story in *Shivḥey ha-BeSHT*. (On her later website, she sets that date as late as 1760.) Heschel (*Circle,* 174, n. 83) suggests a date as late as 1734 for the birth of R. Yeḥiel Mikhl. If that is true, Altshuler's dating for his son's birth would make more sense.

21. Heschel, *Circle,* 170–74. R. David of Makow (*Shever Poshe'im,* 71b) in Wilensky, *Ḥasidim,* v. 2, 170, quotes a Hasidic tradition that R. Mikhl was a reincarnation of the prophet Habbakuk.

22. R. Yosef of Yampole married the daughter of R. Barukh (Altshuler, 58, n. 128). This may confirm the sense of an ongoing non- or anti-Mezritch strain within early Hasidic leadership.

23. Schorr, *Ketavim,* 465, n. 53 (*Beyt Aharon ve-Yisra'el* 132:66).

24. *Zemir 'Aritsim u-Ḥarvot Tsurim,* based on Is. 25:5 and Josh. 5:2, printed in Aleksnits, 1772.

25. This sermon is not dated, but it is part of a group belonging to 1773 and '74 and quite clearly belongs to the group.

26. It is not clear whether the group of sermons preserved in *Shemu'ah Tovah* is complete or whether an earlier part of the original manuscript might be missing. In at least one place, he states, "as I have said above," regarding an item not found in the present group. On the other hand, it is likely that these sermons were preached only during the summer months, when the Sabbath is longer. Perhaps only the sermons for the first two Sabbaths of the book of Numbers (*be-midbar* and *naso*) are missing.

27. *Shemu'ah Tovah* 5a.

28. See Scholem, "Three Types," and discussion by Green in "Typologies."

29. The undated letter of R. Eleazar, son of R. Elimelekh of Lezajsk, referred to above, is an important piece of evidence in trying to determine this question. He seems to use the terms somewhat interchangeably. But when discussing the right of the particularly pious to abandon the custom of Ashkenaz and pray according to the Lurianic tradition, he adds the statement that "there are some who are not on the rung I described who pray in this version. They join themselves to the elevated *ḥasidim*, and they too are called *ḥasidim*" (Wilensky, *Ḥasidim,* v. 1, 172).

30. Within the Maggid's own writings, see the very useful list of parables concerning

sons and fathers in Schatz-Uffenheimer's edition of MDL, index s.v. *mashal*. Judaism contains a long history of this typology of son vs. servant. It has been discussed at length by Idel in *Sonship*.

31. *Shemu'ah Tovah* 5a: וז"ש לא ע"ה חסיד, והוא כי מדריגת החסידות לא ישיג רק מי שכבר שלט בתאוותו החמרית ונפרד ממנה ונתדבק אל השכליות אשר משם יעלה בסתר המדריגה להשיג מעט מידיעתו ית׳ רוממותו וגדולתו ואז יתלהט ויכסוף רצונו לעשות נחת רוח ליוצרו, משא"כ במי שעדיין לא נפרד מהתאווה החומרית הארצית שזהו לא יוכל להיות חסיד כנ"ל, וזהו ולא עם הארץ שהוא הנדבק בארציות, לא יוכל להיות חסיד.

32. I quote the entire verse, which is partially shortened in the printed sermon. The word *sarav* is especially significant here.

33. These are the seventy heavenly princes or angels that rule over the seventy nations of humanity according to rabbinic sources, including Shemot Rabbah 21:5, Tanḥuma *be-shalaḥ* 13, etc. The word *sarim* could refer to either heavenly or earthly rulers, and I am suggesting that the ambiguity in Levi Yitsḥak's usage is intentional.

4. THE HASIDIC TSADDIK AND THE QUEST FOR MODELS

1. The claim that the Hasidic *tsaddik* is indeed the only proper leader for the Jewish people is also central to the writings of R. Ya'akov Yosef of Polonnoye. Ya'akov Yosef does not yet consistently use the term *tsaddik* to describe this figure; that seems to have emerged in the school of the Maggid. See the extensive discussion in Dresner, *The Zaddik*, and Green, "Typologies."

2. For examples of this dichotomy in the TYY, see 228, *bo*; 282, *yitro*; 547, *tsav*, where they are compared to Noah and Abraham.

3. Dov Baer, *Or Torah*, 119, *tehillim*, quoting b. Berakhot 34b. Here the Maggid is close to the view expressed by Levi Yitsḥak in the above-quoted sermon recorded in *Shemu'ah Tovah*, preached right after the Maggid's death. For a parallel, see TYY 382, *yitro*.

4. KL 1:20, *noaḥ*; based on Zohar 1:106a, etc. See the many sources quoted by Rand ad loc.

5. *No'am Elimelekh*, 455–6, *shelaḥ*. Translated in *Speaking Torah, shelaḥ*. The Hebrew *me-'olam* in the original remark means "never." Playing on the later, and especially Eastern European understanding of the word *'olam* (*oilem* in Yiddish), he is reading it as "the public" or "ordinary people."

6. On the BeSHT's view of how to preach, see the story of the preacher who spoke ill of Israel in *Shivḥey ha-Besht*, 235–36; *In Praise*, 182–83. See also his parable about preachers in TYY 659, *kedoshim*. Despite this and other quotations, this distinction did not always work for the Toledot himself, who was known to have been of sterner disposition. But see TYY, *naso*, 843, where he commends Aaron for having been a man of *ḥesed*, thus beloved by others and able to raise them up. Other leaders, he notes, do in fact love their hearers, but that love is not reciprocated, as the preacher is "reproving them about heavenly matters." In the end, he is less successful in getting them to change their ways.

He is likely speaking here from experience. On the broader background of preachers' styles in pre-Hasidic Eastern Europe, see Piekarz, *Bi-Yemey Tsemiḥat ha-Ḥasidut*, 96–172.

7. KL 2:47, ḥukkat.

8. This linkage is stated explicitly in a letter by R. Yitsḥak Eisik of Zhidachov, included in *Darkhey Yesharim* by R. Menaḥam Mendel of Premishlany (Chernovtsy, ed., 1855, 11b).

9. This positive approach to preaching, followed almost universally in Hasidism, stands in sharp contrast to that which dominated within the *Mussar* movement as it arose in late nineteenth-century Lithuania. There the preacher saw his task as one of breaking down the stubborn ego of his hearers, bringing them to tearful repentance and to a willingness to rebuild their moral character from the ground up.

10. The notion that a *tsaddik* is one who has eyes that see only the good in people is widespread in early Hasidic sources. It is especially identified in many tales with the character of R. Zusya of Anipol.

11. KL 2:73–74, *pinḥas*. Angels obviously don't need to eat. Abraham's act of feeding them as soon as they arrived was a way of demonstrating to them how fragile humans are, being dependent on material sustenance. It is worth recalling, by the way, that these angels were on their way to punish the wicked of Sodom, for whom Abraham was soon to intervene in another way as well. This motif in Levi Yitsḥak's writings will be treated more fully below in chapter 9.

12. KL 2:132–3, *shoftim*. The concluding quotation is from b. Soṭah 8b. Emphasis added.

13. This psychological role of the *tsaddik* as moral healer is most fully portrayed by R. Naḥman of Bratslav in his well-known reading of the verse beginning *azamrah*, Psalm 146:2. See *Likkutey MoHaRaN* 1:272.

14. It appears in the first section of *Ge'ulat Yisra'el*, compiled by Yehoshu'a Avraham be Yisra'el and published in Ostrog, 1821. This section was reprinted under the new title *Pitgamin Kaddishin*, Warsaw, 1887 et seq. It should be noted that 1821 is only thirteen years after Levi Yitsḥak's death, a time when many who had known him were still alive. This, along with the contents of these teachings themselves, gives strong reason to lend them credence. The work is divided into two sections, one a collection of teachings by various Ukrainian *tsaddikim* but featuring especially the line extending from the Maggid to Levi Yitsḥak and on to his most important disciple R. Aharon of Zhitomir. It seems likely that the editor was working directly from oral or written sources collected within that circle. The second section of the volume contains the earliest printed material from the circle of R. Pinḥas of Korzec.

15. b. Berakhot 10a.

16. *Heh* bowing to *vav* is found in Vital's *Peri 'Ets Ḥayyim*, Purim 6. It is frequently referenced in the writings of the *Toledot*. See TYY 748, *emor*, and references assembled there in n. 349.

17. *Ge'ulat Yisrael, Levi Yitsḥak* #5. An interesting parallel to this defense of wandering

tsaddikim is found in DME, by the Baʿal Shem Tov's grandson Efrayim of Sudilkow. See there, 463a, *masaʿey*, and also 455a, *liqqutim*. Emphasis added.

18. Dov Baer was an exception, having an early established "court" in Mezritch and later in Rovno. This may have been due to a physical disability, which would have made regular travel difficult.

19. Compare this to Menaḥem Naḥum's comparison of the *tsaddik* to a peddler, quoted below in chapter 7.

20. *Ge'ulat Yisra'el #18.*

21. KL 1:20, *noaḥ*.

22. Based on Vital, *Shaʿar ha-Pesukim*, bereshit #6.

23. See Green, *Devotion*, where I long ago suggested that the Hasidic Abraham had a certain typological closeness to the Pauline Abraham, based on the Christian reading of Genesis 15:1.

24. KL 1:49, *lekh lekha*. This is linked by Levi Yitsḥak to the well-known rabbinic reading of Gen. 2:4 (BR 12:9) that treats *be-hibare'am*, "as they were created," as an anagram for Abraham. This passage is a much more radical example of "Incarnational Hasidism" than the Abraham text from *Or ha-Me'ir* quoted by Magid on page 24 of his book, *Hasidism Incarnate*. On the related notion of Abraham as an *adopted* son of God, see Idel, *Sonship*, 133–4. For an account of Abraham's birth that parallels or imitates the New Testament story of the Christ child, see the long passage from *Sefer ha-Yashar* (Venice, ed.,1624, 18a–19a) quoted by Ginzberg in *Legends of the Jews*, v. 1, 207–9, and v. 5, 217, n. 48.

25. Compare b. Sukkah 49b.

26. KL 1:34, *lekh lekha*.

27. See the treatment by Or N. Rose in "Protest or Discernment" in *Be-Ron Yaḥad*, Green and Mayse, eds.

28. See discussion above in chapter 1 and below in chapter 11.

29. KL 1:191–92, *shemot*. This source is discussed more fully below in chapter 10, n. 60–61. Compare also Moses' mind "turned upward" here to the reference below in chapter 6 to the *tsaddik*'s self-negation because his mind is turned upward rather than downward.

30. KL 186–88, *yitro*. The "thick cloud" is the less-than-perfect vision, perhaps even using anthropomorphic imagery, needed to communicate with the people. Moses seeks to reach beyond this but is instructed not to place himself out of reach.

31. KL 2:42–43, *koraḥ*. Might we extend this to see a claim here that the Maggid's son, the "Angel," was not an appropriate heir to leadership any more than were Moses' sons? If Levi Yitsḥak was, as I argue here, a strong advocate for going forth and spreading the teachings, i.e., expanding the movement, perhaps he saw the quietism of the Angel as standing in his way. This difference is also reflected in the respective literary styles of the Maggid's collected teachings in MDL and the notably clearer and more accessible

versions of the same ideas in KL.

32. b. Shabbat 115a

33. KL 1:360, *terumah.*

34. ST 39–40. The comment on the *shekhinah* and the Western Wall is from Tanḥuma, *shemot* 10.

35. See above, chapter 3.

36. b. Berakhot 31b–32a. For two modern treatments of this theme, see Anson Raytner, *Arguing with God*, and Dov Weiss, *Pious Irreverence.*

37. Despite Moses' being always designated as *rabbenu*, "our teacher," not as *tsaddik*, in traditional sources.

38. KL 2:38, *shelaḥ*. For an enlightening discussion of this Torah passage, very much in Levi Yitsḥak's spirit, see Muffs, *The Personhood of God*, 100–101.

39. See the discussion in Magid, *Hasidism Incarnate.*

40. KL 1:247–8, *be-shalaḥ*. The Talmudic reference משה שפיר קאמרת is to b. Shab. 101b. It is used this way already in *Shney Luḥot ha-Berit*, *Shavu'ot*, *Torah Or*, and is widely quoted in early Hasidic literature in discussions of the *tsaddik*. See, for example, DME 176, *yitro*, and NE, 312, *tetsaveh.*

41. Tikkuney Zohar 69, 112b.

42. Midrash Tehillim ad loc. For a full discussion of this theme in early rabbinic sources, see Meeks, "Moses as God and King."

5. THE MEZRITCH CIRCLE: A LATER LOOK

1. Several fascinating accounts of R. Shlomo's death are collected in *Shema' Shelomo*, part II, 20d–21b. These also include the tradition within Karlin that he died a martyr and was thought to be the martyred Messiah ben Joseph. I have heard Schorr recount that the Jews of Ludmir regularly referred to his burial place as "the grave of Messiah ben Joseph."

2. This *'aliyah* has been much discussed in the scholarship on early Hasidism. See Etkes, "On the Motivation for Hasidic Immigration (*'aliyah*) to the Land of Israel." See also the early treatment by Halpern, "Ha-'Aliyot ha-Rishonot shel ha-Ḥasidim," as well as those by Assaf, "She-Yaṣa Shemu'ah she-ba Mashiaḥ Ben David," and Haran, "Mah Heni'a et Talmidey ha-Maggid La-'alot le-Erets Yisra'el?" On R. Menaḥem Mendel and the unique Hasidic community that he and the Kalisker created there, see the insightful introduction by Glazer to the translation of *Pri ha-Arets* in his *From Tiberias, With Love*, v. 1, as well as the second volume in that series (2020), coedited with Nehemia Polen. The second volume is a collection of essays on R. Avraham Kalisker and selected translations from his *Ḥesed le-Avraham*. That volume arrived too late for full consideration here of the important articles by Mayse and Polen, adding much clarity to issues around the controversy discussed in this chapter. Generally we are in agreement about the main

outlines of that conflict.

3. The degree of independent authority R. Shne'ur Zalman enjoyed increased gradually. At first, he was clearly R. Menaḥem Mendel's representative "on the ground" in Reisin, the personal bond between the master in Tiberias and his disciples remaining strong. In 1785–86, however, both the Vitebsker and the Kalisker wrote to Shne'ur Zalman urging him to play a stronger role. See the discussion by Etkes, *Shneur Zalman*, chapter 1b, disagreeing with some of the views of Haran in the article cited below, n. 8.

4. See Etkes, *Rabbi Shneur Zalman*, chapter 2, "A Leader of Hasidism," 22–63.

5. On ḤaBaD history, including this period, see also Dov Baer Levin, *Toledot ḤaBaD be-Russia ha-Tsarit*, part 1.

6. On the Chernobyl dynasty and its history, see Sagiv, *Dynasty*, as well as brief remarks in the final section of my introduction to *The Light of the Eyes*. A memoir of Hasidic life in Chernobyl is Mekler's *Fun Rebin's Hoif.*

7. Wilensky, *Ḥasidim*, v. 2, 196. See above, chapter 2, n. 11.

8. On this dispute, see Haran, "R. Abraham of Kalisk and R. Shneur Zalman of Liadi—A Friendship Cut Off."

9. Darkening the bright light, or obvious meaning, of Hasidic teachings. Based on an ancient mythic view that the sun enters an encasement as it sets and therefore cannot be seen at night. See b. Nedarim 8a.

10. b. Ḥullin 137b. There it means that biblical and rabbinic Hebrew usages are to be distinguished, but here he means that "the light of Torah," the teachings of our Hasidic masters, should not be confused with the "language of the sages," the abstruse and potentially misleading symbolic language of Lurianic Kabbalah. He is interestingly admitting that the BeSHT and the Maggid had created a sort of new religious language, one that spoke more directly than that of the prior mystical tradition.

11. *Geshem*, the word for "rain," here mean "the corporeal," as in *gashmi*, "physical," as opposed to *ruḥani*, "spiritual." He means to say that the symbolic language of Kabbalah is too likely to be taken literally, especially by an "inadequate" generation of hearers, and thus "corporealized," leading people to think of God in overly physical terms. This was considered particularly dangerous because Kabbalah is filled with sexual imagery. There is evidence of both internal Hasidic concern and anti-Hasidic accusation that the popularization of mystical teachings would lead to a coarse vulgarization of such symbols. See discussion below in chapter 10. This suspicion is likely related to the leftover impact of Sabbatian and Frankist teachings, which tended to use such sexual symbolism in especially bold ways. Among the most extreme examples of this is the treatise *Va-Avo ha-Yom el ha-'Ayin*, which modern scholarship has confirmed as authored by R. Yonatan Eybeschutz.

12. Based on Job 15:5. His choice of *leshon 'arumim* may mean that one can refer to the deeper secrets in hints, but the surface meaning of one's words should lead people to proper emotions and behavior. Note that reference to *guf* and *middot*, "body and

emotions" (or "moral qualities"), locates the discussion in the two lower triads of the Kabbalistic *sefirot* (*ḤaGaT NeHI*), as distinct from *ḤaBaD*, reflecting a preference for contemplation of the highest intellectual realms. This is precisely the point of departure between the Kalisker and R. Shne'ur Zalman.

13. This book demands too much learning; the Hasidic message in it is overly intellectualized. But the verse he chooses here (Is. 29:13) is regularly found in early Hasidic texts to refer to "learned" (or "routinized") religious behavior, precisely the sort of Judaism that the BeSHT's teachings were created to oppose. Study of your book, in other words, will lead people in precisely the wrong direction.

14. The full text of the letter is published in Hilman, *Iggerot Ba'al ha-Tanya u-Veney Doro*, 105–7. See also Mondshine, *Masa'*.

15. See treatment by Etkes in *Shneur Zalman*, 244–45, as well as that by Schorr in Mark and Horen, eds., *Levi Yitsḥak*, n. 34. For a listing of all the books known to have received approbations from Levi Yitsḥak, see Cooper, 74, n. 23, in the same volume.

16. Mondshine, *Masa'*, 51, n. 178, quoting *ReMaḤ Otiyyot*.

17. Heilman, *Bet Rabbi*, 126. See also *Zikhron Tov* 6, #10. There R. Yitsḥak of Neskhiz recalls that when he asked Levi Yitsḥak, his prospective grandfather-in-law, what he thought of the writings of Shne'ur Zalman, Levi Yitsḥak replied with high praise for his halakhic work, *Sefer Birkat ha-Nehenin*. This is clearly a backhanded slap at the *Tanya*. This account, though recorded later, should be added to my other suggestions of reasons to think that Levi Yitsḥak was less than happy with that work, and that R. Shne'ur Zalman knew what he was doing by avoiding asking him for an approbation for it.

18. R. Shlomo of Karlin had died in 1792, killed in Ludmir in the course of the Russian-Polish war. His place was taken by R. Asher, son of his master R. Aharon of Karlin. It is noteworthy that there was also a marital connection between Karlin and Miedzybozh. In 1786, R. Dov Baer (later of Tulchin), the son of R. Shlomo Karliner, was married to a daughter of R. Barukh, who had no sons. See Schorr, *Ketavim*, 411.

19. There are various Hasidic stories in which R. Barukh speaks ill of Levi Yitsḥak and, when challenged, takes it back and shows that he meant only the highest praise or good wishes. One such account is found in *Zikhron Tov* 6, #9. This rivalry is also reflected in a letter to Levi Yitsḥak by Ya'akov Yitsḥak of Lublin, a younger disciple of the Maggid who struggled to stay neutral in this dispute. In the letter, he says, "It is not my way to become involved in any dispute or argument, especially between two great *tsaddikim*, God forbid." He then goes on to apologize for having visited R. Barukh but not Levi Yitsḥak during a trip to Ukraine. The letter is undated but was written after 1800. The letter is printed in *Tseror ha-Ḥayyim*, edited by N. N. ha-Kohen, 1913 (reprinted Jerusalem, n.d.), 88.

20. On R. Asher and the history of Karlin-Stolin in general, see Schorr, *Ketavim*, as well as Brown, *Like a Ship*. R. Aharon of Karlin and the Lechowiczer went to R. Baruch in Miedzybozh in 1802, seeking to reignite the controversy against R. Shne'ur Zalman

over issues of faith vs *hitbonenut*. See Schorr in the *Levi Yitsḥak* volume, Mark and Horen, eds., 53ff.

21. The differences among the disciples of the Maggid had already been noted by their enemy R. David of Makow. After the Maggid's death and the original bans of 1772, he says, "they followed the way of lies, and God scattered them into varying types [*minim*, possibly a pun on 'heretics']. One sect prays with sharp swords [an allusion of Hasidic rules for slaughter], but another, called ḤaBaD, is wicked in a different way. One contemplates [*meḥashev*] and the other worships [*'oved*]." This keen observer understood the difference between the more contemplative and devotional trends within the Maggid's school. See Wilensky, "The Polemic," 153.

22. Eventually, the ḤaBaD supporters among them became settled in Safed (some of them later creating a community in Hebron) while the followers of R. Avraham were in Tiberias.

23. Kalisker's letter is printed in Hilman, #100, 169–71.

24. R. Avraham was well aware of this. He refers to that connection in the opening of his own letter. The betrothal was between either Yosef or Eliezer, one of the sons of Levi Yitsḥak's son Meir, to Sarah, the daughter of Dov Baer, later to be the *rebbe* of Lubavitch. The actual wedding took place in Zlabin in the summer of 1807. See Mondshine, *Masa'*, 49. For a first-hand account of Levi Yitsḥak's attending this wedding (or a second marriage with the Schneersohns?), see the account by Yitsḥak of Neskhiz in *Zikhron Tov* 6, #10.

25. With regard to the controversy over funding for *erets yisra'el*, Levi Yitsḥak remained faithful to supporting the followers of Shne'ur Zalman, as did his son R. Yisra'el of Pikov after his father's death. See Mondshine, *Masa' Berdychiv*, 48–49, for a full description of that journey, including a discussion of the fundraising controversy.

6. TRANSLATING THE TRANSCENDENT

1. By this I mean the *kavvanot* and *yiḥudim*, linked to each word of the liturgy and each ritual act, so emphasized by the Lurianic Kabbalah. See the discussion by Weiss, "The Kavvanoth of Prayer in Early Hasidism."

2. The Ba'al Shem Tov first achieved notice as a Kabbalist and spiritual teacher who eschewed the ascetic path. See his very sharp remarks in this regard in his letter to his disciple R. Ya'akov Yosef of Polonnoye, translated in Etkes, *The BeSHT*, 180–81.

3. *Shivḥey ha-BeSHT*, 64; *In Praise of the Ba'al Shem Tov*, 31.

4. For two examples, see the novels *The Tremble of Love* (2017) by Ani Tuzmanand and *Adele* (2018; Hebrew) by Yochi Brandes, both creations of a Ba'al Shem Tov for the feminist era.

5. See above, chapter 2, n. 24.

6. Dov Baer was not a rabbi, and the teachings attributed to him do not evidence a

high degree of Talmudic learning regarding the legal heart of the Talmudic corpus, but he surely knew and used the essential *terminology* of Talmudic discourse. He was very learned, like a good mystical preacher of his age, in Talmudic legends (*'Eyn Ya'akov*), in the Zohar and other Kabbalistic works, and what are called *sifrey yere'im*, writings of the pious. The latter included Elijah De Vidas's *Reshit Ḥokhmah*, the writings of the MaHaRaL of Prague (both sixteenth century), and the *Shney Luḥot ha-Berit* of Yeshayahu Horowitz (seventeenth century).

7. Chief among these were Avraham Azulai and Yeshayahu Horowitz.

8. The anti-Hasidic polemicist R. David of Makow records the very interesting statement that R. Levi Yitsḥak made to him in 1778: that he had not looked at the Lurianic writings for twelve years, since coming to the Maggid. While R. David is to be considered an inaccurate witness on many matters, this seems like a rather specific statement, an unlikely fabrication. If true, it would be an indication that the Maggid discouraged his students (or at least this leading one) from studying the Lurianic corpus, or perhaps that the disciple felt he no longer needed it after encountering the Maggid and his own unique religious language. See Wilensky, "The Polemic," 151.

9. It seems clear that he read somewhat widely in early (pre-Zoharic) Kabbalistic literature. It is impossible to know exactly which works he might have read in manuscript, but a few key works of this early period were available in print. These include the writings of Naḥmanides, along with some comments on them, as well as Ya'akov Bar Sheshet's *Sefer ha-Emunah veha-Bitaḥon,* first published in the Kabbalistic miscellany *Arzey Levanon*, along with some other important sources. See Menaḥem Lorberbaum's "'Attaining the Attribute of 'Ayin': The Mystical Religiosity of *Maggid Devarav le-Ya'aqov*." See also Netanel Lederberg's *The Gateway to Infinity: Rabbi Dov Baer, the Maggid Mesharim of Mezhrich.* Hillel Zeitlin's "The Fundaments of Hasidism" is his own reconstruction of early Hasidic teaching, largely based on the Maggid. It is available in English in his *Hasidism for a New Era*, 71–117.

10. On this and other matters concerning the Maggid's language, see Mayse, *Speaking Infinities* and "Beyond the Letters."

11. On the place of letters in the BeSHT's legacy, see Idel, *Hasidism*, and the treatment of Horen, *Ziqqato shel ha-BeSHṬ la-Qabbalah ha-Lurianit.*

12. Among the Maggid's students, Ze'ev Wolf of Zhitomir makes this process a key concern of his sermons in his *Or ha-Me'ir*.

13. The corpus of what actually constitute the Maggid's writings remains highly problematic. Many essentially anonymous teachings are attributed to the BeSHT in one collection, to the Maggid in another, etc. See Mayse, *Speaking Infinities* and "Beyond the Letters." On issues related to manuscript research in early Hasidic sources, see also Moseson in his dissertation "From Spoken Word to the Discourse of the Academy: Reading the Sources for the Teachings of the Besht" and recent article "From Private Letter to Communal

Document: On the Multiple Versions of the Letter of the Besht."

14. Solomon Maimon, *Autobiography*. The chapter is conveniently reprinted in Gershon Hundert's *Essential Papers on Hasidism*, 11–24. See also the new translation by Yitshak Melamed and Abraham Socher, *The Autobiography of Solomon Maimon* (2018). A similar report of such practice exists concerning the Maggid's disciple R. Ḥayyim Ḥaykl of Amdur.

15. Gellman discusses the various communities around Ya'akov Yitsḥak, the Ḥozeh of Lublin, the youngest member of the Maggid's circle in his *The Emergence of Hasidism in Poland*.

16. KL 1:3, *bereshit*.

17. The tetragrammaton or four-letter name of God is popularly linked to the verb "to be." In the causative (*hif'il*) construction, it could mean "He causes to be" or "brings about."

18. The opening Bereshit teachings of both *Toledot Ya'akov Yosef* and *Me'or 'Eynayim* also serve as "introductions" in this sense, seeking to set the tone and announce key motifs for the entire volume.

19. KL 1:420–21, *shir ha-shirim*. This passage likely contains a polemical note, favoring the approach of the Maggid over that associated with Pinḥas of Korzec and others, insisting on repair of the *middot*, emotional and moral issues, before daring to "ascend" in this way. On these two approaches within Hasidism, see Heschel's remarks in his "Pinḥas of Korets" in *Circle*. There is rather little talk of Hasidism as a path of moral self-improvement, *tikkun ha-middot*, in *Kedushat Levi*, when compared with such parallel Mezritch school works as *Me'or 'Eynayim* or *Or ha-Me'ir*.

20. In reading both the Maggid and Levi Yitsḥak this way, I am in strong disagreement with the writings of Piekarz in his important study *Between Ideology and Reality*, where he reads talk of self-negation in early Hasidic sources largely as ethical instruction toward humility rather than as reflecting mystical experience. These categories, of course, were not clearly distinguished from one another in the minds of the Hasidic authors, and there are indeed passages that can be read that way. But the broader evidence, including that of the passages I am discussing here, convince me (along with Margolin, Kaufmann, and others) of the more fully mystical reading.

21. KL 1:269, *be-shallaḥ*; 1:309, *mishpatim*. *Histaklut* as a mystical technique plays an important role in the Maggid's thought as well. See MDL #21 as well as Schatz-Uffenheimer's index, s.v. *histaklut*. The gaze, both human/divine and internal to divinity, has a long history within Kabbalah. See discussion by Wolfson in *Through a Speculum That Shines*, index, s.v. *histaklut* and elsewhere. "There is no place devoid of Him" is derived from Tikkuney Zohar 25; it becomes a popular watchword in Hasidic sermons.

22. KL 1:198, *shemot*.

23. See Matt, "Ayin," 86, on the permutation of אני to אין, based on Gikatilla, *Sha'arey Orah*, Warsaw 1883, 103a. The Maggid also discusses returning *aniy* to *ayin* in *Or Torah*

168, *emor*. See further TYY 636, *kedoshim*; ME 429–34, *naso* #2.

24. *Temurato* in the verse refers to a substitute animal replacing one designated for sacrifice. But Kabbalistic tradition refers to "palaces of transformation" using the same word. The soul is transformed as it passes through these realms.

25. KL 1:72, *va-yera*, based on Bereshit Rabbah 56:2. The Maggid has a reading of this verse in *Or ha-Emet* 41a. R. Ḥayyim Ḥaykl also interprets it, with similar mystical intent. See translation and discussion of it in Schatz, *Hasidism*, 70–72. For Menaḥem Naḥum of Chernobyl's reading, see ME 2:428 and 454. The latter is translated in *Speaking Torah*, v. 2, 177–78.

26. For Levi Yitsḥak on the letter *alef*, see KL 1:32, *lekh lekha*.

27. KL 1:363, *ki tissa*. The play of *alef* and *pele* is first found in Zohar 3:193b. Quotation of it by the BeSHT is found in TYY 1374, *kuntres aḥaron*. For further meditations on this theme, see KL 2:178, *yom ha-kippurim*.

28. This seems to be the case for the Maggid himself and most of the Hasidic schools. *Ayin* or *keter* is beyond counting, and the difference is made up by including *da'at* as one of the ten *sefirot*. But there may have been some conflict about this. See the very sharp comment opposing this view in KL 2:215, *likkutim*. On the Kabbalistic history of counting or not counting *keter* (= *ayin*), see Tishby, *Wisdom*, v. 1, 242–46, and Matt, "Ayin."

29. The Maggid's teachings on this point are, as stated above, abstruse and inconsistent. For an attempt to make philosophic sense of them, see Lorberbaum, "Attaining." In some of those texts, *ḥokhmah* is identified with *ayin* while *malkhut* or *shekhinah* represents *yesh*.

30. See the discussion by Loewenthal in *Communicating the Infinite*, 147–67.

31. For a comparison of the Maggid's abstract theology to that of Maimonides, see Lorberbaum, "Attaining."

32. The influence of the author of Tikkuney Zohar, a Kabbalist familiar with philosophic issues, should not be underestimated. This can be seen even in the famous *Pataḥ Eliyahu* passage, widely used liturgically in Sephardic/Hasidic circles. On the Tikkuney Zohar, see Ro'i, *Ahavat ha-Shekhinah*.

33. On Cordovero's thought, see Ben-Shlomo, *Torat ha-Elohut shel R. Moshe Cordovero*, and Sack, *The Kabbalah of Rabbi Moshe Cordovero*.

34. KL 2:215, *likkutim*. For a parallel within the Maggid's school to this theology of inner gaze, see Ḥayyim Ḥaykl of Amdur, *Ḥayyim va-Ḥesed* #27, on Eccles. 7:11.

35. On the history of this phrase and its use in early Hasidic sources, see Green, "The Hasidic Homily," 261, n. 26.

36. KL 2:185–6, *likkutim*. See also KL 2:123, *'ekev*. Interestingly, self-negation results in pleasure. For further discussion of pleasure in the devotional life, see below, chapter 12.

37. This *bon mot* is pre-Hasidic, listed in Buxtorf's 1648 guide to Hebrew proverbs. It is found in TYY 285, *bo*; 588, *tazri'a*, without attribution to the BeSHT. *Me'or 'Eynayim* and others regularly refer to it as BeSHTian.

38. The first two letters of *shema'*, *shin* and *mem*, constitute the word *shem*, "name."

The third letter is called *'ayin*, or "eye."

39. KL 2:105, *va-etḥanan*

40. On esotericism in Naḥmanides, see Halbertal and Feldman, "Tradition, Closed Knowledge, and the Esoteric," and further remarks in his *Naḥmanides: Law and Mysticism* and *By Way of Truth.*

41. KL 1:388, *pekudey*. The moment of return from an experience of mystical self-negation is key to understanding much of Kabbalistic mythology. The Zohar's constant depictions of the emergence of the *sefirot* out of sublime mystery may reflect this process, projecting the mystic's own experience of the reemergence of self out of nothingness. See discussion in Green, "Hillel Zeitlin and Neo-Hasidic Readings of the Zohar."

42. KL 1:324, *terumah.*

43. KL 2:259, *likkutim.* For discussion of the inner eye in earlier Jewish sources, see Wolfson's treatment of the theme in Yehudah ben Barzilai of Barcelona, Yehudah Halevi, and others in his *Speculum*, 148–67, and index, s.v. "eyes."

44. See further discussion of reentry in Green, "Hillel Zeitlin and Neo-hasidic Readings of the Zohar."

45. KL 2:212, *likkutim.*

46. The reference to "stripping off the physical," *hitpashtut ha-gashmiyyut*, is one Levi Yitsḥak uses elsewhere as well. See KL 2:310, *purim* 1. It is of medieval origin, and also enters into the halakhic literature via *Tur Oraḥ Ḥayyim* 98. It is a term that does not particularly reflect the ethos of the Ba'al Shem Tov and stands at the very center of the debate over diverse understandings of Hasidic mysticism. See the discussion in Green, "Buber, Scholem, and the *Me'or 'Eynayim.*"

47. KL 1:189, *shemot.* See also 2:215, *likkutim*: *da'at* draws one toward the *'ayin.*

7. THE MYSTIC AND THE RELIGIOUS REVIVAL

1. These are listed by Schatz-Uffenheimer in her edition of *Maggid Devaraw le-Ya'akov*, index, s.v. *mashal.*

2. This very important passage is found, with some variations, both in *Kitvey Kodesh*, 1862, 11, and in *Shemu'ah Tovah* 49b. See also the reconstructed version of *Shemu'ah Tovah* found in Derbarmdiger's *Yalkut Kedushat Levi*, 64–65.

3. b. Ḥagigah 13a, quoting Ben Sira, 3:21. I think this is also the meaning of the very obscure reference to Manoaḥ in this text. He was acting out of ignorance in inquiring of the angel's name (Jud. 13:17), reaching beyond the level of knowledge permissible to him. See also KL 354, *ki tissa*, and 2:178, *yom ha-kippurim*, where the same teaching on the *alef* is applied to the *alef* of *eḥad* in reciting the *shema'*.

4. See the anonymous *Ma'arekhet ha-Elohut*, chapter 7 (ed. Mantua 82b), and the discussion by Tishby in *Wisdom*, v. 1, 234.

5. This renders the blessed Holy One, or *tif'eret* in the sefirotic scheme, into something

reminiscent of *kavod nivra'*, the "created glory," in the thought of Sa'adya Gaon and his successors among medieval Jewish philosophers. But is this a statement of great theological radicalism by the Maggid or simply the result of imprecision in the rather poor linguistic toolkit of the writer?

6. KL 1:6–7, *bereshit.* Hence the hidden Godhead may be referred to by the rather Maimonidean term *sibbat ha-sibbot*, "the Cause of Causes," but here being used in a Kabbalistic context.

7. See my commentary to this text in *Keter,* chapter 11.

8. *Tikkunim* 1 (17a). This text is reprinted in many Sephardic and Hasidic prayerbooks and is still recited daily in many Sephardic/Mizraḥi communities and prior to the Friday afternoon service in the Hasidic rite.

9. See treatment by Tishby in *Wisdom*, v. 1, 246–51.

10. See above, chapter 3.

11. *Shemu'ah Tovah* 70, ed. Derbarmdiger, 47. On the Midrashic source and its history in Jewish mystical literature, see Wolfson, "The Image of Jacob."

12. Ze'ev Wolf of Zhitomir in *Or ha-Me'ir* 812, *rosh ha-shanah,* translated in *Speaking Torah*, v. 2, 173.

13. *Imrey Tsaddikim*, 25.

14. See below, chapter 9, n. 31.

15. b. Berakhot 17b.

16. Tikkuney Zohar 10, 25b.

17. In addition to various references in KL, see Shne'ur Zalman's *Tanya*, 43, and *Iggeret ha-Kodesh*, 18; TYY and *Me'or 'Eynayim*, index, s.v. *ahavah ve-yir'ah.*

18. KL 1:55, *lekh lekha.* The fact that *yir'ah* is an anagram of *re'iyah*, "seeing," is used by Levi Yitsḥak.

19. In Jewish sources, it is first articulated in the eleventh century by Baḥya Ibn Paquda, who wrote in Muslim Spain, a region where Sufi devotionalism was widespread. From the beginning, it may be said, this sort of religious psychology transcended the boundaries between traditions.

20. The place of fear of punishment was much discussed within the Maggid's circle. For a total dismissal of its value, see ME 388–91, *likkutim*, s.v. *ve-natan.* By contrast, R. Avraham Kalisker suggests that one needs to begin with it every day, growing from there into a higher sense of awe (Letter #59, quoted by Schorr, *Ketavim*, 507). Levi Yitsḥak seems at a midpoint between these two views.

21. KL 2:207, *likkutim*. See the fuller version in KL 2:123, *'ekev*. This dichotomy relates also to the reading of Song of Songs 1:5–6, quoted in the preceding chapter. The higher *yir'ah* is often defined by the Zoharic phrase *be-gin de-ihu 'ikkara ve-shorsha de-khulhu 'almin,* "because He is the essence and root of all the worlds." This is awe before a more abstract and less personified perception of divinity.

22. See treatment of "A Dudele" by Lukin and Wigoda, "Darey Ma'alah 'Im Darey

Matah," in Mark and Horen, eds., *Levi Yitsḥak*, 438–40.

23. A medieval Hebrew proverb, often attributed to the Talmud. Compare b. Berakhot 6a.

24. See Zohar sources referenced by Hecker in "Kissing Kabbalists."

25. ST 24b. Compare to KL 2:6, *shavuʿot*, and 2:182, *ve-zot ha-berakhah.*

26. Especially the *Shaʿar ha-Ahavah* of *Elijah De Vidas's Reshit Ḥokhmah.*

27. A classic Kabbalistic formulation based on Tikkuney Zohar 57.

28. KL 2:185–86, *likkutim*, based on Zohar 1:11b and 3:225a.

29. KL 2:207, *likkutim*. See the fuller version in KL 2:123, *ʿekev*. This dichotomy relates also to the reading of Song of Songs 1:5–6, quoted in the preceding chapter. See also KL 1:327, *tetsavveh*, where *yir'ah* is described as a mystical self-transcendence that unites all creatures.

30. See Green, "The Hasidic Tzaddik," in the forthcoming Idel festschrift volume.

31. The *pidyon nefesh* was a praxis that Hasidism had inherited from Kabbalists who preceded them. It is documented in Central Europe in the century proceeding Hasidism. See treatments by Rubenstein in "Notes," 93–94, and Hundert, *Jews in Poland-Lithuania in the Eighteenth Century.*

32. KL 1:85, *ḥayyey sarah*; 1:121, *va-yetse*. Interestingly, only R. Avraham David Wahrmann of Buchach says that he went to Berdychiv to study with Levi Yitsḥak for a quarter of a year partly "for the sake of livelihood, for example to learn the magical practices [*segulot*] and healings that the rabbi practiced. But the year became confused and I did not learn this from him. I recall only the words of Torah that he spoke." Quoted in *Tif'eret Bet Levi*, 25, from his *ʿEzer be-Kodesh* on *ʿEven ha-'Ezer*, 76. We do not know exactly what נתבלבלה עלי השנה means, but it is notable that the only report of Levi Yitsḥak's having such powers results in a failure to learn them.

33. b. Moʿed Katan 16b.

34. KL 1:421, *shir ha-shirim*. Compare this to *Kedushat Levi* on Abraham and Melchizedek, to be discussed below in chapter 11. Perhaps he is here also responding to voiced concerns about the difference between his path and that of his close Mezritch friend Shne'ur Zalman, who refused to offer prayers or blessings regarding worldly matters. He may be the greater *tsaddik*, Levi Yitsḥak is saying, but I am one who can be of greater help to you.

35. A lost text reconstructed from fragments by Mordecai Margaliot, translated by Morgan as *Sepher ha-Razim, The Book of the Mysteries.*

36. DME 544–45, *haftarah ki tetse,* based on m. Avot 1:3. For English translation see *Your Word is Fire,* 82.

37. KL 1:317–8, *shir ha-shirim.*

8. THE QUESTION OF MIRACLES

1. Heilman, *Bet Rabbi*, 3b. See the extended discussion and contextualization of this source in Schorr, *Ketavim*, 437–38, n. 71–72.

2. There are exceptions, but these tend to be "generic" Hasidic miracle tales, meaning that they could have been told of anyone, having no particular relationship to the character of Levi Yitsḥak. Once Levi Yitsḥak was such a famous name, mostly toward the turn of the twentieth century, all sorts of miracles were attributed to him. Such is the case with most of the tales found in the Levi Yitsḥak chapter of works like Tsaylengold's *Me'orot ha-Gedolim*. A Yiddish version of that chapter was printed in Bilgoray under the title *Nif-lo'os Kedushas Levi*. This is not to be confused with the Yiddish *Niflo'os Beys Halevi*, which is nothing other than an augmented translation of Gutmann's *Tif'eret Bet Levi*! Both of these are reprinted together in the *Sippurim Nifla'im be-Yiddish* series, Brooklyn 1987, v. 2.

3. Levi Yitsḥak's one prior publication, his brief commentary on the Six Remembrances (Mezirov, 1794), to be discussed below, was also something quite out of the ordinary. It may be the only commentary ever published on that text as a separate work.

4. See the very full discussion of the MaHaRaL's Purim treatise *Or Ḥadash* in Orit Ramon's *Maharal in New Light*. Like others, she shows, Maharal used the Esther story as a jumping-off point for a discussion of political philosophy.

5. The term *nes nistar* is a coinage of the RaMBaN, thought to be one of his most distinctive contributions to the history of Jewish thought. For extended discussion of the meaning of this term in the RaMBaN's writings as well as its later misappropriation, see Berger, "Miracles and the Natural Order in Naḥmanides," in Twersky, *Naḥmanides*, 107–28; Halbertal, *Truth*, 149–80. See also Pedaya, *Ha-RaMBaN*, index s.v. *nes*, as well as the particularly lovely excursus on Naḥmanides's idea in R. Baḥya ben Asher's introduction to his commentary on *parashat ki tissa*.

6. See the discussion of the MaHaRaL's influence on early Hasidism by Safran, *Hasidism: Continuity or Innovation*, 47–144, as well as prior comments in Green, "Levi Yitshak of Berdichev on Miracles," in *The Heart of the Matter*, essentially an earlier version of the present chapter.

7. b. Shabbat 88a.

8. The word *megillah* actually derives from the root *g-l-l*, meaning "to roll." *Megalleh*, "reveal," is from *g-l-h*.

9. KL 2:342, *kedushat purim* 2:8.

10. y. Megillah 4:5. Maimonides, *Mishneh Torah*, *hilkhot megillah*, and *ḥannukah* 2:18.

11. KL 2:275–8, *kedushah le-ḥannukah*. MaHaRaL 59 distinguishes Hanukkah from Purim. Hanukkah was in fact a revealed miracle, referring to the miracle of the lights. This was possible because the Second Temple still stood. Purim takes place in *galut*, where only hidden miracles are possible. Hence its heroine is named Esther, etc.

12. KL 2:297–307, *kedushah le-hannukah* 5.

13. See MDL 27–28, #14, and 54, #35, where the Maggid says that Israel in exile are

capable of receiving only hidden miracles, those deriving from *malkhut,* indicated by the name *adonay*, but not revealed miracles, which depend on the name YHWH. On the source of this view, see Halbertal, *Truth*, 158–162.

14. This parallels the view of the RaMBaN in his comment to Gen. 17:1. See Halbertal, *Truth*, 159.

15. That is why the time for lighting Hanukkah candles is "עד שתכלה רגל מן השוק," playing on *regel/hergel.*

16. Halbertal, *Naḥmanides*, chapter 4, "Miracles and the Chain of Being."

17. This is frequently illustrated in the early Hasidic sources by pointing out that הטבע, "nature," and *Elohim* bear the same numerical value. It is found in TYY 33, introduction, but goes back to Cordovero's *Pardes* 12:2.

18. Psalm 145:19 thus reads, "[God's] will is made by those who fear Him." More on this below. The No'am Elimelekh's version of this same idea is expressed in "עיני ה׳ אל צדיקים" (Ps. 34:17), read as "The eyes of God belong to the righteous." "It is in the hands of the *tsaddikim* to make eyes for blessed Y-H-W-H." NE 74, *ḥayyey sarah*. He most surprisingly reads the morning blessing *pokeaḥ 'ivrim*, "who opens the eyes of the blind," as referring to the *tsaddik*'s ability "to open the eyes above to pay attention to Israel."

19. KL 2:338, *kedushat purim* 2:5.

20. See MDL 49, #30. One is here tempted to ask whether Levi Yitsḥak is a very subtle reader of the RaMBaN with regard to the question of the human role in effecting one sort of divine interference or another. RaMBaN, following Ibn Ezra, ties the ability to effect miracles to one's level of *devekut.* Compare the discussion by Halbertal, *Truth*, 167–73. My sense is that what we have here is a rediscovery by Levi Yitsḥak within the general thought-world of Kabbalah rather than a careful reading of particular sources.

21. KL 2:322–34, *kedushat purim* 1:5, based on m. Shekalim 5:1.

22. KL 2:353, *kedushat purim* 3:2, based on b. Sanhedrin 92b. These passages reflect the same atmosphere as found in R. Naḥman of Bratslav's daring images of music surrounding the messiah in his *Megillat Setarim.* See Mark, *Megillat Setarim*, 54.

23. Note the parallel to Levi Yitsḥak's younger colleague R. Naḥman of Bratslav *dancing* in order to defeat the tsar. See Green in *Tormented Master*, 143, and the fuller discussion by Fishbane, "To Jump for Joy."

24. b. Mo'ed Katan 16b; see also Green, "The Hasidic Tsaddik."

25. It is interesting to compare LY's usage of the Mo'ed Katan passage with that of the *Me'or 'Eynayim.* The latter quotes it quite frequently but always in an apologetic context to show that it is not really the *tsaddik,* but God who is negating the decree. See discussion in the "Tsaddik" section in Green, introduction to *The Light of the Eyes.*

26. The reader familiar with contemporary academic treatments of Jewish mysticism will notice that the term "theurgy" has been absent from my discussion here. See below in chapter 10. In the Hasidic sources, the effect of human devotion upon the divine realm,

thus energizing the release of blessing to this world as well, is referred primarily to the prayers and deeds of the *tsaddik*. There is little distinction I can find between this and the hidden miracle. Hence, I prefer to use the term found in the sources. The world is daily sustained by the hidden miracle of God's responding to the *tsaddik*'s prayers.

27. Note how different this reading of Korah is from that of his early sermon in *Shemu'ah Tovah*, quoted above in chapter 3. But this is unsurprising. The preacher faces the same readings each year and interprets them according to the needs of the hour.

28. Based on the experience of this little community in the Holy Land, R. Avraham Kalisker was to write uniquely about *dibbuk ḥaverim*, the intense brotherhood among *ḥasidim*. See discussion by Hundert, *Toward a Biography of R. Abraham Kalisker*, 89–109.

29. *Avkat rokhel*, based on Song of Songs 3:6.

30. Hebrew obscure: ומושל משלים אני גם בגילוי.

31. Heb.: אני תולה כל הדברים בי.

32. *Siftey Ṣaddiqim* 62b. This work was written by Pinḥas of Dinovitz in the early 1820s (he refers to Avraham Yehoshu'a Heschel of Opatow, who died in 1825, with the blessing of the living) but remained in manuscript for forty years. It is generally treated as an authentic early collection, unaltered by its publishers.

9. AN EMERGING RELIGIOUS PERSONALITY

1. ST 35a.

2. See the thirteenth-century Ya'akov Bar Sheshet's *Sefer ha-Emunah veha-Bitaḥon*, once attributed to Naḥmanides and therefore published in Chavel's edition of *Kitvey RaMBaN*. The classic academic treatment of *bitaḥon* is that of Werblowsky, "Faith, Hope, and Trust."

3. Schatz-Uffenheimer, *Hasidism*, 86. This view is central to her phenomenological linking of Hasidism to seventeenth-century Christian Quietism.

4. KL 1:262–64, *be-shalaḥ*. Emphasis added.

5. See chapter 1. (Although published in Levi Yitsḥak's ninth year as rabbi of Berdychiv, the book gives the impression of having been written earlier, closer to his appointment there.)

6. Included in KL 2:496–97, *beyt ha-levi*.

7. Tanḥuma emor 22; b. Yoma 86a.

8. This sermon is also the first teaching attributed to Levi Yitsḥak in *Ge'ulat Yisra'el*, 6.

9. See Scholem, *The Messianic Idea in Judaism*.

10. This remains true also for Levi Yitsḥak's younger contemporary Naḥman of Bratslav. See his very strongly mystical teaching on messiah found in *Likkutey MoHaRaN* 2:61, translated in my *Tormented Master*, 321–22. This requires a rethinking of Weiss's view, based on Scholem's hypotheses, that Bratslav, being based on faith in God and the

tsaddik rather than upon a quest for unitive mystical experience, required a return to a need for messianism that had been reduced in the Mezritch school. Such a rereading of R. Naḥman also comports with the important advances Mark has made in interpreting his teachings as deeply intertwined with his own personal mystical and visionary experiences.

11. I again need to remind the reader that we are dealing with emphasis and frequency of expressed concern, not with absolutes. *Of course*, one can find evidence of historical and collective messianism in any collection of Hasidic sermons. On the influence of the MaHaRaL of Prague over this aspect of Levi Yitsḥak's thought, see the essay by Rahmani in *Levi Yitsḥak*, Mark and Horen, eds., 247–61.

12. Bereshit Rabbah 14:9

13. b. Berakhot 6a.

14. The *Ge'ulat Yisra'el* recounting of this teaching (12b) adds a brief prayer spoken by R. Zusya of Anipol in the same spirit: "Lord of the World! Your people Israel are surely good! Should You say otherwise, God forbid, Your own *tefillin* would be unfit for use!"

15. Here, too, the question of audience is all important. Elimelekh is writing for his disciples, future *tsaddikim*. So too is the Maggid (if he wrote at all); he is speaking to members of his small circle. Levi Yitsḥak is sometimes (not always) addressing a broader community of Jews, reaching out to build the wider movement.

16. I am speaking here of the bulk of the teachings by each of these preachers. Clearly one could find individual statements by each that would contradict this assertion.

17. KL 1:243, *bo*.

18. KL 1:193, *shemot*; 1:424, *shir ha-shirim*; 2:174, *shabbat shuvah*.

19. KL 2:3, *be-midbar*.

20. *Ge'ulat Yisra'el* 11, #15.

21. The evolution of Levi Yitsḥak's somewhat modest challenges to God into the literary and poet Levi Yitsḥak of the mid twentieth century openly demanding divine justice and placing God on trial has been thoroughly documented by Mark in "Din Torah 'im ha-El," his own contribution to the Levi Yitsḥak volume, which he also coedited.

22. KL 2:69, *balak*.

23. *Ge'ulat Yisra'el*, 3. Levi Yitsḥak, #22. Of course, Levi Yitsḥak knew very well that writing is forbidden on the festival of Rosh Hashanah even when it does not occur on the Sabbath!

24. KL 2:74, *pinḥas*. See also KL 1:210, *shemot*, and 2:175, *shabbat shuvah*. Elsewhere, however, LY quotes the Talmud (b. Ber. 30a) to the effect that God regrets having created the evil urge and thus blames Himself for the sins of humans. *Siftey Tsaddikim* 20a.

25. See above chapter 6, n. 2.

26. *Tsava'at RiYVaSH* #9; *Likkutim Yekarim* #23.

27. Several recent studies by Moshe Idel have emphasized the possibly non-Jewish and multi-ethnic sources of the BeSHT's religious attitudes. Much more work needs to

be done in further exploring these avenues of influence.

28. From the *seliḥot* liturgy, based on Ps. 143:2.

29. KL 2:173, *rosh ha-shanah.*

30. ST 21b–25b, *va-etḥanan.*

31. KL 2:103–4, *va-etḥanan.* This comment occurs in the context of why Jews move about so much while in the act of prayer, something for which, as we will recall, Levi Yitsḥak himself was well known and which was to get him in trouble.

32. ST 40a.

33. KL 2:288, *ḥanukkah* #5.

34. KL 2:367–68, *purim* #3.

10. PLEASURES SUBLIME AND WORLDLY IN THE RELIGIOUS LIFE

1. This aspect of Kabbalah has been extensively discussed in the writings of Moshe Idel and especially by Jonathan Garb, *Manifestations of Power in Jewish Mysticism.*

2. Sifrey *ha'azinu* 319; b. Shabbat 89a. See the important discussion of these and related sources in Heschel's *Heavenly Torah,* 104–26.

3. On *ta'anug*, but touching more broadly on the whole question of pleasure and its mutuality in the religious life as reflected in the Hasidic sources, see Idel, "*Ta'anug*: Erotic Delights from Kabbalah to Hasidism," a most important treatment to which I shall refer further in this chapter. I disagree with a number of Idel's readings, essentially around the question of whether *ta'anug* necessarily refers to erotic pleasure. On *sha'ashu'a*, see Liebes, *Zohar ve-Eros.*

4. b. Shabbat 88a. Compare Zohar 1:89a.

5. Naḥmanides, Commentary to Ex. 29:46. RaMBaN's articulation of the *mitsvot* as fulfilling a divine need becomes the key idea in R. Meir Ibn Gabbai's *'Avodat ha-Kodesh*, a *summa kabbalistica* that was written early in the sixteenth century in the generation preceding that of Cordovero and Luria, influencing both. Ibn Gabbai's teachings were passed on to Hasidism via extensive quotations in Isaiah Horowitz's *Shney Luḥot ha-Berit.* On the importance of this idea among Kabbalists of the generation following the expulsion from Spain, see Gottlieb, *Meḥkarim*, 29–38.

6. b. Berakhot 7a. R. Yishma'el here is understood to be Yishma'el the High Priest, as opposed to the frequently quoted *tanna,* since only he could enter the Holy of Holies. Akatriel, while technically an angel named "the crowning of God," is taken here to be a vision of God.

7. KL 1:397, *pesaḥ.* "Israel above" refers to the *sefirah tif'eret*, the aspect of Divinity that represents the personified deity, the blessed Holy One, also called Israel the Elder, *yisra'el sabba.*

8. "The blessed Holy One desires [or 'longs for'] the prayers of the righteous." b. Ye-

vamot 64a. Heschel's *Torah min ha-Shamayim* sees this worldview present in the school of R. Akiva, thus linking up the Akiva/Yishma'el typologies to the dispute between Maimonides and Naḥmanides on the nature of God and the admissibility of divine need. On this question as a key motif in Heschel's own theology, see Green, "God's Need."

9. See Green, *Keter*, chapters 1–6.

10. That *kavvanah* is expressed in concentration on specific prescriptions of devotional intent, called *kavvanot,* especially following the Lurianic innovations of the sixteenth century reflected in *Sefer ha-Kavvanot.* From ancient times, the term contains within it aspects of both "intention" and "intensity." On the range of meanings of *kavvanah,* see Enelow, "Kawwana: The Struggle for Inwardness in Judaism."

11. *Mishneh Torah, teshuvah* 10. See discussion in Green, "Judaism as a Path of Love," 98.

12. This understanding of the creation of humans, defining its purpose in essentially spiritual/erotic terms, is ubiquitous in the Kabbalistic sources. It is spelled out with particular clarity in R. Meir Ibn Gabbai's *'Avodat ha-Kodesh* 4:3–12. I have translated and annotated these chapters to be published under the title *Secrets of Creation,* accompanied by a contemporary response by astrophysicist Howard Smith and illuminations by artist Debra Band (forthcoming).

13. See TYY 526, *emor*, for one of many examples.

14. See especially his statement, "Why do Israel pray and yet messiah has not arrived? Because they do not lengthen [their recital of] *ahavah rabbah* ['with great love'] that precedes the *shema'*, representing the kisses that precede conjugal union, in order to arouse Her desire." Quoted in TYY 275, *va-era.* See discussion in Green, introduction to *The Light of the Eyes,* 20.

15. English translation available in Etkes, *The Besht,* 277.

16. And thus require immersion in the *mikveh* according to Hasidic practice. Ideally, a *ḥasid* will immerse in the *mikveh* every morning before prayer. That implies a need to cleanse oneself from possible seminal emission during the night. This is a Hasidic revival of an ancient Jewish practice that had been set aside and is one of the distinctive hallmarks of the Hasidic way of practicing Judaism. On the question of male immersion in Hasidism, see Wertheim, *Law and Custom in Hasidism,* 102–5.

17. Based on Ex. 21:10, regular conjugal relations and fulfillment of one's wife's sexual needs is counted as a positive commandment, obligating every married man, even where the obligation to "be fruitful and multiply" does not apply.

18. KL 1:435–46, *metsora'.* In another passage (1:441, *aḥarey*), however, he admonishes his hearers to approach their wives purely for the sake of the *mitsvah,* with no thought of their own pleasure at all, seeming to believe that such "pure" sexual relations are possible.

19. KL 1:173–74, *va-yeḥi*; 1:433, *tazri'a*; *Ge'ulat Yisra'el* #4. But see also KL 1:25, *noaḥ*, and the sources quoted in n. 14 above and KL 1:181, *va-yeḥi.* These are perhaps best resolved by KL 1:288, *yitro*, where Levi Yitsḥak describes in detailed stages the pleasure God seeks

to give the *tsaddik* in response to that which the *tsaddik* offers Him.

20. He is reading *asis* as though a *hif'il*, or causative form.

21. KL 2:349, *purim*, emphasis added. A somewhat more accepting attitude regarding spiritual pleasure as the only truly fulfilling pleasure is found in KL 1:334, *tetsaveh*. Moses' days of *milu'im* (the seven days preceding Aaron's consecration as high priest) are thus named because they were the time devoted to only truly *fulfilling* the singular human pleasure of serving God.

22. KL 2:23, *naso*, emphasis added.

23. MDL #53. For an interesting comment on the mutuality of sexual pleasure as a metaphor for the divine-human relationship, see ST 51a.

24. The point is not just a grammatical one. *Zot* regularly is used to refer to *shekhinah* in the Zohar and throughout Kabbalistic writings. The Maggid reads it, quite shockingly, to mean that YHWH is transformed from "male" into "female" by the act of receiving our blessing. His reading of the verse in English would sound like "The [all-powerful] Y-H-W-H has become a [needy and receiving] female! We are truly astonished by this!"

25. KL 1:434, *tazri'a*. This text also quotes Ps. 45:10 and may be a different version of that quoted above from *Ge'ulat Yisra'el*. See also *Tif'eret 'Uziel, ve-zot ha-berakhah*, translated in Green et al., *Speaking Torah*, v. 2, 150. See Idel's treatment of this passage in *Ta'anug*, 121. Needless to say, the giving and receiving of pleasure are as hopelessly intertwined in the intimacies of the eros of the divine/human relationship as they are in the act of physical love. See also KL 1:417–8, *shir ha-shirim*. Here we find a depiction of intense erotic love: we are to love God like the bride loves her spouse. We love Him just because He loves us, not for any rewards. To indicate this, we kiss Him on the mouth, not on the hand, meaning that we look for no reward. (Here Levi Yitsḥak is actually quoting RaSHI on the Song of Songs verse. He might not have had the boldness to have said this on his own.) In the very next text, KL 1:418, *shir ha-shirim*, we find a very subtle treatment of eros. There are two kinds of love that God has for us. One is represented by kisses, a love that stems from before creation. Here no *shefa'* (or semen) passes between the lovers. This is described as being like a kiss between two (male) friends! Then there is a second form of love once we are created and exist as separate beings. He hints but won't quite say outright that this is like conjugal union, including the flow of *shefa'*. The inconsistency of the sources on these matters is demonstrated by a passage found in ST 82b to the effect that one cannot say to God, "I love You," but only, "I love serving You."

26. Heb.: *naḥat ruaḥ ve-ta'anug*. *Ge'ulat Yisra'el* #4, emphasis added. Just above that, in #2, the editor recalls a teaching of Levi Yitsḥak's in which Israel are called God's children only when they serve Him wholeheartedly, without any thought of reward. To serve for reward is to relate to God as a servant rather than as a son.

27. The words literally mean "remember" or "mention" and "keep" or "observe." The word *zakhor*, however, is consonantally equal to *zakhar*, "male." For the Kabbalists, these

two elements of Shabbat were the male and female aspects of the deity coming into union. See discussion by Ginsburg, *The Sabbath*, 109ff.

28. Bringing about that flow of energy is "being male," *zakhar.* See extended treatment in Ibn Gabbai, *The Secret of the Sabbath.*

29. KL 1:359, *ki tissa*. See also KL 1:275–76, *be-shalaḥ*, in contrast, for example, to ME *va-yakhel I*, translated in *Light of the Eyes*, 493–94.

30. TYY 310, *bo*; 451, *mishpatim.*

31. KL 1:440, *aḥarey*. The teaching is incomplete, but this appears to be its thrust. Here Levi Yitsḥak is going against a very long and fully articulated Kabbalistic tendency to defend and identify with Aaron's sons. On Nadav and Avihu in the Hasidic imagination, see Mayse, "Like a Moth to the Flame," as well as Kara-Ivanov Kaniel, "Consumed by Love: The Death of Nadav and Avihu as a Ritual of Erotic Mystical Union." Another passage where Levi Yitsḥak demurs strongly from the idea of serving through corporeal things is found in KL 1:241, *bo.*

32. KL 1:426, *shemini*, emphasis added.

33. KL 1:303, *yitro.*

34. R. Hayyim Tirer of Chernovtsy, *Sidduro shel Shabbat*. Cited by Idel, *Hasidism*, 129. Note the seamless flow between "love" and "being a part of." The mystic understands that there is a relationship called "love" in which there ultimately is no Other. See also the treatment of this source in Green, *Devotion*, 87, n. 103. For discussion of this in a contemporary theological context, see Green, "Judaism as a Path of Love."

35. See discussion by Idel in his *Hasidism,* 139f. See also the sources he brings there, 328, n. 246.

36. ST 41b. Note *sha'ashu'a* here in a non-erotic context. See also ST 55b, a very strong statement on God's desire for *ta'anug*. We are here to be *mashpi'a* to that desire; God becomes the female, the *needy* one, *'ani ve-evyon*, without us! See also KL 1:100, *toledot*, as well as Rand's note in KL 1:179, *va-yeḥi*, and the other similar sources quoted there. In these passages, Levi Yitsḥak is making quite explicitly the point that "Israel sustaining their Father in Heaven" is again and again understood as their providing pleasure for Him. This very powerfully reverses the dynamic of "thirst for God"; here God is the thirsty one.

37. See an especially beautiful expression of this in *Yosher Divrey Emet* by R. Meshullam Feibush of Zbarasz, #5.

38. This language is already found in the old rabbinic sources. See b. Berakhot 32a, where God says to Moses, "You have given Me life by your words."

39. MDL #123, found also in ST 55b. For another use of the cow and calf metaphor, see KL 1:219, *va-era*. See also KL 1:408, *pesaḥ*, one of many passages attesting to God's great pleasure in doing good for His beloved children. We are permitted to petition God in prayer for our good since we know that God is a parent who takes great pleasure in giving to His children. Hence these prayers too are "for the sake of heaven." On the possible

roots of Levi Yitsḥak's emphasis on Israel's sonship in the writings of the MaHaRaL of Prague, see Raḥmani, "Sanegoran shel Yisra'el," in Mark and Horen, eds., *Levi Yitsḥak*, 253–61. My own sense is that here the Maggid's influence is decisive. But it may be that he, in turn, was influenced by reading the MaHaRaL.

40. KL 1:331, *tetsaveh*. But in 1:289, *yitro*, He does so in order to increase our joy in the process of striving to become close to Him.

41. KL 1:266, *be-shalaḥ*. The parable is found in several early collections of Hasidic teachings.

42. Here too, as discussed above, we may detect in Levi Yitsḥak a bit of disdain toward the obvious miracle. This is the "child-like" side of God, "giving in" to the obvious needs of Israel.

43. KL 1:296–7, *yitro*. This would contradict his reading of "He held the mountain over their heads," quoted earlier in chapter 8. But preaching does not make for consistency.

44. TYY 111, *lekh lekha*. See also 285, *bo*.

45. TYY 588, *tazri'a*.

46. Translated in *The Light of the Eyes*, 100–101.

47. The key work on this subject is *In All Your Ways Know Him* by the late and much lamented Tsippi Kaufmann.

48. This assertion stands at the core of the great debate between Gershom Scholem and Martin Buber on the meaning of Hasidic devotion. See discussion in Green, "Buber, Scholem, and the *Me'or 'Eynayim*."

49. ME 22, *bereshit* #5.

50. See discussion in Green's introduction to *The Light of the Eyes*, 63–65, and ME *Pinḥas* #1, 624–33. The quotation from the BeSHT is otherwise known only from a single reference in the TYY 479, *va-yakhel*.

51. He means Solomon, the purported author of Proverbs. Perhaps he thought the verse was in the Psalms.

52. KL 1:441, *aḥarey*; emphasis added. This text is also quoted by Kaufmann in *Be-Khol*, 199, n. 71.

53. Emphases added. This may be seen as an unusual instance of what today is called "predicate theology": the phrase "God is good" is turned around to mean that the good (in this case, "the tasty") is God.

54. ME, *Mattot*, emphasis added. *Light of the Eyes*, 639. See sources in b. Ta'anit 11a–b.

55. KL 1:17, *bereshit*. See a parallel text in R. Yitsḥak of Radwil's *Or Yitsḥak* and the treatment of it by Schatz-Uffenheimer in *Hasidism as Mysticism*, 129.

56. For Levi Yitsḥak's view, see KL 1:123–4, *va-yetse*. On Menaḥem Naḥum, see the treatment in Green, "Buber, Scholem, and the *Me'or 'Eynayim*" as well as in the introduction to *The Light of the Eyes*.

57. KL 1:417, *shir ha-shirim*. He is referring to a folk etymology linking *tefillah* and

naftulim, "wrestling" (as in Gen. 30:8), the basis of the name Naftali.

58. KL 191–92, *shemot*. This source has been quoted above in chapter 4, n. 28.

59. *Amtaḥat Binyamin* 12d. Quoted by Rand in KL 1:192, n. 19.

60. See discussion above, chapter 6.

61. This question of the intended audiences for particular teachings or statements found within Hasidic writings is one that has been ignored or undertreated by scholarship in the field. There are cases where it can be more easily determined. Regarding ḤaBaD, for example, there is a great difference between what R. Shne'ur Zalman wrote in the *Tanya*, intended for the widest distribution, and the much more Kabbalistically inclined teachings in many of his *ma'amarim*, many of which remained unprinted until the late twentieth century. *No'am Elimelekh* has been shown (see following note) to serve as a treatise intended entirely as a training manual for future would-be *tsaddikim*, those who surrounded its author. But works like the *Me'or 'Eynayim* or *Kedushat Levi 'al ha-Torah* are compendia put together and published after the preacher's death. The one who composed these sermons for preaching or taught them to his students is considered the author of the teachings, but the degree to which he was the one who committed them to writing in Hebrew varies greatly and is mostly unknown. Often the volumes were edited by the authors' heirs. Their intent was to gather and preserve as much of the *tsaddik*'s teachings as they could, without any thought of distinguishing among intended audiences. See the discussion around this issue regarding ḤaBaD and Karlin in Schorr, *Ketavim*, 505–6.

62. I am grateful to Ebn Leader for this understanding of the *No'am Elimelekh*. See his "Leadership as Individual Relationships" in *Be-Ron Yaḥad*, 177–202.

11. DEFENDING THE COMMANDMENTS

1. As my student Ariel Mayse has argued, there is an embrace of legal diversity and flexibility in Hasidism, which amplifies what is already there in the tradition. But it has interesting and well-defined boundaries. The legal decisors within Hasidism did not feel themselves bound to any particular legal code when it came to ritual matters but more to the cultures/texts of Lurianic ritualization. See his initial treatment of this theme with Maoz Kahana in "Hasidic Halakhah: Reappraising the Interface of Spirit and Law," as well as Mayse, "The Ever-changing Path: Visions of Legal Diversity in Hasidic Literature," and his forthcoming further studies of the subject.

2. The Zohar, actually composed in late thirteenth-century Spain, was thought to be the work of its second-century hero, R. Shim'on ben Yoḥai. In Hasidic circles, it was considered authoritative, and its views were sometimes followed even in opposition to more normative halakhic sources. See discussion by Jacob Katz in *Halakhah and Kabbalah* and Yisrael Ta-Shma in *Ha-Nigleh sheba-Nistar*. The Lurianic sources, mostly still unprinted in the early years of Hasidism, are often referred to by members of the Maggid's circle as

ketavim, "writings." See, however, the statement by Levi Yitsḥak quoted by R. David of Makow, referred to above in chapter 6, n. 7.

3. Parallel, I am suggesting, to that discussed by Liebes in his "Zohar as Renaissance."

4. See the discussion in Green, "The Hasidic Homily." The strength of this transmission varied greatly. Many later collections of Hasidic homilies overuse such devices as gematria (numerology) or *notarikon* (secrets unpacked by abbreviation), indicative of a decline of literary imagination. But in the writings of some later masters, including the Polish school following the revival in Kock (including both Ger and Izbica), the creative and often radically innovative reading of scripture remained alive and well.

5. On the process of spiritualization of the tradition within Judaism, and especially Hasidism, see Margolin, *Mikdash Adam*.

6. See above, chapter 1.

7. This terminology originates in the early fourteenth-century Tikkuney Zohar 25b and is widely found throughout later Jewish pietistic literature, constantly referred to in the early Hasidic sources. See for example *Tanya* 1:40.

8. Of course, "excessive" is a relative term. While there are early Hasidic sources that militate against guilt over minor infractions of *halakhah*, there was also a tendency to add certain *ḥumrot*, or extra strictures, as a sign of Hasidic piety. Speaking very generally, I would say that the extreme emphasis on *kavvanah* is most strongly expressed in such figures as Menaḥem Mendel of Vitebsk, Ḥayyim Ḥaykl of Amdur, and Menaḥem Naḥum of Chernobyl. Over against them, and perhaps concerned by their views, were Levi Yitsḥak, R. Shne'ur Zalman, and Elimelekh of Lezajsk.

9. See Tikkuney Zohar #29, 73a.

10. See Horowitz, *Shney Luḥot ha-Berit*, Yoma, *Derekh Ḥayyim* 16 (163). Quoted in the name of the BeSHT in *Degel Maḥaneh Ephraim* 328, *koraḥ*.

11. See Schatz, *Hasidism*, 310–25. See also Weiss, "Torah Study in Early Hasidism," in his *Studies*, 56–68.

12. This version of Talmud Torah and disputes about it reach back to the age of the Zohar. See Katz, *Halakhah ve-Kabbalah*, for a discussion of competing modes of Torah study in the course of later Jewish history.

13. See discussion by Cooper, cited above in chapter 1.

14. See especially 310–52.

15. Margolin, *Mikdash Adam*; Kaufmann, *Be-Khol*, indices s.v. *Schatz*.

16. See the teachings of the Maggid on the saying of R. Akavya ben Mehallalel in m. Makkot 3:16, found in *Or Torah* 147a and translated in Schatz, *Hasidism*, 136–37. The point of the teaching is that the *mitsvot* are not limited to the traditional 613 but that every act is potentially a *mitsvah*.

17. Here it is good to remind ourselves that there is little inner consistency to be found in the thought of a man who has left us only sermons, each one preached before

a particular audience on a particular day. The background and circumstances of each *derashah* are almost entirely lost to us. Thus, there are some passages in *Kedushat Levi* that could have been lifted right out of the *Me'or 'Eynayim* and vice versa. See, for example, *Kedushat Levi* 11:135–36, *va-yeshev*, on the *kavvanah* of raising sparks through eating. In pointing to differences, I am looking at the preponderance of evidence, not at absolutes.

18. b. Makkot 23b.

19. The Talmudic passage suggests only the correspondence of the positive commandment to the human limbs; the 365 prohibitions represent the days of the solar year. By the time of the Zohar (see 1:170b for *gid ha-nasheh*), however, the "sinews" have been added to the "limbs." See the classic presentation of this in Vital's *Sha'arey Kedushah* 1:1.

20. From the Shabbat and Festival morning liturgy.

21. *Kedushat Levi* 1, *bereshit*, 1:9–10. See also KL 2:246, *likkutim, cv. zakhor ve-shamor.* "His deeds" in this verse is perhaps being read as "its deeds," referring to the people. Israel becomes powerful, in the worldly sense as well, by performing the *mitsvot.*

22. *Kedushat Levi* 12:98, *va-etḥanan.*

23. The ritual forms fulfilled on Sukkot and Hanukkah immediately come to mind. *Imrey Tsaddikim* includes long discussions by Levi Yitsḥak on the *mitsvot* of these festivals, showing his significant Talmudic erudition.

24. *Kedushat Levi* 11:3, *bereshit.* Note that our pleasure in doing the *mitsvah* is not considered worthy of mention here. The actual effect our deeds have on the inner divine world is not apparent to us. Of course, the true Kabbalist sought to know precisely what those effects were and how they came about. Here we see a clear example of the Hasidic retreat from Kabbalah as a system of esoteric knowledge, sufficing instead with a general aura of mystery and wonder. "Reverse alphabet" means reading from the end of the alphabet backwards (A = Z, B = Y, etc.), a system of deriving meaning called אתב"ש, which was quite widely used in Kabbalah.

25. *Kedushat Levi* 1:120, *va-yetse*, based on a nice reading of אשר צפנת ליראיך (Ps. 31:20).

26. m. Avot 4:2

27. KL 1:111, *va-yetse. Sekhel gadol yoter* does not mean "greater rational understanding," but refers to a deeper sense of spiritual awareness. This use of *sekhel* is typical of the Maggid's school.

28. KL 1:36–9, *lekh lekha.* See my prior treatment of this text in *Devotion*, 20–22. This is parallel to the discussion of the two types of *tsaddik*, above in chapter 4, n.3, and Levi Yitsḥak's preference for the "lesser," the one who can bring blessing into this world.

29. KL 2:309–10, *kedushat purim* I, and elsewhere. Levi Yitsḥak's Abraham is a unique religious personality. Living before the calendar of festivals was set, he could celebrate Pesaḥ and Yom Kippur on the same day, depending upon which religious instinct was aroused in him. See KL 1:406, *derushim le-pesaḥ.*

30. Such *mitsvot* as the sabbatical and jubilee years, tithing, etc. apply only to Jews living

inside the Land of Israel. One might think that we too, living outside the Land, would do better to worship by devotion alone since we cannot fulfill all of the commandments. But that option is closed off after the giving of the Torah.

31. The sense that visionary experience is of a lower order than abstract insight is consistent with much of Kabbalistic tradition, which located vision in the *hekhalot* that lie beneath *shekhinah*. See Tishby, *Wisdom of the Zohar*, v. 2, 587–614. The intellectualist bias is deeply rooted in both esoteric and exoteric aspects of the Jewish tradition.

32. In the New Testament, Melchizedek is mentioned only in Hebrews, but there extensively in chapters 5–7. See esp. 7:11.

33. An ancient text referred to as the "History of Melchizedek" is present in many languages associated with the Eastern church traditions. It may have originated in Jewish apocryphal literature but only survives in heavily Christianized versions. This text, and the tradition stemming from it, was especially popular in the Russian church and led to the widespread use of the name. See Bőttrich, "Melchizedek among Russian Saints: The History of Melchizedek between Jews and Slavs."

34. See discussion in Green, *Devotion*, 22–33, but especially ME *va-yera, cv. kiyyem avraham* (in English, *The Light of the Eyes*, 214–16). Christian doctrine, especially that of the Eastern Orthodox churches, gives to its priests the power of blessing and of sanctification (declaring something holy), far more than is included in the title "rabbi." In Judaism, the power of blessing still lies within the hands of the historic priestly tribe as descendants of Aaron. The now familiar act of the rabbi pronouncing blessing over the congregation is a modern innovation. Sanctification (as in *kiddush ha-ḥodesh*, for example) could be performed by the central rabbinic court in ancient times. But there they spoke as representatives of the people, not necessarily as "clergy."

35. Shne'ur Zalman of Liadi, who rejected what he saw as an over-emphasis on *kavvanah* in early Hasidic circles and insisted on the concrete act as the center of the *mitsvah*, in fact took a more extreme position. See Schatz-Uffenheimer, *Hasidism*, chapter 12, "Ḥabad: Anti-spiritualism as a Quietistic Value," 255–89; Elior, *Unity of Opposites: The Mystical Theosophy of ḤaBaD*, 116–86 (Hebrew); and further discussion by Loewenthal, *Communicating the Infinite*, 86–90. For Levi Yitsḥak's place in this debate, see also the important parallel discussion in KL 1:213–5, *va-era*. There he decries those who seek to serve God by separating themselves from this world. "One who is detached from this world, not performing any service [*'avodah*], passing his days in vanity, represents 'the end of days,' the other [i.e., demonic] side. A person is holy by separating from the *desires* of this world and by serving God through the *deeds* of Torah, prayer, and charity [*tsedakah*, 'righteousness']." (Emphasis added.)

36. KL 2:309–13, *kedushat purim* 1:1.

37. See especially KL 2:237–38, *likkutim, shabbat*. Levi Yitsḥak's treatment of the correspondence between the body and the *mitsvot* is based on the discussion in Vital's *Sha'arey*

Kedushah 1:1 and many other Kabbalistic sources.

38. See the sources from *Degel Maḥaneh Ephraim* 140, *va-era*, and others cited and discussed in Green, *Devotion*.

39. ME 51–52, *va-yera*. Light of the Eyes, 214–15.

40. b. Shabbat 31b.

41. *Ge'ulat Yisra'el* #16.

12. INTERPRETING TORAH

1. See the prior discussion in Green, "Hasidism and Its Changing History."

2. b. Bava Metzia 59a–b.

3. See especially the passages from R. Meir Ibn Gabbi and R. Isaiah Horowitz quoted near the end of Scholem's "Revelation and Tradition as Religious Categories in Judaism."

4. Be-Midbar Rabbah 13:15. The fourteenth-century Tikkuney Zohar was constructed to illustrate this point in a Kabbalistic context, each of its seventy chapters offering a distinctive reading of Genesis 1:1. This was outdone by R. Nathan Shapira of Cracow (seventeenth century), whose *Megalleh 'Amukot* proposes 252 readings of a single verse in Deuteronomy!

5. b. Makkot 22b.

6. *Degel Maḥaneh Ephraim* 269, *shemini*, emphasis added. This early work still uses the term *ḥakhamim* rather than the *tsaddikim* more common in the Maggid's school, but it is clearly the Hasidic master that he has in mind. See also parallel in *bereshit*, s.v. *zeh sefer*. See the discussion in Green, "Hasidism and Its Changing History."

7. See Heschel, "Rabbi Naḥman of Kosow," in *Circle*, 133, n. 87.

8. This quip is first recorded in the responsa of the twelfth-century Tosafist Rabbenu Tam. *Shiltey Giborim* to the *Mordekhai*, b. Gitin 85a.

9. KL 2:254–5, *likkutim*.

10. For a directly opposing view, see R. Levi Yitsḥak's friend Elimelekh of Lizhensk in NE 584, *ha'azinu*.

11. b. Sanhedrin 89a.

12. KL 1:320–1, *terumah*, quoting b. Shevu'ot 15a and b. Sanhedrin 89a. Emphasis added.

13. b. Berakhot 26a.

14. See above, chapter 3, n. 13.

15. *Peri 'Ets Ḥayyim, sha'ar yamim tovim* 4:5.

16. The four-fold language here echoes the four worlds of Kabbalistic metaphysics.

17. KL 1:398–9, *derushim le-pesaḥ*.

18. This view of revelation and authority is interestingly comparable to Franz Rosenzweig's well-known distinction between *Gebot* and *Gesetz*, "commandment" and "law," in understanding the Torah. "Law" has been finally stated and exists separately from the

original lawgiver, whereas "commandment" implies that the Commander remains personally present as the act is carried out. See Rosenzweig's essay "The Builders: Concerning the Law" in his *On Jewish Learning* (New York: Schocken), 1955, 72–92.

19. b. Mo'ed Katan 16b.

20. KL 1:298, *yitro*, emphasis added. See also KL 2:272, *likkutim*, *avot*.

21. KL 1:347–8, *purim*. This remarkable assertion does not appear in the 1798 *Kedushat Purim*, where he discusses the same Talmudic passage, perhaps indicating that it was a later insight.

22. See Levi Cooper's exhaustive survey of Levi Yitsḥak as a halakhist in "Rabbanut, Halakha, Lamdanut" in Mark and Horen, eds., *Levi Yitsḥak*, referenced above in chapter 1.

23. See y. Shekalim 6:2 (49d), Sotah 8:1 (22d), Devarim Rabbah 3:12 (ed. Lieberman 89), and discussion by Heschel, *Heavenly Torah*, 333–4. See also Zohar 2:84a, 114a, 3:112a.

24. This language describes the poetic line arrangement of the text as written in a Torah scroll. In the Torah text, this rule is applied only to Exodus 15, the Song at the Sea.

25. There is no such verse in the Bible. This is the Isaiah verse as reread in Va-Yikra Rabbah 13:3, where "new" is added.

26. These are Maimonides's 13 Articles of Faith. He assumes that the Talmud would need to accord with the views of Maimonides.

27. Mekhilta, *be-shalaḥ* 2. Ezekiel's opening vision is taken to be the fullest scriptural revelation of the upper universe. As such, it stood as the basis of later visions of the *merkavah* or divine throne. The "handmaiden"—perhaps a stand-in for Israel herself—saw even more. Here the event of the sea's splitting and its graphic representation in the Torah scroll are interestingly comingled.

28. KL 2:246–7, *likkutim*. He seems to be reading "from Me" to mean that the new Torah will be revealed from within the old. Or perhaps *me-iti* is to be read as *me-oti*, "from within my letter." For other references to black fire and white fire, see KL 2:13–14, *shavu'ot*, and 2:240, *likkutim*. A somewhat longer record of this teaching is recorded in *Imrey Tsaddikim*, 8. He connects it also to the diminishing and future fulfillment of the moon (*levenah* = *levanah*).

29. The comparison with today's physicists' quest for "dark matter" cannot be resisted. "In the future" (the scientists' messianic age?), all will be revealed. Will the dark turn out to be light? Only the student of the Zohar's *butsina de-kardinuta* ("Lamp of Darkness") knows for sure.

30. That text is written in dual columns, called "brick over brick." The teaching fits less well to that way of writing, probably indicating that the other was the original.

31. b. Berakhot 17a. "Brick over brick" means that this poem is written in two parallel poetic columns.

32. "Fear of God" here might also be translated as "piety" or "reverence." He seems to be pointing to three levels of *yir'ah*: the lowest is fear of being cut off or distanced from

God (fear of punishment for sin is usually disregarded as too lowly for consideration in this list). The second is the awe before God's presence, apprehension of divine power. The third, beyond our grasp, defies definition.

33. *Siftey Tsaddikim* 32d. See also page 41 for a somewhat garbled parallel. R. Naḥman of Bratslav offers a similar interpretation of the Berakhot passage in *Likkutey MoHaRaN* 1:21.

34. Moshe Idel has treated this theme in "Ottiyot Levanot." Although apparently unaware of the *Siftey Tsaddikim* version, he interprets the text precisely as unpacked by it.

13. LOOKING INTO THE FUTURE?

1. b. Baba Metsi'a 59a–b.

2. KL 2:272, *likkutim*. Emphasis added. See also parallel in KL 1:312, *mishpatim*.

3. KL 1:188, *ḥayyey sarah*; 2:101, *va-etḥanan*.

4. b. Shabbat 105a.

5. *Toledot Aharon*, by Aharon of Zhitomir, in Levi Yitsḥak's name. *Likkutim*, s.v. *Torah Tsivvah*. See also KL 1:306–7, *yitro*.

6. See the discussion by Lorberbaum, "'Ayin."

7. This is then manifest in the union of *binah* (as *'olam ha-mahashavah*) and *malkhut* (*'olam ha-dibbur*). That is what makes Torah the vehicle for human apprehension of and absorption into the mind of God.

8. *Keter*, which is usually seen as the locus of divine will, setting the emanation process in motion, has now effectively disappeared, enveloped (but de facto "lost") within *eyn sof*. The relationship between *keter* and *ḥokhmah* in the Maggid's writings is subtle and inconsistent. See the treatment by Mayse in *Beyond the Letters*, 14–15, 202, and 237–38. Yehuda Liebes has suggested to me a parallel to R. Naftali Bachrach. See his "Li-Demuto, Ketavav, ve-Kabbalato shel Ba'al 'Emek ha-Melekh," n. 116–7 and 131. In the psychological reflection of the cosmic structure, *kadmut ha-sekhel*, or pre-conscious mind, plays a major role. But this remains quite elusive when referring to the divine mind and in any case is usually not defined as will.

9. MDL 21, #7. The quotation is from Bereshit Rabbah 8:7, one of the interpretations of "Let us make man" (Gen. 1:27). God's desire even to create humanity derives from the will of the righteous and their desire to serve him. The Maggid also has (MDL 257–262, #161) an opposite interpretation of this verse, in which God arouses in the righteous a desire for petitionary prayer. Since they are ever satisfied with their lot, they might stop praying. But God, who "longs for the prayers of the righteous," creates this desire within them. See discussion of this passage by Schatz in *Hasidism*, 156. The presence of two such different readings of a verse shows the great influence of contemplation of scripture in shaping the thought of such a homiletic thinker. He seems to be pondering the verse in

two very different directions, and both are recorded by his disciples.

10. b. Bava Batra 10a.

11. KL 2:272–3, *likkutim*.

12. In a passage we read above, that was only the "lesser" side of God, God acting in a state of *katnut* to please the will of His child. This was the God of the Reed Sea crossing as distinct from Sinai (KL 1:296–97, *yitro*. See above chapter 10, n. 33). But here and elsewhere he goes beyond that. On the need for the *tsaddikim* to implant will in God, see also *Ḥayyim va-Ḥesed* #7. This was a teaching of the Maggid that seems to be widespread among his disciples. It is his own theological "tempering" of the BeSHT's ability to perform wonders, part of the transition from *ba'al shem* to *tsaddik*. See the discussion by Weiss in "The Great Maggid's Theory."

13. b. Ḥagigah 14b.

14. KL 1:109, *va-yetse*.

15. A good summary of this discussion can be found in Jacobs, *Seeker of Unity*, 49–63.

16. TYY 119, *va-yera*. *Torey Zahav, ha'azinu*, among others, quotes it in the name of the BeSHT.

17. KL 1:344, *derushim le-purim*.

18. KL 1:291, *yitro*. Here we are also reminded of God's ability to write in His book on Yom-tov or Shabbat only for the sake of saving a life, quoted above.

19. KL 1:279–80, be-*shalaḥ*.

20. KL 1:339, *derushim le-purim*. (This is not the Purim teaching published by Levi Yitsḥak in 1798, but a portion of the posthumous *Kedushat Levi*.)

21. *Siftey Tsaddikim* 17b, 41b.

22. Mondshine, *Masa' Berdychiv*, 49.

23. NE 540–41, *va-etḥanan*. Cited by Mark in *Levi Yitsḥak*, 366. The description of Moses as *ish ha-elohim*, meaning "husband of the *shekhinah*," is well-known from the Zohar. There *Elohim* is the lowest rung in the sefirotic world, and Moses is identified with the rung of Her divine spouse, the blessed Holy One. Building on that opening, R. Elimelekh is in fact making a much more daring claim.

24. See Green, *Tormented Master*, Appendix I, "Faith, Doubt, and Reason."

BIBLIOGRAPHY

PRIMARY SOURCES

Section 1: Classical Rabbinic Sources

Mishnah

Jerusalem Talmud

Babylonian Talmud

RaSHI and Tosafot to the Talmud

Tosefta

Mekhilta

Sifrey

Bereshit Rabbah

Shemot Rabbah

Va-Yiqra Rabbah

Be-Midbar Rabbah

Devarim Rabbah

Midrash Tehillim

Tanḥuma

Section 2: Medieval and Early Modern Sources (pre- and non-Hasidic)

Note: Parentheses indicate first publication; edition consulted listed as necessary.

Arzey Levanon. (Venice, 1601).

Baḥya ben Asher. *Bi'ur 'al ha-Torah*. (Naples, 1492).

______. Edited by C. Chavel. Jerusalem: Mossad ha-Rav Kook, 1971.

Bar Sheshet, Ya'akov. *Sefer ha-Emunah veha-Bitaḥon*. (Venice, 1601).

Caro, Yosef. *Shulḥan 'Arukh*. (Venice, 1565).

Cordovero, Moshe. *Pardes Rimmonim*. (Salonika, 1584).

De Vidas, Eliyahu. *Reshit Ḥokhmah*. (Venice, 1579).

Gikatilla, Yosef. *Sha'arey Orah*. (Mantua, Riva di Trento, 1561).

Horowitz, Yeshayahu. *Shney Luḥot ha-Berit*. (Amsterdam, 1648).

Ibn Gabbai, Meir. *ʿAvodat ha-Kodesh*. (Venice, 1545?).

_____. *Sod ha-Shabbat: The Mystery of the Sabbath*. Translated by Elliot Ginsburg. Albany: State University of New York Press, 1989.

_____. *Secrets of Creation*. Selection from *ʿAvodat ha-Kodesh*. Translated and annotated by A. Green, with commentary by H. Smith and illuminations by D. Band (Forthcoming).

Ibn Paquda, Baḥya. *Ḥovot ha-Levavot*. (Naples, 1490).

Isserles, Moshe. *Mappah la-Shulḥan ʿArukh*. (Cracow, 1569–71).

Luria, Yiṣḥaq (attributed). *Sefer ha-Kavvanot*. (Venice, 1620).

Maʿarekhet ha-Elohut. (Ferrara, 1557).

Maimon, Moshe ben (Maimonides). *Mishneh Torah*. (Rome, 1469).

Naḥman, Moshe ben (Naḥmanides). *Perush ʿal ha-Torah*. (Rome, 1469).

Peri ʿEtṣ Hadar. (Venice, 1718).

Sefer ha-Razim. Edited by Mordecai Margaliot. Jerusalem: Yediʿot Aḥaronot, 1966.

_____. *Sepher ha-Razim: The Book of the Mysteries*. Translated by M. Morgan. Chico CA: Scholars' Press, 1983.

Shelomo ben Yiṣḥaq (RaSHI). *Perush ʿal ha-Torah*. (Rome, 1469).

Spira, Nathan Neta. *Megalleh ʿAmukot*. (Cracow, 1637).

Tikkuney Zohar. (Mantua, 1558).

Vital, Ḥayyim and Shmu'el (attributed). *Peri ʿEts Ḥayyim*. (Korzec, 1782).

_____. *Shaʿar ha-Pesukim*. (Jerusalem, 1863).

_____. *Shaʿarey Kedushah*. (Amsterdam, 1715).

Yehudah Loew ben Bezalel (MaHaRaL). *Or Hadash*. (Prague, 1600). ed. Bnei Brak, 1972

Zohar (Mantua, 1558–60; Cremona, 1560).

_____. Translated by Daniel Matt et al., vols. 1–12. Stanford: Stanford University Press, 2004–2017.

Section 3: Hasidic Sources

Alpha Beta. Tzvi Hirsh of Nadworna. (Nowy Dwor, 1799).

Amtaḥat Binyamin. Binyamin of Zalozhtse. Commentary on Kohelet. Minkovtsy, 1796.

ʿAvodat Yisraʾel. Yisraʾel Hapstein of Kozienice. (Josefow, 1842). Jerusalem: Siftey Ṣadiqqim, 1993.

Buṣina Di-Nehora. Barukh of Miedzhybosh. (Lviv, 1880).

_____. *he-Ḥadash*. Brooklyn: Makhon Beʾer Yiṣḥaq, 1998.

_____. *ha-Shalem*. Lviv: R. Margulies, n.d.[1930?].

Degel Maḥaneh Efrayim. Moshe Ḥayyim Efrayim of Sudilkow. (Korzec, 1810). Jerusalem: Makhon Siftey Tsaddikim, 2012.

Geʾulat Yisraʾel. Yehoshuʿa Avraham ben Yisraʾel. (Ostrog, 1821).

Ḥesed le-Avraham. Avraham ha-Mal'akh. (Chernovtsy, 1851).

Iggeret ha-Kodesh. Shneur Zalman of Liadi. (Slawuta, 1797). Brooklyn: Kehot, 1973.

Imrey Tsaddikim. Warsaw, 1896.

Kedushat Levi. Levi Yitsḥaq of Berdichev. (Slawuta, 1798; Berdychiv, 1811). Edited by Michael Aryeh Rand. Jerusalem: Makhon Hadrat Ḥen, 2010.

Keter Torah. Meir ben Levi Yitsḥak. (Mezirov, 1803; Zhitomir, 1806).

Kitvey Kodesh. Dov Baer of Mezritch. Lviv, 1862.

Likkutey MoHaRaN. Naḥman of Bratslav. (Ostrog, 1808; Mogilev, 1811).

Likkutim Yekarim. Edited by Meshullam Feibush Heller of Zbarash. (Lviv, 1794) Jerusalem: Menaḥem Roth, 1974.

Maggid Devarav le-Ya'aqov. Dov Baer of Mezritch. (Korzec, 1781). Edited by Rivka Schatz-Uffenheimer. Jerusalem: Magnes Press, 1978.

Me'or 'Eynayim. Menaḥem Naḥum of Chernobyl. (Slawuta, 1798).

_____. Edited by Yitsḥaq Shim'on Oesterreicher. Jerusalem, 2012.

_____. Jerusalem: Peer Mikdoshim, 2015.

No'am Elimelekh. Elimelekh of Lezajsk. (Lviv, 1788). Edited by Gedalyahu Nig'al. Jerusalem: Mossad Harav Kook, 1978.

Or ha-Emet. Dov Baer of Mezritch. (Zhitomir, 1901). Brooklyn: Y. M. Wieseltier, 1960.

Or Torah. Dov Baer of Mezritch. (Korzec, 1804) Jerusalem, 1968.

Peri ha-Arets. Menaḥem Mendel of Vitebsk. (Kapust, 1814).

Pitgamin Kaddishin. Yehoshu'a Avraham ben Yisra'el. (Partial reprint of *Ge'ulat Yisra'el*). Warsaw, 1887.

Shema' Shelomo. Shelomo of Karlin. (n.p., 1928).

Shemen ha-Tov. Tzvi Yeḥezkel Mikhelson. (Piotrkov, 1905).

Shemu'ah Tovah. Dov Baer of Mezritch and Levi Yiṣḥaq of Berdichev. (Warsaw, 1938) Brooklyn, 1983.

Shivḥey ha-Besht. (Kapust, 1815).

_____. Edited by Avraham Rubenstein. Jerusalem: Reuven Mass, 1991.

_____. *In Praise of the Baal Shem Tov*. Translated and edited by Dan Ben-Amos and Jerome R. Mintz. Northvale, NJ: Jason Aronson, 1993.

Shivḥey Tsaddikim. Anonymous. (Warsaw, 1883).

Sidduro shel Shabbat. Hayyim Tirer of Chernovtsy. (Mohilev, 1813).

Siftey Tsaddikim. Pinḥas of Dinovitz. (Lviv, 1865).

Tanya (Likkutey Amarim). Shne'ur Zalman of Liadi. (Slawuta, 1797), Brooklyn: Kehot, 1973.

Tif'eret 'Uziel. Uziel Meisels. (Warsaw, 1863).

Toledot Ya'akov Yosef. Ya'akov Yosef of Polonnoye. (Korzec, 1780) Jerusalem: Eichen, 2011.

Torey Zahav. Binyamin of Zalozhtse. (Mohilev, 1816). Jerusalem: Makhon Ṣimḥat 'Olam, 2013.

Tsava'at Ha-RiVaSH. (n.p. [Russia/Poland], 1793). Brooklyn: Kehot, 1975.
Tseror ha-Ḥayyim. edited by N. N. ha-Kohen, n. p., 1913 (reprinted Jerusalem, n.d.).
Yosher Divrey Emet. Meshullam Feibush of Zbarasz. (Mukachevo, 1905).
[Sefer ha-] Zekhirot. Levi Yitsḥak of Berdychiv. (Mezirov, 1794).
Zikhron Tov. Anonymous. (Piotrkow, 1892).

SECONDARY SOURCES

Alfasi, Yiṣḥaq. *Encyclopedia of Hasidism.* Jerusalem: Mossad Harav Kook, 1986 (Hebrew).
Altshuler, Mor. *Rabbi Meshulam Feibush Heller and His Place in Early Hasidism.* Jerusalem: Hebrew University, 1995 (Hebrew).
Anonymous. *Niflo'os Beys Halevi.* (n.p., n.d) (Yiddish).
Anonymous. *Niflo'os Kedushas Levi.* Bilgoray (n.d.) (Yiddish).
Anonymous. *Sippurim Nifla'im be-Yiddish.* Brooklyn, 1987, v. 2.
Anonymous. *Toldot Ha-Meḥabber* in Mukachevo 1939 edition of *Kedushat Levi.*
Assaf, David. "'Bat? Dino Le-halka'ah: He-Ḥasid ke-Adam Metsaḥek ["A Girl! He Ought to Be Whipped!": The Hasid as Homo Ludens]." In *Let the Old Make Way for the New: Studies in the Social and Cultural History of Eastern European Jewry Presented to Immanuel Etkes*, edited by David Assaf and Ada Rapoport-Albert. Jerusalem: Zalman Shazar Center, 2009 (Hebrew).
_____, and Raya Haran. "'She-Yatse'ah Shemu'ah she-Ba Mashiaḥ Ben David': Or Ḥadash 'al 'Aliyat ha-Ḥasidim bi-Shenat 5537." *Zion* 61, no. 3 (1996): 319–46.
Ben-Shlomo, Yosef. *Torat ha-Elohut shel Rabbi Moshe Cordovero.* Jerusalem: Mossad Bialik, 1965.
Berger, David. "Miracles and the Natural Order in Nahmanides." In *Rabbi Moses Nahmanides (Ramban): Explorations in His Religious and Literary Virtuosity*, edited by Isadore Twersky, 107–28. Cambridge: Harvard University Press, 1993.
Berger, Israel. *'Eser Tsaḥtsaḥot* (part of his *Sefer Zekhut Yisra'el*). Piotrkow: Ḥ. H. Palman, 1913.
Bőttrich, Christian. "Melchizedek among Russian Saints: The History of Melchizedek between Jews and Slavs." In *The Bible in Slavonic Tradition* (*Studia Judeoslavonica* #9). Leiden: Brill, 2016.
Brown, Benjamin. *Like a Ship on a Stormy Sea: The Story of Karlin Hasidism.* Jerusalem: Zalman Shazar Institute, 2019 (Hebrew).
Cooper, Levi. "Rabbanut, Halakha, Lamdanut: Hebetim 'Alumim be-Toldot ha-Rav Levi Yitsḥak mi-Berdychiv." In *Rabbi Levi Yitsḥak mi-Berdychiv*, edited by Zvi Mark and Ro'i Horen. Rishon Le-Zion, Israel: Yedioth Aharonoth, 2017.

Derbarmdiger, Michael, ed. *Yalkut Kedushat Levi*. Brooklyn: Mekhon Kedushat Levi, 2004.

Dresner, Samuel H. *Levi Yizhak of Berdichev*. New York: Hartmore House, 1974.

______. *The Zaddik: The Doctrine of the Zaddik According to the Writings of Rabbi Yaakov Yosef of Polnoy*. New York: Schocken, 1974.

Elior, Rachel. *Unity of Opposites: The Mystical Theosophy of Ḥ aBaD*. Jerusalem: Mossad Bialik, 1992 (Hebrew).

Enelow, Hyman. "Kawwana: The Struggle for Inwardness in Judaism (Meditation as a Preparation for Prayer.") Reprinted in *Zen and Hasidism*, 98–194. Hoboken, NJ: Ktav, 1978.

Etkes, Immanuel. *The Besht: Magician, Mystic, and Leader*. Waltham, MA: Brandeis University Press, 2005.

_____. "The Early Hasidic 'Court.'" In *Text and Context: Essays in Modern Jewish History and Historiography in Honor of Ismar Schorsch*, edited by Eli Lederhendler. New York: Jewish Theological Press, 2005.

_____. "On the Motivation for Hasidic Immigration ('aliyah) to the Land of Israel." *Jewish History* 27, nos. 2–4 (2013): 337–35.

_____. *Rabbi Shneur Zalman of Liady: The Origins of Chabad Hasidism*. Waltham MA: Brandeis University Press, 2015.

Fishbane, Michael. "To Jump for Joy." *Journal of Jewish Thought & Philosophy* 6, no.2 (1997): 371–87.

Garb, Jonathan. *Manifestations of Power in Jewish Mysticism*. Jerusalem: Magnes Press, 2005 (Hebrew).

Gellman, Uri. *The Emergence of Hasidism in Poland*. Jerusalem: Zalman Shazar Institute, 2018 (Hebrew).

Ginsburg, Elliot. *The Sabbath in Classical Kabbalah*. Albany: State University of New York Press, 1989.

Ginzburg, Louis. *Legends of the Jews*. 7 vols. Philadelphia: Jewish Publication Society of America, 1947.

Glatzer, Nahum Norbert. "A Study of the Talmudic-Midrashic Interpretation of Prophecy." In *Essays in Jewish Thought*. Tuscaloosa: University of Alabama Press, 1978.

Glazer, Aubrey, and Nehemia Polen, eds. *From Tiberias, With Love*. Louisville, KY: Fons Vitae, 2019.

_____. *idem*., volume 2. [Boston:] Academic Press, 2020.

Goldfrank, David. "The 'Judaic-Reasoning Novgorod Heretics' and Some Echoes of Spain in Late Medieval Russia." *Russian History* 44, no. 4 (2017) 547–69.

Gottlieb, Ephraim. *Meḥkarim be-Sifrut ha-Kabbalah*. Tel Aviv: University of Tel Aviv, 1976.

Green, Arthur. "Around the Maggid's Table: Tzaddik, Leadership, and Popularization in the Circle of Dov Baer of Miedzyrzecz." In *The Heart of the Matter*. Philadelphia: Jewish Publication Society, 2015.

_____. "Around the Maggid's Table: Tzaddik, Leadership, and Popularization in the Circle of Dov Baer of Miedzyrzecz." *Zion* 78, no. 1 (2012): 73–106 (Hebrew).

_____. "Buber, Scholem, and the Me'or 'Eynayim." In *Swimming against the Current: Reimagining Jewish Tradition in the Twenty-First Century: Essays in Honor of Rabbi Chaim Seidler-Feller*, edited by David N. Myers and Shaul Seidler-Feller. Boston: Academic Studies Press, forthcoming.

_____. *Devotion and Commandment: The Faith of Abraham in the Hasidic Imagination.* Cincinnati: Hebrew Union College Press, 1989.

_____. "God's Need for Man: A Unitive Approach to the Writings of Abraham Joshua Heschel." *Modern Judaism* 35, no. 3 (2015): 247–61.

_____. *A Guide to the Zohar*. Stanford: Stanford University Press, 2004.

_____. "The Hasidic Homily: Mystical Performance and Hermeneutical Process." In *As a Perennial Spring: A Festschrift Honoring Rabbi Dr. Norman Lamm*, edited by Bentsi Cohen, 237–64. New York: Downhill Publishing LLC, 2013.

_____. "The Hasidic Tsaddik and the Charism of Relationship." in *Essays in Honor of Moshe Idel* (forthcoming). Jerusalem, 2022.

_____. "Hasidism and Its Changing History." *Jewish History* 27, nos. 2–4, Special Issue: Toward a New History of Hasidism (2013): 319–336.

_____. "Hillel Zeitlin and Neo-Hasidic Readings of the Zohar." *Kabbalah* 22 (2010): 59–78.

_____. "Judaism as a Path of Love." In *Be-Ron Yaḥad: Studies in Honor of Nehemia Polen*, ed. Ariel Evan Mayse and Arthur Green. Boston: Academic Press, 2019.

_____. *Keter: The Crown of God*. Princeton: Princeton University Press, 1997.

_____. "Levi Yizhak of Berdichev on Miracles." In *The Heart of the Matter*. Philadelphia: Jewish Publication Society, 2015.

_____. "R. Levi Yitsḥak of Zelichow." In *Ḥiddushim: The Hebrew College Jubilee Volume*. Boston: Academic Press, 2022.

_____. *The Light of the Eyes: Homilies on the Torah*. Translation, Introduction and Commentary. Stanford, CA: Stanford University Press, 2021.

_____. *Speaking Torah: Spiritual Teachings from around the Maggid's Table*. Woodstock: Jewish Lights, 2013.

_____. *Tormented Master*. Tuscaloosa: University of Alabama Press, 1978.

_____. "Typologies of Leadership and the Hasidic Zaddiq." In *The Heart of the Matter*. Philadelphia: Jewish Publication Society, 2015.

_____. "*Ẓaddiq* as Axis Mundi in Later Judaism." In *The Heart of the Matter*. Philadelphia: Jewish Publication Society, 2015.

_____. *Conduct Literature (Regimen Vitae): Its History and Place in the Life of BeSH-Tian Hasidism*. Jerusalem: Mossad Bialik, 1989 (Hebrew).

Gries, Ze'ev. *The Hebrew Book: An Outline of Its History*. Jerusalem: Mossad Bialik, 2015 (Hebrew).

Grossberger, Ephraim. "Le-Hagdil Torah ule-Ha'adirah." *Or Yisrael* 27 (Nissan 2002): 192–210.

Grossman, Avraham. "From Father to Son: The Inheritance of the Spiritual Leadership of the Jewish Communities in the Early Middle Ages." *Zion* 50 (1985): 189–220 (Hebrew).

Halbertal, Moshe. *By Way of Truth: Nahmanides and the Creation of Tradition*. Jerusalem: Shalom Hartman Institute, 2005 (Hebrew).

_____. *Nahmanides: Law and Mysticism*. Yale University Press, 2020.

Halbertal, Moshe, and Jackie Feldman. "Tradition, Closed Knowledge, and the Esoteric: Secrecy and Hinting in Nahmanides' Kabbalah." In *Concealment and Revelation: Esotericism in Jewish Thought and Its Philosophical Implications*, 83–92. Oxford: Princeton University Press, 2007.

______. "Ha-'Aliyot ha-Rishonot shel ha-Ḥasidim le-Erez Yisrael." Jerusalem, 1946.

Haran, Raya. "R. Abraham of Kalisk and R. Shneur Zalman of Liadi—A Friendship

______. *Pinkas Va'ad Arba' Aratsot*. Revised edition by I. Bartal. Jerusalem, 1990.

Halpern, Israel. "Rabbi Levi Yizḥaq of Berdichew and the Edicts of His Times." *Tarbiz* no. 28 (1958): 90–98.

Cut Off." In *Kolot Rabbim: The Rivkah Schatz Memorial Volume*, v. 2, 399–428 (Hebrew).

______. "Mah Heni'a et Talmidey ha-Maggid La-'alot le-Erets Yisra'el?" *Cathedra* 76 (1995) 77–95 (Hebrew).

Heilman, Avraham Shemu'el. *Bet Rabbi*. Berdychiv, 1902.

Hecker, Joel. "Kissing Kabbalists: Hierarchy, Reciprocity and Equality." *Studies in Jewish Civilization* 18 (2008): 171–208.

Heschel, Abraham Joshua. *The Circle of the Baal Shem Tov*. Edited by Samuel H. Dresner. Chicago: University of Chicago Press, 1985.

_____. *Heavenly Torah*. Translated by Gordon Tucker and Leonard Levin. New York: Continuum, 2005.

_____. *Torah min ha-Shamayim*. New York: Soncino Press, 1962.

Hilman, David Tzvi, ed. *Iggerot Ba'al ha-Tanya u-Veney Doro*. Jerusalem, 1953 (Hebrew).

Horen, Ro'i. *Zikkato shel ha-BeSHṬ la-Kabbalah ha-Lurianit*. PhD diss., Ben-Gurion University, 2017.

Hundert, Gershon, ed. *Essential Papers on Hasidism*. New York: New York University Press, 1991.

_____. *Jews in Poland-Lithuania in the Eighteenth Century*. Berkeley: University of California Press, 2006.

_____. *Toward a Biography of R. Abraham Kalisker*. Master's Thesis, Ohio State University, 1971.

_____, ed. *The YIVO Encyclopedia of Jews in Eastern Europe*. New Haven: Yale University Press, 2008.

Huss, Boaz. "A Sage is Preferable to a Prophet: Rabbi Shimon bar Yochai and Moshe Rabbeinu in the Zohar." *Kabbalah* 4 (1999): 103–9.

Idel, Moshe. *Ben: Sonship and Jewish Mysticism*. London: Continuum, 2007.

_____. *Hasidism: Between Ecstasy and Magic*. Albany: State University of New York Press, 1995.

_____. "*Ta'anug*: Erotic Delights from Kabbalah to Hasidism." In *Eros and Sexuality in the History of Western Esotericism*, 111–51. Leiden: Brill, 2008.

_____. "White Letters: From R. Levi Isaac of Berditchev's Views to Postmodern Hermeneutics." *Modern Judaism* 26, no. 2 (2006): 169–92.

Jacobs, Louis. *Seeker of Unity*. New York: Basic Books, 1966.

Kara-Ivanov Kaniel, Ruth. "Consumed by Love: The Death of Nadav and Avihu as a Ritual of Erotic Mystical Union." *Te'udah*, 26 (2014): 585–653.) (Itamar Gruenwald Festschrift).

Katz, Jacob. *Halakhah and Kabbalah*. Jerusalem: Magnes, 1984 (Hebrew).

Kauffman, Tzippi. *In All Your Ways Know Him: The Concept of God and Avodah be-Gashmiyut in the Early Stages of Hasidism*. Ramat Gan: Bar-Ilan University Press, 2009 (Hebrew).

_____. "On the Portrait of a *Tsaddiq*: R. Zusha of Annopol." *Kabbalah* 30 (2013): 273–302 (Hebrew).

Klier, John. *Russia Gathers Her Jews: The Origin of the "Jewish Question" in Russia, 1772–1825*. DeKalb, IL: Northern Illinois University Press, 1986.

Laytner, Anson. *Arguing with God: A Jewish Tradition*. New York: Jason Aronson Incorporated, 1997.

Leader, Ebn. "Leadership as Individual Relationships." In *Be-Ron Yaḥad: Studies in Jewish Law and Theology in Honor of Nehemia Polen*, edited by Ariel Evan Mayse and Arthur Green. Boston: Academic Studies Press, 2019.

Lederberg, Netanel. *The Gateway to Infinity: Rabbi Dov Baer, the Maggid Mesharim of Mezhrich*. Jerusalem: Rubin Mass, 2011 (Hebrew).

Levin, Dov Baer. *Toledot ḤaBaD be-Russia ha-Tsarit*. Brooklyn, 1988.

Lieberman, Hayyim. "Seder Ha-Rabbanut Shel Rabbi Levi Yitsḥak." In *Ohel Rahel*. Brooklyn, NY: Gross Bros. Printing, 1980.

Liebes, Yehudah. "Zohar ve-Eros." *Alpayyim* 9 (1994): 67–119.

_____. "The Messiah of the Zohar." In *Studies in the Zohar*. Albany: State University of New York Press, 1993.

_____. "Zohar as Renaissance." *Daʿat* 46 (2001): 5–11 (Hebrew).

_____. "Towards a Study of the Author of *ʿEmek Ha-Melekh*: His Personality, Writings, and Kabbalah." *Jerusalem Studies in Jewish Thought* 11 (1993): 101–37 (Hebrew).

Loewenthal, Naftali. *Communicating the Infinite: The Emergence of the Habad Schoo*l. Chicago: University of Chicago Press, 1990.

Lorberbaum, Menahem. "Attaining the Attribute of 'Ayin': The Mystical Religiosity of *Maggid Devarav le-Ya'aqov*." *Kabbalah* 31 (2014): 169–235 (Hebrew).

Mach, Rudolf. *Der Zaddik in Talmud und Midrasch*. Leiden: Brill, 1957.

Maciejko, Paweł. *The Frankist Movement in Poland, the Czech Lands, and Germany (1755–1816)*. Oxford: Oxford University Press, 2003.

_____. *The Mixed Multitude: Jacob Frank and the Frankist Movement*. Philadelphia: University of Pennsylvania Press, 2001.

Magid, Shaul. *Hasidism Incarnate*. Stanford: Stanford University Press, 2015.

Maimon, Solomon. *An Autobiography*. Translated by Michael Shapiro. Chicago: University of Illinois Press, 2001.

______. *The Autobiography of Solomon Maimon: The Complete Translation*. Edited by Yitsḥak Y. Melamed and Abraham Socher. Princeton: Princeton University Press, 2019.

Margolin, Ron. *Mikdash Adam* [The Human Temple]. Jerusalem: Magnes Press, 2005 (Hebrew).

Mark, Zvi. *Megillat Setarim: The Secret Messianic Vision of Rebbe Naḥman of Breslov*. Ramat Gan: Bar Ilan University Press, 2006 (Hebrew).

_____. "Din Torah 'im ha-El." In *Rabbi Levi Yitsḥak mi-Berdichev*, edited by Zvi Mark and Roʾi Horen. Rishon Le-Zion, Israel: Yedioth Aharonoth, 2017.

_____, and Roʾi Horen, eds. *Rabbi Levi Yitsḥak mi-Berdychiv*. Rishon Le-Zion, Israel: Yedioth Aharonoth, 2017.

Matt, Daniel C. "*Ayin*: The Concept of Nothingness in Jewish Mysticism." In *Essential Papers on Kabbalah*, edited by Lawrence Fine. New York: New York University Press, 1995.

Mayse, Ariel Evan. *Beyond the Letters: The Question of Language in the Teachings of Rabbi Dov Baer of Mezritch*. PhD diss., Harvard University, 2015.

______. "'Like a Moth to the Flame': The Death of Nadav and Avihu in Hasidic Literature." In *Be-Ron Yaḥad: Studies in Jewish Law and Theology in Honor of Nehemia Polen*, edited by Ariel Evan Mayse and Arthur Green. Boston: Academic Studies Press, 2019.

______. "Moving Mezrich: The Legacy of the Maggid and the Hasidic Community in the Land of Israel. In *From Tiberias with Love*, v. 2, 129–82. Louisville: Fons Vitae, 2019.

______. "The Ever-Changing Path: Visions of Legal Diversity in Hasidic Literature." *Conversations* 23 (2015): 84–115.

______. *Speaking Infinities: God and Language in the Teachings of Rabbi Dov Ber of Mezritsh*. Philadelphia: University of Pennsylvania Press, 2020.

Mayse, Ariel Evan, and Maoz Kahana. "Hasidic Halakhah: Reappraising the Interface of Spirit and Law." In *AJS Review* 4, no. 2 (2017): 375–408.

Meeks, Wayne. "Moses as God and King." In *Religions in Antiquity: Essays in Memory of Erwin Ramsdell Goodenough*, edited by Jacob Neusner. Leiden: E. J. Brill, 1968.

Mekler, David L. *Fun Rebin's Hoif*. New York: Jewish Book Publishing Co., 1931.

Mondshine, Yehoshua. *Masa' Berdychiv: The Journey of Our Elder Lord, Teacher, and Rabbi to Berdychiv, Breslov, and Miedzhybosh in the Year 5570*. Jerusalem: K'ramim Institute, 2016 (Hebrew).

Moseson, Elly. *From Spoken Word to the Discourse of the Academy: Reading the Sources for the Teachings of the Besht*. PhD diss., Boston University, 2017.

______. "From Private Letter to Communal Document: On the Multiple Versions of the Letter of the Besht." *Kabbalah* 47 (2021).

Muffs, Yochanan. *The Personhood of God: Biblical Theology, Human Faith, and the Divine Image*. Woodstock, VT: Jewish Lights Publishing, 2009.

Nadav, Mordecai. *The Jews of Pińsk, 1506 to 1880*. Edited by Jay Mirsky and Moshe Rosman. Stanford, CA.: Stanford University Press, 2008.

Pedaya, Ḥaviva. "The Ba'al Shem Tov, R. Jacob Joseph of Polonnoye, and the Maggid of Mezhirech: Outlines for a Religious Typology." *Da'at* 45 (2000): 25–73 (Hebrew).

______. *Nahmanides: Cyclical Time and Holy Text*. Tel Aviv: Am Oved, 2003 (Hebrew).

Petrovsky-Shtern, Yohanan. "The Drama of Berdichev: Levi Yitsḥak and His Town." *Polin* 17 (2004): 83–94.

______. "Ḥasidei De'ar'a and Ḥasidei Dekokhvaya': Two Trends in Modern Jewish Historiography." *AJS Review* 32, no. 1 (2008): 141–67.

Piekarz, Mendel. *Between Ideology and Reality: Humility, 'Ayin, Self-Negation, and Devequt in Hasidic Thought*. Jerusalem: Mossad Bialik, 1994 (Hebrew).

______. *The Beginning of Hasidism: Ideological Trends in Drush and Musar Literature*. Jerusalem: Mossad Bialik, 1978 (Hebrew).

Polen, Nehemia, and David Maayan. "Theology, Succession, and Social Structure in the Dispute between R. Abraham Kalisker and R. Shne'ur Zalman." In *From Tiberias with Love*, v. 2, 183–203.

Polonsky, Antony. *The Jews in Poland and Russia*. Portland, OR: Oxford, 2010.

Raḥmani, Shaḥar. "*Sanègoran shel Yisra'el*." In *Rabbi Levi Yitsḥak mi-Berdychiv*, edited by Zvi Mark, and Ro'i Horen. Rishon Le-Zion, Israel: Yedioth Aharonoth, 2017.

Rapoport-Albert, Ada. "Hasidism after 1772: Structural Continuity and Change." In *Hasidism Reappraised*, edited by Ada Rapoport-Albert. London: Littman Library, 1996, 76–140.

_____. *Women and the Messianic Heresy of Sabbatai Zevi 1666–1816*. Translated by Deborah Greniman. Oxford: Littman Library of Jewish Civilization, 2011.

Ramon, Orit. *Maharal in New Light*. Jerusalem: Zalman Shazar Center, 2017 (Hebrew).

Ro'i, Biti. *Ahavat ha-Shekhinah*. Ramat Gan: Bar Ilan University Press, 2017.

Rosenzweig, Franz. "The Builders: Concerning the Law." In *On Jewish Learning*, 72–92. New York: Schocken, 1955.

Rosman, Moshe, and Murray Jay Rosman. *Founder of Hasidism: A Quest for the Historical Ba'al Shem Tov*. University of California Press, 1996.

Rubenstein, Avraham. "Notes on a Collection of Testimonies against Ḥasidism" *Tarbiz* 32 (1962): 80–97.

Sack, Bracha. *The Kabbalah of Rabbi Moshe Cordovero*. Beer Sheva: Ben Gurion University Press, 1995 (Hebrew).

Safran, Bezalel. *Hasidism: Continuity or Innovation*. Cambridge: Harvard University Press, 1988.

Sagiv, Gad. *Dynasty: The Chernobyl Hasidic Dynasty and Its Place in the History of Hasidism*. Jerusalem: Magnes Press, 2014 (Hebrew).

Schatz-Uffenheimer, Rivka. *Hasidism as Mysticism: Quietistic Elements in Eighteenth-Century Hasidic Thought*. Princeton: Princeton University Press, 1993.

Scholem, Gershom. "The Legend of the Thirty-Six Righteous." In *The Messianic Idea in Judaism*. New York: Shocken, 1971.

_____. *On the Mystical Shape of the Godhead: Basic Concepts in the Kabbalah*. New York: Schocken, 1991.

_____. "Revelation and Tradition as Religious Categories in Judaism." Translated by Michael A. Meyer. In *The Messianic Idea in Judaism and Other Essays on Jewish Spirituality*, 282–303, 363. New York: Schocken Books, 1971

_____. *Three Types of Jewish Piety*. Zurich: Rhein Verlag, 1971.

Schorr, Avraham Abish, "Rabbi Levi Yitshak mi-Berdychiv Beyn Tsaddikey Doro: Maḥlokot ve-Haskamot." In *Rabbi Levi Yitsḥak mi-Berdichev*, edited by Zvi Mark and Ro'i Horen. Rishon Le-Zion, Israel: Yedioth Aharonoth, 2017.

______. *Ketavim*. Jerusalem: Makhon Bet Aharon ve-Yisra'el, 2018.

Ta-Shma, Yisrael. *Ha-Nigleh sheba-Nistar*. Israel: Ha-Kibbutz ha-Me'uhad, 1995.

Teller, Adam, "Tradition and Crisis? Eighteenth-Century Critiques of the Polish-Lithuanian Rabbinate." *Jewish Social Studies* 17, no. 3 (2011): 1–39.

Tishby, Isaiah. *Wisdom of the Zohar: An Anthology of Texts*. 3 vols. London: Littman Library, 1989.

Tsaylengold, Aharon. *Me'orot ha-Gedolim*. Bilgoray, 1911. Jerusalem: Karmel, 1997.

Urbach, Ephraim. "*Halachah* and Prophecy." *Tarbiz* 18, no. 1 (1946): 1–27 (Hebrew).

Walden, Aharon. *Shem ha-Gedolim he-Ḥadash*. Warsaw, 1864.

Weiss, Dov. *Pious Irreverence: Confronting God in Rabbinic Judaism*. Philadelphia: University of Pennsylvania Press, 2017.

Weiss, Joseph. "The Beginnings of Hasidism." *Zion* 16 (1951): 46–105 (Hebrew).

_____. *Studies in Eastern European Jewish Mysticism*. London: Oxford University Press, 1985.

_____. "Torah Study in Early Hasidism." *Ha-Tzufah* 4, no. 5 (1966).

_____, and Joseph Dan. "The Kavvanoth of Prayer in Early Hasidism." In *Studies in East European Jewish Mysticism and Hasidism*, edited by David Goldstein, 95–125. Liverpool University Press, 1997.

Werblowsky, R. J. Zwi. "Faith, Hope, and Trust: A Study of the Concept of Bittaḥon." In *Papers of the Institute of Jewish Studies*, 95–139. Jerusalem: 1964.

Wertheim, Aaron. *Law and Custom in Hasidism*. Translated by Shmuel Himelstein. Hoboken, NJ: Ktav, 1992.

Wigoda, Michael. "Darey Ma'alah 'Im Darey Matah." In *Rabbi Levi Yitsḥak mi-Berdichev*, edited by Zvi Mark and Ro'i Horen. Rishon Le-Zion, Israel: Yedioth Aharonoth, 2017.

Wilensky, Mordecai. *Ḥasidim and Mitnaggedim: A Study of the Controversy between Them, 1772–1815*. Jerusalem: Mossad Bialik, 1970 (Hebrew).

______. "The Polemic of R. David of Makow against Hasidism." *PAAJR* 25 (1956): 137–56.

Wolf, Barukh. "Iggeret ve-Sefer." In *Heikhal ha-BeShT* 17 (2006): 147–64. (Hebrew).

Wolf, Yasny, ed. *Yizkor-bukh fun der Zhelekhover Yidisher Kehile*. Chicago: Tsentraler Zhelekhover Landsmanshaft, 1953.

Wolfson, Elliot R. "The Image of Jacob Engraved upon the Throne of Glory." In *Massu'ot: Studies in Kabbalistic Literature and Jewish Philosophy in Memory of Ephraim Gottlieb*, edited by Michal Oron and Amos Goldreich, 131–85. Jerusalem: Bialik, 1994 (Hebrew).

______. *Through a Speculum That Shines: Vision and Imagination in Medieval Jewish Mysticism*. Princeton, New Jersey: Princeton University Press, 1994.

Ya'ari, Avraham. "Ha-Defus ha-'Ivri be-Berdychiv." *Kiryat Sefer* 21 (1944/45) (Hebrew).

Zeitlin, Hillel. "Fundaments of Hasidism." In *Hasidism for a New Era: The Religious Writings of Hillel Zeitlin*, edited by Arthur Green. New York: Paulist Press, 2012.

INDEX